Why People Radicalize

**Perspectives on Justice and Morality**
*Carolyn Hafer and Mario Gollwitzer*
Series Editors

**Books in the Series**
*Unequal Foundations: Inequality, Morality, and Emotions Across Cultures*
Steven Hitlin and Sarah K. Harkness

*Why People Radicalize: How Unfairness Judgments are Used to Fuel Radical Beliefs, Extremist Behaviors, and Terrorism*
Kees van den Bos

*The Moral Punishment Instinct*
Jan-Willem van Prooijen

# Why People Radicalize

*How Unfairness Judgments are Used to Fuel Radical Beliefs, Extremist Behaviors, and Terrorism*

**KEES VAN DEN BOS**

PROFESSOR OF SOCIAL PSYCHOLOGY

EMPIRICAL LEGAL SCIENCE AT UTRECHT UNIVERSITY

THE NETHERLANDS

OXFORD
UNIVERSITY PRESS

Oxford University Press is a department of the University of Oxford. It furthers
the University's objective of excellence in research, scholarship, and education
by publishing worldwide. Oxford is a registered trade mark of Oxford University
Press in the UK and certain other countries.

Published in the United States of America by Oxford University Press
198 Madison Avenue, New York, NY 10016, United States of America.

Library of Congress Cataloging-in-Publication Data
Names: Bos, Kees van den, author.
Title: Why people radicalize : how unfairness judgments are used to fuel radical beliefs,
extremist behaviors, and terrorism / Kees van den Bos.
Description: New York, NY : Oxford University Press, [2018] |
Includes bibliographical references and index.
Identifiers: LCCN 2018009454 | ISBN 9780190657345 (hardcover : alk. paper)
Subjects: LCSH: Radicalism—Psychological aspects. | Terrorism—Psychological
aspects. | Judgment.
Classification: LCC HN49.R33 B67 2019 | DDC 303.48/4—dc23
LC record available at https://lccn.loc.gov/2018009454

9 8 7 6 5 4 3 2

Printed by Sheridan Books, Inc., United States of America

# CONTENTS

This book focuses on the issue of why people radicalize. This issue includes the question of why sometimes Muslims or those who identify with right-wing or left-wing politics can be tempted to engage in violent extremism and be sympathetic to terrorist acts. The book argues that part of the answer to these important yet complex and multifaceted topics lies in people perceiving certain things in their world as profoundly unfair. For example, they feel that their group is being treated in blatantly unfair manners, or they judge crucial moral principles to be violated.

The book makes the case that these unfairness judgments threaten people's sense of who they are and jeopardize their beliefs about how the world should look. Furthermore, these judgments are not merely perceptions, but instead feel real and genuine to those who constructed them. As a result, these unfairness judgments can fuel people's radical beliefs, extremist behaviors, and support for terrorist acts. This book explains how this fueling process takes place.

This book argues that unfairness-inspired fueling of radicalization is especially likely when people feel uncertain about themselves and when they are insufficiently able to control their self-centered impulses. For example, when people are not able to manage their emotional reactions of anger toward those who are different from themselves, this can exacerbate various radicalization processes. As such, personal uncertainty and insufficient self-correction can dramatically enhance rigid thinking, strong defensive reactions toward those who are from different cultures or subcultures, and violent rejection of law and democratic principles.

The book discusses each aspect of this line of reasoning in detail. In doing so, the book grounds each aspect and provides in-depth insight into the many details important for the understanding of Muslim, right-wing, and left-wing radicalization. The book draws novel conceptual conclusions and suggests usable practical implications. The book pays close attention to the important nuances and caveats that are relevant when applying these insights to processes of radicalization. I also discuss explicitly both strengths and possible limitations of the line of reasoning conveyed here, hence offering a balanced treatment of current insight into the social psychology of radicalization and unfairness.

I wrote the book based on my expertise as a fairness researcher and my experiences of giving advice on radicalization (and associated issues of extremism and terrorism) to the Dutch government and the National Coordinator for Security and Counterterrorism. Based on this expertise and these experiences, I aimed to convey a convincing and an engaging line of reasoning to a broad audience of not only radicalization and fairness researchers in particular, and university psychologists and other scientists more generally, but also politicians and policy decision makers, lawyers and judges, police officers and counter-radicalization officials, civil servants and social workers, parents and teachers, students and professionals, and others who are interested in radicalization, extremism, terrorism, and unfairness.

The book consists of 12 chapters, arranged in four parts, introducing the topic of radicalization, focusing on its antecedents, examining its core components, and offering reflections on the subject. Each part of the book consists of three chapters, and each chapter contains six sections, enhancing the readability of this book. The book includes 12 figures that illustrate key elements of the line of reasoning presented here. All in all, this scholarly yet accessible book should give the reader basic and in-depth insights into why people radicalize and how judgments of unfairness can fuel radical beliefs, extremist behaviors, and support for terrorism.

I put this book together because there is good scientific evidence that can help to explain why people radicalize and even why they start sympathizing with extremist and terrorist movements. Furthermore, it is captivating to see how what normally are commendable psychological processes pertaining to issues of fairness, justice, and morality can lead people astray and in fact steer them into adopting radical, extremist, and terrorist views.

Importantly, I try to understand radicalization, extremism, and terrorism as a research psychologist and law professor. Of course, trying to understand these topics as a scientist and scholar is not the same as sympathizing with radicals, extremists, or terrorists as a person. Quite the contrary, I hope that the insights into Muslim, right-wing, and left-wing radicalization put forward in this book help to prevent, attenuate, and counter these important instances of radicalization.

# PART ONE

# Introducing Radicalization

# A Framework for Understanding Radicalization

## 1.1 INTRODUCTION

Radicalization and associated issues such as extremism and terrorism are important problems in our world. These issues are the core topics of this book. Specifically, I examine how perceptions of unfairness play a key role in our understanding and possible prevention of various radicalization processes, including processes that lead to violent extremism and terrorist acts. Various radical belief systems are associated with the problems of radicalization, extremism, and terrorism. For example, these belief systems include extreme Muslim beliefs as well as radical right-wing and left-wing beliefs.

Muslim radicalization and terrorism are responsible for terrible events such as the coordinated attacks by al-Qaeda on the United States on 9/11 (2001), the murder of Theo van Gogh in Amsterdam (2004), the bomb attacks in Madrid (2004) and London (2005), the assault on the offices of the French satirical weekly newspaper *Charlie Hebdo* in Paris (January 2015), and the terrorist acts in the same city (November 2015). These forms of radicalization and terrorism are currently associated with the violent behavior by the Islamic State in Iraq and Syria (since 2014).

Right-wing radicalization and extremism are linked to the attack on the Murrah Federal Building in Oklahoma by Timothy McVeigh and Terry Nichols (1995) and the shootings by Anders Breivik in Norway (2011). They are currently also associated with the notable fact that since 9/11, right-wing extremists have committed at least 19 lethal terrorist attacks in the United States.[1]

Left-wing radicalization and terrorism are accountable for the bombings, assassinations, kidnappings, bank robberies, and shoot-outs with police by the Red Army Faction (*Rote Armee Fraktion* or Baader-Meinhof Group) in Germany (1970–1995) and the Red Brigades (*Brigate Rosse*) in Italy (1970–1988). Radical left-wing beliefs are also associated with violence by terrorist and guerilla movements such as the Revolutionary Armed Forces of Colombia (*Fuerzas Armadas Revolucionarias de Colombia*, FARC) (1964–2017), the Peruvian Shining Path (*Partido Comunista del Perú* or *Sendero Luminoso*) (since 1980), and animal rights extremism in the Netherlands (Netherlands General Intelligence and Security Service, 2009).

This book focuses on why people radicalize and engage in extremist or terrorist behaviors. The first chapter seeks to introduce and define the concept of radicalization and associated issues. In doing so, it introduces a

1. Data retrieved from http://securitydata.newamerica.net/extremists/deadly-attacks.html on August 20, 2015.

framework that is used in the book to understand the process of radicalization, including extremist behaviors and terrorism.

## 1.2 DEFINITIONS AND PHASES OF RADICALIZATION

Various definitions exist for the concepts of radicalization, extremism, and terrorism. In this book I rely on the Netherlands General Intelligence and Security Service (2007a, 2007b, 2009) and concentrate on those instances of *radicalization* that can be defined as processes of growing willingness to pursue and/or support radical changes in society (if necessary in an undemocratic manner) that are in conflict with or could pose a threat to the democratic legal order.

One core topic that I address in this book is that it is pivotal to differentiate between those individuals and organizations who operate within the law and those involved in activities that go beyond the law, breaking or violating it. It is also very important to distinguish clearly between violent and nonviolent acts. As such, I distinguish between activism, extremism, and terrorism.

I define *activism* as a state in which individuals or groups of individuals seek to realize their goals through extra-parliamentary activities, but in doing so remain within the law. I talk about *extremism* when I focus on individuals or groups who deliberately overstep the bounds of the law to commit illegal, sometimes violent, acts. Furthermore, again relying on the Netherlands General Intelligence and Security Service (2009), I refer to *terrorism* when I describe individuals or groups who are engaged in ideologically motivated violence or other destructive acts—whether actual, planned, or threatened—against persons, property, or the fabric of society, committed with the aim of bringing about social change, causing serious public disquiet, or influencing the political decision-making process.

Viewed in this way, activism, extremism, and terrorism constitute different phases of growing radicalization. Figure 1.1 illustrates these different phases. Radicalization processes include extremism and

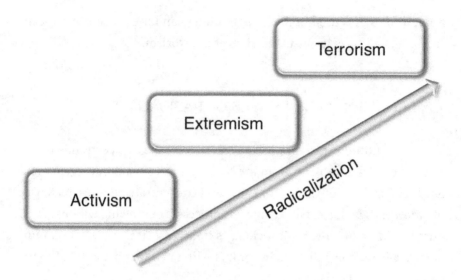

**Figure 1.1 Phases of Radicalization.**
Different concepts of the radicalization process on which this book focuses. In this process, activism, extremism, and terrorism constitute different phases of growing radicalization. The book aims to study full processes of radicalization, with special emphasis on extremism and terrorism.

terrorism as key and salient phases that often constitute focal points of attention. Hence, my aim in this book is to study full processes of radicalization, with special emphasis on extremism and terrorism.

In studying these issues, it is important to note that radical views are not necessarily bad (see, e.g., Israel, 2001, 2006, 2011), especially not when they adhere to principles of constitutional democracy and stay away from violent behavior. Furthermore, radicalization does not necessarily culminate in violent extremism, nor does it need to result in terrorism. I also note explicitly that what defines a terrorist movement is sometimes dependent on time. For example, my grandfather and other people from the Dutch resistance during the Second World War were called "terrorists" and were treated accordingly by the Nazi Germans who invaded the Netherlands from 1940 to 1945. This noted, the radical views and extremist behaviors I am focusing on in this book tend to be more closely related to violent and antidemocratic illegal behavior that is typically associated with the general gist of most terrorist movements to create terror among demo-cratically chosen governments and among citizens that can and should be viewed as innocent people (De Graaf, 2010). I also note that in this book I am adopting a predominantly descriptive perspective. In Part Four (Chapters 10–12) I address some of the normative issues that follow from the line of reasoning that I present in this book.

## 1.3 KEY THEME

Although I am comfortable with defining radicalization and associated topics like I did in the previous section, I also note explicitly that the problems of radicalization, extremism, and terrorism are complex and involve many determinants and that many pathways lead to different outcomes and different behavioral responses among different groups of radical persons (McCauley & Moskalenko, 2008; Moghaddam & Marsella, 2004).

That is why I review several instances of radicalization, extremism, and terrorism in this book and note important issues of how to define and conceptualize the different thoughts, feelings, and behaviors of people involved in various phases of radicalization. In doing so, I review core theories that have been proposed to study the radicalization process. I also discuss important empirical studies that have been conducted to test these theories.

The multifaceted quality of radicalization, extremism, and terrorism also implies that policy decision makers and others who want to handle or deal with these problems are faced with a formidable task. Indeed, in my country the Netherlands it is told that a tough and firm decision maker who was then the National Coordinator for Security and Counterterrorism looked at the potentially large number of youngsters who may be vulner-able to radicalization, sighed, and stated: "I want to know what these guys think!"

With this heartfelt statement, this counterterrorist decision maker conveyed that he wanted to know why people radicalize. Indeed, it can well be argued that one of the most important problems the world is confronted with and one of the most challenging problems that modern science faces concerns the issue of what drives radicalization, extremism, and terrorism. This book focuses on this issue.

In answering the question of why people radicalize, I argue that we need to know the relevant psychological processes underlying radicalization and associated issues such as extremism and terrorism. This book discusses these processes. By bringing together thus-far scattered in-depth insights into the psychology of radicalization and going beyond earlier insights and reviews that have examined this topic, I scientifically ground and explicate some of the core reasons for why people radicalize.

Importantly, I cannot and will not discuss all determinants of radicalization, nor can I focus on all pathways leading to growing radicalization. Instead, this book notes that an important reason why people radicalize lies in their perceptions of unfairness. Especially when one focuses on earlier phases of radicalization, perceptions of unfairness (and associated experiences such as injustice, the opinion that some issues are immoral, and the general feeling that things are "not right") are key to understanding radicalization, extremism, and terrorism. As Moghaddam put it in 2005: "In order to understand the actions of the few who climb to the top of the staircase to terrorism and plunge into terrorist acts, one must begin by considering the conditions of life and the perceptions of justice among the millions on the ground floor" (p. 166).

Both macro-oriented societal sciences (such as sociology) and more micro-oriented behavioral sciences (such as psychology) make clear that the experience of unfairness and injustice is often a key antecedent of societal and social change (Folger & Cropanzano, 1998; Klandermans, 1997; Layendecker, 1981; Tyler, Boeckmann, Smith, & Huo, 1997). After all, experiencing that something is unfair and unjust in society provides major impetus to the realization that this needs to be addressed and that hence change is needed, for example, in politics or political movements. On a more micro-level, experiencing that another person is treating you or your group in an unjust and unfair manner usually results in strongly felt emotions and the wish to do something about this, such as fight against the unfairness (Van den Bos & Lind, 2002, 2009). This book focuses on people's perceptions of unfairness as they pertain to the radicalization process. In fact, these unfairness perceptions are the key theme of this book.

Understanding perceptions in general, and perceptions of unfairness in particular, can be complex, in part because these perceptions can be biased in important ways. What is unfair is really in the eye of the beholder, but because these perceptions are deeply felt as real and genuine, they tend to have real consequences (Thomas & Thomas, 1928) and can fuel radical beliefs and extremist and terrorist behaviors in important ways. The study of radicalization therefore needs constant updating and refined understanding of what is driving people's perceptions of unfairness and what psychological processes and potential biases influence these perceptions. The current book does precisely this and aims to provide an accessible, advanced, and up-to-date treatment of what is going on inside people's heads with respect to fairness issues and radicalization, what leads them to believe that something is fair or unfair, what the variables are that impact this psychological process, and what the consequences are of these perceptions for processes having to do with radicalization, extremism, and terrorism. The next section introduces a framework that is used in this book to understand the radicalization process, including behaviors of extremists and people's sympathy for terrorist movements.

## 1.4 A FRAMEWORK OF GROWING RADICALIZATION

As mentioned, this book focuses on the issue of how people use judgments of unfairness to fuel radical beliefs and extremist behaviors. In the view portrayed in this book, radicalization, extremism, and terrorism are multifaceted phenomena and are caused by many different factors. One of these factors is the experience that things are unfair. The current book focuses on this experience by considering how normal psychological processes pertaining to the experience of unfairness may lead people to adhere to abnormal extremist beliefs and to engage in abnormal terrorist behaviors.

In this way, this book focuses on the issue of how people use judgments of unfairness to fuel radical beliefs and extremist behaviors.

Figure 1.2 summarizes the process of growing radicalization on which this book focuses. The framework delineated in the figure indicates that there are many different events that people may interpret as unfair. These experiences include events that signal that people are treated in unfair ways by other important individuals, such as societal authorities (Tyler & Lind, 1992). Experiences of unfairness also include the feeling of being deprived as an individual or as a group member of important goods or immaterial issues compared with other individuals and other groups (Crosby, 1976; Stouffer, Suchman, DeVinney, Star, & Williams, 1949; Runciman, 1966). And people experience that things are unfair when their outcomes are worse than the outcomes of other persons who performed equally well or who bring equally important inputs to social exchange relationships (Adams, 1965; Blau, 1964). Furthermore, the book notes that immoral events are among the worst kinds of experiences that people can have (Greene, 2013; Haidt, 2003a; Skitka, 2002). In this book, I argue that experiences of unfair treatment, relative deprivation, inequitable distribution of outcomes, and immorality fuel the radicalization process such that

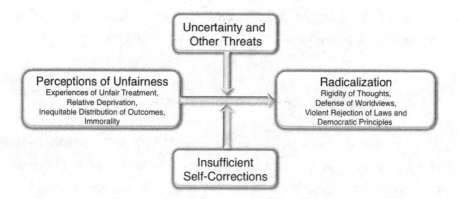

**Figure 1.2 Growing Radicalization.**
The process of growing radicalization on which this book focuses. The framework proposes that various perceptions of unfairness exacerbate important components of radicalization. The model further assumes that insufficient self-corrections, uncertainty, and other threatening information strengthen this process.

the presence of these perceptions of unfairness is likely to aggravate the radicalization process and increase the chances that people become more radicalized.

As Figure 1.2 indicates, core components of radicalization on which this book focuses include rigid thoughts by people (Dechesne, 2001; Peterson & Flanders, 2002; Rock & Janoff-Bulman, 2010; Rokeach, 1948). I also focus on people's willingness to strongly defend these thoughts and beliefs as well as their ideas of how they think the world should look and their intention to defend their own culture or subculture (Becker, 1973; Greenberg, Koole, & Pyszczynski, 2004; Greenberg, Solomon, & Pyszczynski, 1997; Kruglanski et al., 2014; Pyszczynski, Solomon, & Greenberg, 2003). People's violent rejections of law and democratic principles also constitute important components of radicalization on which this book focuses.

I note in this book that when for motivational or cognitive reasons people are inclined to correct in insufficient ways for their self-serving or hedonic impulses (Van den Bos, Peters, Bobocel, & Ybema, 2006), perceptions of unfairness are likely to have an especially strong influence on people's tendencies to engage in radical thoughts and radical behaviors. Furthermore, when people feel uncertain about themselves or are encountering other threatening information (Van den Bos & Lind, 2002, 2009), the chances that radicalization will be exacerbated are increased.

In summary, Figure 1.2 depicts the radicalization process on which this book focuses. The model illustrated in the figure proposes that various perceptions of unfairness exacerbate important components of radicalization. The model further assumes that insufficient self-corrections, uncertainty, and other threatening information strengthen this process. Taken together, the various components in Figure 1.2 illustrate the key theme in this book, namely that experiences of unfairness (Finkel, 2001) and injustice (Lind & Tyler, 1988) in society may be important drivers of social unrest and the deeply felt need for societal change (Layendecker, 1981). These experiences can be genuinely felt and, when coupled with a sense of frustration (Folger, 1977) and deprivation (Runciman, 1966), may serve as pivotal antecedents of enhanced radicalization, particularly when people are unable or unwilling to correct for their self-centered impulses (Van den Bos et al., 2006), feel uncertain about themselves (Hogg, Kruglanski, & Van den Bos, 2013; Van den Bos & Lind, 2002), and live in insecure conditions (Moghaddam, 2010).

## 1.5 THE PROCESS OF ATTENUATING RADICALIZATION

Importantly, this book not only focuses on the issue of how radicalization grows and develops but also explores how we can prevent more extreme forms of radicalization. In addition, the book attempts to explore how we can deradicalize people after extreme forms of radicalization have taken place. Prevention of radicalization can be more doable than deradicalization after people have become radicalized, but both forms of attenuating radicalization are explored here. Moreover, the book argues that fairness perceptions play an important role in the process of attenuating radicalization. The book does this by relying on the psychological analysis of how and why people think and react after they are radicalized, as described in the previous section.

Figure 1.3 illustrates the process of attenuating radicalization on which this book focuses. The book argues that various perceptions of fair treatment are likely to have a damping effect on the prevention or attenuation of radicalization. Experiences of fair treatment on which this book focuses include the receiving of mutual respect (Miller, 2001; Tyler, 2006; Tyler & Lind, 1992). A core issue in the experience of fair treatment includes being allowed opportunities to voice one's opinions about important issues and important decisions to be made (Folger, 1977; Van den Bos, 1999, 2005). Fair treatment also includes receiving due consideration such that one's views are listened to by important decision makers and societal authorities (Tyler, 1987, 1989). Overall impressions of fairness also are part of the experience of fair treatment (Lind, 2001).

The book further proposes that enhanced brain capacity may strengthen the positive influence of issues of fair treatment on the

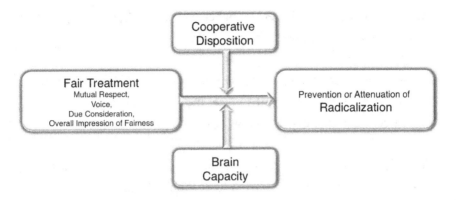

**Figure 1.3  Attenuating Radicalization.**
The process of prevented or attenuated radicalization that is discussed in this book. The framework argues that different elements of fair treatment increase the chances that radicalization is prevented or attenuated. The model also notes that increased brain capacity and cooperative disposition strengthen this process.

prevention or attenuation of radicalization. For example, the book argues that when people have more cognitive capacity available (Van den Bos et al., 2006) and have sufficient working memory (Schmader, Johns, & Forbes, 2008), this increases the chances of fair treatment being picked up by individuals such that they are less likely to radicalize or even may be tempted to start a process of deradicalization. A cooperative disposition is also very important in this respect (Van den Bos et al., 2011).

Deradicalization may be a daunting task. However, with that being said, the notions of fairness and justice may help in deradicalization processes. Consider, for example, the story of Maajid Nawaz as described in his book *Radical* published in 2013. Nawaz learned about the radical Islamist movement Hizb ut-Tahrir, a London-based Islamist group, spreading throughout Europe and Asia in the 1980s and 1990s. At age 16, he was already a ranking member in Hizb ut-Tahrir. He quickly rose through the ranks to become a top recruiter and a charismatic spokesman for the cause of uniting Islam's political power across the world. Nawaz was setting up satellite groups in Pakistan, Denmark, and Egypt when he was rounded up in the aftermath of 9/11 along with many other radical Muslims. He was sent to an Egyptian prison, and he came out of prison completely

changed, convinced that his entire belief system had been wrong and determined to do something about it:

> I had always been taught—and had passionately believed—that the
> presence of Islamism meant justice and the absence of it created
> injustice. But now I began seeing things differently.
>
> I'd only joined HT [Hizb ut-Tahrir] because of the fire that injustice
> had lit inside me. And as I started to decouple justice from Islamism
> in my mind, it was the beginning of the end of my belief in Islamism.
> If justice and Islamism were separated, then not only was it possible
> to have one without the other, it also meant that there were situations
> where *the two might come into conflict.* (Nawaz, 2013, p. 192)

As a result of these notions of fairness and justice, Nawaz met with activists
and heads of state, built a network, and started a foundation (Quilliam)
to combat the rising Islamist tide in Europe and elsewhere, using his intimate knowledge of recruitment tactics in order to reverse extremism and
persuade Muslims that the "narrative" used to recruit them (i.e., the West
is evil and the cause of all of Muslim suffering) is false (Nawaz, 2013).

These are merely some insights from one person who indicated to
have gone through a deradicalization process. Obviously, how to achieve
successful deradicalization is a very difficult issue. In fact, one can go so
far as to label the question of how to deradicalize people as the proverbial
"million-dollar question" in the psychological literature on radicalization
(and a million dollars is probably a huge underestimation). Against this
background, the insights from Nawaz's *Radical* (briefly cited here) are one
indication that although the process of deradicalization may be tough, the
experience of fair treatment may be key to successful deradicalization.
I try to ground and develop this proposition in this book.

In summary, Figure 1.3 depicts the process of prevented or attenuated
radicalization on which this book focuses. The model portrayed in this
figure shows that different elements of fair treatment increase the chances
that radicalization can be prevented or attenuated. The model also notes

that increased brain capacity and cooperative disposition strengthen this process.

## 1.6 OVERVIEW

This book provides an analysis of the radicalization process that applies to various forms of radicalization such as Muslim, right-wing, and left-wing radicalization. The book notes that radicalization processes of different individuals and different groups may vary in important ways. Because of the complex nature of radicalization processes, this book does not provide a comprehensive list of do's and don'ts about how to treat radicals, nor is it the purpose of the book to provide a complete review of all the literature that is available on the important and multifaceted issues of radicalization, extremism, and terrorism. The problem of radicalization is too complicated, and there are too many different groups of radicals and too many different types of radicalization processes out there, to provide clear-cut, "one-size-fits-all" kinds of answers to these problems, let alone to try to come up with *the* answer to the question of why people radicalize.

The aims of this book, therefore, are explicitly more modest: It aims to scientifically ground and explicate some of the core reasons why people radicalize. In doing so, it brings together thus-far scattered in-depth insights into the psychology of radicalization and tries to go beyond earlier insights, empirical articles, and review publications that examined this topic. The book aims to provide an advanced and up-to-date treatment of the psychology of unfairness judgments, the social psychological variables that influence the effects of these judgments, and the conceptual and normative implications that follow from this study. By providing an in-depth analysis of how people use judgments of unfairness to fuel radical beliefs and extremist behaviors, the book tries to provide some of the answers to the big and important question of why people radicalize.

Part One introduces the topic of radicalization and associated issues such as extremism and terrorism. As such, Chapters 1 to 3 discuss the broad question of how we can best understand radicalization. The current chapter introduces a framework that is used in this book to delineate the radicalization process. Chapter 2 discusses relevant instances of radicalization, extremism, and terrorism, particularly as they pertain to people's perceptions that things are not fair. After this, Chapter 3 introduces some important theories that have been developed to try to understand the issues of radicalization, extremism, and terrorism. In this way, the reader is introduced to the broad array of radicalization instances and theories about radicalization.

Parts Two and Three serve as the scientific backbone of the book. These parts discuss relevant scientific notions, principles, and processes that I argue are needed to understand the psychology of radicalization properly. In particular, Part Two focuses on key antecedents of the radicalization process as studied in this book. Chapter 4 describes the core factor in the radicalization process on which this book focuses, namely how people use judgments of unfairness to fuel radical beliefs, extremist behaviors, and terrorism. In particular, I note that various experiences of unfairness and injustice in society may be important drivers of social unrest and the deeply felt need for societal change. These experiences can be genuinely felt and, when coupled with a sense of frustration and deprivation, may serve as pivotal antecedents of enhanced radicalization. This process is especially likely to occur, I argue, when people feel uncertain about themselves and live in insecure conditions or are otherwise threatened (Chapter 5), particularly when people are unable or unwilling to correct for their self-centered impulses (Chapter 6).

Part Three concentrates on core components of what people think, feel, and do after they are radicalized. As such, this part of the book portrays a psychological depiction of how radical people think and react. Rigidity of thoughts (Chapter 7), or "cognitive rigidity," is an important component of how radical people reason. Enhanced defense of these thoughts and beliefs, including the strong affective feelings that people tend to experience during these experiences of "worldview defense," play important roles in this process (Chapter 8).

A crucial step in processes of radicalization is when people move from nonviolent ways of social activism to more violent forms of showing societal disengagement, unrest, and protest. A noteworthy tipping or break point is whether people's acts occur within or outside the law. Accepting that one lives in a democratic society and hence needs to adhere to principles of constitutional democracy and stay away from violent, illegal behavior is key to the prevention of radical and terrorist behavior. Denoting others' opinions as blatantly wrong may be conducive to starting to think that democratic principles are irrelevant and hence can be broken, if needed in violent manners. I argue that, psychologically speaking, this process, including the rejection of majority rule in a democratic society, can be a crucial step in enhanced radicalization. As such this book distinguishes between different types or different phases of radicalization and different forms of extremism (such as violent versus nonviolent forms) and explicitly distinguishes between acts that fall within the law and those that go beyond it (Chapter 9).

Part Four closes the book by drawing conclusions and reflecting on what we have learned. Chapter 10 discusses conceptual implications that scientists and others may learn from this book. The chapter also discusses important limitations of what is presented here. This discussion is presented in such a way that future researchers can derive testable hypotheses from it that can be examined in future research studies. The book also discusses in a straightforward and scientific way the limitations of the approach, perspectives, and standpoints ventilated here. In particular, the book notes that different psychological processes are probably important in different phases of radicalization. As such, this book focuses especially on the first, foundational phase of radicalization in which perceptions of unfairness and feelings of deprivation dominate (Moghaddam, 2005) and hence may be less applicable to more extreme forms of radicalization.

I also discuss what we can do about radicalization on the basis of the insights presented in this book. As such, Chapter 11 identifies some important ways of dealing with radicalization, extremism, and terrorism and discusses practical implications that policy decision makers and others may derive from the book in their attempts to develop measures to counter sympathy for extremist beliefs and support for terrorist behaviors. I note that prevention and fighting of radicalization obviously are very challenging tasks but may be possible when lessons learned from the psychology of fairness judgments (discussed in this book) are taken into consideration and are combined with the classic ideal of Scientific Enlightenment that focuses on the application of critical rationalism to problems of civilization (Popper, 1945, 1959; see also Hume, 1777; Kant, 1784; Rousseau, 1762; Smith, 1759; Voltaire, 1763) and with modern insight into the power of conscious, deliberative thought (Baumeister & Masicampo, 2010) and the cooperative disposition of many people (Staub, 2015; Van den Bos & Lind, 2013). Furthermore, prevention may be best achieved by trying to nourish agreement with democratic values (Moghaddam, 2005). This may be realized by adherence to fair and just treatment in mature interactions in which both respect and acceptance of responsibilities are important. Thus, the book argues and grounds the proposition that perceptions that things are unfair may fuel growing radicalization, whereas perceptions that things are fair may prevent or decrease radicalization.

The book ends by drawing final conclusions and putting forward some final notes. In Chapter 12 I discuss approaches of how to study radicalization and what the implications of this study are for empirical research in the areas of the behavioral and social sciences and the domains of law and human behavior and society. Taken together, these chapters aim to enhance our understanding of why people radicalize. In doing this, the book grounds how judgments of unfairness can feed radical thoughts, extremist acts, and sympathy and active support for terrorism.

# Instances of Radicalization, Extremism, and Terrorism

## 2.1 INTRODUCTION

In this chapter I focus on issues of radicalization (including notable instances of extremism and terrorism) as they apply to perceptions of unfairness (and related constructs such as feelings of personal uncertainty, other threatening information, and rigidity of people's thoughts). As such, it is not my aim to provide a complete review of all instances of radicalization that are out there. Instead, I discuss some instances of Muslim radicalization, right-wing radicalization, and left-wing radicalization that are relevant to the book's line of reasoning as this is illustrated in Figure 1.2. The instances I review include some issues of activism, important examples of terrorism, and most notably instances of extremism. As such, I try to review the full range of the radicalization process as shown in Figure 1.1, with special emphasis on issues of terrorism and, particularly, extremism.

Thus, in this chapter I review radical beliefs, extremist behaviors, and terrorist acts associated with Muslims as well as people from the right wing and left wing of the political spectrum (however hard this sometimes may be to define). In reviewing the radical beliefs and behaviors associated with these beliefs, I try to show that perceptions that things are unfair play a crucial role in the different radicalization processes that are discussed here. I ground this insight in part on what I saw as a researcher conducting or supervising research for Dutch ministries and government agencies. In these research projects, I saw the important role that perceptions of unfairness play in the radicalization of Muslims, right-wing extremists, and left-wing extremists. It is the radicalization processes of these groups of people on which I focus in this book.

I also pay appropriate attention to the radicalization of other groups and individuals in this book, but I concentrate primarily on Muslim, right-wing, and left-wing radicalization. I complement these insights with what other research projects and other researchers teach us about various radicalization processes. I also rely on basic and fundamental scientific literature that helps me in my quest to push forward the science of radicalization processes by focusing on what key antecedents (see Part Two) and core components (see Part Three) of radicalization we can distinguish and what good, reliable scientific insights tell us about these antecedents and components (see Part Four).

## 2.2 MUSLIM RADICALIZATION

As noted, my fascination with radicalization processes was influenced heavily by research projects that I performed in collaboration with Dutch ministries and associated organizations. For example, in a research project that Annemarie Loseman, Bertjan Doosje, and I conducted for the National Coordinator for Security and Counterterrorism in the Netherlands, we interviewed 131 Muslim youngsters from the Netherlands by means of survey questionnaires assessed on the Internet, measuring their susceptibility to adopting radical attitudes and behaviors (Doosje, Loseman, & Van den Bos, 2013). We also conducted qualitative in-depth personal interviews with Muslim radicals, including Salafists, at various mosques and other places (Van den Bos, Loseman, & Doosje, 2009).

In these research projects on radical attitudes among Muslims in the Netherlands, we found that unfairness perceptions played an important role in the radicalization process of these Muslims. That is, our Muslim respondents indicated that the Prime Minister of the Netherlands was not advocating or defending their rights. They noted, for instance, that this person or other politicians did not seem to allow for the Sugar Feast or other important Muslim holidays to be turned into official national holidays. The Muslim citizens also looked at judges and police officers and how they as members of their group were treated by those officials, relative to how members of other groups were treated. They also pointed at work managers in Dutch society, such as the manager from the local grocery store who did not want them to have an internship or a side job at that store. I discuss the unfairness experiences of these Muslim respondents in detail in Chapter 4, the chapter that is dedicated to an in-depth review of the psychology of perceptions of unfairness. Here, I note that perceptions of unfairness played a key role among Muslim respondents and Muslim radicals in the Netherlands.

In other research projects in other countries with other radical Muslims, we also saw important suggestions that perceptions of unfairness fueled Muslim radicalization. For instance, Meertens, Prins, and Doosje (2006) cite important evidence indicating that when individual Muslims or groups of Muslims feel that they are being suppressed or treated unfairly, this often leads to the legitimization of violent behavior. A clear example of this statement is seen in the perceptions of unfairness that are present

among core members of al-Qaeda, perceptions that have fueled the violent behavior of the terrorist organization.

   Al-Qaeda is known for several extremist acts and terrorist attacks in
several places around the world. Al-Qaeda's main terrorist act was the
attack on the World Trade Center on September 11, 2001. Other terrorist
attacks by al-Qaeda took place in 1992 on a hotel where US troops had
stayed in Aden, Yemen; the US embassies in Nairobi, Kenya and Dar es
Salaam, Tanzania in 1998; and the bombing of the USS Cole in 2000.[1]
One could well say that al-Qaeda originated out of the hate by the leader
of al-Qaeda, Osama bin Laden, for the United States. As Bodanksy
(2001) notes: "Bin Laden hates the United States passionately and
considers it his principal enemy. He accuses the United States—the locus
of Westernization and modernity—of being the source of all crises and
trouble afflicting the Muslim world" (pp. ix–xx). Furthermore, Mustafa
Kamil, one of Bin Laden's supporters, stressed that Muslims must resort to terrorism as the sole viable and effective means of meeting such
challenges as "the enslavement of mankind, the unfair killing of the
oppressed on earth, the corruption of man and land, and the prolifera-
tion of destructive weapons that are used only by the tyrants" (Bodansky,
2001, p. 403). Thus, observers of al-Qaeda note that perceptions of unfairness and associated emotional reactions play a key role among the
members of the terrorist organization.

   Similarly, Stern (2004) cites a member of an extremist Muslim group in
Pakistan who expressed his feelings of unfairness by stating that America
is a terrorist country and that the West is trying to force its capitalist ideology on Islam. The person further noted that there is less poverty in
America because Americans profit from the poverty of the developing
countries and care only about their own well-being and maximization
of their own wealth, at the expense of others. This capitalist ideology
was considered very unfair by the person quoted. The feelings this radical Muslim expressed are an example of a comparison between his own

---

1. See https://en.wikipedia.org/wiki/Al-Qaeda. See also Bodansky (2001) and Stern (2004).

country and the Western world in general and the United States specifically, suggesting that experienced unfairness can be derived from making
comparisons with countries objectively removed from one's own country.

Interestingly, the role of unfairness perceptions can also be seen in response to the actions the United States undertook in reaction to 9/11.
According to Stern and Berger (2015), the 2003 invasion of Iraq further
spurred the felt injustice and justification of violent responses in return.
As the authors notices: "Iraq would be a lightning rod for jihadists, who
flocked to a country where they had not been able to operate successfully before in order to confront American troops. But the invasion re-
inforced jihadi claims about America's hegemonic designs on the Middle
East, providing a recruiting bonanza at a time when the terrorist needed
it most" (Stern & Berger, 2015, p. 18). These perceptions of unfairness
created opportunities for the rise of al-Qaeda in Iraq and later for the rise
of Islamic State (IS) in Iraq and Syria.

IS (or DAESH, which stands for *Dawlat Islāmiyya Irāq Shām*, which
in turn refers to Islamic State in Iraq and Syria [ISIS], or Islamic State
of Iraq and the Levant [ISIL]) has been responsible for the attack on the
French satirical magazine *Charlie Hebdo* in 2015, the killing of tourists
in a hotel in Tunis in the same year, and the bombing of the airport in
Brussels in 2016. Although IS has been categorized as a form of radicalization inspired by extreme religious beliefs, United Nations political
advisor Ghassan Salamé interestingly noted that IS radicalization often is
not driven by the religion itself, but that religion comes later, as some sort
of legitimization of extremist views and associated violent behaviors.[2]
When Salamé's perspective is correct, this would imply that religion is
not a source of IS identification but rather a tool to mobilize people to
join IS.

Perceptions of unfairness also play a crucial role in the radicalization
associated with IS. For example, experts warn that it is not really possible

2. See the interview in the *Tegenlicht* documentary posted on January 31, 2016 at YouTube,
https://www.youtube.com/watch?v=9OlgweIjBdM).

to beat IS without addressing the feelings of humiliation and deprivation among Sunni Muslims who are associated with IS.[3]

Importantly, one should not consider all radical and extremist Muslim groups as one and the same. For example, al-Qaeda and IS each stand for several subgroups. Furthermore, al-Qaeda and IS have different ideological backgrounds and different perceptions of what are the right and wrong things to do. This can cause not only frustration among the different groups but also a split, and it can even result in a war on its own.

For instance, the first meeting between Osama bin Laden and Abu Musab al-Zarqawi, a crucial person in the rise of IS, revealed fundamental differences between the two. Stern and Berger (2015) states that Bin Laden was put off by Zarqawi's commitment that all Shiite Muslims must be killed. In later years, Bin Laden expressed his frustrations in letters stating that he was deeply troubled by jihadi groups that targeted Muslim civilians. These clashes about what is fair, just, and moral behavior are important and, I argue in this book, can serve as important tools that can have important roles in processes of deradicalization. For instance, this may lead to the important breakdown of the belief that extreme Muslim ideology can and should be equated with fairness and justice.

In the previous chapter I discussed the case of Nawaz (2013), whose attenuated radicalization was inspired by a similar breakdown between justice and his radical belief in Islam. And in the spring of 2014, IS and al-Qaeda officially separated. Many observers of this separation suggested that this occurred because IS was even too extreme for al-Qaeda (Stern & Berger, 2015).

Another relevant example of an extreme Muslim group for which perceptions of injustice and deprivation have led to extreme actions is the Taliban. The Taliban is also a prime example of how rigid thoughts are a core component of radicalization processes, as discussed in detail in Chapter 7. And it is another example of how different radical Muslim groups may clash, in part because of things they see as fair or unfair. This

3. Experts cited in the newspaper *NRC* on June 11, 2016. See also Roy (2017).

also can be seen with the rise of the Mujahideen versus the Taliban, which originated in the Soviet-Afghan War in the years between 1979 and 1989.[4]

The communist government of Afghanistan, being backed up by the Soviet Union, fought against an insurgent group of Muslim Afghan warriors, the Mujahideen. The Mujahideen were supported by the United States, and in the end, the Mujahideen won and seized power in Afghanistan. During the Soviet-Afghan War, millions of Afghans fled to Pakistan. In Pakistan, the Afghan civilians sent their children to schools named "madrasas." These schools gave the refugees food and shelter, but also taught the children an extreme form of Islam.

In Afghanistan, the Mujahideen were now in control, but this did not restore peace. On the contrary, the people of Afghanistan accused the Mujahideen of brutality, ceaseless fighting, and corruption. To put an end to these unfair acts, the students of the madrasas, and one student in particular, Mohammed Omar, started a politico-religious force. This force became known as the "Taliban," which translates as "students" (Blanchard, 2008). For example, the Taliban claimed that a local governor had abducted and raped two teenage girls. In response to this act of unfairness, the Taliban freed the girls and hanged the governor. Mohammed Omar started the movement with fewer than 50 armed madrasas students, but within a few months 15,000 madrasas students had joined the Taliban in Afghanistan, attesting to the attractiveness of entitative groups that fight unfairness and injustice.

Since then, however, the Taliban has been accused of brutal treatment of Afghan civilians. They denied their people food and harshly enforced their interpretation of the Islamic Sharia law. For example, they forced women to wear a burka and denied them access to health care, education, and work. To further pursue their political and ideological goals, the Taliban also committed a huge number of violent and terrorist acts. This illustrates one of the core themes of this book, namely how rigid and extreme notions of what is right and wrong may sometimes convert into

4. See https://en.wikipedia.org/wiki/Taliban and https://en.wikipedia.org/wiki/Mujahideen. See also Blanchard (2008).

brutal and violent acts to defend what is seen as right and to fight against what is perceived to be wrong. These issues also play an important role in right-wing radicalization.

## 2.3 RIGHT-WING RADICALIZATION

Another important form of radicalization comes from people on the political right. For instance, in our own research of extreme right-wing attitudes among "autochthonous" citizens of the Netherlands, we derived our insights from large-scale online survey questionnaires (Doosje, Van den Bos, Loseman, Feddes, & Mann, 2012) as well as in-depth interviews with extreme youngsters from groups such as *Voorpost*[5] or people associated or formerly associated with *Nederlandse Volks-Unie*, a Dutch political extreme-right party with sympathy for Nazi ideas (W. van den Bos, Van Dijk, Westenberg, Rombouts, & Crone, 2009). In these studies we found that unfairness perceptions played a key role in right-wing radicalization. For example, the right-wing autochthonous respondents tended to note that how they were treated relative to Muslims in the Netherlands was really unfair, not deserved, and not right. Some of our right-wing respondents indicated that Muslims were taking away important material goods, such as jobs and housing, and also immaterial goods, such as access to potential dates. I return to this issue in Chapter 4, where I discuss the psychology of unfairness perceptions in detail.

Here I note that similar reactions were recently found in the Netherlands when Dutch citizens were interviewed about individuals who seek asylum in the country. For example, when a major of a town in the Netherlands agreed with the building of an asylum center after she received this request from the province, a local Dutch woman stated: "We have fought for many years to be able to build houses. Everything they [the city government] could counteract, they counteracted. And NOW, now when they want to have an asylum center, they want to realize it within this short amount of

5. See https://en.wikipedia.org/wiki/Voorpost.

time. I find it inconceivable."[6] Another Dutch citizen noted: "People who seek asylum pay lots of money to cross over to this country. This implies they have money. And if they arrive here they get more money. We have to pay for that. I find this truly ridiculous."[7] Clearly, perceptions of unfairness play an important role in what is generally known as processes of right-wing radicalization.

Indeed, there is an abundance of unfairness perceptions among various forms of instances of right-wing thought. These instances range from right-wing political ideas and associated activism that clearly act within the boundaries of constitutional democracy. There are also more extreme movements and radical individuals who can or are tempted to break the law and act in violent manners to convey what they think is right and to protest against what they see as wrong. Perceived unfairness as impetus for right-wing politics can be seen, for example, in the French *Front National*, the Dutch *Partij voor de Vrijheid* (PVV), and the British National Party (BNP).

Copsey (2004) studied the BNP as a form of contemporary British fascism and noted the important role that the quest for legitimacy played in the rise of the party. As such the development of the BNP can be seen as an interesting form of right-wing radicalization. Copsey identifies the reemergence of popular racism as the most obvious factor of the electoral advance of the BNP in May 2003. He notices that this popular racism was not focused on a single issue, such as anger toward asylum seekers. In fact, Copsey (2004) interestingly states that: "The popular racism that occasioned the party's success in Burnley was grounded more in feelings of resentment toward the local Asian community and perceptions that the funding distribution between wards was unfair. We need only reflect for a moment on its May 2003 campaign slogan of 'Vote for a fairer Burnley.' This had little to do with asylum-seekers—it's key demands were for a more equitable distribution of public monies, withdrawal of funding to the town's translation unit and the creation of the special unit at Burnley

6. See https://www.youtube.com/watch?v=rT8I4ZLYKo0, retrieved on June 6, 2016.

7. Interview in *De Volkskrant* on September 19, 2016.

police station to deal with 'anti-white' racism" (p. 146). In short, various issues related to perceived fairness and unfairness can be seen in the growth of the BNP, such as perceived unfair distributions, perceptions of inequity, and searches for legitimacy.

Right-wing radicalization, thus inspired by various perceptions of unfairness, may turn into violent and antidemocratic behavior and even terrorism. For example, in the early 1980s right-wing terrorism started to spread throughout Europe. Germany, France, Italy, and Turkey have all known far right-wing extremist groups (Copsey, 2004; Hoffman, 1982). For instance, in August 1980 a group of right-wing terrorists exploded a bomb at a railroad station in Bologna, Italy, killing 85 people and injuring more than 180. According to the Italian police, the perpetrators were Valerio Fioravanti and Francesca Mambro, two members of the neofascist organization *Nuclei Armati Rivoluzionari* (or Armed Revolutionary Nuclei [NAR]).[8] Another example of right-wing radicalization is the *Nationaldemokratische Partei Deutschlands* (or National Democratic Party [NDP]) in former West Germany.

The political system of West Germany after the Second World War was marked by a close alliance with the United States and a shrinking of ideological differences (Nagle, 1970). This is why the birth of a new party, the NDP, which was a fusion of the last survivors of right-wing extremism, was hardly noticed when the party started to develop in 1964. The party's appeal, however, rose toward to the end of the 1970s, and several terrorist cells associated with the party were formed. These cells have been responsible for several bombings, including the Oktoberfest bombings of 1980 (Hoffman, 1982).

Nagle (1970) notices that the formation of the NDP should be seen as a reaction to the governmental crisis in Germany. Looking at the reasons that Germany was in a governmental crisis may thus well explain why the NDP was formed. Nagle (1970) identifies the growing economic difficulties and the perceived lack of protection of small businessmen, including farmers, as the most important contributors. Indeed, economic protectionism for

8. See https://en.wikipedia.org/wiki/Right-wing_terrorism#Italy. See also Hanley (1997).

small businesses was an important component of NPD policy. The NPD stated in their Manifest of 1965: "Germany needs a healthy agriculture for the defense of its political independence.... The agricultural sector, therefore, needs a guaranteed income in order to insure its continuing existence in our industrial society. Therefore, through energetic representation in the Common Market, we demand also an end to that unfair competition which over and over is prejudicial towards our farmers, despite their diligence" (Nagle, 1970, p. 114). Nagle also notes that uneasiness about the alliance with the United States and several scandals concerning the military policy lay at the basis of the crisis.

Another interesting instance of right-wing radicalization is found in Brazil during the early 1960s, culminating in the military rule of the country during 1964 and 1985 (Skidmore, 1988). In the early 1960s, right-wing individuals in Brazilian society, including important leaders of the Brazilian military forces, perceived the ruling of João Goulart as a socialist threat. Large demonstrations opposing this threat were held, the so-called *Marchas da Família com Deus pela Liberdade,* or marches for family and God for freedom. Following these marches, authoritarian military dictatorship began in 1964 with a coup d'état led by the Armed Forces against the administration of President Goulart, who had assumed the office after being vice president, upon the resignation of the democratically elected president Jânio Quadros. The military regime ended when José Sarney took office as president on March 15, 1985. During the period of Brazilian military government, bombing attempts happened in which far-right militaries engaged in the repression were actively involved. The Brazilian case is interesting because it shows how perceptions that things go wrong and associated societal protest can be transformed into violent action, including bombing attempts.

Some forms of religious extremism can be associated with politically right-wing radicalization. A special or an interesting extremist group in this respect is the Ku Klux Klan (KKK).[9] The KKK is the name of three

9. See https://en.wikipedia.org/wiki/Ku_Klux_Klan. See also Du Bois (1935), Farmer (2005), MacLean (1995), and McVeigh (2009).

different past and present extremist groups in the United States. They are known for their brutal actions. To cite Du Bois (1935): "Armed guerrilla warfare killed thousands of Negroes; political riots were staged; their causes or occasions were always obscure, their results always certain: ten to one hundred times as many Negroes were killed as whites. . . . Masked men shot into houses and burned them, sometimes with the occupants still inside. They drove successful black farmers off their land. . . . Generally, it can be reported that in North and South Carolina, in 18 months ending in June 1867, there were 197 murders and 548 cases of aggravated assault" (pp. 674–675).

Farmer (2005) also notices that "the targets of KKK activities in the 1920s were not exclusively racial, and certainly included black, but also everything and everyone else that conservative extremists at the time viewed as unchristian, un-American or immoral. The list of targets therefore also included Catholics, Jews, Mexicans . . . , dance halls, movie theaters, businessmen charged with corrupting young women . . . , thieves, bootleggers, and doctors who performed abortions" (p. 208).

KKK ideology has been motivated by perceptions of unfairness in important ways. For example, in 1923 D. C. Stephenson, the then-new grand dragon of the KKK, addressed the largest Klan rally ever held in the United States. In his speech, entitled "Back to the Constitution," Stephenson denounced political corruption and American imperialism abroad and called for an end to deficit spending. He addressed the crowd in Kokomo, Indiana's Malfalfa Park in the following way:

> The constitution must be vitalized to compel common economic justice with respect to currency and credit. Otherwise, in another fifty years, this nation will be experiencing all the agonies of class conflict that can end only in economic chaos and political revolution. More and more will the great middle class be wiped out. Already the tendency is dangerously toward an unproductive dividend-clipping aristocracy of wealth, with every billion that it gains through manipulation of money and monopolization of credit adding by

inverse ratio to the numbers whose unjust impoverishment becomes a menace to the nation. (McVeigh, 2009, p. 4).

Another example is the way the KKK viewed the role of women. In the line of good Protestant living, they believed women should take care of their households and should not be distracted from their "cardinal functions," which included childbearing and childrearing. Surprisingly enough, the KKK did encourage suffrage for Protestant white women. This was an opinion that was deeply felt, as a quote of Athens, Georgia, Klan leader W. R. Tindall illustrates. That is, in 1924 there was a plan to levy taxes on women voters and Tindall responded to this plan with the following words: "unfair, unjust, and contrary to our principles of government" (MacLean, 1995, p. 116).

Right-wing terrorism is motivated by a variety of far-right ideologies and beliefs, including anticommunism, neofascism, neo-Nazism, racism, and xenophobia. Right-wing terrorists aim to overthrow governments and replace them with nationalist or fascist-oriented governments. The core of this movement includes neofascist skinheads, far-right hooligans, youth sympathizers, and intellectual guides who believe that the state must rid itself of foreign elements in order to protect *rightful* citizens. However, they usually lack a rigid ideology, especially when compared with Muslim radicalization and left-wing radicalization.[10]

Furthermore, Muslim radicalization often occurs in groups. This also is the case for processes of right-wing radicalization, but right-wing extremists also include many lone actors or lone wolves, isolated individuals with extreme ideas but not close, proximate relationships with groups or organizations sharing their ideas. Examples of these are Timothy McVeigh and Terry Nichols, who are responsible for the 1995 bombing of the Murrah Federal Building in downtown Oklahoma City in 1995. McVeigh and Nichols were angry at the federal government's handling of the 1992 FBI standoff with Randy Weaver at Ruby Ridge as well as the Waco siege in

10. See https://en.wikipedia.org/wiki/Right-wing_terrorism. See also Moghadam (2006).

1993. McVeigh decided to bomb a federal building as a response to these raids.[11]

Another example of a right-wing lone wolf is the Norwegian Anders Breivik. In 2011, he set off a car bomb in the heart of Oslo's government district, killing eight people and injuring 200. After this, he went to the island of Utøya, where the youth of the Norwegian Labour Party had gathered for their annual retreat, and there he killed 67 youngsters by gun shots. Ninety minutes before Breivik's attack on Oslo, he distributed a 1,518-page document by means of email. In this Manifesto he describes the assault on Western values by feminists, deconstructionists, the Frankfurt School, Islam, the European Union, the United Nations, and many other sources. Breivik expresses utter contempt for Norwegian women in the document. He also believes that Muslim men are violent and lawless but writes affectionately of the Muslim friends he had as a teenager (see Carle, 2013). For now, I conclude that perceptions of unfairness and associated psychological reactions such as emotional responses and rigid (and sometimes conflicting) thoughts play a role in right-wing radicalization.

## 2.4 LEFT-WING RADICALIZATION

Processes of radicalization and perceptions of unfairness also play a role among those on the political left. One of the most well-known left-wing groups born out of perceived unfairness is the Occupy movement. This movement started on September 17, 2011, when people occupied Zuccotti Park in New York City to protest against economic unfairness and the unequal distribution of wealth in America. In an interview with the *Daily Telegraph* on October 29, 2012, Andrew Haldane, the Executive Director of Financial Stability at the Bank of England, stated that the protesters had been right about bankers' behavior and were correctly trying to persuade bankers to behave in a more moral way.

---

11. See https://en.wikipedia.org/wiki/Oklahoma_City_bombing. See also Associated Press (2001).

Perceptions of unfairness play a role in left-wing radicalization that not only involves nonviolent protest but also includes violent behavior. For example, in a research project for which I chaired the supervision committee for the Netherlands Ministry of the Interior and Kingdom Relations, it was found that individuals and organizations involved in what I label as left-wing radicalization pertaining to asylum and animal rights basically had one of two starting points for their processes of radicalization (IVA, 2010). In both starting points, perceptions of unfairness play a crucial role.

Characteristic of one starting point route is that people experienced emotions, including sorrow and feelings of frustration, about the perceived suffering and injustice done to animals and foreigners in the Netherlands. The other starting point relies less heavily on emotions and is characterized by people having developed critical views about society, sometimes strong ideological views, that serve as impetus for an ideologically based striving for more just treatment of animals and people who seek asylum in the Netherlands. In technical terms one can thus say that both "affective-experiential" and "cognitive-rationalistic" processes (see Van den Bos & Lind, 2009) can play a role in left-wing individuals getting involved in radicalization regarding asylum and animal rights.

Whatever route or starting point that the left-wing radicals whom we studied followed, the radicalization processes have been known to result in violent behavior (IVA, 2010; Netherlands General Intelligence and Security Service, 2010). For example, these groups of left-wing radicals often engage in so-called "home visits," in which they go to the houses of individuals working for companies that are perceived to treat animals in the wrong way. Or they visit the homes of civil servants who are active in governmental agencies responsible for handling asylum applications. Quite often these home visits end up in violations of the personal space of the individuals under attack, including the smashing of individual properties or the throwing of paint or lumps of clay from the individuals' gardens to the private houses of the individuals. In a legal sense these demonstrations often are minor misdemeanors only, but these radical behaviors can create deep feelings of fear or even terror among the targeted individuals and the families of those individuals.

The Netherlands General Intelligence and Security Service (2014) notes that left-wing activism and extremism in the Netherlands currently is a multifaceted phenomenon that clearly involves extremists, who legitimize the use of violence, but that also includes activists, who want to act within the law. Importantly, left-wing radicals, and especially those who are tempted to engage in violent behavior, often seem to act in the ways that they do because they feel morally superior (Netherlands General Intelligence and Security Service, 2010). One could say that quite often their reasoning can be captured in statements saying that these kinds of radicals convey the following: "This is wrong, and therefore I am in my right to do something about this, even when I then would break the law."

I come back to the issue of perceived moral superiority in Chapter 4, where I discuss this observation and its implications in more detail. Here I focus on an interesting, and I think important, example of growing left-wing radicalization observed in the Netherlands in recent years. An outcome of this radicalization process was observed on August, 26, 2016, when the Dutch newspaper *NRC* reported that the home of the director of the Repatriation and Departure Service, a high civil servant of the Ministry of Safety and Justice in the Netherlands, was besmirched with red paint. According to the article, an action group, which calls itself "Demolish the Deportation Machine," has claimed responsibility for this act. The action group has been active for several years and opposes the Dutch detention and deportation policy. In 2008, the action group published a list of more than 100 companies and dozens of organizations and persons involved in this policy.

The Repatriation and Departure Service is responsible for the returning of individuals who are denied asylum in the Netherlands. The director of the service whose house had been besmirched with paint was being watched for months by left-wing extremists. The director had gained their attention when she planned to attend a charity run for refugees. This upset the activists, who perceived her as an important symbol of an inhumane asylum policy. They started a campaign against the director's participation in the charity run. Interviews in which the director advocated the official Dutch repatriation policies were distributed. Hateful reactions soon followed. An activist wrote: "Almost every sentence of the director of the Dutch part of the European deportation system is full with lies and twits of reality." Another activist said: "Scandalous, you should not be participating in a charity run and deport people into distress several days after."

In the end, according to the organization of the charity run, the director decided after a series of "intimidating messages and signals" not to participate. This was perceived as a victory by an action group that calls itself "Stop Deportations!", who viewed their protest actions as "completely just." They also commented that they were "forced" to engage in this protest behavior and that the director should "learn something out of this, namely what it feels like when you should do something you rather would not because you were forced to do it." Other action groups have been distributing lists of companies that have contributed to the building of repatriation centers as well as lists of private addresses of officials associated with the policies that they deem unfair and unjust. As a result, for example, a can of butyric acid was thrown into the hallway of an advice bureau in Arnhem that was involved in the building of a detention center.

The private address of the Director of the Repatriation and Departure Service was spread on the Internet, suggesting that everyone who is bothered by the Service or does not agree with the work of the Service should pay the director a visit. In line with the theory of symbolic interactionism (Blumer, 1969; Mead, 1934), the director is the personification of the system that the actions groups loathe. "It is contaminated work," reported a spokesperson of the No Border Network anonymously on Facebook. According to the No Border Network, the Repatriation and Departure Service has no "existence right" and "does not fit in a world without borders that we seek." These reasoning processes of these left-wing extremists indeed reflect important notions of perceived moral superiority that serve to justify the privacy-intruding and violent behaviors associated with these processes of left-wing radicalization.

Another example of left-wing radicalization is the *Rote Armee Fraktion* (or Red Army Faction [RAF]). This group of left-wing terrorists was very active in the 1970s in West Germany (De Graaf, 2010; Kellen, 1990).

The RAF is probably one of the most well-known examples of left-wing radicalization in which activism gradually developed into clear acts of terrorism.

The origins of the RAF can be traced back to the student protest movement in West Germany in which there was anger at the postwar denazification in West and East Germany, which was perceived as a failure because former Nazis held positions in government and economy. The radicals further regarded the conservative media as biased. And some radicals used the supposed association of large parts of society with Nazism as an argument against any peaceful approaches. The radicalized members were influenced by many writings of communist authors and critical and philosophical reflections on society.[12]

In the end, the RAF engaged in a series of bombings, assassinations, kidnappings, bank robberies, and shoot-outs with police over the course of three decades. Their activity peaked in late 1977, which led to a national crisis that became known as the "German Autumn." The RAF has been held responsible for 34 deaths. These include the violent kidnapping and eventual killing of the president of the German Employers' Association, Hanns Martin Schleyer, a former officer of the SS and NSDAP member. This also involved the killing of Jürgen Ponto, the head of Dresdner Bank, who was shot in front of his house. One of those involved in the latter act was the sister of his goddaughter.[13]

As we have seen in other instances of radicalization, perceptions of unfairness were present in the RAF radicalization process. This is obvious when we view the many writings of the RAF members and their predecessors talking at length about the many instances of unfairness and injustice they perceived in Western capitalist countries. We can also see evidence for the role of perceptions of unfairness and injustice when we look at a letter that Gert Richard Schneider wrote to his parents, long before he became a notable member of the RAF.

12. See https://en.wikipedia.org/wiki/Red_Army_Faction. See also Aust (1985, 2009).
13. Ibid.

In the letter Schneider explained why he had quit his academic study and instead had started to work as a laborer. He told his parents that this choice was based on a conscious analysis and developing process. This process let him to the conclusion that an unfair situation was taking place in society, which had made him unwilling to become "someone big" in society. According to him, the "big" people kept everyone else "small." The big people owned the most, whereas 80% of the people were laborers, the "small" ones. According to Schneider, the current economic crisis was coming from this disproportional distribution of ownership, and the laborers were the ones paying for it. This is why he chose to live like a laborer. He chose to be at the side of the barricades at which, according to him, the oppressed were fighting to the extent that they eventually would change the system. This is just an example of how an individual's perception that things in society are unfair formed the basis of the person making certain choices that eventually led him to radicalize and become a notorious member of a far-left militant group (Pekelder, 2007).

The notion of perceived unfairness was also a major source of protest and anger that led to the uprising of the *Fuerzas Armadas Revolucionarias de Colombia* (or Revolutionary Armed Forces of Colombia [FARC]), a guerrilla movement, known to have employed terrorist acts (Livingstone, 2004). For example, the distribution of land in Columbia was seen as unfair and unjust. Molano (2000) states that after a new conservative government was formed in 1946, this government used political violence to regain the oligarchy's land and to remain in power. The resistance that this caused was further spurred by the murder of a charismatic Liberal and land-reform movement leader (Molano, 2000). Quoting Chernick, Tellidis and Toros (2015) note: "The political and social goals of the FARC have been striving for since its incipience have hardly changed: Broadly speaking, they consist of political inclusion, equal access to state resources, including solving the agrarian problem, as well as reforming the structure of the state forces" (p. 132).

Another political goal of the FARC is to provide relief from the daily discrimination of women. According to them, women should fight for equal treatment and should join the FARC. A leader of the FARC explained why a woman had joined FARC: "A woman perceives injustice through every pore in her body; from the moment she is born, she is discriminated against" (Stanski, 2005, p. 139). The FARC is a guerrilla movement that has been active since 1964 and is known to have employed terrorist acts (Livingstone, 2004). The perceptions of unfairness prevalent among members of the FARC hence can lead to a better understanding of this movement and their actions.

Another example of the extreme left is *Sendero Luminoso* (or Shining Path), founded in the late 1960s in Peru. Shining Path is a terrorist group known for its brutality and the slaughtering of many people. The leader and founder of Shining Path, Abimael Guzmán, was inspired by Mao Zedong's Cultural Revolution and wanted to overthrow the government of Peru and to replace it with a communist government. Part of his motivation for wanting to do this (in violent ways, if necessary) was discontent with the unfair existence of class differences and imperialism. Maoism and other communist theories do not, however, completely account for the views and actions of Guzmán, in part because his background as belonging to the elite and being a light-skinned, well-educated man distanced him from the peasants he was fighting for (Starn, 1995). For example, while claiming to stand up for the peasants, Guzmán was characterized by a complete lack of interest in the traditions and culture of the native Peruvian people (Starn, 1995).

Scientific analyses of the Shining Path suggest that the movement was attractive to the poorest people of Peru because it meant an escape from the hardships of daily life, including national corruption, poverty, and despair. Starn (1995) says: "The Shining Path offered the possibility of mastery over the unmasterable, a magnetic promise in the face of chaos and trauma in years of official corruption and economic crisis among the hardest in Peru since the Chilean invasion at the end of the nineteenth century" (p. 418). "The seeming unknotting of tangles" of Peruvian history "by the nimble metaphysics of a universal Marxism" was conducive in conveying this illusion of mastery goals (Starn, 1995, p. 418).

Not unlike right-wing radicalization, left-wing extremism also includes lone actors, individuals with extreme ideas but not close or immediate relationships with groups or organizations that influence or coordinate their behaviors. For example, Volkert van der Graaf is a Dutch environmental and animal rights activist who, on May 6, 2002, went out on his own to shoot Pim Fortuyn, the leader of a right-wing political party (*Lijst Pim Fortuyn,* or List Pim Fortuyn [LPF]) in the Netherlands.

Fortuyn was killed at the shooting. In part because the killing took place only nine days before the elections of Dutch Parliament, the brutal assassination of an important political leader had a huge impact on Dutch society. Although Van der Graaf was very active in domains such as animal rights and environmental issues and was working with several organizations focusing on these issues, most of his activities were concentrated on working within these organizations in setting up legal procedures against animal abuse and violations of environmental laws. In contrast to this, the killing of Fortuyn was meticulously planned only by himself, and he did all this on his own, much to the surprise of his friends, fellow activists, and also his girlfriend. The assassination clearly was the result of one person acting in a violent and extremist way.

During the handling of his criminal case, as a result of which he was convicted and sentenced to 18 years of prison, Van der Graaf admitted to having acted alone, without the help of others. To the court he stated that he acted in the way that he did because of the general stigmatizing political views of Fortuyn (who had called Islam a retarded culture), the polarizing way in which Fortuyn promoted those views, and the huge amount of political power that he was expected to have in the near future. According to the Public Prosecutor,[14] Van der Graaf wanted to stop the danger and threat to society that Fortuyn was posing. He wanted to stop Fortuyn from exploiting Muslims as "scapegoats" and weaker members of society. As a result of these perceptions and ideas, he killed Fortuyn. Clearly, perceptions that things are not right and need to be corrected can lead left-wing extremists to act in violent, illegal, and immoral ways.

14. Quoted in the Dutch newspaper *Trouw* on November 25, 2002.

## 2.5 CORE PROPOSITION

The aim of this chapter was to provide a brief review of radical beliefs, extremist behaviors, and terrorist acts that have been reported to be associated with perceptions of unfairness. As such, the chapter aimed to ground a core proposition of this book, namely that perceptions of unfairness play a crucial part in processes of growing radicalization.

What the chapter showed is that unfairness perceptions indeed fuel the radicalization of Muslims, such as Salafists in the Netherlands; extremist Islamic groups in Pakistan; the Taliban in Afghanistan; al-Qaeda in Kenya, Tanzania, and the United States; and IS in Iraq, Syria, and various other countries, including in Western Europe. Indeed, in our modern world, unfairness-inspired processes of Muslim radicalization seem to be everywhere.

We also saw that perceptions of unfairness play an important part in the radicalization of those on the right or the extreme right of the political spectrum, such as members of political parties or movements such as *Front National* in France; the BNP in the United Kingdom; and the PVV in the Netherlands. I also discussed responses of Dutch citizens opposing arrival of asylum-seeking refugees and examined extreme right-wing movements such as *Nederlandse Volks-Unie* and *Voorpost* in the Netherlands and *Marchas da Família com Deus pela Liberdade* in Brazil. Furthermore, I discussed right-wing extremist or terrorist groups such as NAR in Italy; the KKK in the United States; the NDP in Germany; and right-wing lone wolves such as Anders Breivik in Norway and Timothy McVeigh in the United States.

Moreover, perceived unfairness also plays a crucial role in left-wing radicalization such as in Occupy movements in Hong Kong and different Western countries. We also saw instances of violent extremism with respect to asylum rights and home visits regarding animal rights; instances of left-wing radicalization associated with groups such as No Border Network in Europe and Stop Deportations in the Netherlands. I also reviewed relevant left-wing extremism and terrorism such as the RAF in

Germany (and elsewhere), the FARC in Columbia, and Shining Path in Peru, as well as murderous left-wing lone actors such as Volkert van der Graaf in the Netherlands.

I note explicitly that the instances that I discussed here do not constitute a full list of all instances in which Muslim and right- and left-wing radicalization may be associated with perceptions of unfairness. I also state explicitly that the instances reviewed are not meant to be representative of the radicalization processes of these groups or that there are no meaningful differences between these groups or different times in history associated with the groups. I further note that I could also have focused on other groups involved in radicalization than Muslims or those on the right or the left of politics. And I stipulate that, for the moment, I skip some important definitional issues (such as how to categorize right- and left-wing political groups or whether to label some radical acts as instances of activism as opposed to extremism or terrorism).

All this said, I think it is reasonable to conclude that the condensed review of concrete and specific instances of Muslim and right- and left-wing radicalization presented in this chapter suggests that perceptions of unfairness indeed seem to be related to several concrete and specific instances of important radicalization processes. The implication is that when people perceive things as very unfair, they seem to be more likely to develop radical beliefs and to engage in extremist behaviors and terrorist acts.

## 2.6 TAKING PEOPLE SERIOUSLY: SERIOUS RESPECT AND SERIOUS RESPONSIBILITIES AS ADVANCED GOLDEN RULE

In this book I study the proposition that unfairness perceptions play a pivotal role in various radicalization processes by adopting the view that we should take people seriously. That is, if we want to truly understand processes of radicalization in such a way that we can significantly prevent, attenuate, and fight violent extremism and terrorism, then we should pay in-depth attention to what is driving radicalizing persons. This does not imply that I sympathize with radicals, extremists, or terrorists, but it does mean that as a scientist I seriously examine and scrutinize the thoughts, feelings, and behaviors of radicalizing persons in order to understand what is going on. In other words, when we really want to be able to prevent and counter violent extremism and terrorism, we should take people seriously.

In particular I argue that taking people seriously involves at least three things. First, it implies that we should incorporate a systematic analysis of how radicalizing persons interpret the world. Thus, we should examine what radicalizing persons think, what they feel, and how they behave. This psychological analysis includes the study of how fair or unfair radicalizing individuals and group members perceive certain things to be and how this influences their feelings and subsequent behaviors.

Second, I argue that taking people seriously implies that we should take seriously the implications that follow from the psychological science of people's fairness and unfairness judgments. That is, this science indicates that people value the experience of fairness so much, and hate to be treated in unfair manners, because they want to be taken seriously as full-fledged members of society whose views are genuinely valued and whose opinions are given serious and due consideration (Lind & Tyler, 1988; Tyler, 1987, 1989; Tyler & Lind, 1992). Being treated in a fair manner by societal authorities and other important people in your group and world signals that you are a worthy person who is taken seriously by important social referents (Lind, Kanfer, & Earley, 1990; Tyler, 1987, 1989). This experience has many positive effects on many reactions of many people (Van den Bos, 2005, 2015; see also Ellis & Abdi, 2017; Mirahmadi & Farooq, 2010). This analysis does not imply that we should treat radicalizing extremists in a fair manner and then everything will be hunky dory. Not at all. But the current book makes a case for the importance of being taken seriously that is conveyed by fair treatment by society and significant social figures.

Third, taking people seriously does not imply that we need to pamper people and give in to whatever they want, casually ignoring the serious problems their wishes and their behaviors may cause to society at large. Instead, in my perspective, taking people seriously implies that we should point people not only to their rights but also to their responsibilities and their duties, which go together with being a mature grown-up and a valuable full-fledged citizen of society.

Philosophical insight has yielded the "Golden Rule." This principle holds that we should treat others as we would wish to be treated ourselves (more on this in Flew, 1979). Here I would like to argue for what I call an "Advanced Golden Rule." With this rule I mean that we not only need to pay attention to the rights, perceptions of being valued, and all positive things that follow from the experience of being treated in fair manners that we should consider in the prevention of radicalization processes, but also that we need to emphasize the responsibilities, duties, and other things that take up time and energy and involve important levels of self-control among the persons who potentially may radicalize.

In short, when we want to prevent and fight radicalization, we need to go to the sources of the radicalization processes. These sources include experiences of severe unjust treatment, deprivation as a group, perceptions of immorality, and other instances of unfairness. Focusing on this issue implies an analysis that will reveal the social importance of being taken seriously as a valuable person. Importantly, taking people seriously also implies that we are able to point people at their duties and obligations as citizens of democratic legal states. All this suggests that we need to invest in neighborhoods and social contacts because this is the smart thing to do, and that we simultaneously should not pamper or overindulge radicalizing people and should clearly let them know when they are going too far.

Obviously, the statements in this section form only an abbreviated version of the line of reasoning that I want to convey in this book. To provide a more detailed and nuanced analysis of my arguments, it now is time to discuss earlier theories that focused on the relationship between unfairness perceptions and radicalization (Chapter 3), followed by an in-depth and up-to-date discussion that focuses on perceptions of unfairness (Chapter 4) and what factors may strengthen or weaken the effects of these perceptions (Chapters 5 and 6). Taken together, perceptions of unfairness coupled with moderating variables can culminate in core aspects of human radicalization, including rigidity of thoughts (Chapter 7), strong defense of people's cultural worldviews (Chapter 8), and ultimately the violent rejection of law and democratic principles (Chapter 9). It is to a discussion of these issues that we now turn.

# A Review of Radicalization Theories

## 3.1 INTRODUCTION

In this chapter I review core theories of radicalization, with a special emphasis on those theories that examine extremism and terrorism and, in
particular, those that include perceptions of unfairness as one of the core
mechanisms that fuel radicalization. After all, the suggestion that follows
from Chapter 2 and other observations of radicalization is that perceiving
that things are unfair and not right tends to feed various processes of radicalization. It should not come as a surprise, therefore, that many of the
radicalization theories that have been proposed over the years pay special
attention to the issue of perceived unfairness. The current chapter reviews
these theories and also pays appropriate attention to other variables that
are important in this respect, such as how people respond to threats and
how they can react in rigid ways.

A lot has been written about the issue of radicalization. The review
presented in this chapter is not intended to be exhaustive. There are simply
too many theories out there to review them all. Also, the review of the
theories that are discussed will be necessarily brief. There are many details
that are important in each of the theories briefly reviewed here, and the
reader is kindly requested to refer to the original publications that discuss
the important details of the various theories.

Thus, the review provided is neither exhaustive nor extensive. What
the current chapter does is portray the broad array of relevant theories
that have been published over the years. This will give the reader a good
overview of what is out there and a good handle on the relevant scientific fields of investigation (for other reviews, see, e.g., Bongar, Brown,
Beutler, Breckenridge, & Zimbardo, 2007; Moghaddam & Marsella, 2004;
Rahimullah, Larmar, & Abdalla, 2013; Reich, 1990; Victoroff & Kruglanski,

2009). This will also ground the discussion of perceived unfairness and other relevant factors in the chapters that follow the current chapter.

Specifically, this chapter starts with reviewing models that focus on the radicalization process. These process models are discussed in Section 3.2 and encompass a staircase approach to terrorism (3.2.1), a model that focuses on individual and socialization dynamics of jihadist terrorism (3.2.2), a model that examines individual, group, and mass dynamics of political radicalization (3.2.3), and an approach to transformative learning that studies the processes of personal change associated with radicalization (3.2.4).

The chapter goes on to examine factors that motivate the radicalization process. Section 3.3 discusses some of these factors. This discussion includes people's quest for significance (3.3.1) and factors that serve as trigging points in processes of radicalization (3.3.2).

Different models of radicalization have focused on how fairness can impact different radicalization processes, and Section 3.4 reviews some of the important fairness models. This includes a review of an approach that examines perceptions of procedural unfairness and democracy (3.4.1), a discussion of how symbols of injustice play a role in radicalization processes (3.4.2), how revolutions tend to be legitimized (3.4.3), and how moral disengagement plays a pivotal role in different processes of radicalization (3.4.4).

Variables from within a society as well as from outside society can constitute important issues in radicalization processes. Section 3.5 reviews some of these internal and external influences. This includes homegrown terrorism (3.5.1) and how internationally oriented Internet, media, and social media can influence processes of radicalization (3.5.2).

## 3.2 PROCESS MODELS

### 3.2.1 Staircase to Terrorism

One of the most important models in the study of radicalization is Moghaddam's (2005) staircase approach. The model examines the social and psychological processes that lead to terrorist acts. In this psychological approach, terrorism is seen as the last step in the process of radicalization.

In his model, Moghaddam uses the metaphor of a narrowing staircase, which he conceives of as having a ground floor and five higher floors. Each floor is a step further to the last floor, terrorism. Moghaddam seeks to explain why some people climb the whole staircase, whereas most do not. As it turns out, various issues of fairness, justice, and morality play essential roles in this process, with different notions of fairness, justice, and morality playing an important role at different floors.

The model finds it important to start at the basis and to look at the people on the *ground floor*. After all, most people are on the ground floor. Psychological interpretation of material conditions is important at this floor. In this interpretation process, feelings of fair and just treatment tend to dominate among the majority. Perceived deprivation can be prevalent among some people at the ground floor. Those people are the most likely to move on to the higher floors in the model. Moghaddam uses the French Revolution as an example of how collective mobilization and abnormal action can be the result of experiences of relative deprivation.

Persons who perceive doors to be open to the *first floor* are motivated by the options they see to fight the unjust situation that they perceived at the ground floor. Whether or not they perceive those options as available to them depends on two psychological factors: how they see possibilities to personal mobility to improve their situation and their perceptions of procedural justice. A key factor affecting perceived procedural justice is whether people receive or are denied opportunities to voice their opinions in decision-making processes.

If persons are denied voice opportunities or otherwise are refused meaningful participation in decision making, they can excessively blame "the other." For example, people living in the Middle East can blame the United States for things that are wrong in their personal living conditions. People at this floor then start to express a Freudian-like displacement of aggression, which is characteristic of the *second floor*. For instance, persons at this floor can be tempted to show aggression toward groups to which they do not belong (out-groups). Quite often this displacement of aggression is channeled through support for institutions and organizations that nurture authoritarian attitudes and extremist behavior, including educational systems that encourage rigid, us-versus-them thinking and fanatical movements.

At the *third floor*, terrorist organizations arise as a parallel world with its own morality. Because of this parallel morality, people in terrorist organizations feel that they are morally engaged and that this justifies their actions. The goal is to keep the parallel world as secret and isolated as possible. Some members of terrorist groups could even continue to live a normal life, without telling their spouses and closest friends about the parallel world that they entered.

Those who have climbed to the *fourth floor* are part of a tightly controlled group. New recruits are being socialized into the traditions, methods, and goals of the terrorist organization. Leaving the group often means being in a world in which the government does not allow them to voice their opinions or to let them participate in the decision-making progress. This is why the individuals on the fourth floor find themselves staying in a tightly controlled group from which they, after a certain point, cannot exit alive. The fourth floor is characterized by solidification of categorical thinking and the perceived legitimacy of the terrorist organization.

The *fifth floor* is defined by being psychologically prepared to commit acts of terrorism. Two psychological factors lie at the basis of this willingness: the social categorization between the group to which one belongs (the in-group) and groups to which one does not belong (out-groups) and the exaggeration of the differences between those groups. This increases psychological distance between the different groups. This distance is needed to sidestep inhibitory mechanisms that would prevent the actual engagement in terrorist acts.

While most floors in the staircase model focus on what people do when they are engaged with extremist movements or terrorist organizations, Moghaddam notes that the majority of people are at the ground floor. What matters most on the ground floor are perceptions of fairness. As Moghaddam notices, even the poorest of the poor can feel that they are not unjustly treated. This is why Moghaddam proposes that counterterrorism should focus on long-term solutions of improving the conditions on the ground floor. One way to implement these long-term solutions is to focus on supporting contextualized democracy through procedural justice, including opportunities to voice opinions in important legal and political issues.

Moghaddam's model is related to, and in important ways grounds, the line of reasoning put forward in this book. In fact, the current book is indebted to many models discussed in this chapter, and particularly Moghaddam's (2005) groundbreaking publication (see also Moghaddam, 2006, 2008, 2010; Moghaddam & Harré, 2010; Moghaddam & Love, 2011; Moghaddam & Marsella, 2004). Having said that, the present book focuses not on stepwise development but instead on more gradual growing of radicalization. Furthermore, whereas many floors in Moghaddam's model concentrate on what people do and think after they are affiliated with terrorist organizations (Floors 3-5), the current book examines in detail why exactly radicalization takes place at various phases and what details and specifics are important in the processes that lead up to people possibly affiliating with terrorist groups and their actual engagement in terrorist acts (either when affiliated with groups or as lone actors). The current book does all this by providing updated insights that we now realize are important in processes of radicalization, including people's engagement in extremist movements and terrorist behaviors.

### 3.2.2 Individual and Socialization Dynamics of Jihadist Terrorism

Kepel and Rougier (2016) are leading a network of researchers for the European Commission in a project that adopts a Scientific Approach to Finding Indicators of and Responses to Radicalization (SAFIRE). The project focuses on jihadist terrorism and identifies various individual paths and socialization dynamics behind this form of radicalization. As such, SAFIRE analyzes individual differences as well as the wider social background behind and around the emergence of radicalization and the use of violence (see also Kepel, 2017).

Kepel and Rougier (2016) note that in dynamic processes of socialization, strong feelings of injustice are often coupled with self-efficacious individuals and enabling environments. For example, the European Commission's Expert Group on Violent Radicalisation (2008) emphasizes the leading role of ideological activists in terrorist enterprises and that these activists are motivated by idealism and a strong sense of justice. According to the Expert Group, these individuals are often resourceful, educated, and well integrated and are sometimes even considered as role models in their communities. Young people can also look for collective recognition and adventure, and group dynamics influence this process in important ways. Furthermore, youngsters can be frustrated (see also Folger, 1977). When coupled with a history of delinquency or other personal difficulties, this can lead them to engage in different paths of radicalization that ultimately can lead to militancy and terrorism.

The Expert Group on Violent Radicalisation (2008) argues that radicalization is a complex outcome, often the result of a combination of personal and social factors. A shared sense of injustice regarding how the constituencies that the terrorists claim to represent are treated is one important factor in this respect, particularly when this is coupled with social or societal exclusion and real or perceived humiliation among the constituencies. Ideology plays an important role in this process, both as a factor that motivates behavior and as a factor that inhibits moral concerns (see also Kramer, 1990; Wardlaw, 2009). This is especially true in the case of jihadist Salafist ideology, which divides the world into two antagonistic parts. In this respect, the Expert Group draws an analogy between European nationalist, right-wing, and left-wing terrorist groups in the 1960s and 1970s and Muslim extremists that nowadays find useful rhetorical narratives in a specific jihadist ideology to justify purely criminal acts that otherwise would lack any support from their own group or large parts of society.

Specifically, the Expert Group points out that within several Muslim communities worldwide there tends to exist a global mood that is characterized by widespread feelings of inequity and injustice and a very acute sense of marginalization and humiliation. These perceptions and feelings are often underestimated by Western observers. The wide-spread feeling of humiliation and uncertainty basically rests on an array of specific local circumstances. As with earlier forms of radicalization in the 1960s and 1970s, it offers fringe groups an opportunity to justify their recourse to terrorism. Importantly, such terrorist violence is condemned by large majorities in most countries of the Muslim world as well as within Muslim communities inside Europe, according to the Expert Group.

The work by the Expert Group on Violent Radicalisation is related to another radicalization model that Kepel and Rougier (2016) discuss: the four-stage model by Borum (2011a, 2011b). In an attempt to try to understand the events of 9/11, Borum—a psychologist by education with professional experience as a police officer and police instructor—developed a training heuristic for law enforcement. The result is not a formal social science theory (Borum, 2011a, 2011b) but provides an interesting conceptual model for the emergence of a terrorist mindset focusing on main turning points in the radicalization process. The four-stage process begins when people interpret or frame some unsatisfying event, condition, or grievance as being unjust and not fair. The injustice is blamed on a target policy, person, or nation. The responsible party is then denigrated and often demonized. This facilitates justification or impetus for aggression. Thus, we see some important overlap between SAFIRE and related approaches (Borum, 2011a, 2011b; Expert Group on Violent Radicalisation, 2008) and the work by Moghaddam (2005) and the current book.


## 3.2.3 Individual, Group, and Mass Levels of Political Radicalization

A conceptual line of work that not only focuses on individual and group mechanisms of radicalization but also examines what masses do and how people engage in these masses is provided by McCauley and Moskalenko (2008, 2011; see also McCauley, 2007a, 2007b, 2017; McCauley & Segal, 2009). These authors focus on the issue of political radicalization. They do not propose a single theory to explain the radicalization process, in part because the authors view this as too daunting or too difficult a task. Instead, the authors identify several mechanisms that they consider to be major contributors to the process of political radicalization. These mechanisms hang together somewhat loosely but are arranged at three different levels, focusing on the individual level, the group level, or the mass level.

At the *individual level*, McCauley and Moskalenko (2008) note that people may feel that they are personal victims. For example, suicide terrorists often cite revenge for attacks on loved ones as a motive for self-sacrifice. Individuals may also hold important political grievances that may move them to individual radical action and violence. Furthermore, an individual's progress into a terrorist group is typically slow and gradual, with many smaller tests taken before being trusted in more important missions and with many nonviolent tasks done before being asked to use guns or bombs. Indeed, it is rare that an individual moves from sympathizer to activist by suddenly undertaking some major risk or sacrifice. Moreover, individuals are often recruited to a terrorist group via personal connections with existing terrorists, in part because no terrorist wants to try to recruit someone who might betray the terrorists to the authorities. In practice, this means recruiting from the network of friends, lovers, and family.

At the *group level*, McCauley and Moskalenko (2008) observe that groups of strangers who discuss political issues often show increased agreement about the opinion at issue and a shift toward increased extremity in the average opinion of group members. Frequently, political radicalization takes place under isolation and threat. The result often is a strong sense of cohesion among the group members. For example, isolation is characteristic of terrorist cells, whose members can trust only one another. Because the terrorists depend on one another for their lives in fighting the enemy, extreme interdependence produces extreme group cohesion. The resulting group's consensus about value and morality acquires enormous power, including the power to justify and even require violence against those who threaten the group. Groups can also be in competition for the same base of sympathizers and can gain status by more radical action in support of the cause. For instance, groups can compete over who can claim credit for a particular suicide terrorist attack. Radical groups can also be in competition with state power. For example, the power of the state can be perceived as squashing the group, such as when some form of police response is perceived to include extreme violence or severe violation of civil or human rights. The result can be an increase in sympathy for the victims of state repression. Similarly, Della Porta (1995, 2009) discusses a number of examples of people for whom the death or imprisonment of a fellow group member was the instigation for joining a terrorist underground. Within-group competition and differences of political opinion can also produce intense conflict and personal animosities. Group-based action against the state can perhaps help to manage these within-group tensions.

At the *mass level*, McCauley and Moskalenko (2008) note that issues such as in-group identification, patriotism, and nationalism can be very important. For example, the 9/11 attacks and other out-group threats are known to have resulted in increased patriotism among US citizens, increased support for the US President, and a general bolstering of American values. According to McCauley and Moskalenko, mass radicalization by external attack tends to be a reliable effect. The authors also often observe that when group conflict involves prolonged violence, group members become more extreme in their negative perceptions of one another. This tendency can become so extreme that the enemy is no longer seen as human. A famous instance of such dehumanization and its relationship with violent behavior is represented in Ulrike Meinhof's renowned quote from *Der Spiegel* (June 15, 1970):

> Wir sagen, natürlich, die Bullen sind Schweine, wir sagen, der Typ in der Uniform ist ein Schwein, das ist kein Mensch, und so haben wir uns mit ihm auseinanderzusetzen. Das heißt, wir haben nicht mit ihm zu reden, und es ist falsch überhaupt mit diesen Leuten zu reden, und natürlich kann geschossen werden.

In my translation into English:

> We state that Cops are Pigs, we note that the character in uniform is a pig, not a human being, and we have to face him as such. That is, we should not discuss with him, and it is wrong to discuss with these folks at all, and of course there can be shootings.

In conflicts with states and out-groups, radical groups also tend to value those who gave up their lives for the cause and hence cherish the memory of their martyrs. McCauley and Moskalenko (2008) note that the empirical study of martyrdom is underdeveloped. In fact, with many of the mechanisms that they propose, systematic data are lacking, in part because data can be hard to obtain with many terrorists.

McCauley and Moskalenko's work is an example of an approach to radicalization in which experiences of injustice and perceptions of unfairness are not core propositions. Nevertheless, with many mechanisms that they discuss, the issue of perceived unfairness seems to be prevalent. This seems to be the case with the mechanisms of personal victimization and political grievances, for example. The authors also reflect explicitly on the role of unfairness and injustice when they discuss the issue of social movements. McCauley and Moskalenko (2008, p. 416) note that "radicalization of many kinds may be associated with a syndrome of beliefs about the current situation and its history (Eidelson & Eidelson, 2003): We are a special or chosen group (superiority) who have been unfairly treated and betrayed (injustice), no one else cares about us or will help us (distrust), and the situation is dire—our group and our cause are in danger of extinction (vulnerability)."

To conclude, McCauley and Moskalenko do identify perceptions of injustice and unfairness as possible incentives of political radicalization, but these perceptions do not seem to serve a central role or are not made explicit in the mechanisms they propose. They do note, however, that the mechanisms they have identified are not exhaustive.

### 3.2.4 Transformative Learning

Wilner and Dubouloz (2011) apply transformative learning theory to radicalization. As such, they examine the cognitive processes and other processes of personal change associated with radicalization. The theory views radicalization as a personal (and at times, interpersonal) process in which individuals adopt extreme political, social, and/or religious ideals and aspirations and in which the attainment of particular goals justifies the use of indiscriminate violence. The theory assumes that radicalization is both a cognitive process and an emotional process. Both cognitions and emotions can prepare and motivate people to pursue violent behavior.

Transformative radicalization is not a theory that focuses strongly on perceptions of unfairness and injustice. Rather, the theory focuses on learning processes because it is assumed that terrorists have to learn how to behave as a terrorist. An important aspect of this learning process is not only obtaining the skills required to participate in violent behavior but also internalizing the rationalization that legitimizes the violent activity. Thus, people who contemplate killing citizens in campaigns of political violence do so because they come to believe that murder is feasible and just (Wilner & Dubouloz, 2011). Furthermore, the authors argue that images of conflict that purport to show injustices carried out against Muslims are internalized as accurate information.

The issue of transformative radicalization is important, in part because it examines explicitly whether people transform abruptly and quickly into radicals and terrorists or whether this is a gradual process that takes time. For example, a transformative crisis or other trigger event can be abrupt and focused in time, causing an instant disorientation in belief and knowledge systems. According to transformative theory, people can respond to this by searching for new meaning perspectives almost immediately. These are examples of trigger events and abrupt forms of radicalization.

Transformation can also be a more gradual and cumulative process. In this case, radicalization is assumed to be the product of many small, successive, and incremental events that trigger change. These events may be difficult for people to interpret. During these episodes of distortion, people experience contradictions in what to do, which can cause feelings of anxiety. What results is a feeling of self-doubt, confusion over identity, and intense personal debate. Eventually, a tipping point is reached whereby radicalizing people can come to realize that the old reality simply no longer exists and a new one must be established. This realization facilitates the process of identifying with the newly internalized reality and encourages an exploration of new roles and new social values (Wilner & Dubouloz, 2011).

Both abrupt and gradual radicalization can occur. However, Wilner and Dubouloz (2011) argue that individuals' joining terrorist groups typically is the result of a slow and gradual process (see also Horgan, 2005, 2009; McCauley & Moskalenko, 2008).

## 3.3 MOTIVATING FACTORS

### 3.3.1 Significance Quests

One of the most prolific writers and prominent scholars of radicalization and terrorism is Arie Kruglanski. Kruglanski and colleagues (2014) have developed a model of radicalization and deradicalization based on the notion that the quest for personal significance constitutes a major motivational force that may push individuals toward violent extremism (Dugas & Kruglanski, 2014; Kruglanski et al., 2013; Kruglanski, Chen, Dechesne, Fishman, & Orehek, 2009; see also Bélanger, Caouette, Sharvit, & Dugas, 2014; Kruglanski, Crenshaw, Post, & Victoroff, 2008; Kruglanski & Fishman, 2006, 2009; Webber, Babush, et al., 2018).

The model defines radicalization as a movement in the direction of supporting or enacting radical behavior. The model notes that goals play an important role in human behavior (Kruglanski et al., 2002; Shah, Friedman, & Kruglanski, 2002). Behaviors that one would describe as radical undermine other goals that matter to most people. Thus, terrorism is described as radical because it runs counter to common norms or concerns. Terrorist acts, while serving a given end, undermine other goals that matter to the large majority of people. For example, living and not dying is among the more important goals that people have. The behaviors of suicide bombers, who kill themselves for their terrorist movements, are inconsistent with this ultimate or final goal. Therefore, one might label such behaviors as counterfinal (Kruglanski et al., 2014).

The significance quest model proposes that commitment to focal goals shifts among terrorists compared with other normal people. The model submits that the reason for terrorist acts is a disproportionate commitment to ends served by the extreme behavior that prompts a devaluation or a forceful suppression of alternative considerations (Shah et al., 2002). The model argues that the focal goal to which political radicals and terrorists are committed is a general motivating force that the authors call the quest for significance. The quest for significance is the fundamental desire to matter, to be someone, to have respect (Kruglanski et al., 2014).

Here I note that respect is a central part of the literature on fair treatment (Tyler & Lind, 1992; Van den Bos, Van der Velden, & Lind, 2014) and hence a focal issue of the current book (see Section 2.6). Furthermore, respect and fair treatment are so important to people because they signal to them that they are full-fledged and valued members of their group, sub-culture, or society. The current book also includes a discussion of how people respond to psychological threats (see Chapter 5) and how they defend their cultural worldviews (see Chapter 8). These issues are related to Kruglanski's work on significance quests (see also Hogg, Kruglanski, & Van den Bos, 2013).

The significance quest model observes that various terrorist goals have been listed in the literature. These include things such as honor, vengeance, religion, loyalty to the leader, and perks in the afterlife (Kruglanski et al., 2014). The model assumed that the quest for significance is underlying all these goals. From that perspective, the various specific motivations mentioned in the terrorism literature are special cases of the significance quest.

The Kruglanski et al. (2014) model of radicalization and deradicalization contains three crucial components: (1) the motivational component (the quest for personal significance) that defines a goal to which one may be committed, (2) the ideological component that in addition identifies the means of violence as appropriate for this goal's pursuit, and (3) the social process of networking and group dynamics through which the individual comes to share in the violence justifying ideology and proceeds to implement it as a means of significance gain.

Kruglanski et al. (2014) note that a terrorism-justifying ideology typically contains three essential ingredients. These ingredients are related to the issues of unfairness, injustice, and immorality (discussed in Chapter 4): There is the element of grievance (injustice, harm) believed to have been suffered by one's group (e.g., religious, national, ethnic); there is a culprit presumed responsible for the perpetrated grievance (e.g., the United States, Israel, Christians, Crusaders, Jews); and there is a morally warranted and effective (hence, significance-promoting) method of removing the dishonor created by the injustice, namely terrorism, for which the implementer is accorded reverence and appreciation from the group.

In particular, Kruglanski et al. (2014) propose that where the shared reality of one's group—its core beliefs—highlights a grievance suffered by the group at the hands of alleged perpetrators, it is often coupled with advocacy of strikes against the enemy as a way of redressing the presumed injustice; dealing the enemy a humiliating loss thus "levels the playing field" as it were and removes the stain of lost significance that one's group has suffered.

The significance quest in itself, however, does not suffice for a person to radicalize. Kruglanski et al. (2014) notices that the "significance quest alone does not drive people toward violence; the choice of how to achieve significance is dependent on adopted ideologies and the means they recommend for significance attainment" (p. 428).

The Taliban can be seen as a good illustration of the model by Kruglanski et al. (2014) and the three intertwining forces that arouse and maintain roads to terrorism. The first one, the motivational force, is a significance loss or gain. The fact that the Mujahideen, once in power, have acted brutally and corruptly against the Afghan people can be viewed as a significance loss. The second force is ideological. Kruglanksi et al. (2014)

note that the significance quest alone does not drive people toward violence; the choice of how to achieve significance is dependent on adopted ideologies and the means they recommend for significance attainment. The students of the madrasas had learned and adopted the ideologies from an extreme form of Islam. These values guided them in their actions and could explain how they, for example, were able to deny health care and education to their own women. The last force is a social force. The madrasas can be identified as the place where the students and future members of the Taliban formed their shared reality and social network. On top of that, the ideologies they adopted and the social network they built were intertwined with the madrasas.

## 3.3.2 Triggering Factors

Many theories of radicalization distinguish between different stages or phases in processes of radicalization. A relevant issue in all these models is what the factors are that trigger people to move from one phase or stage to another. Feddes, Nickolson, and Doosje (2015) focus on this issue explicitly (see also Doosje, Zebel, Scheermeier, & Mathyi, 2007; Feddes, Mann, & Doosje, 2015; Van Bergen, Feddes, Doosje, & Pels, 2015).

Feddes et al. (2015) note that although the radicalization process is not the same for everyone, it is possible to identify several stages. Based on existing models of radicalization (e.g. Borum, 2011b; Moghaddam, 2005; Precht, 2007; Sageman, 2004; Schmid, 2013; Silber & Bhatt, 2007; Wiktorowicz, 2004), the authors identify four stages in the radicalization process.

In the *first stage* people are starting to become sensitive to radicalization. In the views of Feddes et al. (2015), this "sensitivity stage" in fact precedes the actual radicalization process.

In the *second stage* people orient themselves to the particular type of radicalization that appeals to them. In this "orientation stage," people actively search for information relating to the radical ideology they are attracted to. They also start to develop radical perspectives on how they see and interpret the world. Feddes et al. note that moving from the first to the second stage is a crucial step. Wiktorowicz (2004) has called this a process of cognitive opening because it constitutes the moment that individuals are going to ask questions about their existence and are becoming open to alternative worldviews.

In the *third stage* people are actual members of (virtual or real) radical groups. This "membership stage" is characterized by the further development of ideological thinking, indoctrination, and possibly the increasing willingness to view violence as permissible. If attitudes to violence become more positive, this increases the chances that people take the step to the next stage.

In the *fourth stage* extremist action takes place. In this "action stage," the actual steps are being taken to prepare, plan, and commit acts of violence and other extremist behaviors. In contrast with this book, Feddes et al. (2015) view this stage as not being part of a radicalization process but instead as being a stage of extremism.

Feddes et al. (2015) note that radicalization tends to be a nonlinear and dynamic process (Bartlett, Birdwell, & King, 2010; De Wolf & Doosje, 2015; Feddes et al., 2013; King & Taylor, 2011; McCauley & Segal, 1989). That is, growing radicalization does not necessarily need to develop in continuous ways such that people slowly but gradually move from sensitivity to orientation, followed by membership and finally extremism. In fact, some people radicalize, but a lot more people do not. And sometimes the radicalization process takes some time, whereas at other moments it takes place very rapidly. These observations raise the question of why this is the case. To answer this question Feddes et al. examine triggering factors: defining events that spur processes of radicalization.

Specifically, Feddes et al. (2015) distinguish between two types of trigger factors: turning points and catalysts. Turning points are events that lead people to become more open to new ideologies or new worldviews. As such, they can alter the direction in which people develop. Thus, turning points can lead to rapid growth of radicalization, but they can also start a process of deradicalization (Demant et al., 2008; McGloin, Sullivan, & Piquero, 2009; Rutter, 1996; Van der Valk & Wagenaar, 2010a;

Wiktorowicz, 2004; Zammit, 2013). Someone can move quite suddenly, for example, from the stage of orientation to membership. And people can deradicalize, for instance when they switch from orientation back to sensitivity.

Catalysts are another type of triggering factors, according to Feddes et al., and are defined as events that reinforce or attenuate the radicalization process (Christmann, 2012; Veldhuis & Bakker, 2007; Veldhuis & Staun, 2009). In contrast to turning points, catalysts do not alter the direction in which persons are developing, but instead strengthen or weaken the direction of growing or attenuating radicalization that already has taken place.

Besides triggering factors, Feddes et al. (2015) also pay attention to root factors of radicalization. Root factors are defined as more structural or long-term circumstances that underlie radicalization and that have a high chance of leading to growing radicalization (King & Taylor 2011; Kruglanski & Fishman, 2009; Moghaddam, 2005; Veldhuis & Staun, 2009). Triggering factors, in contrast, are concrete events that provide the final push to move from one phase to another.

One could say that the current book treats perceptions of unfairness and injustice as root factors that underlie many instances of radicalization, at least partially. The book also notes that because of the hot-cognitive or emotion-arousing quality of unfairness perceptions (Van den Bos, 2007), experiencing that something is blatantly unfair can serve as a turning point that spurs radicalization. Unfair events in the life of a person may also increase the radicalization process or lead to further deradicalization and hence act as catalysts of radicalization.

Feddes et al. (2015) identify three levels, each with their own triggering factors. Triggering factors at the micro-level take place at the personal level and involve identity, relative deprivation, feelings of exclusion, feelings of humiliation, and direct experiences with discrimination, racism, and exclusion. Micro-factors also include confrontation with death, problems at home, loss of a job, dropping out of school, and confrontations with authorities. Triggering factors at the meso-level have to do with the social processes in the direct social environment of people. Examples of meso-level factors are social networks that can push people to become a member of an extremist group. For example, individuals can be influenced by friends and people that are important to them and join an extremist group because of that. Cutting ties with social bindings, getting married, participating in training, and being exposed to propaganda are other examples of meso-level factors. Triggering factors at the macro-level are events at national or global levels. Well-known examples of macro-level triggers are the conflicts between Israel and Palestine and between the Syrian government and Sunni Muslims. Observed attacks on the group one identifies with, as well as government policies that are or are not focused on one's own group, are other examples of macro-level triggers.

Importantly, Feddes et al. (2015) propose a topology consisting of individual differences and associated motives that can strengthen or weaken the effects of the proposed triggering factors. This topology is very relevant to the current book, in part because one type of radical person that the topology distinguishes is motivated by a quest for justice for oneself and/or one's own group. Thus, this type of *justice seeker* is particularly sensitive to events or other triggers pertaining to unfairness done to oneself and/or one's group.

Feddes et al. (2015) speculate that particular events related to relative deprivation are of special importance to justice seekers, for example, when they perceive that they themselves (individual deprivation) and/or their own cultural group (group deprivation) are being disadvantaged and feel like they and/or their group deserve better (Buijs, Demant, & Hamdy, 2006; Kepel, 2004; Moghaddam, 2005; Van den Bos et al., 2009). As such, the authors hypothesize that justice seekers are especially sensitive to trigger factors at those micro-, meso-, and macro-levels that are related to injustice done to themselves (individual deprivation) and/or to their own group (group deprivation).

On a micro-level, this would imply, for instance, that events that relate to the social status of individuals matter. Furthermore, the loss of a job or quitting school can cause frustration about one's own status or about one's group and its place in society. And confrontational experiences with authorities and experiences of discrimination can evoke a sense of injustice, which can serve as a trigger in the radicalization process (e.g., Abbas, 2007; Richardson, 2012; Van der Valk & Wagenaar, 2010a; Woodlock & Russell, 2008). At the meso-level, recruiters and propaganda can amplify a sense of injustice (Campbell, 2015; Wiktorowicz, 2004), and this can have macro-level implications because these kinds of events can be interpreted as attacks on the group as a whole (Buijs et al., 2006; Horgan, 2008; Precht, 2007).

Interestingly, Buijs et al. (2006) have labeled justice seekers as "political radical activists," and Linden (2009) denotes this type of radical as a "revolutionary." In contrast, this book adopts a more general approach and points to the more general role that various perceptions of unfairness and injustice play with many different radical people and various radicalization processes, not only radical activists or revolutionaries.

Another type of radical that Feddes et al. (2015) distinguish is the radical who *seeks identity*. Research from developmental psychology and social psychology has shown that the development and maintenance of a positive identity is important to people (Erikson, 1968; Tajfel & Turner, 1979). Furthermore, in general, people have a strong tendency to be part of a group (Baumeister & Leary, 1995). And, importantly, we know that justice matters to people in part because fair treatment signals inclusion in the group or society, whereas unfair treatment is linked with social and societal exclusion (Lind & Tyler, 1988). Identity seekers are sensitive to triggering factors related to social identity and social binding.

The third category of radical that Feddes et al. (2015) distinguish is the individual who, above all, is driven by a search for significance, meaning, and support. *Significance seekers* can do this in their attempts to deal with personal crises. According to Kruglanski et al. (2014), the experience of significance and meaning is key in the radicalization process for significance seekers. The theory by Kruglanski and colleagues was discussed at length in the previous section of this chapter. Here I note that significance seekers are assumed to be sensitive to personal triggers and triggers related to an ideology that offers meaning and significance (Kruglanski, Gelfand, & Gunaratna, 2012; see also Heine, Proulx, & Vohs, 2006).

The fourth and last type of radical that Feddes et al. (2015) distinguish is the person who is seeking sensation and thrills (Bjørgo & Carlsson, 2005). Frequently, these radicals (often men) want to show their manliness by going on radical adventures. This category of *sensation seekers* is sensitive to triggers related to violence, tension, romance, and sensation.

Feddes et al. (2015) notice that the occurrence of one or even several triggering factors does not necessarily mark the start of a radicalization process, but that focusing on specific events that can be defined as trigger factors will be helpful in recognizing and addressing radicalization. They further note that gender and age are often important moderators, such that terrorists are mainly men between the ages of 18 and 30 years (De Graaf, 2012; see also El-Said & Barrett, 2017; Jacques & Taylor, 2013; Monahan, 2012).

Adolescence is a period in which people are more vulnerable to radicalization (Bhui, Dinos, & Jones, 2012; Bhui et al., 2014) and criminality (Hoffmann & Cerbone, 1999). Moreover, it turns out that as people get older, they often distance themselves from extremism (Monahan, 2012) and extremist groups (Farrington, 1987). The relation between level of education and radicalization turns out to be ambivalent. Schmid (2013) has concluded, based on an overview of radicalization literature, that there are both highly and lowly educated terrorists.

## 3.4 FAIRNESS ISSUES

### 3.4.1 Procedural Unfairness and Democracy

Moghaddam (2005) proposed that the best way to address the issue of radicalization is to start at the ground floor: to keep people from experiencing unjust or unfair treatment. This can be done by promoting democracy. Tyler, Schulhofer, and Huq (2010) and Li (2009) have focused on these issues. Tyler et al. (2010) do not examine processes of radicalization or deradicalization, but instead examine the interesting issue when members of the Muslim American community voluntarily cooperate with police efforts to combat terrorism. As it turns out, this is an issue that is directly related to perceptions of fairness.

Tyler and colleagues (2010) observe that previous studies have emphasized two mechanisms by which policing can reduce levels of social disorder. The authors label these mechanisms as the instrumental model and the normative model. In the instrumental model, people estimate the expected costs and benefits of compliance with the law or cooperation with the police, and they comply or cooperate only when the benefits outweigh the costs. Reasons for cooperation from this perspective include the fear of punishment or unwelcome policing measures and the expectation of individual or communal benefits following successful police efforts to control crime (Posner, 2007).

The normative model of Tyler et al. emphasizes self-regulatory as well as normative motivations. This model proposes that people comply and cooperate when they believe authorities are legitimate and entitled to be obeyed. The model argues that when authorities are viewed as more legitimate, their rules and decisions are more likely to be accepted. The model further links the legitimacy of institutions to the concept of procedural fairness (Sunshine & Tyler, 2003; Tyler, 2006; Tyler & Fagan, 2008).

Tyler et al. (2010) note that the fairness of police procedures depends on the manner in which street stops are conducted, whether the police are neutral and transparent in their application of legal rules, whether they explain their actions and seek input from community members before making decisions, and whether they treat people with dignity and respect. Judgments about procedural fairness and procedural justice have been found to influence the perceived legitimacy of law enforcement and thus to affect willingness to comply and to cooperate (Tyler, 2009). Viewed from this perspective, perceptions of procedural fairness and justice play a key role in people's willingness to cooperate with the police and, by extension, with antiterror policing and associated government policies.

Using data from telephone interviews with 300 Muslim Americans in New York City from March 2009 to June 2009, Tyler et al. (2010) found a robust correlation between perceptions of procedural justice and both perceived legitimacy and willingness to cooperate with antiterrorism policing. Thus, the procedural justice of police activities is the primary factor shaping legitimacy and cooperation with the police. The authors found little evidence that evaluations of either the severity of terrorist threats or of police effectiveness play a significant role in determining willingness to cooperate. Furthermore, religiosity, cultural differences, and political background had weak relations with cooperation. These results suggest the importance of procedural justice considerations in the design of antiterrorism policing strategies concerning Muslim Americans within the United States. These results support the normative model by finding that the procedural justice of police activities is the primary factor shaping legitimacy and cooperation with the police. Thus, Tyler and colleagues explicitly relate perceptions of fairness, and especially perceptions of procedural fairness, to the legitimacy of government and democratic constitutions. Interesting in this respect is Li's (2009) analysis of whether democracy reduces or promotes transnational terrorist incidents. To this end, Li assessed different effects of democracy on transnational terrorism among 119 countries from 1975 to 1997.

Li (2009) notes that there are different arguments to propose that democracy will either reduce or promote transnational terrorism. The first argument expects that democracy reduces transnational terrorism. After all, democratic societies offer access for citizens to seek recourse to their grievances. Furthermore, democratic rules ensure the nonviolent resolution of conflicts of interest. Hence, groups in democratic societies are more likely to consider nonviolent alternatives that are easier to pursue than terrorist activities to further their interest.

The second argument suggests that democracy in fact can encourage terrorism. This argument puts forward that democratic countries provide relatively more freedom of speech, movement, and association. Democracies also permit parochial interests to get organized and reduce the costs of conducting terrorist activities.

In examining these contrasting predictions between democracy and terrorism, Li (2009) observes that previous empirical work used aggregate

indicators of regime type. Earlier research also failed to separate the positive and negative effects of democracy. To address these issues, Li examines
the different mechanisms by which democracy can affect transnational
terrorism.

The findings presented by Li (2009) suggest that democracy can
reduce terroristic acts. For example, her findings suggest that democratic participation reduces transnational terrorism. This is because
democratic participation increases political efficacy of citizens as
well as their levels of satisfaction with government. Democracy also
reduces grievances and thwarts terrorist recruitment. Public tolerance
of counterterrorist policies is also raised because of democratic participation. These findings seem to fit the results obtained by Tyler et al.
(2010) regarding perceptions of procedural fairness, legitimacy, voluntary compliance with policing measures, and acceptance of government and law.

However, Li (2009) also points to some evidence that democracy
can encourage or facilitate the occurrence of terrorist acts. For instance, because democracy facilitates freedom of speech, association,
and movement, terrorism can be a more serious option than an easier
course of action in democracies and open societies. Li (2009) also
notes that institutional checks and balances that are fundamental in democracy can create frustration of marginal groups. Civil liberties, like
freedom of speech, also seem to contribute in some way to the awak-
ening of terrorism. Institutional constraints can weaken the ability of
governments to fight terrorism, making this a very tough task for the
governments involved.

Li's (2009) main conclusion is that democracy in itself is no panacea
to terrorism because different aspects of democracy may evoke different
reactions to radicalization and terrorism. Paying appropriate attention
to the specific mechanisms involved and how these mechanisms affect
the behavior of various individuals and groups is crucial in this respect.
Perceptions of procedural fairness may serve a pivotal role in these
mechanisms (Tyler et al., 2010; see also Moghaddam, 2005).

## 3.4.2 Symbols of Injustice

Important stimuli can also function as symbols of injustice or justice. These symbols can serve important functions in processes of radicalization, extremist behavior, and the fight against terrorism.

For example, in Chapter 2 we saw that a director of the Dutch Repatriation and Departure Service, who is responsible for the returning of individuals who are denied asylum in the Netherlands, is perceived by left-wing activists as an important symbol of inhumane asylum policies. This fits with the theory of symbolic interactionism (Blumer, 1969; Mead, 1934). Related to this, the relational model of authority points to the important role that authorities play in society and in social groups (Tyler & Lind, 1992). How fairly such authorities are treating you or others is thus an important signal of how much the authority is valuing and respecting you as an important, full-fledged member of society or the group in which the person is an authority (see also Section 2.6).

Thus, the relational model of authority proposes that individuals care about procedural justice because procedural justice conveys a symbolic message to justice recipients about their relationship with the entity enacting justice, especially with respect to their inclusion in the group (Tyler & Lind, 1992). Procedural fairness has important informational value for citizens interacting with legal authorities (Tyler, 2006), and procedural fairness helps people to evaluate how societal authorities regard and value them (Lind & Tyler, 1988). Perceptions of procedural justice and injustice thus can serve as important symbols that signal important information about relationships with society and social groups.

Githens-Mazer (2008) shows how symbols can serve as the basis for perceptions of injustice and the associated radicalization of North African Muslims who are living in Britain. The author notes that injustice is a motivating factor for growing radicalization among these Muslims. Symbols, memories, and myths are key to perceiving injustices because these communicate a history in which people who belong to a particular group can collectively recognize past injustices. The symbols, memories, and myths also connect those past injustices with contemporary individual experiences of deprivation and other forms of injustice.

In the case of North Africans living in the United Kingdom, immigrants who are now in their mid-30s have had to flee their country because of the Afghanistan and the Algerian civil wars. Githens-Mazer (2008) states that this experience serves as a narrative explaining the injustices that forced these immigrants to leave their homeland. This experience is constantly retold, according to Githens-Mazer, which causes the perceptions of injustice to be salient and a key component of the social identity of the immigrants.

This experience and the associated perceptions of injustice can persist over generations. This can also be seen in other cases, such as the case of Irish Americans' support for the Irish republican movement. Individuals who had been removed by birth from the domestic Irish experience by three to four generations, and who may have had little to almost no contact with an indigenous Irish population, still felt compelled to provide monetary, moral, and physical support to Irish republicans (Githens-Mazer, 2008). For example, after the start of "the Troubles" in Northern Ireland in 1969, Irish Americans contributed to the Irish Northern Aid Committee (NORAID), an Irish American organization that raised funds for the Provisional Irish Republican Army (Githens-Mazer, 2008).

In the Netherlands a process related to what Githens-Mazer (2008) is describing led to perceptions of severe injustice, which ultimately led to terrorist behaviors. In the aftermath of Indonesian decolonization, the Dutch government transported military personnel and their families from the Indonesian South Moluccas to the Netherlands. The personnel were discharged on arrival and housed in camps, including the Westerbork camp, from which Jews and gypsies were transported to the Nazi death camps in the Second World War. The way in which all this was done was perceived to be unfair and unjust and was generally experienced as a breach of promise.

The process of retelling these experiences of injustice, not unlike what Githens-Mazer (2008) is talking about, led to growing tension and grievance among the South Moluccans now living in the Netherlands. In the 1970s this fueled a series of terrorist attacks, with the general purpose being the realization of the self-proclaimed Republic of the South Moluccas (or *Republik Maluku Selatan* [RMS]).

For example, on the morning of May 23, 1977, four armed South Moluccans took hostage 105 children and their five teachers at a primary school in Bovensmilde, a small village in the Netherlands. When the hostage-taking began, the children were forced to cover the windows with newspapers, preventing the outside world from knowing what was happening inside. Two days later, there were elections for the national parliament. To increase pressure on the government and the Prime Minister, Dries van Agt, the children were forced to shout out of the windows: "Van Agt, we want to live." Two days after this, all the children were released. Four teachers were retained as hostages. Fifteen days later, marines attacked the school and the Moluccans surrendered. The four attackers were convicted, with sentences varying from 6 to 9 years.[1] As it happens, in high school I became friends with one of the children who was taken hostage, and I saw how jittery this experience made him for the first couple of years that followed, although he, his brother, classmates, and teachers all made it through the whole hostage crisis without permanent physical harm.

Symbols and metaphors pertaining to what is just and what is the right thing to do can also serve important roles in attempts at deradicalization and counterterrorism. For example, Kruglanski, Crenshaw, Post, and Victoroff (2008) examine from a psychological perspective the use of metaphors in framing counterterrorism. One major counterterrorism metaphor is that of war, which has been adopted by the US government since the 9/11 attacks.

This metaphor reasons that wars are fought by states. The enemy who is responsible for terrorist attacks is thus an identifiable entity whose interests fundamentally oppose one's own. The conflict is zero-sum because the outcome will be victory for one side or the other. There is no

---

1. See https://en.wikipedia.org/wiki/1977_Dutch_school_hostage_crisis. See also Githens-Mazer (2008) and Rasser (2005).

compromise, and the war metaphor is totalistic and extreme, according to Kruglanski et al. (2008).

Kruglanski and colleagues (2008) note that this metaphor has helped to guide policy but has also met challenges because of lack of fit and the availability of counter-analogies with different lessons of history. In fact, a problem with most metaphors, according to Kruglanski et al., is that they capture some aspects of counterterrorism's effects while neglecting others.


### 3.4.3 The Legitimization of Revolution

An issue that is related to some extent to the role of perceptions of injustice and growing radicalization is the subject of injustice and the support and legitimization of revolution. J. Martin, Scully, and Levitt (1990) are among the many that theorized about this issue (see, e.g., Layendecker, 1981). J. Martin and colleagues studied some aspects of this theorizing by means of an exploratory study using content analyses of the speeches and writings of 22 leaders of violent 20th-century revolutions.

The theorizing of J. Martin et al. (1990) is interesting for the current book because it explicitly and in detail reviews and criticizes theories of injustice in their application to how leaders of violent, 20th-century revolutions use claims about injustice to delegitimatize a status quo system of reward distribution, to justify bloodshed, to assess the balance of power, and to envision a perfectly just future. As such, J. Martin et al. propose that perceptions of injustice will play a role in how leaders of revolutionary movements will look at the past, the present, and the future.

When looking at the past, perceptions of injustice were assumed to be delineated by the leaders in their attempts to criticize the status quo. Content analyses of the speeches and writings of the leaders of violent 20th-century revolutions showed that a wide range of material and ideological or emotional outcomes were mentioned by the leaders in their speeches and writings. The distributive justice rule that was cited in this respect had to do with too much inequality between groups. Indeed, inequality is among the core justice principles that people refer to (see, e.g., Layendecker, 1981; Messick, 1993).

When looking at the present, J. Martin et al. (1990) proposed that perceptions of injustice thus formed are used in attempts to mobilize people and other resources for revolutionary purposes. Two activities are assumed to be crucial to the process of encouraging people to take the risks associated with joining a violent revolutionary movement. First, there needs to be an assessment of the balance of power between the revolutionary group and the enemy that gives the revolutionaries the credible hope that they can win. Second, and perhaps more important, the possibility of bloodshed has to be justified. For example, violence is justified by claims that it is a means to a just end or by claims that it is a just defense against an actual or anticipated attack by an enemy (Walzer, 1977). Furthermore, violence by the revolutionary group can be portrayed or seen as a justifiable response to other kinds of violence. This use of violence can have great symbolic qualities for the people involved in the revolutionary movement (Bourdieu, 1977a, 1977b).

Content analyses indeed suggested that violence on the part of the revolutionary group was justified as a means to a just end and as a defense against the actual and symbolic violence of the enemy. In contrast, the enemy's ends and the enemy's defense against the revolutionaries' violence were described as unjust. These findings are in accordance with just war theories (see, e.g., Walzer, 1977).

When looking at the future, J. Martin et al. (1990) assumed that revolutionary movements aim to envision a perfectly just world. After all, a delineation of the injustice of the status quo gains force when it is contrasted with a revolutionary vision of an ideal world. Content analyses suggest that these offered an unexpectedly simplified vision of perfect justice. Again, a wide range of material, ideological, and emotional outcomes were mentioned, and all these outcomes were again related to one rule of distributive justice: to decrease inequality.

J. Martin et al. (1990) concluded that although interesting, their study is an exploratory study using archival data. A different sample of leaders from other centuries or different political orientations may have produced different results, generating a different set of ideas. That said, the conceptual line of reasoning that follows from the work by J. Martin et al. is interesting and underscores the importance of notions of injustice in attempts to understand support for revolutionary ideas and movements. This obviously is important for the understanding of radicalization processes.

### 3.4.4 Moral Disengagement

In processes of growing radicalization, people need to be able to engage in what observers would call immoral acts: violent courses of action targeted, for example, at innocent citizens or people working for government agencies in democratic societies. Dehumanization is a key aspect here, as we saw in the work of Moghaddam (2005) and McCauley and Moskalenko (2008). Bandura (1999) has proposed an elaborate set of conceptual thoughts on this issue (see also Bandura, 1986, 1990; Bandura et al., 1996).

Dehumanization refers to how the perpetrators view the persons they mistreat. Bandura (1999) notes that self-censure for cruel conduct can be disengaged by stripping persons of human qualities. When dehumanized, they are no longer viewed as human beings with feelings, hopes, and concerns but are instead viewed as subhuman objects. We saw an example of this in the 1970 *Der Spiegel* piece in which terrorist Meinhof talked about police officers as pigs who can be targeted in shootings.

It is easier to brutalize people when they are viewed as lesser humans or as nonhuman forms. Blaming one's adversaries or circumstances is an expedient that can help in this self-exonerative purpose. According to Bandura (1999), in this process people view themselves as faultless victims driven to injurious conduct by forcible provocation. Bandura (1986, 1990, 1999; Bandura et al., 1996) proposes that a crucial precondition before dehumanization can take place is that people can disengage themselves from moral self-sanctions.

In his theory of moral self-disengagement, Bandura (1986, 1990, 1999; Bandura et al., 1996) notes that in the course of socialization, people adopt moral standards that serve as guides and as major bases for self-sanctions regarding moral conduct. In this self-regulatory process, people monitor their conduct and the conditions under which it occurs, judge it in relation to their moral standards and perceived circumstances, and regulate their actions by the consequences they apply to themselves (Bandura, 1999).

People refrain from behaving in ways that violate their moral standards because such conduct will bring self-condemnation. The constraint of negative self-sanctions for conduct that violates one's moral standards operates anticipatorily. In the face of situational inducements to behave in inhumane ways, people can choose to behave otherwise by exerting inhibiting self-influence. Self-sanctions keep conduct in line with personal standards. It is through the ongoing exercise of self-influence that moral conduct is motivated and regulated. This capacity for self-influence gives meaning to moral agency. Self-sanctions mark the presence of moral oughts. The exercise of moral agency can inhibit people from behaving inhumanely (Bandura, 1999).

One way in which people engage in processes of disengagement is by cognitively reconstructing the behavior under consideration. According to Bandura (1999), people do not ordinarily engage in harmful conduct until they have justified to themselves the morality of their actions. In this process of moral justification, detrimental conduct is made personally acceptable by portraying it as serving socially worthy or moral purposes. People then can act on a moral imperative and preserve their view of themselves as moral agents while inflicting harm on others.

Euphemistic language is often used to make harmful conduct respectable and to reduce personal responsibility for it. Furthermore, terrorists see their behavior as acts of selfless martyrdom by comparing them with widespread cruelties inflicted on the people with whom they identify (Bandura, 1999).

People can also engage in moral disengagement by obscuring or minimizing the agentive role in the harm they cause. According to Bandura (1999), this is because moral control operates most strongly when people acknowledge that they cause harm by their detrimental actions. People will behave in ways they typically repudiate if a legitimate authority accepts responsibility for the effects of their conduct.

Under displaced responsibility, people view their actions as stemming from the dictates of authorities; they do not feel personally responsible for the actions. Because they are not the actual agent of their actions, they are spared self-condemning reactions. Bandura (1999) notes that self-exemption from gross inhumanities by displacement of responsibility is most gruesomely revealed in socially sanctioned mass executions.

The exercise of moral control is also weakened when personal agency is obscured by diffusing responsibility for detrimental behavior and by disregarding or distorting the effects of one's actions. When people pursue activities that are harmful to others for reasons of personal gain or social pressure, they avoid facing the harm they cause, or they minimize it. If minimization does not work, the evidence of harm can be discredited. Bandura (1999) proposes that as long as the harmful results of one's conduct are ignored, minimized, distorted, or disbelieved, there is little reason for self-censure to be activated.

Bandura (1999) notes that disengagement practices will not instantly transform considerate persons into cruel ones. Rather, the change is achieved by gradual disengagement of self-censure. According to Bandura (1999), the process of radicalization involves a gradual disengagement of moral sanctions from violent conduct (see also Sprinzak, 1990, 2009). It begins with prosocial efforts to change particular social policies and opposition to officials, who are intent on keeping things as they are. Embittering failures to accomplish social change and hostile confrontations with authorities and police lead to growing disillusionment and alienation from the whole system. Escalating battles culminate in terrorists' efforts to destroy the system and its dehumanized rulers.

Bandura (1999) notes that psychological theorizing and research tend to emphasize how easy it is to bring out the worst in people through dehumanization or other means. As such, sensational negative findings receive the greatest attention (see, e.g., Milgram, 1974). However, what is not often noticed is the evidence that most people refuse to behave cruelly when the situation is personalized, such as when they have to inflict pain by direct personal action and when they see the suffering they cause (Bandura, Underwood, & Fromson, 1975). Thus, an understanding of when people engage or do not engage in processes of disengagement may be crucial for our insights into both the radicalization process and the possible attenuation of radicalization.

## 3.5 INTERNAL AND EXTERNAL INFLUENCES

### 3.5.1 Homegrown Terrorism

Muslim-oriented terrorism not identified with terrorist groups like al-Qaeda or Islamic State does not necessarily have to take place in the Middle East or have to be committed by residents of the Middle East. People born in the West can also sympathize with the ideas and values of Muslim terrorism and commit terrorist acts in their home country. These terrorists are often called "homegrown terrorists," individuals who are born and bred in the country in which they ultimately engage in terrorist acts or are sympathetic to the idea of committing terrorist acts in their country (see also Buijs, Demant, & Hamdy, 2006).

An example of homegrown terrorism is the suicide-bombing in 2005 in central London, killing 52 people. Three of the four terrorists were British born. Furthermore, the Frenchman Salah Abdeslam and the Belgian Abdelhamid Abaaoud were involved in the terrorist attack in November 2015 in which 129 people were killed in Paris.

Homegrown terrorists are highly valuable to terrorist organization like al-Qaeda because they are often able to travel freely in Western countries, know the Western habits, and speak the language fluently. An illustration of this is the fact that Osama bin Laden personally recruited and selected four men from Germany to help plan the 9/11 attacks. These men spoke English, were educated, and were familiar with Western values and habits. One of them, Mohamed Atta, was even reported to have helped the hijackers to blend in by helping them dress in Western clothes and by teaching them how to order food. Precht (2007) notices that intelligence information indicates that homegrown terrorism is a rising problem.

Precht (2007) has identified four overlapping phases that are typical for the radicalization process of homegrown Muslim terrorists. These phases can take several months to a few years. Furthermore, Precht considers background, trigger, and opportunity factors as major influences on the Western terrorist. Precht identifies a couple of indicators that are specific to the different phases.

The first phase, that of preradicalization, is not yet characterized by specific signs of radicalization. In this phase several background factors are assumed to be important. One of the factors is the experience of discrimination, alienation, and perceived injustices. Among the injustices experienced are the widespread stop-and-go searches used in many countries, which are perceived by Muslims as unfair and discriminatory. Furthermore, most radicals have a Muslim background with which they struggle in the Western world. The experience of personal traumas, harsh living environment, and the presence of peers, leading to segregation and parallel societies, are also among the background factors, as is the absence of a critical debate among Muslims about Muslim terrorism.

The second phase, conversion and identification, is dominated by a changed appearance, a gradual rejection of the Western lifestyle, and a change of personality and religiosity. Trigger factors important in the second phase include the perception of Western foreign policy and single provocative incidents. For instance, Western forces in Iraq and Afghanistan are seen by many Muslims as occupiers of Muslim land and are a source of anger. Pictures from the Abu Ghraib prison and Guantanamo Bay and television broadcasts from battle zones in Afghanistan, Iraq, Algeria, Chechnya, Kashmir, Gaza, Somalia, Sudan, and other areas contribute to an image of violence, maltreatment, and injustices toward Muslims. The West is perceived as pro-Israel and as having double standards with regard to the Muslim world. This view of Western foreign policy seems to play a crucial role in creating anger, especially among younger generations of Muslims. Precht (2007) notes that the official motivation for the London suicide bomber Mohammad Sidique Khan was the perceived injustices carried out by the West against Muslims around the world.

The myth of jihad and the desire for activism is also important in the second phase. Precht (2007) observes that according to the ideology of militant Muslims and violent jihad, Islam is under constant threat and every good Muslim must fight these hostile forces. Jihad is portrayed as a fight between good and evil. This myth is being reproduced by propaganda and preachers and among groups of young people. According to Precht, the myth of jihad is appealing to some young Muslims who have a desire to do something and act against the perceived injustices and threats against Islam and react against the society in which they live. The presence of charismatic persons or spiritual advisors is also important in the second phase.

The third phase, indoctrination, is characterized by an increased isolation from the former life, meetings in private locations, and travels to Muslim countries. Because in the third phase the newly acquired identity takes over from the former identity, group bonding plays an extremely important role in this phase. Locations and venues like mosques, schools, and (when applicable) prisons offer great opportunities to meet like-minded people. Internet and satellite channels can also constitute opportunity factors and as such serve as places to meet like-minded people. The last phase, action, is the actual participation in a terrorist act (Precht, 2007).

## 3.5.2 Internet, Media, and Social Media

Ideas about radicalization and the perceptions of unfairness associated with these ideas not only are communicated from person to person in processes of interpersonal communication but also are conveyed and spread by means of various sources of media. For example, books and pamphlets are written and distributed among Muslim, right-wing, and left-wing extremists and potential or would-be extremists. Thus, traditional media can have an important role in the spreading of ideas about at least some forms of radicalization.

Importantly, the Internet and the use of social media play crucial roles in the spread of information and communication about modern forms of radicalization, extremism, and terrorism. In fact, many important sources of information on which this book is grounded rest on ideas developed and research findings obtained before the Internet and the use of social media became so prevalent in our modern world. For example, important insights on which I developed the current book come from a research project that Annemarie Loseman, Bertjan Doosje, and I presented in 2009. Since then, the use of the Internet and in particular social media has become more widespread, and this is pivotal for our understanding of processes of radicalization.

Related to this, J. Martin et al. (1990) observed, much to their surprise, that relatively few social comparisons were made in the speeches and writing of the 20th-century revolutionary leaders whom they analyzed. The authors had expected that in a revolutionary context, the leaders would mention a wider range of material and demographic dimensions for comparison, pointing to how their group or movement was faring less well compared with other groups in terms of important material outcomes (such as food, shelter, jobs, and property) and ideological and emotional outcomes (such as individual emotional well-being, including feelings of freedom; Foa & Foa, 1974; Schwinger, 1980). In contrast to expectations, few social comparisons were made in the content analyses presented by J. Martin et al. (1990). The relevance of social comparisons may have increased over the past 20 years, in part because the Internet and social media have made it much easier to engage in processes of social comparison and to communicate the outcomes of these processes to other members of the own group. It is my hypothesis that feelings of unfairness that can arise as a result of comparing one's own group with other groups are easily and frequently spread through the Internet and social media.

Social media—defined here as websites, applications, and electronic devices that enable users to create and share content and to participate in social networking—has become an integral part of daily life. It is therefore not surprising that social media also plays a role in the radicalization process of many individuals these days. Thompson (2011) has argued that the use of social media tools by individuals and organizations to radicalize individuals for political and social change has become increasingly popular as the Internet penetrates more of the world and mobile computing devices are more accessible. She concludes that social media is an effective tool to use to radicalize and recruit members into a cause, in part because nowadays it is almost always available and is easily accessible.

Chebib and Sohail (2011) have analyzed the Egyptian Revolution of 2011 to try to understand how social media has contributed to this revolutionary process. These authors conclude that the first and foremost reason why social media have facilitated the revolution is its ease of accessibility. This is a conclusion that Thompson (2011) supports. For example, al-Qaeda developed its own online magazine, intended to stimulate young English-speaking men to become homegrown terrorists. Furthermore, Thompson states that people in Western countries, where the Internet and social media are most easily accessible, are most likely to be recruited and radicalized via the Internet (see also Emerson, 2002; Gartenstein-Ross & Grossman, 2009; King & Taylor, 2011; Schuurman, 2017).

Thompson (2011) has identified another important quality that makes social media an easy contributor to the radicalization process. Thompson notices that social media, because it connects people easily, serves as a platform for like-minded people to meet and to create a movement. On top of that, social media serves as the binding factor. Through social media, ideas are easily spread and discussed. In this way, processes of groupthink are facilitated by social media, and this may lead to growing radicalizing.

Chebib and Sohail (2011) also note that social media can put one's own group first and can help to overcome social differences and physical distances. This means that social media narrows the communication gap, which implies that people from all sorts of backgrounds can be connected. Moreover, the authors notice that emotions communicated through social media tend to be contagious and that social media serves as the means of transmitting these emotions. As a result, strong emotional words that people use in their postings on social media will influence the emotions of the postings of their friends.

Another feature of social media is the uncontrollable information flow (Chebib & Sohail, 2011). Thus, social media serves as a platform for both emotional expressions and uncontrollable information flow, so the density of social connections is increased. These qualifications make social media a major facilitator for radicalization. Both Thompson (2011) and Chebib and Sohail (2011) note that an increase in the density of information flow and in emotional perceptions will create a higher probability for radicalization.

To conclude, social media are easily accessible. This accessible platform serves as a facilitator that overcomes social distances and physical barriers where like-minded people can meet and spread information and emotions. Social media can also be used by terrorist organizations to actively recruit people for their organizations. Seen in this light, social media should be regarded as a facilitator to radicalization. Indeed, the Dutch newspaper *de Volkskrant* notes that right-wing resistance messages against refugees and people who seek asylum in the Netherlands are posted on Facebook and ultimately lead to radical acts against these people.[2]

## 3.6 CONCLUSIONS

The current chapter does not provide an exhaustive review of all the radicalization theories that are out there and that have been published over the years. That was not the purpose of the chapter. In contrast, this chapter's aim was to provide a brief review of some earlier theories of radicalization. The various sections reviewed these theories. Here I conclude that perceptions of unfairness and injustice play an important role in many of the conceptual models and theories reviewed. The theories and models highlighted different notions of unfairness and injustice. Now seems the time to systematically address the role that perceptions of unfairness and injustice can play in radicalization processes.

2. *De Volkskrant* (September 16, 2009), Verzet verschuift van internet naar straat.

Thus far, this book has discussed the role that perceptions of unfairness have played in several instances of radical, extremist, and terrorist behaviors (Chapter 2). And the book has reviewed earlier theories that addressed these issues and provided accounts that mostly included the role of perceptions of unfairness and injustice (Chapter 3). Now it is time to examine in detail how the perceiving of unfairness takes place (Chapter 4) and what are the important moderators that influence the effect that these perceptions can have on the radicalization process and associated extremism and terrorism (Chapters 5 and 6). These topics are the subject of the next chapters and the following part of this book.

# PART TWO

# Key Antecedents
# of Radicalization

# Perceiving Unfairness

## 4.1 INTRODUCTION

As should be clear by now, a central topic on which this book focuses is the notion that the experience that things are unfair is a major factor in processes of radicalization and growing adherence to extremist ideas and the development of sympathy for terrorist movements. As Chapter 2 showed, this notion is prevalent in various instances of radicalization, extremism, and terrorism. And Chapter 3 observed that several theories noted the significance of the experience of unfairness and how this plays an important part in the study of radicalization and associated issues such as extremism and terrorism. In the current chapter I zoom in on the experience of unfairness. As such, my aim is to provide a systematic treatment of the literature on experiences of unfairness and to delineate how these experiences are related to issues of radicalization, extremism, and terrorism.

Focusing on the topic of perceptions of unfairness is important because although the psychology of radicalization clearly involves more than merely the experience of unfairness, it nevertheless seems to be the case that perceptions that things are not fair play a key role in at least some phases of the radicalization process. This applies particularly to the early phases in which normal people may be tempted to embrace radical ideas and condone violent strategies in the pursuit of those ideas. Furthermore, the science of how people form the impression that things are unfair is fascinating. The literature on this topic is not without its complexities, but it also gives clear answers as to what factors play a crucial role in the construction of judgments of unfairness. Thus, this chapter focuses on the science of how people form judgments of unfairness.

Because the issue of how people use judgments of unfairness to fuel radical beliefs and extremist behaviors is at the core of the present book, one could say that the current chapter provides the basic building block on which this book is founded: the perception that things are unfair and unjust. To this end, the chapter introduces core concepts that play an important role in perceiving unfairness. These issues include perceptions of unfair procedures or (to use the term that I prefer) experiences of unfair treatment (Section 4.2), being deprived as an individual or as a group of important goods and resources (Section 4.3), and the experience of inequitable distribution of important outcomes (Section 4.4). The chapter also incorporates notions of immorality into the antecedents of radicalization, including violations of moral convictions and breaches of what is morally right and good (Section 4.5). In this way the current chapter highlights that several perceptions of unfairness serve a pivotal role in the radicalization process. Implications of this observation for how to study and possibly intervene regarding radicalization are discussed (Section 4.6).

## 4.2 UNFAIR TREATMENT

At the core of the perception that things are unfair are experiences that someone has treated you in an unfair and unjust manner (Lind & Tyler, 1988; Tyler & Lind, 1992; Van den Bos, 2005, 2015; see also Finkel, 2001; Miller, 1999). The literature on treatment fairness (or "procedural justice," as it is often called) tends to focus on either the positive effects of fair treatment on people's reactions (e.g., Lind & Tyler, 1988; Tyler & Lind, 1992; Tyler, 2006) or the negative effects of unfair treatment on human responses (e.g., Folger, 1977, 1984).

On the positive side, fair treatment entails getting respect from important people, including societal authorities such as politicians, police officers, and judges (Tyler & Lind, 1992). Fair treatment also encompasses getting appropriate opportunities to voice one's opinions about key issues, including important decisions that are to be made (Lind, Kanfer, & Earley, 1990; Tyler, 1988). Pivotal is that voiced opinions are given due consideration by those who make decisions or are otherwise important for the people involved and who were voicing their opinions (Tyler, 1989). Experiences of fair treatment are also formed by people's overall impression of fairness (Lind, 2001, 2002; see also Finkel, 2001).

On the negative side, unfair treatment involves the absence of respect or being treated with blatant disrespect. Unfair treatment also includes the denial of important voice opportunities or, when voice is allowed, inappropriate consideration of the views ventilated. Furthermore, people tend to be quite good at forming overall impressions indicating that how they are treated is "fishy" and not really fair.

In short, there are several criteria that people can use to form the judgment that they have been treated in either fair or unfair ways (see, e.g., Leventhal, 1980; Lind & Tyler, 1988; Van den Bos, Van der Velden, & Lind, 2014). For now I assume that the absence or denial of respect, voice, due consideration, and overall impressions of fairness serves a key role in the radicalization processes on which this book focuses. Figure 1.3 discussed in Chapter 1 lists these four criteria of treatment unfairness.

Experiences of unfair treatment play such a central role in the psychology of protest and violent behavior (Klandermans, 1997) because being denied fair treatment by important people signals that one is not deemed worthy as an individual nor as an important member of one's group or society (Lind & Tyler, 1988). So, for example, when an important member of your group, such as your group leader or your supervisor at the place where you work, treats you with disrespect and is not interested in your opinions about important matters, this conveys that this person does not consider you to be a full-fledged member of the group. Similarly, when important people in society, such as police officers, judges, or employers, treat you rudely and in an overall unfair manner, this implies that you are not considered as an important member of society by those individuals or institutions conducting the unfair treatment (Tyler & Lind, 1992). After all, social inclusion is a key element of what we humans are striving for. Hence, being socially excluded hurts (Eisenberger, Lieberman, & Williams, 2003).

Related to this, the psychology of treatment fairness has revealed that fair and unfair treatment serve pivotal roles in how we deal with alarming events in our worlds (Van den Bos, Ham, Lind, Simonis, Van Essen, & Rijpkema, 2008). Figure 4.1 illustrates this alarm-system perspective on the role of fair and unfair treatment in the radicalization process. The model portrayed in this figure focuses on what happens when people encounter alarming events. Economic and financial problems can constitute alarming events, and so does social rejection or being ostracized from important groups or social relationships. Failure to have successes in school or important societal contexts also is alarming to many people, in part because this installs a fundamental sense of personal uncertainty among the people involved (Van den Bos, 2009a; Van den Bos & Lind, 2002).

Alarming events tend to trigger processes of sense-making (Van den Bos & Lind, 2009). People want to understand what is causing the alarming events and what they can do about it. They want to know how they or their group can cope. To do this, people start to search for information and vigorously process the information they encounter and have at hand. Information that they are treated in fair or unfair manners is especially important then.

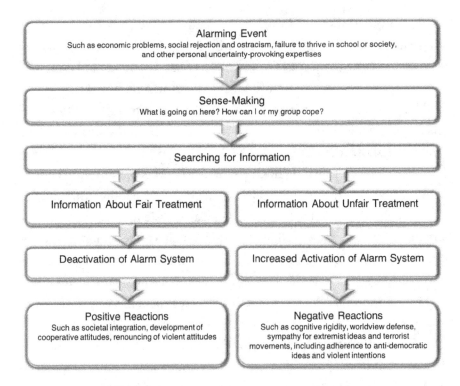

**Figure 4.1 Alarm-System Perspective on the Role of Fair and Unfair Treatment in the Radicalization Process.**
This model explains why experiences of fair and unfair treatment matter so much to people and are assumed to have a central role in radicalization. The model proposes that people try to make sense of alarming events and that information about fair treatment encountered in processes of sense-making will calm people and hence yield positive reactions, whereas information about unfair treatment will lead to increased activation of the alarm system and hence instigate negative reactions among humans. (Based on Figure 19.1 presented in Van den Bos, 2015. Used by permission of Oxford University Press.)

Because treatment fairness has important informational value for people, it follows that people are susceptible to issues of treatment fairness in many alarming or sense-making triggering situations (Van den Bos et al., 2008). That is, because of the strong connection between treatment fairness and the essence of what we humans are, I assume that when people encounter information that they are treated unfairly, this will increase the activation of the human alarm system (Eisenberger et al.,

2003). In processes of radicalization this may have all sorts of negative consequences, such as people responding in cognitively rigid ways to their environments, with increased worldview defense reactions, and even with enhanced sympathy for extremist ideas and terrorist movements. A strong and long-lasting activation of the human alarm system may lead to adherence to antidemocratic ideas and violent intentions to realize those ideas. Figure 4.1 shows these effects.

What Figure 4.1 also highlights is that when people encounter information that they are treated fairly in alarming situations, this may in fact be helpful to deactivate the human alarm system. As a result, people are more likely to show positive reactions, such as integration in society, the development of cooperative attitudes, and the renouncing of previously held violent attitudes associated with extreme or rigid ideas. It is my assumption that the experience of fair treatment has a special role in the prevention of radicalization and in processes of deradicalization, such that fair treatment may well prevent the likelihood of extremist ideas and behaviors to develop or—after these ideas and behaviors have been developed—the significant attenuation of these ideas and behaviors.

Importantly, some of the implications that follow from an alarm-system perspective on treatment fairness and a sense-making view on the radicalization process stand in contrast to the view that humans are primarily interested in material gain and try to achieve this gain by rational means. A basic assumption underlying the alarm-system model is that people are individuals who are frequently busy appraising what is going on in their social surroundings and how to behave in these surroundings (Van den Bos, 2015). This suggests that the *Rational-Economic Man* view that one finds so often in the fields of business, economics, law, and elsewhere in society (see Kahneman, Knetsch, & Thaler, 1986) should be replaced or at least complemented by a view of humans as *Social-Appraising Individuals* (Van den Bos, 2015; Van den Bos & Lind, 2013). The current book aims to develop these sense-making and social-appraising processes for the issue of radicalization.

As noted, I argue that the experience of unfair treatment has a special role in growing radicalization (Moghaddam, 2005). Treatment fairness is assumed to be especially important for processes of attenuating radicalization (Tyler, Schulhofer, & Huq, 2010). I also stipulate that in processes of growing radicalization, other experiences of unfairness also are important. One of these issues is the experience of relative deprivation, on which the next sections focuses.

## 4.3 RELATIVE DEPRIVATION

In addition to paying appropriate attention to experiences of fair treatment, social psychologists have proposed a number of other theories and conceptual frameworks that deal with people's concerns about justice. Two of the most important theories are relative deprivation theory and equity theory. These theories focus on the outcomes that people receive or do not receive. These outcomes can be material in nature, such as financial outcomes, including salary and other payments. The outcomes can also be of a more immaterial quality, such as status and recognition at one's workplace or in one's society.

The experience of relative deprivation was famously proposed by Stouffer, Suchman, DeVinney, Star, and Williams (1949) in their study of military personnel. These authors observed that although personnel from the US military police were promoted more slowly than officers from the Air Force, the police officers were more satisfied with their salary, status, and rank than the air corpsmen. The explanation Stouffer et al. developed for these and other observations relied on the concept of referent comparisons. That is, it is essential to realize that social judgments are shaped not only by absolute standards but also by standards set by social comparisons (Pettigrew, 2015). Stouffer reasoned that the military police compared their promotions with other military police and not with those from the Air Force, whom they rarely met or did not know much about. Thus, the concept of relative deprivation holds that people judge outcomes as unfair when the outcomes they actually receive fall short of the outcomes they expected to receive (see, e.g., Crosby, 1976; Gurr, 1970; Runciman, 1966; Smith, Pettigrew, Pippin, & Bialosiewicz, 2012; Stouffer et al., 1949).

Developing the concept of relative deprivation further, Crosby (1976) stated that for an individual to feel resentment about missing out on something, at least five conditions must be met. That is, the person involved (1) should observe that someone else possesses what the person is missing, (2) wants to have the missing outcome, (3) feels entitled to it, (4) thinks it is feasible to obtain the outcome, and (5) does not feel personally responsible for not having the desired outcome. In this way, Crosby developed an egoistical model of relative deprivation. This model focuses heavily on self-involved individuals who want to obtain things that other persons already have.

Importantly, Runciman (1966) noted that relative comparisons are made not only between a person and other persons but also between groups. For example, it is one thing when a woman perceives that her salary is lower than that of her colleagues working in the same organization, but it is another thing when the same woman experiences being deprived of a higher income because of the group or groups to which she belongs, such as her gender, ethnic background, age, or social class. Group deprivation is also apparent when teenagers envy wealthy characters from other groups in movies or on television. Thus, relative deprivation can be caused by interpersonal comparisons and by intergroup comparisons. Runciman therefore distinguished between personal deprivation (what he called "egoistic" relative deprivation) and group-based deprivation (what he labeled as "fraternalistic" relative deprivation).

Merton (1938) used the concept of relative deprivation to understand social deviance. In doing so, he relied on the work by the famous sociologist Émile Durkheim (1897), who put forward the notion of "anomie" to convey circumstances in which society provides little moral guidance to individuals and in which social bonds between an individual and the community are broken down and hence there are conditions of societal derangement. Indeed, relative deprivation is important because people who perceive that they or their group are deprived of things deemed valuable in society—whether money, justice, status, or privilege—may join social movements with the hope of redressing their grievances. It should not come as a surprise, therefore, that relative deprivation is a potential cause of social movements and societal protest (Klandermans, 1997). Extreme conditions or radical perceptions of relative deprivation may lead to political violence such as rioting, civil wars, and terrorism (Gurr, 1970; Merton, 1938).

The notion of relative deprivation has important implications for the study of radicalization and associated issues such as extremism and sympathy for terrorist movements. For example, it is not only or primarily people's objective or absolute deprivation that determines justice-based grievance but also or especially the relative injustice experienced, for example, by the deprived conditions that people perceive they are encountering relative to other individuals or other groups. Thus, studying objective conditions is important, for instance, because unfairness perceptions of radicalizing persons can be correct, at least partially. However, describing these objective conditions does not provide the sole or even the most important answer to the issue why people radicalize. People's perceptions of their social conditions are key to the understanding of the radicalization process.

Because these perceptions are relative, this also implies that those individuals from radical groups who are themselves relatively well off, and hence can imagine that they may succeed in improving their conditions, may show extreme levels of grievance and resentment, for example, when it turns out that they will not get access to a good job or high societal status after all (see also Crosby, 1982, 1984; Klandermans, 1997). This is related to the frustration effect whereby repeated denial of deserved and just treatment may lead to extreme levels of grievance (Folger, 1977). Indeed, quite often individuals with relatively high levels of education are the ones who in the end engage in terrorist behaviors. This is not only because some terrorist attacks involve elaborate cognitive capacities and developed skills but also because these individuals are more likely to experience barely missing out on important progress, wanted goods, and desired social standing.

In our own research of extreme right-wing attitudes among autochthonous citizens from the Netherlands and radical attitudes among Muslims in the Netherlands we found that perceptions of relative group deprivation played a key role in the radicalization processes of these two groups (Van den Bos, Loseman, & Doosje, 2009). We also observed some important differences between the two groups. That is, the right-wing autochthonous respondents tended to attribute the cause of their group deprivation to Muslims and indicated that Muslims were taking away important material goods, such as jobs and housing, and also immaterial goods, such as access to potential dates. Thus, one could say that the right-wing citizens were experiencing group deprivation targeted at another group in society. One could label this as an instance of horizontal group deprivation.

Interestingly, the Muslim respondents were not so much oriented or focused on right-wing groups. In contrast, in their experiences of group deprivation the Muslim citizens were oriented on important authorities in society, such as the prime minister or managers from organizations, and attributed their group deprivation to those societal authorities. For example, the Muslim respondents we interviewed indicated that the Prime Minister of the Netherlands was not advocating or defending their rights. They noted, for instance, that this person or other politicians did not seem to allow for the Sugar Feast or other important Muslim holidays to be turned into official national holidays. In their experiences of relative group deprivation, the Muslim citizens also looked at judges and police officers and how they as members of their group were treated by those officials, relative to how members of other groups were treated. They also pointed at work managers, such as the manager from the local grocery store who did not want them to have an internship or a side job at that store. In short, the experiences of group deprivation among our Muslim respondents seemed to be oriented at societal authorities. One could call this an instance of vertical group deprivation.

Figure 4.2 shows the horizontal and vertical instances of group deprivation we observed in our research in the Netherlands. This figure is not meant to imply that no vertical orientation takes place among right-wing autochthonous Dutch citizens, nor that no horizontal orientation occurs among Dutch Muslims—certainly not. However, for the moment I conclude that both horizontal and vertical deprivation seem to play an important role in the psychology of radicalization.

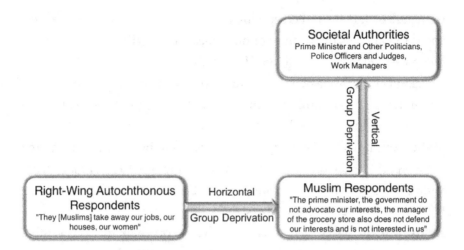

**Figure 4.2  Horizontal and Vertical Group Deprivation Among Right-Wing Autochthonous and Muslim Respondents.**
This model distinguishes horizontal group deprivation, found especially among right-wing autochthonous respondents in the Netherlands who experienced that Muslims were taking away important material or immaterial goods, and vertical group deprivation, observed particularly among Muslim respondents who perceived important societal authorities not being interested in them and not defending their rights.

I also state explicitly that there well might be significant distaste of the elite and the status quo among those from right-wing movements as well as those with lower educational levels and Muslims living in Western countries (see, e.g., Hulst, Van den Bos, Robijn, Romijn, Schroen, & Wever, 2018). All these observations suggest to me that horizontal and vertical aspects of cultural and subcultural differences (see also Triandis & Gelfland, 1998) need to be included in the study of radicalization, extremism, and terrorism.

## 4.4 INEQUITABLE OUTCOMES

Although issues of unfair treatment and relative deprivation are critical in understanding grievance, social protest, and radicalization, and have captured the appropriate attention of justice scholars, they comprise only part of the story: Perceptions of unfairness also include questions about the fairness or inequity of outcomes and the distribution of those outcomes (Deutsch, 1975, 1985; Homans, 1961).

The outcomes that people obtain matter to them, in part because of instrumental or economic reasons (Walster, Walster, & Berscheid, 1978). For example, the income that people receive tends to be positively related to their emotional well-being. This effect tends to be there at least up to a certain point. After this point increased income is not further associated with increased well-being (Kahneman & Deaton, 2010). In interactions between citizens and the social system, an important determinant of satisfaction with the system and its leaders is the outcomes obtained (Leventhal, Karuza, & Fry, 1980). Indeed, outcomes influence attitudes toward leaders (Michener & Lawler, 1975) and trust in government (Katz, Gutek, Kahn, & Barton, 1975). Moreover, discontent with the courts is often assumed to be linked to instrumental concerns about the outcomes delivered by the court (Grootelaar & Van den Bos, 2016). Outcomes surely matter because of financial motives, although research also suggests that self-interest is a less potent motive of human behavior than is often thought to be true (Miller, 1999). One reason for this is that in isolation outcomes do not mean that much to people. For outcomes to become meaningful, we need to compare them with other outcomes.

One way in which we compare outcomes is temporal. For example, people may have become accustomed to getting better outcomes in the past, and hence their current outcomes feel not right and indeed unfair and unjust (Van den Bos et al., 2005). Or people somehow may have built up the expectation that they will get better outcomes in the future and hence may become deeply frustrated when these outcomes are not realized in actuality. Thus, outcomes and outcome fairness play an important role in human reactions because those outcomes can fall below people's expectations. Indeed, expectations provide an important reference point on which people base the evaluations of the outcomes that they receive or hope to receive (Thibaut & Kelley, 1959). Outcomes that fall below people's expectations are easily perceived as unfair and can be a cause of great grievance. These expectation-based feelings of unfairness may exacerbate the radicalization process, such that when expectations exceed the actual outcomes young people receive, this may be a great source of frustration.

Another potent way in which we compare outcomes is social. Social comparisons tend to be more directly related to judged fairness than expectations are (Austin, McGinn, & Susmilch, 1980; Blau, 1964). Theories of distributive justice highlight that it is not only or primarily the individual outcomes that people receive that determine their reactions but also the distributions of outcomes in the social context in which people find themselves. Thus, it is not so much one's own salary, for example, that determines levels of outcome fairness or outcome satisfaction, but rather it is the knowledge that someone else's salary is much better that negatively influences fairness and satisfaction ratings. Equity research has shown that outcomes frequently are evaluated in terms of where the outcome falls relative to the outcome of others (Adams, 1965; Messick & Sentis, 1983): Outcomes are judged as fairer and more satisfying when outcomes are equal to, as opposed to different from, outcomes of comparison others. It is on this social comparison that most equity theories focus.

Simply put, equity theories note that people judge an outcome as fair when the ratio of their own inputs and outputs equals the ratio of inputs and outputs of comparison others (e.g., Adams, 1965). Thus, when evaluating whether your outcome is fair, you compare your own outcome with the outcomes that other people receive, and you correct this comparison of outcomes by evaluating the amount of time, energy, talent, and other inputs that you put into obtaining your outcome and the inputs another person or other persons put into this. Thus, when another person is comparable to you in terms of inputs, your outcome should be comparable to the outcome of the comparable other person in order to label your outcome fair and equitable. When the other person's outcome is better than yours, his or her inputs should be greater to justify this unequal distribution of outcomes (Adams, 1965).

Presumably because we humans are social animals (e.g., Aronson, 1972), it is the social comparison–based quality of outcome distributions that tends to have strong and powerful effects on human reactions. These effects can be observed in many different social situations, including intimate relationships, in which social comparison–based information about inequity has been found to influence marital satisfaction (see, e.g., Van Yperen & Buunk, 1991). Social comparison information also plays a strong role in processes of radicalization. For example, the perception that comparable others in society are receiving better outcomes can be an important source of dissatisfaction and grievance.

Furthermore, peer opinions about what constitutes good outcomes and what are reasonable inputs to obtain these outcomes can influence evaluations of one's own outcomes and associated affective and emotional reactions (Folger, Rosenfield, Grove, & Corkran, 1979). People who have been radicalized or who are tempted to radicalize may well be more likely to be affected by persons with whom they can easily compare themselves. For instance, a person such as Nawaz (2013) who used to live in similar circumstances and who had radicalized before but now regrets having done so may well be a more powerful source of information for radical youngsters in Western societies than the government of those societies. Thus, social comparison information can lead to both growing and attenuation of the radicalization process.

The comparison of one's own outcomes and inputs with the outcomes and inputs of others creates the likelihood of systematic psychological biases in the evaluation process. For example, it can be tempting to underestimate the time, energy, and talent of other people and to overestimate one's own inputs. It can also be tempting to compare one's own outcomes with those of others and think that "if only" things would have been a little bit different, then one's own situation, including one's own outcomes, could have been much better (Folger, 1986). The next chapters focus on the issue of biased information processing in some detail.

Here I note that not only biases but also the presence or absence of relevant information, and especially social comparison information about others' outcomes, has important consequences for how people respond to their outcomes. For example, it can be argued that complete information about another person's outcome is often missing. It quite frequently happens, for instance, that we do not know the exact salary that our colleagues are earning at the company where we work. Research suggests that in such circumstances of missing relevant information, we start to rely on information that is available in the situation at hand (Van den Bos, Lind, Vermunt, & Wilke, 1997). Most notably, information about how fairly we have been treated tends to be widely available and easy to process. This may be one reason why human reactions tend to show such strong and reliable reactions of treatment fairness (Van den Bos, 2001a, 2015). This suggests that a careful analysis of information processes people are going through is of essential importance when we want to understand the fairness judgments they are forming—for instance, when undergoing processes of radicalization.

## 4.5 IMMORALITY

An important component in the process of radicalization can be the feeling that things are not right and, in fact, are morally wrong. One reason for this is that morality and moral concerns are strongly related to the essence of who we as humans are (Haidt, 2003a). We want to be moral beings and want to be seen as such (Cramwinckel, Van Dijk, Scheepers, & Van den Bos, 2013). Building up moral credentials that we are good people hence is very important to us (Monin & Miller, 2001).

Moral concerns constitute a pivotal force of human behavior, in part because we have elaborate reasoning skills and sophisticated cognitive skills that allow us to come to important conclusions about what is right or wrong. Morality is also important for its own sake, not only because of evolutionary concerns, but also because we deeply and innately care about morality and about what is right (Greene, 2013). Thus, although it may be very difficult to falsify that self-interest is not underlying moral concerns, my hypothesis is that quite often we see the best of what humans can achieve when they act in moral ways and go out of their way to take principled standpoints in matters of what should be done. For example, this inspired important behaviors of resistance heroes in my country during the Second World War. The fact that people often may act out of more mundane reasons or plain self-interest, as opposed to genuine altruistic motives and high moral principles, does not negate the observation that true moral concerns exist and that morality has inspired some of the most important and indeed most beautiful instances of human behaviors this world has ever encountered.

Perceiving that things are morally wrong upsets us, in part because these immoral events threaten our notion that we live in a world that is understandable and predictable. After all, we want to make progress toward the attainment of our goals, and we can best do this in a world where we know we can have a personal contract that in the long run our efforts will pay off and will be rewarded (Van den Bos, McGregor, & Martin, 2015). This notion of a personal contract applies to our own relationship with the world but also is relevant for how we view how others are faring. Thus, when we experience immoral acts that are directed toward us, this is upsetting, captures our attention, and instigates important behavioral tendencies to do something about this or (when meaningful opposition is not deemed possible) to leave the situation and seek circumstances that feel more right to us. Also, immorality directed at our group can trigger similar reactions. And so can immoral acts that are not directed toward ourselves or our own group but that are just wrong and hence need to be corrected. This can be seen, for example, when people like Bob Geldof fight poverty in Africa. In short, experiences that things are immoral can deeply concern us.

One of the reasons why perceiving immorality is upsetting presumably is that this is directly related to strongly felt moral emotions. In fact, core emotions such as anger and disgust are strongly associated with important moral codes of how to behave (Rozin, Lowery, Imada, & Haidt, 1999). We indeed judge persons and groups by relying on the emotions and affective feelings these individuals and groups trigger among us (Giner-Sorrola, 2012). Moral emotions thus play an important role in our emotional life (Gray & Wegner, 2011; Moll, De Oliveira-Souza, Zahn, & Grafman, 2008; Prinz & Nichols, 2010).

Moral reasoning also motivates people to approve or disapprove of certain behaviors. In fact, people often feel mandated to take firm stances with regard to important moral issues (Skitka, 2002). It should not come as a surprise, therefore, that people may feel the inclination to protest and fight against what they see as morally wrong. This morality-based opposition clearly has yielded behaviors that are important and good for society at large.

Importantly, although I hypothesize that true moral concerns have an impact on what we do, I also note that we sometimes "underdo" it and act too little out of moral concerns. This is quite obvious when we observe human behavior in the real world, including our own behaviors at certain times. Interestingly, we also sometimes "overdo" it and behave too much in principled ways. Haidt (2012), for example, notes that moral righteousness can lead people to react too quickly to other points of view. Thus, because we not only adhere to certain political or religious beliefs but in addition are convicted that these beliefs are right, we can easily be tempted to infer that other points of view are not right. This may lead to the denigration of those other views without (and this is crucial) appropriate attention to the validity of the views in question.

I am not implying here that views different from ours always have a kernel of truth and cannot be wrong. Quite the contrary, I hate such simple-minded postmodern kinds of reasoning styles in which "anything goes." The crucial point I am trying to make here is that sometimes morality can lead us to derogate other points of view without giving those views full consideration. Focusing on our own moral values and extensive reasoning processes concerning why these values are valid and honorable can lead us to overlook the possible importance of other viewpoints out there.

This line of reasoning fits with a proposition formulated by Haidt (2001), who argued that in many circumstances our intuitions or gut feelings may precede our reasoning of what is right and wrong. In fact, Haidt proposes that feelings and moral emotions provide meaningful input for how to interpret moral issues. This probably is the case because in many circumstances information about moral issues is not available or is too complex to digest in all its nuances. Feelings and emotions then serve as important sources on which people build their moral judgments

(Van den Bos, 2003). Thus, when a certain situation feels right, you infer that the situation probably is moral. And when another event makes you disgusted, you tend to conclude that the event in all likelihood is wrong. This perspective is related to Hume's (1739) take on the role of emotions and moral judgments.

An important reason why we sometimes act in moral righteous ways and do not pay appropriate attention to others' views is that our own moral judgments feel right and genuine (Higgins, 1996; Higgins, Idson, Freitas, Spiegel, & Molden, 2003). Moral information that is easier to process seems to have a higher likelihood to be judged as being moral compared with information that is more difficult to process (see, e.g., Laham, Alter, & Goodwin, 2009). I note explicitly that the issue of the relationship between fluency of cognitive processes and moral judgment is awaiting definitive evidence (see, e.g., Jiang & Hong, 2014), but for now I propose that we seem to be attuned to make it easy for ourselves, especially when our thoughts are preoccupied or when we find ourselves in dire circumstances, and it is in these kinds of circumstances that we may be tempted to process information about other people in superficial ways and think of our judgments as correct and true.

In all likelihood, what people think is right or wrong is typically the result of an interplay between moral emotions and moral reasoning (Greene, 2005; Greene, Sommerville, Nystrom, Darley, & Cohen, 2001; Van den Bos, 2003). This interplay can obtain complex forms in different situations. In trying to understand these forms, it is important to study carefully what important psychological functions morality and moral judgments fulfill.

One important psychological function of morality has to do with the groups to which people belong versus the groups to which they do not belong (Greene, 2013; Giner-Sorrola, 2012). We have a tendency to be more positive about our own groups than about other groups (Tajfel & Turner, 1979). In fact, in competition with other groups, we tend to be more competitive than in interaction with other individuals (Schopler et al., 2001). This effect, known as the interindividual-intergroup discontinuity effect (Wildschut et al., 2003), could well explain how normal and decent individuals can be lured into competitive mindsets in which they want to outperform other groups, either by ethical means or—if that would not be possible—by not so ethical means.

Related to this, Greene (2013) postulates that in situations in which we interact with others who are members of our own group, we tend to act in cooperative and moral ways. This effect seems to be there, according to Greene, even when we are under time pressure or when our cognitive capacities are taxed in other ways. Thus, we tend to show loyalty to our own group. Indeed, group affiliation serves important and positive psychological functions for people. However, a not-so-nice implication of this loyalty to our own group is that this can easily lead to hostility toward other groups.

I argue here that this reliance on feelings of "Do you belong to my moral tribe, yes or no?" plays an important role in the radicalization process, particularly when this process pertains to hostility between communities. Especially when affiliation with your own group is very important to you, there is the likelihood that you are tempted to develop aversive feelings against groups that are not your own. In other words, it is under these circumstances that in-group love at least sometimes tends to imply out-group hate (Halevy, Bornstein, & Sagiv, 2008). Other groups may also be seen, then, as not so moral as your own group.

Perceived moral superiority and group identification may help people to downplay rule-breaking behavior of in-group members (Iyer, Jetten, & Haslam, 2012). Moral superiority may also underlie people's inclination to think that others are more influenced by egoism-based considerations, whereas they themselves are more influenced by considerations of right and wrong (Peters, Van den Bos, & Bobocel, 2004). Related to this, people may be tempted to engage in processes of moral disengagement in which they convince themselves that ethical standards do not apply to them. People do this by rethinking or reframing their own destructive behavior as being morally acceptable, something that is achieved by inhibiting mechanisms of self-condemnation and not thinking in moral terms about immoral conduct (Bandura, 1986, 1999; Bandura, Barbaranelli, Caprara, & Pastorelli, 1996).

Processes of moral superiority, and especially individual moral superiority, have been observed in my country with respect to left-wing radicalization pertaining to asylum and animal rights (IVA, 2010; Netherlands General Intelligence and Security Service, 2010). Radical individuals ventilated thoughts that how the government is treating people who seek asylum in The Netherlands or how commercial companies are treating animals is clearly wrong. These individuals therefore felt entirely justified and entitled to do something about these issues, even when this implied that they then broke the law or acted in antidemocratic or even violent ways to achieve their goals. These perceptions of moral righteousness are deeply felt and tend to legitimize violent behavior or other conduct that violates democratic values. Why this is the case and how this works psychologically are the subject of the next section.

## 4.6 PERCEPTIONS THAT FEEL GENUINE
## AND HAVE REAL CONSEQUENCES

A basic issue on which this book focuses, and on which the entire current chapter concentrates, is that perceptions that things are unfair serve a pivotal role in the radicalization process. The literature reviewed briefly here suggests that treatment unfairness, individual and group deprivation, inequitable distribution of outcomes, and feelings of immorality, moral righteousness, and moral superiority all can have a great impact on people.

In a research project Annemarie Loseman, Bertjan Doosje, and I did for the National Coordinator for Security and Counterterrorism in the Netherlands, we developed a model that aimed to explain the role that these perceptions of unfairness can play in radicalization processes. Figure 1.2 was a condensed version of that model, and Figure 4.3 shows an expanded version of the model, focusing on the antecedents and consequences of unfairness perceptions in the radicalization process.

Important aspects of the model were tested in survey questionnaires assessed on the Internet among 1,086 Dutch autochthonous youngsters, measuring their susceptibility for adopting radical right-wing attitudes

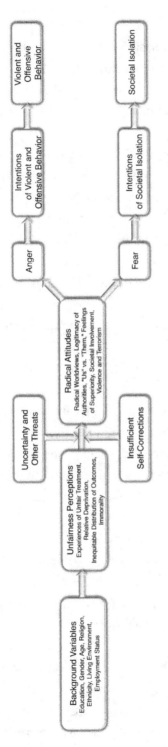

**Figure 4.3  Background Variables, Perceptions of Unfairness, Attitudinal Reactions, and Different Emotional Pathways and Associated Behavioral Intentions and Actual Behaviors in Processes of Radicalization and Societal Isolation.**

This model describes the antecedents and consequences of perceptions of unfairness. The figure illustrates that demographic and other background variables are not sufficient to explain processes of radicalization and societal isolation. Elaborating on Figure 1.2, the model notes that perceptions of unfairness in interaction with insufficient self-corrections and uncertainty and other threats play a crucial role in influencing radical attitudes. When this process is coupled with externally oriented emotions, such as anger, this increases the likelihood of violent and offensive behavioral intentions and actual behaviors associated with radicalization. When combined with internally oriented emotions, such as fear, this increases the chances of intentions and behaviors that isolate people from society. (Based on Figure 2.1 presented in Van den Bos, Loseman, & Doosje, 2009. Used by permission of the Research and Documentation Centre of the Netherlands Ministry of Justice.)

and behaviors (Doosje, Van den Bos, Loseman, Feddes, & Mann, 2012). We also interviewed 131 Muslim youngsters from the Netherlands in the same way (Doosje, Loseman, & Van den Bos, 2013). And we conducted qualitative in-depth personal interviews with 24 radical young persons, both Muslim radicals and Dutch autochthonous right-wing radicals (Van den Bos, Loseman, & Doosje, 2009).

In developing the model depicted in Figure 4.3, I also relied on insights from basic social psychology (e.g., Van den Bos, 2009a; Van den Bos, Peters, Bobocel, & Ybema, 2006) and work on left-wing radicalization such as extremist behaviors regarding asylum and animal rights (e.g., IVA, 2010; Netherlands General Intelligence and Security Service, 2010). Thus, the model that is shown in Figure 4.3 is relevant to different forms of radicalization. The model also has empirical backup. That said, I hasten to add that because practices of radical behavior are complex and multifaceted, many important issues are not known yet and should be studied more carefully (see also Chapter 12).

Following earlier studies on this topic, Van den Bos et al. (2009) identified important demographic and other background variables that could lead to Muslim radicalization and right-wing extremism. These variables include education, gender, age, religiosity, ethnicity, and cultural factors such as under what conditions and where people live and whether they have a job, a side job, or no job at all. These and other background variables are clearly important when we want to understand in detail how and when people will radicalize.

However, not unlike other approaches, we noted in our project that it is impossible to give an "objective" demographic description of radicalization among young people. That is, factors that lead to radical behavior are complex and multifaceted, and it is not possible to point out demographic variables that directly and straightforwardly impact the radicalization process (see also Aly & Striegher, 2012; Krueger, 2007; Krueger & Malečková, 2003; Post, 1990, 2007). Thus, when certain demographic conditions are met, this does not imply that people in fact will engage in radical behavior. Therefore, to obtain good insights into why people engage in radical behavior and start sympathizing with terrorist violence, careful attention should be paid to how people perceive the situation they are in. After all, how people think, feel, and behave is influenced to a large extent by how they interpret situations.

Therefore, the current book notes that people's perceptions, and in particular their perceptions of unfairness, play a crucial role in radicalization processes. Thus, Figure 4.3 illustrates that demographic and other background variables are not sufficient to explain processes of radicalization and societal isolation. Elaborating on Figure 1.2, the model notes that perceptions of unfairness in interaction with insufficient self-corrections and uncertainty and other threats play a crucial role in influencing radical attitudes.

These perceptions of unfairness include perceived unfair treatment, relative levels of individual and group deprivation, inequitable distribution of outcomes, and experiences of immorality. The attitudes we focused on are people's thoughts and feelings about several issues such as radical worldviews, the legitimacy they assign to societal authorities, and the extent to which they engage in "us" versus "them" thinking. The attitudes also include thoughts and feelings about societal superiority and inferiority, being involved in society, and also what people think and how they affectively evaluate violence and terrorism.

As Figure 4.3 illustrates, when this process of unfairness perceptions and attitudinal responses is coupled with externally oriented emotions such as anger, this increases the likelihood of violent and offensive behavioral intentions and actual behaviors associated with radicalization. When combined with internally oriented emotions such as fear, this increases the chances of intentions and behaviors that isolate people from society. Societal isolation can create "lone actor behavior," but more often than not, it is anger and other externally oriented behavioral tendencies that are needed for people to engage in violent and offensive behavior such as terrorist acts. So, extremist and terrorist behaviors are more frequently found in the top-right part of Figure 4.3 than in the lower-right part.

The research findings that my colleagues and I obtained thus far suggest that when basic aspects of a person's life are perceived as unfair, this is likely to result in radical attitudes. Together with sensitivity to personal uncertainty and insufficient self-corrections (topics that will be addressed in the next two chapters), this can easily lead to externally oriented negative emotions (such as anger) and intentions to engage in radical and even violent behavior. In this way, perceptions of unfairness can lead people to hold more positive attitudes about radical issues beliefs, and when associated with externally oriented emotions such as anger, this can lead to extremist and terrorist intentions and actual engagement in these behaviors.

The model depicted in Figure 4.3 does not imply that other variables, such as other emotions besides anger and fear, could not be relevant. For example, Tausch et al. (2011) suggest that feelings of anger are mostly associated with normative behavior (such as in taking part in demonstrations and in signing petitions), whereas contempt would be more associated with nonnormative behavior (such as destroying property or violence against humans). Thus, contempt by radicalizing individuals could well be something that needs to be integrated more fully in analyses of radicalization processes. Other emotions and feelings that are probably relevant include resentment and hate as well as people being upset or finding certain things to be outrageous, to name but a few.

Perceptions of unfairness play such a crucial role in this psychological process, I assume, because fairness refers to very basic norms and values concerning how we humans want to be treated and what should be happening in this world. Many different psychological theories ground this assumption (see, e.g., De Waal, 1996; Greene, 2013; Lerner, 1980; Lind & Tyler, 1988).

Furthermore, compared with more general perceptions of valence that refer to whether things are positive or negative, perceptions of unfairness have a special quality for the perceivers involved. That is, perceptions of unfairness (including perceived unfair treatment, relative deprivation, outcome inequity, and immorality) definitely are related to negative valence but also tend to feel real and genuine in the eye of the beholder. This "It is genuine!" kind of reaction is something unique to perceptions of unfairness in general and to notions of injustice and immorality in particular. Thus, whereas I tend to focus more on the similarities between experiences of unfair treatment, deprivation, inequity, and immorality,

I do note that there can be important psychological and other differences in how these different constructs are perceived and experienced by the individuals involved. Importantly, the more these perceptions feel genuine and real to people, the more likely they are to have real consequences on people's behavior.

I realize that not all who are interested in fighting radicalization and terrorism are enthusiastic about focusing on people's perceptions. I also understand that by emphasizing the role of people's perceptions, I run the risk of being criticized of focusing too much on subjective factors. Related to this, I am well aware that perceptions of unfairness may be biased (e.g., Messick, Bloom, Boldizar, & Samuelson, 1985; Messick & Sentis, 1983). I understand and appreciate these comments. However, ignoring these perceptions (and instead referring to objective factors only or normative approaches of what should be done) may not be a good idea because these perceptions are felt as real and genuine by the individuals who are experiencing them. The emotions that are felt as a result of these perception processes are very real to people as well.

A classic saying holds that although perceptions may be biased or colored, perceptions may be real in the consequences they have on people's reactions and behaviors (Thomas & Thomas, 1928). Therefore, when we would like to understand radical and extremist behaviors, we should take perceptions of unfairness seriously and examine these perceptions thoroughly. An implication of this conclusion is that although focusing on perceptions in this way may make the study of radicalization and extremism more difficult at first, once we understand what is perceived to be wrong, we get hold of a major antecedent of why people may engage in radicalization processes and adhere to extremist movements.

The psychology of how people form and use fairness, justice, and moral judgments is complicated. At the same time, much is known about these processes, and important aspects of how fairness, justice, and morality judgments are formed were reviewed here (for other reviews, see, e.g., Beauchamp, 2001; Cropanzano & Ambrose, 2015; Folger & Cropanzano, 1998; Greene, 2013; Haidt, 2001; Lind & Tyler, 1988; Tyler, 2006; Sandel, 2009; Sinnot-Armstrong, 2008). Thus, I suggest that careful attention to

how situations are perceived and interpreted by people can contribute to
the understanding of radical behavior. Politicians and policy makers can
use this insight, as well as the specifics described in this book, to better
understand and predict the behaviors of potentially radical and extremist
people. Using these insights can lead to a better grounding of the prevention of radical and violent behaviors in our world.

For example, I discussed in this chapter that perceptions of *group*
deprivation seem to be important factors driving Muslim and right-
wing extremism, at least in the Netherlands (Van den Bos, Loseman, &
Doosje, 2009), whereas *individual* notions of immorality are driving important forms of left-wing radicalization regarding animals and people
who seek asylum (IVA, 2010). Because most humans have the potential
to be members of multiple groups, alternative group identities and other
sources of group affiliation can be made salient to those people who are
tempted to identify with radical Muslim and right-wing groups. For instance, when young radicals become older, they often start a family and
hence become responsible for their spouse and children. This may lead
them to be less willing to show actual radical behaviors associated with
Muslim or right-wing extremists (see also Heinsohn, 2005).

Individualistic perceptions of morality may be less easy to alter or to influence. This especially applies to moral convictions and notions of moral
righteousness. When formed, these notions seem quite resistant against
attempts of social influence. After all, why would you be willing to be
influenced by others when you know darn well that this is right and that is
wrong? Moral perceptions tend to be experienced as objectively true. And
you do not negotiate about your moral norms and values. Nevertheless,
the full development of radical attitudes and violent and antidemocratic
behaviors, possibly even terrorist behaviors, implies that people respond
strongly to uncertainty and other threats, and it also involves the presence
of insufficient self-corrections. These topics are discussed in the next two
chapters.

# Uncertainty and Other Threats

## 5.1 INTRODUCTION

Although a central premise of this book is that experiences of unfairness can be important drivers of radicalization processes, I also note explicitly that perceptions of unfairness in general tend not to be enough to lead people into developing radical beliefs and associated extreme feelings and violent behaviors. As the models in Figures 1.2 and 4.3 illustrate, I propose that when the experience of unfairness is coupled with uncertainty and other threatening information, this is likely to exacerbate the radicalization process. Thus, I argue that unfairness perceptions can serve as pivotal antecedents of enhanced radicalization, especially when people feel uncertain about themselves and live in insecure conditions or find themselves in unpredictable situations.

The current chapter focuses on uncertainty as a moderator of the linkage between perceptions of unfairness and the radicalization process. To this end, the chapter introduces the concept of uncertainty and reviews evidence that suggests that under conditions of uncertainty, people are more in need of reassurance that their views on how the world works are valid. They also need bolstering of the positive aspects of their culture and respond negatively toward information that criticizes their culture.

The chapter begins with defining the concept of uncertainty and other threatening information (Section 5.2). I argue that it is important to distinguish between people being uncertain about themselves (personal uncertainty or insecurity; Section 5.3) and people not having enough relevant information available (informational uncertainty; Section 5.4). The two types of uncertainty are not the same and yield predictable differential responses to what people do and on their reactions of cultural worldview defense and associated radicalization processes. Personal uncertainty in particular is an alarming experience with strong affective and emotional reactions and as such can be linked to the human alarm system, a basic system that people use to make sense of their worlds and that I relate in this chapter to processes of radicalization (see Figure 5.1).

Being uncertain about whether one can trust important authorities (such as political authorities or management of work organizations) also has a special place in how people in the modern world respond to what they are experiencing in this world (Section 5.5). The chapter discusses the relationship between uncertainty and the ease of processing of information, arguing that people in general find fluent processing of information to be nice, whereas they judge disfluent processing of information to be aversive. The chapter closes by noting how this experience, when combined with the experience of unfairness, may impact the radicalization process in our modern culture where outcomes are often delayed (Section 5.6).

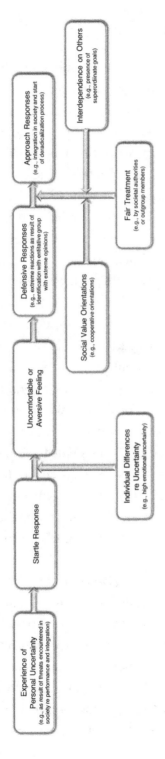

**Figure 5.1 Threat Associated with Personal Uncertainty Transformed into Approach Responses.**

This model describes the consequences of experiences of personal uncertainty. The figure illustrates that spontaneous startle responses are likely to lead to uncomfortable and aversive feelings, especially when people find it difficult to respond in calm ways to uncertain events. These feelings can lead to defensive responses, such as when people start to identify with entitative groups with extreme opinions. Experiences of fair treatment, when combined with cooperative social value orientations and superordinate goals, when being interdependent on others can transform these responses into approach responses, which may be conducive to societal integration and deradicalization. (Based on and extended from Figure 1 presented in Van den Bos, 2009b, and adapted to the radicalization process. Used by permission of Taylor and Francis Ltd.)

## 5.2 DEFINING UNCERTAINTY

It is important to convey how I define uncertainty and what concepts I distinguish in doing so. After all, there are many different types of uncertainties that people can encounter, and it is important not to confuse them (Van den Bos, 2009a; Van den Bos & Lind, 2009). In this book I focus on two important types of uncertainties. One significant type of uncertainty that people often face in our modern world is informational uncertainty. This involves having less information available than one ideally would like to have in order to be able to confidently form a given social judgment. For example, work on human decision making reveals that human judgments are often formed under conditions of incomplete information and that these conditions can lead to predictable effects on human decision and social judgment processes (see, e.g., Kahneman, Slovic, & Tversky, 1982). Thus, when studying how people make social judgments, a pivotal issue is what information people have available.

Informational uncertainty is important and may be what researchers come up with most frequently when they think of the concept of uncertainty, in part because of the success of the decision-making literature and the associated work of Nobel laureates such as Kahneman and Phelps (e.g., Kahneman et al., 1982; Phelps, 1970). This noted, I argue that while informational uncertainty is important, we should not confuse the concept with personal uncertainty. Personal uncertainty is another type of uncertainty, and I think that, compared with informational uncertainty, it is even more important for the understanding of what people do, especially in terms of radicalization.

I define personal uncertainty as a subjective sense of doubt or instability in self-views, worldviews, or the interrelation between the two (Arkin, Oleson, & Carroll, 2009; Van den Bos, 2009a; Van den Bos & Lind, 2009). In my view, personal uncertainty involves the implicit and explicit feelings and other subjective reactions people experience as a result of being uncertain about themselves (Van den Bos, 2001a, 2007; Van den Bos, Poortvliet, Maas, Miedema, & Van den Ham, 2005). Thus, personal uncertainty is the feeling that you experience when you feel uncertain about yourself.

Typically, experiencing personal uncertainty constitutes an aversive or at least an uncomfortable feeling (Hogg, 2007; Van den Bos & Lind, 2002).

The difference between informational and personal uncertainty is related to the distinction between epistemic and affective dimensions of uncertainty. As Michael Hogg (2007) put it, *knowing* that you are uncertain about something is different from *feeling* uncertain. Personal uncertainty involves both stable individual differences, such as differences in emotional uncertainty (Greco & Roger, 2001; Sedikides, De Cremer, Hart, & Brebels, 2009), and situational fluctuations, such as whether people's personal uncertainties have or have not been made salient (Van den Bos, 2001a). After all, personal uncertainty can be produced by contextual factors that challenge people's certainty about what they think, feel, and do, and this can influence their confidence in their sense of self (Hogg, 2001).

The concept of people's selves is very important for understanding personal uncertainty. This is because the self-concept is the critical organizing principle, referent point, or integrative framework for diverse perceptions, feelings, and behaviors (Sedikides & Strube, 1997; see also Loseman, Miedema, Van den Bos, & Vermunt, 2009). The locus of uncertainty can be found in many aspects of the social context, and therefore we are all susceptible to personal uncertainty. However, biographical factors also create stable individual differences in levels of uncertainty, and they can influence people's approach to how they manage uncertainty (Sorrentino, Hodson, & Huber, 2001; Sorrentino, Short, & Raynor, 1984). Furthermore, people strive more strongly for certainty about those aspects of life that are important to them (Hogg & Mullin, 1999).

I propose that experiencing personal uncertainty is a "hot-cognitive" social psychological process (Abelson, 1963; Kunda, 1999), involving a combination of both cognitive and affective reactions (Van den Bos, 2007). I also think that personal uncertainty more often than not involves visceral and intuitive (instead of more reasoned and rationalistic) reactions (Van den Bos, 2009a). Experiencing personal uncertainty about one's attitudes, beliefs, feelings, and perceptions, as well as about one's relationship to other people, is generally uncomfortable or aversive (e.g., Hogg, 2007; Marigold, McGregor, & Zanna, 2009; Sedikides et al., 2009; Sorrentino &

Roney, 1986; Van den Bos & Lind, 2002). It can lead to increased blood pressure and physiological arousal, which may be associated with sustained activation of the hypothalamic-pituitary-adrenal axis in the brain (Greco & Roger, 2003). Personal uncertainty therefore often motivates behavior that seeks to reduce it.

Although experiencing uncertainty may sometimes be sought out and occasionally may instigate contemplation or introspection (e.g., Sorrentino, Bobocel, Gitta, Olson, & Hewitt, 1988; Weary & Jacobson, 1997), I argue that these reactions are more frequently found following informational uncertainty than following personal uncertainty. Whereas people may be able to tolerate informational uncertainties, such as causal uncertainties about what has happened at some point in the past (Weary & Jacobson, 1997) or what will be happening on an upcoming vacation in an exciting environment (Hogg, 2007), I propose that feeling uncertainty about oneself may strongly motivate people to try to get rid of the feeling. In contrast with informational uncertainty, people often find experiencing personal uncertainty an alarming event that does not allow for contemplation and introspection, but that instead requires people to respond rather quickly to what is going on (Van den Bos, 2009a, 2010; Van den Bos, Ham, Lind, Simonis, Van Essen, & Rijpkema, 2008).

As such, my colleagues and I work from the assumption that personal uncertainty activates parts of the human brain that Eisenberger, Lieberman, and Williams (2003) have labeled the "human alarm system." The alarm system is responsible for detecting cues that might be harmful to survival and, after activation, for grabbing and holding attention to these cues and for triggering coping responses that may minimize the threat associated with these cues. Personal uncertainty may be one of these cues that may trigger the human alarm system (Van den Bos et al., 2008), "alerting us when we have sustained injury to our social connections" (Eisenberger et al., 2003, p. 292). From an evolutionary perspective, the working of such an alarm system is adaptive. After all, an activated alarm system prompts the human organism to act and respond more quickly or otherwise more alertly to what is going on in the organism's environment; this in turn makes the survival of the organism more likely.

Furthermore, being uncertain about oneself or being reminded about things one is uncertain about often instigates strong affective-experiential processes (Maas & Van den Bos, 2009). Thus, the idea is that experiencing feelings of uncertainty leads people to start processing information they subsequently receive in experiential-intuitive ways (Epstein & Pacini, 1999), making them react in strong positive affective terms to people and events that bolster their cultural worldviews and in strong negative affective terms to things, individuals, or experiences that violate these worldviews (Maas & Van den Bos, 2009; Van den Bos, 2007).

Therefore, affective responses tend to be good and sensitive indicators of people's reactions to reminders of personal uncertainty (Van den Bos et al., 2005). Measures of more cold-cognitive reactions (such as simple disagreements with other viewpoints) tend to underestimate the effects of personal uncertainty (Van den Bos, 2009a). In other words, while informational uncertainty may involve "cold-cognitive" reactions, personal uncertainty tends to involve "hot cognition," implying a combination of what people think and what they feel (Van den Bos, 2007).

Along similar lines, individual differences in emotional uncertainty tend to predict people's responses to worldview-violating others better than individual differences in cognitive uncertainty (Van den Bos, Euwema, Poortvliet, & Maas, 2007; Van den Bos, Van Ameijde, & Van Gorp, 2006). For example, Greco and Roger (2001) have constructed and validated both an emotional uncertainty scale (which measures the strength of respondents' agreement with items such as "I feel anxious when things are changing" and "I get worried when a situation is uncertain") and a cognitive uncertainty scale (which measures agreement with items such as "I like to know exactly what I'm going to do next" and "When I feel uncertain, I try to make decisive steps to clarify the situation"). In our worldview research studies, we find that the extent to which people consider uncertainty to be an emotionally threatening experience (i.e., emotional uncertainty) tends to explain people's reactions in our studies much better than individual differences in cognitive uncertainty do (Van den Bos et al., 2007; Van den Bos, Van Ameijde, & Van Gorp, 2006).

Related to this, McGregor, Prentice, and Nash (2009) revealed that using the word "insecurity" may convey more clearly to English-speaking participants the startling or threatening meaning of personal uncertainty as this is conveyed, for example, in the Dutch word "onzekerheid" (Van den Bos et al., 2005) or the Turkish word "belirsizlik" (Yavuz & Van den Bos, 2009). Thus, the psychological meaning of exact words used in stimulus materials may need attention in the development of research studies and the interpretation of research findings with different populations, different cultures, and different languages involved.

## 5.3 PERSONAL UNCERTAINTY

Now that we have examined to some extent the role and functioning of different forms of uncertainty, in particular personal and informational uncertainty, we are able to examine the possible roles these forms of uncertainty can have in processes of radicalization. Figure 5.1 summarizes processes that I assume take place when people experience the threat associated with personal uncertainty (see previous section) and how this can lead to defensive processes related to radicalization. The figure also speculates how experiences of fair treatment may possibly transform these defensive responses into approach tendencies associated with deradicalization.[1]

As Figure 5.1 illustrates, in my view people can experience personal uncertainty as a result of different threats people can encounter in society. Quite often these threats may have to do with societal demands on performing well, possibly better than one currently is doing. Important threats may also be related to having to integrate in society and to adapt one's behavior to particular norms and expectations of certain subcultures

1. This model is based on a figure presented in Van den Bos (2009b). The model portrayed in Figure 5.1 is an extended and updated version of the 2009 model, specifically adapted to the process of radicalization.

within society, frequently norms of the majority culture in a certain society. These and other threats quite easily can lead people to become uncertain about themselves and their functioning on various dimensions of performance or social competence in society and in important cultures within the society.

The model portrayed in Figure 5.1 proposes that the experience of personal uncertainty instigates a spontaneous startle response. The startle reflex represents an organism's response to unexpected and intense stimulation, which I argue the experience of personal uncertainty and other psychologically threatening information entail. The startle response that I assume is associated with personal uncertainty can lead to uncomfortable and aversive feelings (Hogg, 2007).

The startle reflex is a relatively primitive response produced by subcortical regions such as the amygdala, and its intensity is influenced by the organism's emotional state (Grillon & Baas, 2003). I argue therefore that individual differences in how strongly or weakly people tend to react to uncertainty in emotional concerns moderate the linkage between startle reactions to personal uncertainty and their uncomfortable and aversive feelings. Figure 5.1 shows this moderating effect of individual differences in uncertainty, including differences in emotional uncertainty (Greco & Roger, 2001).

Uncomfortable and aversive feelings can lead to defensive responses, such as people reacting in extreme ways to different social and societal issues. These extreme reactions are more easily instigated when people identify with entitative groups (Hogg, 2004) that have clear group boundaries and extreme opinions. Highly entitative groups are groups that are well structured with clear boundaries and in which members interact and share group attributes and goals and have a common fate (Hogg, 2014). Because highly entitative groups are the most effective at reducing personal uncertainty, people strive to identify with such groups or strive to accentuate the entitativity of groups they already identify with when they feel uncertain about themselves (Hogg, 2004, 2014). In short, under conditions of personal uncertainty, it becomes attractive to identify with groups that adhere to extreme opinions.

Related to Hogg's work is research by Rieger, Frischlich, and Bente (2017). These authors found that personal uncertainty and authoritarian attitudes shape the evaluation of right-wing extremist Internet propaganda. In their research it was observed that personal uncertainty increased group identification, which ultimately affected the evaluation of right-wing extremist videos addressing the participants' national in-group such that they had less aversion and were more persuaded by the videos.

Building on these insights, the model proposed in Figure 5.1 argues that the experience of personal uncertainty can be a startling experience, triggering defensive responses. The model also proposes that these defensive responses are more likely given relatively high levels of emotional uncertainty, increasing the chances of identification with entitative and extreme groups. Importantly, the model does not stop there, but goes on to argue that people's defensive tendencies can be overcome to some extent by their experiences of fair treatment. That is, when people are treated fairly by societal authorities and/or individuals from out-groups, such as people from the majority group in society, this will lead them to feel valued and judged as full-fledged citizens of society. Viewed in this way, fair treatment signals to people that they are worthy of hearing their opinions and that their opinions should be given due consideration (Lind & Tyler, 1988; Tyler & Lind, 1992). The model shown in Figure 5.1 assumes that this increases the likelihood of approach responses, such as people being more willing to integrate in society and perhaps start processes of deradicalization.

Of course, I realize that deradicalization is a very complicated and multifaceted process. Thus, I put forward explicitly that fair treatment is not enough to instigate reliable deradicalization. For instance, I assume that people's social value orientations moderate the fairness-deradicalization linkage, such that especially those individuals with prosocial values or cooperative tendencies (Van Lange, Otten, De Bruin, & Joireman, 1997) are more likely to show this effect. More people may adopt prosocial or cooperative values than we sometimes realize (Van den Bos et al., 2011), but another condition is also necessary before robust integration or deradicalization is in order. That is, being interdependent on other people, such as when you have to work together with others to reach important, superordinate goals that you cannot attain on your own (Sherif, 1958; see also, Sherif, 1954; Sherif, Harvey, White, Hood, & Sherif, 1961), seems to be another necessary condition. Figure 5.1 shows these processes.

## 5.4 INFORMATIONAL UNCERTAINTY

Informational uncertainty concerns the important question of whether you have enough relevant information to form a reliable judgment and take action accordingly. Key publications in psychology and other behavioral disciplines have revealed that human judgment often takes place under conditions of informational uncertainty (e.g., Kahneman et al., 1982; Tversky & Kahneman, 1974). This also applies to the issue of how people form fairness judgments. Quite often, people do not have the most relevant information available when forming judgments of whether things are fair or unfair (see, e.g., Van den Bos & Lind, 2002; Van den Bos, Lind, Vermunt, & Wilke, 1997). This implies that when we want to understand what people judge to be fair, we have to consider how conditions of informational uncertainty influence the fairness judgment process. Thus, because this book focuses in large part on people's fairness judgments, informational uncertainty is a pivotal issue that we need to address.

Research that my colleagues and I conducted suggests that, in the process of forming fairness judgments, people tend to look first for fairness information that is most relevant in the particular situation in which they find themselves. However, it is not uncommon that people lack information about the most relevant fairness issues. Research findings indicate that in these information-uncertain situations, people start using other information—as substitute information—to assess what is fair. We have labeled this process as the substitutability effect. People substitute one type of fairness information for another, we suggest, to avoid uncertainty about whether their outcomes are fair (Van den Bos, Lind, et al., 1997) and also whether they are being treated fairly (Van den Bos, 1999). Thus, the substitutability effect gives important insight into how people form judgments of outcome and procedural fairness under conditions of informational uncertainty.

Consider the issue of forming judgments whether the outcome that you received is fair or unfair. How do you form such an judgment? One of the most widely accepted answers to the question of what people judge to be fair has been provided by equity theory (e.g., Adams, 1965; Walster, Berscheid, & Walster, 1973; Walster, Walster, & Berscheid, 1978). In essence, equity theory proposes that people judge an outcome as fair when their own outcome-to-input ratio equals some comparative or referent outcome-to-input ratio. This process is frequently driven by social comparison with other people's outcomes and inputs such that people judge their outcome as fair when the ratio of their own inputs and outcomes equals the ratio of inputs and outcomes of comparison others (Van den Bos, 2001b). Equity theory and other related conceptions of outcome fairness and outcome justice emphasize the importance of social comparison information in the process of evaluating outcomes. After all, the comparison of a person's outcome with those of comparison others influences the person's beliefs about the fairness or justice of the person's own outcome and affects how satisfied the person is with the outcome (Messick & Sentis, 1983).

Equity theory has been very influential and has received wide support in many different studies in many different settings and contexts (Berkowitz & Walster, 1976). However, my colleagues and I doubt whether people always (or often) know what outcomes other people have received, which constitutes one of the basic premises of the theory (Adams, 1965; Messick & Sentis, 1983; Walster et al., 1973, 1978). In a research paper published in 1997, we argued that people frequently do not have access to this social comparison information. For instance, in everyday life we often do not know the salaries of the people with whom we work, and even if we do, we may not have a good idea of their contributions. Thus, we argued that social comparison information about outcomes is often not available (Van den Bos, Lind, et al., 1997). We therefore reasoned that in everyday life the issue of how people form outcome judgments is more complicated than is suggested by important articles on equity theory (Van den Bos, 2001b).

Furthermore, we argued that when information about outcomes of others is not available, people would start using information that is available. But what information is available? We suggested that procedural information is frequently present. Then, in many situations people may turn to the fairness of procedures to determine how to react to their outcome. In other words, people may use procedural fairness as a substitute to judge the fairness of their outcome. Therefore, in situations in which a person only knows his or her own outcome (and is not informed about the outcome of another person), we predicted a fair process effect: People will react more positively toward their outcomes following a fair rather than an unfair procedure (Van den Bos, Lind, et al., 1997).

However, we also argued that when a person does have information about the outcome of a comparable other person, he or she will use this social comparison information as a basis for reactions to their outcome. Therefore, we expected less strong fair process effects in situations in which a person knows what outcome the referent other receives. In other words, we predicted that when people had social comparison information about outcomes, there would be less need for procedural fairness to serve as a heuristic substitute in the outcome judgment process (Van den Bos, 2005, 2015).

The results of empirical studies testing these predictions supported our line of reasoning. In particular, our results suggest that when people do not have information about outcomes of others, they use procedural fairness as a substitute to assess how to react to their outcome (yielding fair process effects on their outcome judgments), but they rely less on procedure information when they are informed about the outcome of a comparison other (resulting in nonsignificant fair process effects). More generally, the findings point out that it is important to carefully assess what information is available to people when they are trying to form fairness judgments. The findings also suggest that equity theory is not a descriptive theory of what people judge to be fair, but rather a prescriptive theory. That is, the theory dictates what information people need to judge their outcome as fair or unfair, yet it does not deal with the issue of what happens when important information is missing (Van den Bos, 2001b).

Thus, the results of Van den Bos, Lind, et al. (1997) suggest that classifying information conditions is an important precondition before we as scientists and practitioners can be certain that the processes proposed by equity theory are operating.

Importantly, when people are forming judgments of whether they have been treated fairly or unfairly ("procedural fairness judgments"), issues of informational uncertainty also can play an important role (Van den Bos, 1999). For example, studies on procedural justice have frequently investigated how people react to being allowed an opportunity to voice their opinion versus not being allowed such an opportunity. In general this is now the most accepted manipulation of procedural justice (e.g., Brockner et al., 1998; Lind, Kanfer, & Earley, 1990; Lind & Tyler, 1988; Tyler, 1987; Tyler & Lind, 1992; Tyler, Rasinski, & Spodick, 1985; Van den Bos, Vermunt, & Wilke, 1996).

However, an often-overlooked distinction exists between two types of no-voice procedures both in everyday life and in research studies. One type of no-voice procedure has been used in studies by Folger (1977) and Lind et al. (1990). In both these studies, only participants who got voice were informed about a possibility that participants could get an opportunity to voice their opinion about an important decision the experimenter was going to make, and after this they were informed that they got such an opportunity. Participants in the no-voice condition were not informed about a possible voice opportunity and hence implicitly were not allowed a voice. I labeled this as an implicit no-voice procedure (Van den Bos, 1999, 2001b, 2005).

In other studies, a different type of no-voice procedure has been examined (e.g., Brockner et al., 1998, Study 5; Hunton, Hall, & Price, 1998; Van den Bos, Lind, et al., 1997; Van den Bos et al., 1996; Van den Bos, Wilke, & Lind, 1998; Van den Bos, Wilke, Lind, & Vermunt, 1998): In both the voice and the no-voice conditions, participants were informed that there was a possibility that participants could get an opportunity to voice their opinion about a decision the experimenter was going to make. Participants in the voice conditions were told that they got voice, whereas participants in the no-voice conditions were informed that they did not got an opportunity to voice their opinion. I called this latter procedure an explicit no-voice procedure (Van den Bos, 1999, 2001b, 2005).

On the basis of the substitutability proposition, it can be derived that when information about procedures is not available (as in the case of implicit no-voice procedures), people may find it difficult to decide how they should judge the procedure, and they therefore may use the fairness of their outcome to assess how to respond to the procedure. As a result, the procedural judgments of these people may show strong fair outcome effects. However, persons who are explicitly denied voice have explicit information about procedure and hence have to rely less on outcome information, yielding weaker fair outcome effects on procedural judgments. Findings indeed support this line of reasoning (Van den Bos, 1999, 2005).

Thus, it is important to make a distinction between implicit and explicit no-voice procedures. When information about procedure is not available—as is the case when persons implicitly have not received voice—people may find it difficult to decide how they should judge their procedure. They therefore use the fairness of their outcome, as a substitute, to determine how to respond to the procedure. As a result, the procedural judgments of these people show strong fair outcome effects. However, individuals who have received procedural information, such as persons who explicitly have been denied voice or those who have received voice, have to rely less on outcome information, yielding weaker fair outcome effects on procedural judgments (Van den Bos, 2001b, 2005).

Taken together, I hope to have shown that an important aspect of the fairness judgment process is that it is important to determine in detail what information is known to people and what information is not available or is difficult to interpret (Van den Bos, Wilke, Lind, & Vermunt, 1998). Furthermore, the substitutability hypothesis predicts that in incomplete or insufficient information conditions, people are inclined to use other information—such as procedural or outcome fairness—to substitute for information that would be most directly relevant but that is actually missing (Van den Bos, 2001b, 2005, 2015). This suggests that attending to the nature of fairness and justice information that is actually available may greatly enhance our understanding of people's fairness judgments, including fairness judgments that play a pivotal role in processes of radicalization. Substitution of fairness information also plays an important role when people are forming judgments of whether they can trust others, which is the subject to which I now turn.

## 5.5  UNCERTAINTY ABOUT TRUST

Another substitutability effect plays a role in a pivotal issue for many people in many circumstances, namely the issue of whether they can trust other persons, organizations, or societal institutions with which they are interacting. Answering this question is essential for many people in many different situations, in part because it is related to potential problems associated with social interdependence and socially based identity processes. In fact, the question is so basic to human functioning that it has been termed "the fundamental social dilemma" (Lind, 1995).

The dilemma is "fundamental" because it is concerned with the question of whether one can trust others not to exploit or exclude one from important relationships and groups (see Huo, Smith, Tyler, & Lind, 1996; Lind & Tyler, 1988; Smith, Tyler, Huo, Ortiz, & Lind, 1998; Tyler & Lind, 1992). Answering the question therefore probably involves a search for the most relevant information that is available, and it also entails affective processes.[2] This is in part because ceding authority to another person raises the possibility of exploitation and exclusion, and people therefore frequently feel uneasy about their relationship with authorities (e.g., Tyler & DeGoey, 1996; Tyler & Lind, 1992).

Thus, in many different situations people want to have information about whether they can trust a person who has power over them and can exploit them or exclude them from important relationships or groups. But do people often have direct information about the trustworthiness of such authorities? In a paper that my colleagues and I published in 1998, we

---

2. Therefore, it falls somewhere between informational and personal uncertainty because it probably entails both types of uncertainty in many cases for many people.

suggested that they frequently do not (Van den Bos, Wilke, & Lind, 1998). We also proposed that when people do not have information about the authority's trustworthiness, they still are interested in trying to find out how to judge their interactions and relationship with the authority. How do they do this?

We suggested that in situations in which information about authority's trustworthiness is missing, people refer to the fairness of the authority's procedures to decide how to interpret their relationship with the authority. In other words, in situations in which definitive trust information is lacking, procedural fairness serves as a substitute for deciding how to evaluate one's interactions and relationship with the authority (Van den Bos, 2001b). As a consequence, we expected that when people do not have information about authority's trustworthiness, they would react more positively following their interactions with the authority when the authority had been employing fair as opposed to unfair procedures.

On the other hand, this line of thought also suggested that when people do have direct, explicit information about authority's trustworthiness, they would be less in need of procedural fairness. After all, in those circumstances information about procedural fairness is no longer needed to substitute for missing information about the authority's trustworthiness. We therefore expected that when people do not have information about an authority's trustworthiness, recipients would react more positively toward interactions with the authority when the authority had been employing fair as opposed to unfair procedures, and that less strong fair process effects would be found when people had received direct information about authority's trustworthiness (Van den Bos, 2001b). Findings indeed supported this line of reasoning (Van den Bos, Wilke, & Lind, 1998; see also Van den Bos, Van Schie, & Colenberg, 2002).

In the previously reviewed studies on informational uncertainty and substitutability effects (see previous section), we focused on the content of outcome or process information and on procedural or outcome fairness acting as substitutes when outcome or process information is missing or weak. The studies on uncertainty about trust (Van den Bos et al., 2002; Van den Bos, Wilke, & Lind, 1998) expanded the substitutability line of reasoning to more socially oriented information (trust). It can now be concluded that people especially need procedural fairness when strong, unambiguous outcome fairness information or information about the authority's trustworthiness is lacking. What is especially interesting about the findings is that they provide strong evidence for one answer to the question of why people care about justice (Van den Bos, Wilke, & Lind, 1998). People care about justice, and especially procedural justice, when they do not have direct, explicit information regarding whether they can trust others not to exploit or exclude them from important relationships and groups (Van den Bos, 2001b). The following section discusses what we can conclude from the uncertainty findings reviewed thus far.

## 5.6 REGULATION OF UNCERTAINTY IN DELAYED-RETURN CULTURES

Thus far, we have seen that conditions of uncertainty tend to have strong effects on people's reactions (see Figure 5.1), and we know from earlier chapters that these effects are especially likely to be strong when the uncertainty experience is combined with perceptions that things are unfair and generally not right (see Figures 1.2 and 4.3). Furthermore, I assume that uncertainty about oneself (personal uncertainty) is more threatening than uncertainty about whether one can trust other persons (uncertainty about trust), which in turn is likely to be more threatening than most uncertainty about information (informational uncertainty).

My assumption is based in part on views that suggest that experiences of uncertainty, and especially personal uncertainty, disrupt ongoing processing of information. After all, feelings of uncertainty instigate the notion that something is going on that warrants attention and hence are likely to lead to the interruption of cognitive processes (Van den Bos & Lind, 2013). In general people prefer the fluent processing of information and respond in negative terms to the disfluent processing of information (for another view, see Koerselman, 2016). These effects are there because uncertainty is often linked to possible blockage of attainment of important goals, which is one of the reasons why uncertainty can lead people to respond in extremist ways (see, e.g., Hogg, Kruglanski, & Van den Bos, 2013; McGregor, Hayes, & Prentice, 2015).

To understand the psychological process proposed here, it is important to realize that we humans nowadays live in delayed-return cultures (Woodburn, 1982a, 1982b). In these cultures there is often a delay between the effort people exert and the feedback they receive regarding the outcome of their efforts (L. Martin, 1999). As a result, individuals may experience long stretches of uncertainty between their efforts and their payoff, and they may find at the end of this time that their efforts did not pay off (L. Martin & Shirk, 2006). A good example is attaining a job that one likes. To obtain such a position in society that comes with both financial and emotional benefits, individuals have to undergo years of preparation (i.e., schooling and the training of social skills), during which time they exert immediate effort for an outcome that is both delayed and uncertain (Van den Bos, McGregor, & Martin, 2015). Many people who in the end become extremists may have negative experiences of fulfilling long-term goals, such as finding a fulfilling and valuable job and hence a secure, valued, and respected position in society.

I do realize that sometimes a state of uncertainty may be preferred by people (e.g., Wilson et al., 2005). After all, being completely certain about all or many aspects of one's life may make one's life rather dull. There are clearly instances in which people strive for uncertainty rather than seek to reduce it, and people may want to experience new, uncertain events. I am not denying these effects. However, I also argue that these more positive or approach-oriented reactions to uncertainty are less likely to occur than more negative or avoidance-oriented reactions (Van den Bos, 2009a). Furthermore, when these more positive reactions do occur, I predict that this is more likely to happen in the case of informational uncertainty as opposed to personal uncertainty (Van den Bos et al., 2015).

To conclude, although some philosophers or psychologists may argue that people should accept and, in fact, do accept that they live under conditions of uncertainty, in reality this is not a quest that many people engage in or, when they do engage in it, are successful in. Similarly, some

Zen Buddhists may advocate returning to more immediate-return cultures or contexts, but it is a fact that this is hard to do, and this is a state that is very difficult to obtain. This implies that the issue of uncertainty, and especially personal uncertainty, will play an important role in the delayed-return cultures in which the large majority of humans live nowadays (L. Martin, 1999; Van den Bos et al., 2015). It was the goal of the present chapter to delineate some important issues pertaining to human reactions under conditions of uncertainty. The next chapter will pay appropriate attention to another important moderator of the unfairness-extremism link, namely the issue of insufficient self-corrections.

# Self-Interest and
# Insufficient Corrections

## 6.1 INTRODUCTION

Unfairness perceptions in isolation do not necessarily lead to radicalization, nor is the combination of unfairness with experiences of informational or personal uncertainty or uncertainty about others' trustworthiness always sufficient to instigate or amplify processes of radicalization. People's self-interested motives also play an important role and increase the likelihood that people start radicalizing. In particular, I argue that perceived unfairness and feelings of uncertainty are likely to lead to radicalization when combined with people's tendencies to correct for their self-centered impulses in insufficient ways.

This chapter examines the role of different processes of insufficient self-correction. The chapter begins by exploring how people's reactions may be dominated by their motives of self-interest and how this may impact the radicalization process. The chapter notes that one important reason why people's perceptions of unfairness can be biased is that people tend to balance fairness concerns with other important motives, especially their motive to look after their self-interest. The chapter therefore discusses how people balance the self-interest motive and their fairness concerns (Section 6.2).

To this end, the chapter presents a conceptual model that argues that people's first reactions to arrangements of unfair overpayment may be dominated by their self-interest motives. Most people try to correct for these self-interested or self-centered tendencies, especially when they have enough time to reflect on what is going on and are motivated to engage in these correction processes. In other words, cognitive capacity and motivation influence how people balance self-interest motives and fairness concerns (see Figure 6.1). Full correction of initial self-centered hedonism can be difficult, however, and this explains why people may respond in egoistic ways to arrangements that are unfair yet are advantageous for themselves, resulting in relatively high levels of satisfaction with these unfair outcome arrangements.

Another important form of insufficient correction is found when people respond to people who innocently fell victim to crimes or other misfortunes that are not their fault (Section 6.3). Because these innocent victims can pose a threat to people's belief that the world is a just place where bad things happen only to bad people, people's initial reactions may be dominated by responses of avoidance, resulting in tendencies to blame and derogate the victims for their misfortune. Sufficient cognitive capacity and motivation is needed to start correcting these responses, something that some people can engage in some of the time (see Figure 6.2), but self-correction of avoidance responses to innocent victims is quite often incomplete and insufficient, hence resulting in blaming and derogation of innocent victims.

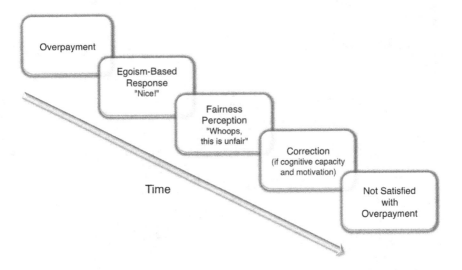

**Figure 6.1  (Insufficient) Correction Processes Regarding Unfair Overpayment and Egoism-Based Responses.**
This model describes people's reactions to arrangements in which they are better paid than comparable other persons. The figure illustrates that spontaneous egoism-based responses ("Hey, this is nice!") may dominate people's first reactions to these arrangements of overpayment. These responses can be corrected when people realize explicitly that the overpayment was not fair ("Whoops, this is unfair"). If people have sufficient cognitive capacity (e.g., their working memory is not taxed) and are sufficiently motivated, self-correction may lead people to be not satisfied with unfair overpayment. Correction is possible yet can be hard to achieve; hence correction of first impulses will often be insufficient.

Interestingly, most (but certainly not all) people seem to be motivated toward the correction of their self-interested intuitions. These self-correction processes are important not only in individualistic contexts, in which people respond on their own to social stimuli, or in interpersonal settings, in which people respond to how others are treated in the situation in which they find themselves, but also in intergroup contexts in which people are responding to interactions with members of other groups (Section 6.3). I present findings that suggest that quite often people may be startled when confronted with potentially threatening out-group members. As a result, people may be tempted to show aversive intuitive reactions targeted at members of other groups. Sufficient cognitive

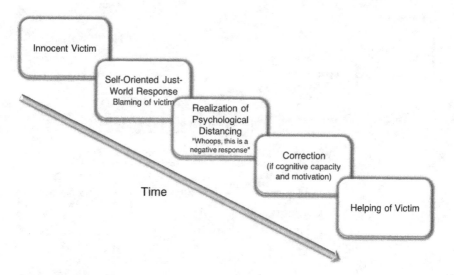

**Figure 6.2 (Insufficient) Correction Processes Regarding Innocent Victims and Self-Oriented Just-World Responses.**
This model describes people's reactions to persons who innocently fell victim to crimes or other misfortune. The figure illustrates that impulsive self-oriented responses (which result in blaming and derogating the victim) may dominate people's first reactions. These responses can be corrected when people realize explicitly that they psychologically distance themselves from the victim ("Whoops, this is a negative response"). If people have sufficient cognitive capacity (e.g., their working memory is not taxed) and are sufficiently motivated, self-correction may lead people to help the victim. Correction is possible yet can be hard to achieve; hence correction of first impulses will often be insufficient.

---

capacity (in the form of sufficient working memory or adequate executive control) and appropriate motivation (in the form of explicitly low levels of prejudice) are needed to start some sort of process to correct these initial, self-centered impulses (see Figure 6.3). Again, correction of initial gut reactions is possible but can be hard, needing sufficient working memory and a lot of motivation. Furthermore, some have argued that self-correction of spontaneous or automatic impulses tends to be impossible (see, e.g., Bargh, 1999).

Situations in which people are interacting and coordinating their behaviors with others are assumed to play a major role in processes of self-correction. People's social values are important in this respect (Section

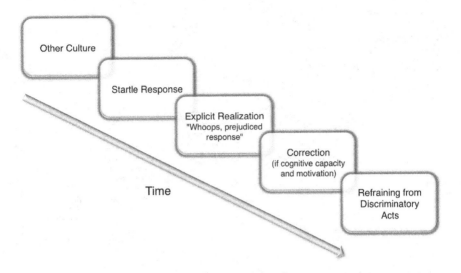

**Figure 6.3 (Insufficient) Correction Processes Regarding Other Cultures and Startle Responses.**

This model describes people's reactions to situations in which they are confronted with persons from other cultures. The figure illustrates that spontaneous startle responses may dominate people's first reactions to these potentially threatening others. These responses can be corrected when people realize explicitly that these are prejudiced reactions. If people have sufficient cognitive capacity (e.g., their working memory is not taxed) and are sufficiently motivated (e.g., adhere to cooperative social values), self-correction may lead people to refrain from discriminatory acts. Correction is possible yet can be hard to achieve; hence correction of first impulses will often be insufficient.

6.5). Recent findings suggest that most (but certainly not all) humans tend to be oriented toward cooperation and as such can be characterized as pro-social beings. Ironically, the social quality of people may inhibit them in showing their prosociality, especially when they are busy trying to sort out what is going on, how to behave in the situation at hand, and how others will view their behaviors. Having made sense of how to interpret the situation at hand and what constitutes appropriate behavior in this situation may help people to free themselves and engage in prosocial behaviors (see Figure 6.4). However, overcoming inhibitory constraints can be difficult, which constitutes another reason why the prosocial quality of people may not always show in public circumstances.

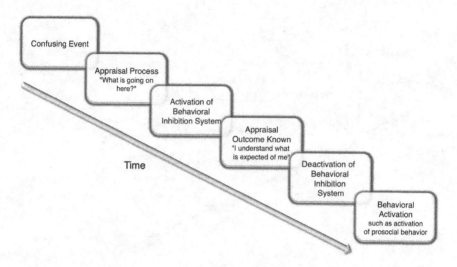

**Figure 6.4 (Insufficient) Correction Processes Regarding Confusing Events and Inhibitory Processes.**
This model describes people's reactions to situations in which they are confronted with confusing events. The figure illustrates that these events instigate appraisal processes ("What is going on here?"). These appraisal processes are facilitated by the activation of the human system that inhibits ongoing behavior. After the outcome of the appraisal process is known ("I understand what is expected of me"), the behavioral inhibition system is deactivated, and activation of outgoing behavior, including prosocial behavior, becomes possible. Appraisal and full deactivation of the behavioral inhibition system are possible yet will not always be achieved.

After we have seen how correction of various sorts of self-interested motives might be possible, but also tends to be very difficult, the chapter closes by discussing some recent advances made in the training of self-correction (Section 6.6.) and how this insight may be relevant for the prevention of radicalization and deradicalization techniques. The chapter does this by noting explicitly that quite often self-correction is very hard and very difficult to achieve, in part because several preconditions have to be met. These preconditions include people's thought processes because their working memory should not be taxed. The appropriate motivational resources in the form of cooperative social values, as well as repeated, intensive, and precisely targeted training techniques, are also

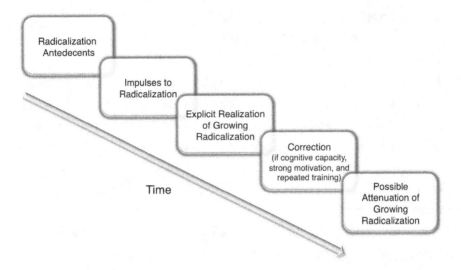

**Figure 6.5 (Insufficient) Correction Processes Regarding Radicalization Antecedents and Associated Impulses.**
This model describes people's reactions to situations in which they are confronted with the various antecedents of radicalization (e.g., perceptions of unfairness) and associated impulses (e.g., anger and other externally oriented emotions) as discussed in this book. The figure illustrates that the impulsive responses can be corrected when people realize explicitly that this is an indication of growing radicalization. If people have sufficient cognitive capacity (e.g., their working memory is not taxed), are sufficiently motivated (e.g., adhere to cooperative social values), and are exposed to repeated training of successful self-correction, then self-correction may lead to attenuated radicalization. Correction is possible yet can be hard to achieve; hence correction of first impulses will often be insufficient.

needed to achieve successful correction processes (see Figure 6.5). Thus, training of self-correction processes may be possible but also tends to be hard and difficult and is in need of constant reinforcement. This fits with the theme of this chapter, namely how self-interest may influence people's initial reactions and how insufficient correction processes may play a role in egocentric human behavior, including behavior of radicals, extremists, and even terrorists. This insight may also be conducive to the possible prevention of radicalization and the initiation of successful deradicalization, however hard this may be.

## 6.2 BALANCING SELF-INTEREST
## AND FAIRNESS CONCERNS

This section focuses on how people balance their egoism-based impulses to arrangements in which they are better off than others and how they may attempt to correct for their impulsive reactions, depending on their current cognitive capacities and their motivations to engage in these correction processes. To this end, I delineate a two-phase model that explains how people deal with motives of both self-interest and justice.

It is my explicit assumption that most people are social beings who tend to care in genuine ways about fairness and justice and in essence are benign creatures who want to do the right thing (Van den Bos & Lind, 2013; Van den Bos, et al., 2011). Research has supported this assumption in important ways (Van den Bos & Bal, 2016). Nonetheless, even social creatures may sometimes be oriented toward their own hedonic responses and the fulfillment of their self-interest concerns. This can be seen when we study how people respond to arrangements in which they are better off than comparable other persons.

For example, Van den Bos, Peters, Bobocel, and Ybema (2006) exposed participants to situations in which there was another person who was comparable to them. That is, this other person performed equally when completing tasks in the experiment and also in other aspects was comparable to the participants themselves. In the 2006 experiments, participants received a certain outcome for their performance in the studies in which they participated. In the experimental condition of primary interest, we informed participants that their own outcome was better than the outcome of the other person. In technical terms this created an arrangement of outcomes that was inequitable yet advantageous to our participants. (Participants in the other conditions were told that their outcome was worse than the other person's outcome, creating inequity that was disadvantageous to our participants, or were informed that their outcome was equal to the other person's outcome, installing an equitable arrangement of outcomes.)

When observing how satisfied people are with these arrangements of advantageous inequity, it can be assumed that there is one source of positive affect and one source of negative affect influencing participants' reactions: (1) the positive source is the egoism-based pleasure of receiving a relatively good outcome, whereas (2) the negative source is the fairness-based feeling of being unfairly advantaged. Furthermore, this assumption can be combined with theories that suggest that people usually will know whether their outcome gives them pleasure before they have insight into the fairness aspects of the outcome distribution (see, e.g., Epley & Caruso, 2004; Epley, Keysar, Van Boven, & Gilovich, 2004; Messick & Sentis, 1979, 1983; Moore & Loewenstein, 2004).

Messick and Sentis, for instance, argue convincingly that the relationship between preference and fairness is such that people generally have more immediate access to or knowledge of their preferences in a situation than access to or knowledge of what is fair. As stated by Messick and Sentis (1983): "One usually knows one's preferences before one knows what is fair" (p. 88). This view led these authors to propose that preference is primary (see also Zajonc, 1980) and that people assess whether and how fairness is relevant in a later phase (possibly almost immediately after preferences are known). Related to this, Moore and Loewenstein (2004) argue that self-interest is automatic, viscerally compelling, and typically unconscious, whereas in contrast, paying attention to fairness concerns is usually a more thoughtful process. Similarly, Epley and Caruso (2004; Epley et al., 2004) propose that people automatically interpret objects and events egocentrically and only subsequently correct or adjust that interpretation when necessary. According to Epley et al. (2004), the automatic default occurs rapidly, but correction requires time and attentional resources.

Building on this line of reasoning, we argued in our 2006 paper that when responding to advantageous inequity, judging the advantage is quick and easy because preferences are primary. Adjusting this appraisal requires cognitive resources because it entails integrating fairness concerns with the initial preference appraisal. We therefore predicted that people should be more satisfied with advantageous inequity when cognitive processing is strongly (as opposed to weakly) limited. Findings across several different experimental paradigms supported our predictions (Van den Bos et al., 2006).

For example, in the first experiment of the 2006 studies, participants read and responded to a scenario in which they received a bonus for their summer job that was twice as large as the bonus that a comparable fellow student received for the same summer job. Half of the participants rehearsed a string of eight symbols while reading and responding to the stimulus materials (creating a condition of high cognitive load among our participants), whereas the other half of the participants rehearsed one symbol only (creating a condition of low cognitive load among our participants). Participants were more satisfied with the arrangement of advantageous inequity under conditions of high cognitive load than under conditions of low cognitive load. Importantly, the cognitive load manipulation did not influence responses of participants who were faced with arrangements that were equitable or inequitable in a disadvantageous way. This suggests that cognitive load especially influences people's responses when they are correcting for their first impulses.

These and other findings suggest that people generally do not like getting outcomes that are advantageous but inequitable in comparison to the outcomes of comparable other persons, but when responding under conditions of high cognitive load, people tend to be satisfied with getting unfair but better outcomes (Van den Bos et al., 2006). Figure 6.1 summarizes in nontechnical terms what I think are the conceptual conclusions from experimental studies such as the 2006 studies.

The two-phase model put forward in Figure 6.1 argues that self-interested responses may dominate first reactions and that correction for genuine fairness and justice takes place somewhat later (Van den Bos & Bal, 2016). The model argues that people's very first reaction when confronted with advantageous inequity is one of pleasure ("Wow, I get more than someone else, that's great!"). This egoism-based, gut reaction perhaps occurs in a rather spontaneous manner that is difficult to control. The model suggests that it is only after this first spontaneous reaction of pleasure that people consider the fairness of the situation ("Hey, but that's not fair!"). This latter, fairness-based reaction is not as automatic and fast as the first egoism-based reaction. People need a little time (perhaps some seconds) and a little more cognitive effort to discover, understand, and respond to the unfairness of a situation in which they are better off than others for no good reason, and this correction process can only take place when people have sufficient cognitive resources available (Van den Bos et al., 2006) and are motivated to do so (Van den Bos et al., 2011).

The model presented in Figure 6.1 suggests at least three conclusions: First, people's gut reaction to distributions of advantageous inequity and other issues may be driven by egocentrism such that people's reptile brain or primitive core leads them to be self-focused and to be pleased with things that are best for them (and not for others). Second, most people are benign beings who intend to do what is good and what is right (Van den Bos & Lind, 2013) and hence try to free cognitive resources that lead them to do the right thing and be oriented toward what others are getting. Thus, quite often, or perhaps even typically, most people tend to correct their self-centered inclinations to include a genuine other-oriented response with appropriate attention to what is fair and just. Third, in the case of radicalization and radical people, correction of self-interested impulses is probably insufficient, causing radical individuals to respond in positive ways to things that are pleasurable for themselves or their own group yet are unfair for society or the world at large. This model of insufficient self-correction hence may play an important and, thus far, relatively unobserved role in the psychology of radicalization.

## 6.3 AVOIDANCE AND APPROACH REACTIONS

Another form of insufficient self-correction that pertains to the balance of egoistic reactions and fairness concerns that I would like to discuss here involves people's reactions to other persons who innocently fell victim to crimes or other misfortune. Although it seems counter-normative to blame innocent victims for their ill fate, it is a well-known fact that people frequently hold victims responsible for their misfortunes and blame them for what has happened. For example, when reading a newspaper article about a girl being robbed or sexually assaulted going home late at night, people often wonder why she had not been more careful (Van den Bos & Maas, 2009). People also are tempted to think in derogatory terms about the personality of the victim (see, e.g., Hafer, 2000a; Hafer & Bègue, 2005; Lerner, 1980; Lerner & Miller, 1978).

These and other findings have been explained by what has become known as just world theory. According to this theory, people have a need to believe in a just world in which individuals get what they deserve (Lerner, 1977; Lerner & Simmons, 1966). When people are confronted with others (such as innocent victims) who get something that they do not deserve, people's principles of deservingness are violated. As a result, people need to restore their belief that the world is a just place in which good things happen to good people and bad things to bad people. Especially when the events that have happened cannot be changed or altered, people often tend to come to the conclusion that victims somehow deserved their ill fate and are to be blamed for what happened to them (Van den Bos & Maas, 2009).

Thus, fitting with a core theme of this book, namely that people are organisms that try to make sense of their world, I note here that one important type of sense-making process revolves around circumstances in which innocent people are victim to terrible crimes such as rape, violence, or other undeserved and unjust experiences. Believing in a just world where good things happen to good people and bad things happen to bad people only implies that people often make sense of these kinds of awful events by trying to compensate the victim or punish the perpetrator. However, if the perpetrator is not likely to be punished, people are tempted to start blaming and derogating the victim for his or her behavior. In this way, people restore their belief in a just world. Thus, somewhat ironically, a justice motive may underlie people's derogatory reactions to innocent victims (Van den Bos & Bal, 2016).

There is plenty of evidence showing that the belief in a just world is influencing people's reactions to victims of rape or other terrible crimes. For example, when a victim is more similar to the observer of the unjust event, the victim is more likely to be blamed and derogated for what happened to him or her (Bal & Van den Bos, 2010). Related to this, when a perpetrator is more similar to the observer and is not caught, the victim is more likely to meet with derogatory reactions. These effects presumably are out there because victims or perpetrators who are more similar to you pose a stronger threat to your personal world. When a perpetrator is not caught, this makes justice concerns more accessible (Hafer, 2000a), and as a result you tend to use more abstract language to describe the victim's behavior and you are more likely to label the behavior and personality of the victim in more negative terms (Van den Bos & Bal, 2016).

A recent research project by Michèlle Bal suggests the important role that avoidance and approach motivation may have in people's responses to innocent victims. Michèlle notes that the typical negative reactions to innocent victims are in essence reactions of people to avoid interactions with the victims and with the thoughts that are associated with them (namely that the world might not be a just place, after all). Supporting this line of reasoning are findings that suggest that the confrontation with innocent victims spontaneously activates avoidance motivation. Findings also show that experimentally induced avoidance motivation enhances blaming and derogation of the victims involved (Bal & Van den Bos, 2018).

For example, Michèlle Bal confronted participants with a video clip about a rape victim who was living in the same city and hence constitutes a big threat to participants' just world beliefs. During this confrontation with the innocent victim, Michèlle unobtrusively manipulated approach motivation toward the victim by asking participants to put their nondominant hand on top of the table and press downward, causing extension of the arm. Earlier research has shown that arm extension produces bodily feedback that unconsciously activates avoidance motivation (Cacioppo, Priester, & Bernston, 1993), presumably because people have learned over the course of their lives to associate arm extensions with the withdrawal from undesired stimuli. In other words, pushing something away from you while watching a video about an innocent victim increased participants' motivation to avoid the victim. Indeed, participants reacted in strong negative terms to the victim in this condition in which avoidance motivation presumably was high (Bal & Van den Bos, 2018).

Interestingly, in another condition Michèlle Bal asked participants to watch the video clip, and while doing so, put their nondominant hand under the table and press upward, causing flexion of the arm during the watching of the video clip. Arm flexion produces bodily feedback that unconsciously activates approach motivation (Cacioppo et al., 1993), probably because people have learned to associate arm flexion with the acquisition of desired stimuli. Thus, pulling something toward you increases the motivation to approach the victim. In line with what could be expected, Michèlle found that participants responded much more positively toward the innocent victim in this condition in which approach motivation can be assumed to be high (Van Prooijen, Karremans, & Van Beest, 2006).

Taken together, these findings suggest that when people are trying to cope with threats to their just world beliefs, impulsive reactions to avoid innocent victims in particular and those less well-off more generally are to be expected. Controlled attempts to increase people's approach motivation may help to start controlling these impulsive effects and respond in more positive terms to those less well off.

The model that is shown in Figure 6.2 illustrates the process that I assume is going on when people respond to innocent victims or others who are less well off. I note explicitly that the model is based on work in progress and in need of strong empirical backup. Having said that, I assume that impulsive self-oriented responses may dominate people's first reactions when they are confronted in vivid and salient ways with persons who innocently fell victim to crimes or other misfortune. These first reactions may result in tendencies to blame and derogate the victims. These responses can be corrected when people realize explicitly that they psychologically distance themselves from the victim ("Whoops, this is a negative response"). If people have sufficient cognitive capacity, such that their working memory is not overloaded, and are sufficiently motivated, for example, when they have adopted a strong approach motivation, then correction processes may lead people to show positive reactions toward the victims, and they may be inclined to help the victims.

As in the previous section, I stipulate that correction is possible yet can be hard to achieve. Thus, correction of first impulses will often be insufficient. This insufficient correction of impulsive reactions to innocent victims fits with the observation that victim-blaming and derogation have often been observed in just world research (Van den Bos & Bal, 2016).

As far as I know, people's belief in a just world has not been examined in empirical radicalization studies (hence why I did not discuss it in Chapters 3 or 4), but here I argue that reacting in negative terms to innocent victims is related to thinking negatively about those well off (including negative reactions to those who are subject to disadvantageous inequity), which in turn is related to what was discussed in Section 6.2, and involves thinking in superior terms of oneself and one's own group. Thinking in terms of superiority plays a crucial role in rigidity of thoughts, defense of cultural worldviews, and other indicators of radicalization (see Figure 4.3). This is an issue that I explore in more depth in the chapters that will follow.

## 6.4 GROUP PROCESSES

Thus far, I have focused in this chapter on how individuals respond to their social environments and primarily on how they interact with other individuals. The notion of people's egocentric first reactions and how they may correct for these impulses also plays an important role in group contexts, for example, in situations in which people respond to people from other groups. This section focuses on these processes, in particular examining people's spontaneous startle responses when they are faced with persons from other cultures as well as when and how they will try to self-correct for these responses regarding other groups.

A classic work in this respect is the 1989 article by Devine on people's stereotypes and their prejudice regarding other cultures and groups. In this paper, Devine distinguishes between people's knowledge of a cultural stereotype and their active endorsement of the stereotype. As such, Devine makes a distinction between negative thoughts about a group to which you do not belong versus evaluating the group in negative ways or acting in negative ways toward the group.

This difference between knowledge and active endorsement of stereotypes is due to the fact that some people are high in prejudice and others are low in prejudice. High-prejudice persons typically evaluate the group under consideration in negative terms. These persons are more likely to act in negative ways toward the out-group under consideration. Low-prejudice persons evaluate the out-group in more positive terms and are inclined to respond in positive, or at least not negative, ways toward the group.

Devine's model assumes that because of socialization experiences, high-prejudice and low-prejudice persons are equally knowledgeable of the cultural stereotype of members from minority groups. Furthermore, because these stereotypes have been frequently activated in the past, these cognitive frameworks constitute a well-learned set of associations that are spontaneously or even automatically activated in the presence of members of the out-group. Importantly, the model proposes that this unintentional activation of stereotypes is equally strong and equally inescapable for high- and low-prejudice persons.

The model by Devine (1989) further explicates that while spontaneous or automatic activation of stereotypes may often be inevitable, high- and low-prejudice persons differ with respect to their active use of the stereotypical beliefs. For example, persons high in prejudice against African Americans may show negative overt behavioral responses to African Americans. In contrast, persons low in prejudice against African Americans belief explicitly that the stereotype is an inappropriate basis for behavior or evaluation and hence experience a conflict between the automatically activated stereotype and their personal beliefs. After all, the stereotype conflicts with their nonprejudiced, egalitarian values. Thus, low-prejudiced persons require intentional inhibition of the automatically activated stereotype in order to show nonprejudiced overt responses. Such inhibition and initiation of new responses involves controlled processes.

Research by Devine (1989) indeed suggests that stereotypes are automatically activated when people are confronted with a member of the stereotyped group and that low-prejudice responses require controlled inhibition of the automatically activated stereotype. This research is important because it suggests that whereas stereotypes are spontaneously or automatically activated (Shiffrin & Schneider, 1977; see also Bargh, 1994), the correction of these responses requires the inhibition of the automatically activated stereotype and the intentional activation of nonprejudiced beliefs.

Devine's work is grounded in the literature on information processing that distinguishes between automatic (mostly involuntary) and controlled (mostly voluntary) processes (see, e.g., Shiffrin & Schneider, 1977). In this literature, automatic processes involve the unintentional or spontaneous activation of some well-learned set of associations or responses that have been developed through repeated activation in memory. They do not require conscious effort and appear to be initiated by the presence of stimulus cues in the environment. A crucial component of automatic processes is their inescapability; they occur despite deliberate attempts to bypass or ignore them. In contrast, controlled processes are intentional and require the active attention of the individual (Devine, 1989; see also Amodio, Harmon-Jones, & Devine, 2003; Devine, 2001, 2003; Devine & Monteith, 1999; Plant & Devine, 2009).

The model put forward by Devine (1989) has been disputed. Indeed, the issue of whether control of automatic responses is possible is a matter of debate, an issue to which I return in the last section of this chapter. Here I note that the model of spontaneous activation of stereotypes and other startling responses to other persons, particularly when they come from other groups, has been supported in important ways by other studies in other research domains.

For example, Gilbert and others have argued convincingly that when people form evaluations of having seen another person performing a certain behavior, they typically draw initial character inferences from the behavior and then correct these initial evaluations by taking into account the influences of external forces that may have influenced the person's behavior (e.g., Gilbert & Osborne, 1989; Gilbert, Pelham, & Krull, 1988). These authors have further put forward that correction requires more cognitive resources than does the forming of initial inferences. As a result, forming person evaluations while simultaneously performing a resource-consuming task should impair the former process more than the latter process. Gilbert et al.'s experiments indeed show that person evaluations are less influenced by external information under conditions of high cognitive load than under conditions of low cognitive load (e.g., Gilbert & Osborne, 1989; Gilbert et al., 1988).

In my own research group, Dragos Petrescu examined how Dutch male students from the White majority group in the Netherlands responded to pictures from a potentially threatening out-group. That is, the participants in a study by Petrescu, Van den Bos, Klumpers, and Kenemans (2018) first contemplated their mortality (a threatening topic) or a neutral control topic. After this, their eye-blink responses to a startle probe were measured while viewing pictures of out-group members (Arabs) and pictures of in-group members (Dutch). As expected, mortality salience produced stronger defensive reactions when participants watched pictures of Arab people, and decreased eye-blink when they watched pictures of Dutch people, but this was only the case for participants reporting relatively low levels of attentional control. This result suggests that responses to threatening conditions are present at a physiological level and may not depend on consciousness. These reflexive processes can subsequently be modulated by effortful, top-down attentional control.

Taken together, I propose a model that is presented in Figure 6.3. This figure illustrates what happens when people are confronted with persons from other groups or other cultures. The model assumes that spontaneous startle responses dominate people's first reactions to potentially threatening other persons. These responses can be corrected when people realize explicitly that these are prejudiced reactions. If people have sufficient cognitive capacity (e.g., their working memory is not taxed) and are sufficiently motivated (e.g., adhere to cooperative social values), self-correction may lead people to refrain from discriminatory acts. The model further assumes that correction is possible yet can be hard to obtain. Therefore, correction of first impulses will often be insufficient.

Applied to the issue of radicalization, the model of insufficient self-correction of individuals' startle impulses activated in group contexts presented in Figure 6.3 suggests that at least some reactions of some radicals may be understood by emphasizing their spontaneous startle responses to others who come from different groups and different cultures than themselves. Especially group-based forms of radicalization (such as right-wing and Muslim radicalization; see Figure 4.2) may be affected by these startle responses. Focusing on the insufficiency of the correction of radicals' spontaneous startle responses may help to understand these forms of radicalization. The issue of cognitive capacity plays an important role in self-correction (Gilbert et al., 1988; Van den Bos et al., 2006). Appropriate motivation in the form of social values is also important, and this is the subject of the next section.

## 6.5 SOCIAL VALUES

How people deal with fairness concerns and how they correct for their impulsive reactions are issues that are influenced by people's social value orientations. Van Lange, Otten, De Bruin, and Joireman (1997) note that traditional theories and insights assume that the principle of rational self-interest or economic man reflects the prevailing motivation among humankind. Indeed, self-interest matters to people (e.g., Walster, Walster, & Berscheid, 1978), and so do financial issues (e.g., Vohs, Mead, & Goode, 2008) and instrumental motives (e.g., Thibaut & Walker, 1975).

Against this background, Van Lange et al. (1997) point out that individuals differ systematically in the manner in which they approach other people, especially in social interactions in which individuals are mutually dependent on each other. Some people are inclined to approach interdependent others cooperatively, whereas other individuals are inclined to approach others in an individualistic way, and some people approach others in a competitive manner. Such individual differences are related to social value orientation, defined as stable preferences for certain patterns of outcomes for oneself and others (McClintock, 1978; Messick & McClintock, 1968; Van Lange et al., 1997).

Thus, Van Lange et al. (1997) use a three-category typology of social value orientation, examining differences between prosocial, individualistic, and competitive orientations. Prosocial or cooperative people tend to favor an equal distribution of outcomes between themselves and others. Individualists tend to maximize their own outcomes with little or no regard for others' outcomes. And competitors tend to maximize their own outcomes relative to others' outcomes, seeking relative advantage over others.

The three social value orientations are predictive of behavior in a variety of social dilemma tasks, with prosocial persons exhibiting clear tendencies toward cooperation (unless others fail to reciprocate), and individualists and competitors exhibiting tendencies toward maximizing their own and relative gain, even when interdependent others evidence high levels of cooperation. Moreover, social value orientations are predictive of helping behavior, judgments of everyday life incidents of cooperation and competition, decisions and judgments regarding commuting choices, and willingness to sacrifice in close relationships (Van Lange et al., 1997).

Interestingly, many research studies have shown that the majority of people tend to adhere to a prosocial orientation (Van den Bos et al., 2011; Van Lange et al., 1997; Van Lange, Agnew, Harinck, & Steemers, 1997; Van Lange & Kuhlman, 1994; Van Lange & Liebrand, 1991a, 1991b). For example, Van Lange et al. (1997) developed a nine-item decomposed game measure of social value orientation by which research participants can be classified as prosocial, individualistic, or competitive depending on whether the majority of their choices are consistent with one of these three social value orientations. Using this measure, several studies have found that the largest group of participants tends to be prosocial, as opposed to individualistic or competitive.

For instance, Van Lange et al. (1997) observed that in a representative sample of the Dutch adult population (N = 1,728), 71.2% of the respondents were prosocial persons or cooperative beings, whereas 21.3% of the respondents were individualistic, and 7.5% of the respondents were competitive. Furthermore, Van Lange (1999) concluded that it is common to find in student samples that more than 50% of the participants can be identified as prosocial. Moreover, the prevalence of prosocial persons tends to be even more pronounced in the adult population in the Netherlands than in student samples in the psychology laboratory (Van Lange et al., 1997). Importantly, similar findings are obtained in the United States and other countries (Balliet, Parks, & Joireman, 2009; Van Lange & Kuhlman, 1994; Van Lange & Liebrand, 1991a, 1991b). Building on these and other insights, I argue that it seems reasonable to assume that many people want to do what is right (Lind & Van den Bos, 2013). In fact, people with positive social values may constitute as much as 90% of the general population in labor organizations (IJfs, 2012).

This said, there are undoubtedly other people who are purposively looking for opportunities to cheat and to engage in fraudulent acts. This group may constitute only 2% of a given labor organization (Lind & Van den Bos, 2013), or perhaps 7% to 10% of society's citizens, and are tempted to adhere to extreme levels of competitiveness, desperately wanting to outperform others. Furthermore, there are perhaps 20% of extreme individualists, who care only about themselves and what they think is right or valuable, ignoring the implications of their thinking for the greater good (Van den Bos & Lind, 2013). However, competitive people and individualists can constitute very salient groups and may have detrimental effects on the coherence of groups, organizations, and societies. For instance, the 2% of employees who actively seek opportunities to cheat can influence an additional 8% in the organization who are inclined to follow fraudulent norms when given the opportunity (IJfs, 2012). Furthermore, extreme individualists can dramatically undermine the necessary level of social coordination between people that is needed for groups and societies to function efficiently and effectively (see also Schelling, 1960; Van Dijk & Wilke, 1993, 1995).

Thus, notwithstanding the prosocial orientation of the majority in many research samples (see also Esposito & Mogahed, 2007), I am definitely aware that some people clearly engage in selfish, exploitative, or even fraudulent behavior (Ariely, 2012). Certainly, there are those with a competitive orientation who would like to outperform others, sometimes even at the expense of some of their own personal gains (Van Lange, Otten, et al., 1997), and these people might be tempted to engage in antisocial and blatantly unfair and unjust behavior (Van den Bos & Lind,

2013), especially when people are in competition with other groups (Van den Bos & Van Laarhoven, 2018; see also Schopler, et al., 2001). In other words, whereas I emphasized in earlier work the positive values of many cooperative people (see, e.g., Van den Bos & Bal, 2016; Van den Bos et al., 2011), here I focus on the darker side of humankind and explore the implications of those social values and associated psychological processes that are relevant to radical and extremist persons.

One implication that I would like to discuss here involves the issue of behavioral inhibition. We humans are creatures who are oriented toward doing things. Yet in many situations we do not know what to do, and then our tendency to act may be inhibited. Especially in confusing, unusual, ambiguous, or otherwise unsettling situations, people try to make sense of what is going on and how to behave. Sense-making and social appraisal are facilitated when ongoing behavioral action is inhibited. Thus, when not knowing how to act, we stop and think for a minute in order to sort out what is going on and how to proceed (Hulst, Van den Bos, Akkermans, & Lind, 2017).

Figure 6.4 illustrates this line of reasoning. The model depicted in the figure examines people's responses to confusing events. The model argues that these events instigate appraisal processes such that people try to determine what is going on in the situation at hand. These appraisal processes are facilitated by the inhibiting of ongoing behavior. After all, it is easier to sort out what is going on and what you should do in the situation at hand when you are not busy with other activities. The model further proposes that after the outcome of the appraisal process is known and people understand what is expected of them, the behavioral inhibition system is deactivated. As a result, activation of outgoing behavior is possible. This includes the possibility of prosocial behavior, for example, because of people's cooperative and prosocial values.

The model depicted in Figure 6.4 also argues that fully understanding what to do and hence full deactivation of the behavioral inhibition system may be possible following confusing events. That being noted, I also propose that in complex social situations in which there is a lot of ambiguity, complete deactivation of behavioral inhibition will not always be achieved by people. For example, in modern societies and our complex world, many things are going on, and it can be difficult for people to make sense of these things and act accordingly.

An implication of this model is that even those with prosocial values may be inhibited to show these values in their behaviors, for example, because they have difficulty determining how to make sense of their social situation, the society in which they find themselves, or the world in which they live. Viewed in this manner, many (but certainly not all) radicals may be viewed as confused individuals. Those individuals may suffer from impaired social or societal coordination (Schelling, 1960) and can be inhibited in showing their social values that in principle could be positive for society at large. That is, our work suggests that too strong activation of the behavioral inhibition system can block prosocial choices and prosocial behavior among those with prosocial values (Van den Bos et al., 2011).

Other radicals and extremists may be characterized by competitive or individualistic values that have mainly negative consequences for society at large. In all likelihood, this group may be very large when compared with representative samples and how these samples adhere to social values (e.g., Van Lange et al., 1997), attesting to the potentially very important role of social values in the process of radicalization.

## 6.6 SELF-CORRECTION

Thus far, in this chapter we have seen various instances in which people can find it difficult to correct for their egocentric impulses. That is, people need sufficient cognitive capacities and strong motivation to counter the hedonistic pleasure of receiving unfair yet advantageous outcomes (Section 6.2), resist the temptation to keep believing in a just world by blaming and derogating innocent victims (Section 6.3), overcome their startle responses to potentially threatening out-group others (Section 6.4), and not being blocked in their activities of social coordination and their prosocial tendencies (Section 6.5). There clearly are examples of people being able to successfully correct for their first, self-centered impulses

(Van den Bos & Bal, 2016; Van den Bos et al., 2006, 2011), but there are also vivid cases in which this turns out not to be successful. I argue here that insufficient self-correction may play a role in various processes of human radicalization. I also wonder whether people can do something against insufficient self-correction.

Obviously, trying to free cognitive capacity or triggering the appropriate non–self-centered motivation may do the trick here. But these are not always easy tasks (see also Paulhus, 1984; Paulhus, Grae, & Van Selst, 1989; Paulhus, Harms, Bruce, & Lysy, 2003; Vohs, Baumeister, Ciarocco, 2005). For example, people may find themselves in conditions in which there clearly is information overload. And activating prosocial motivation may be difficult for some people, especially in situations in which they feel threatened and their self-centered responses tend to be dominant (e.g., Loseman, Miedema, Van den Bos, & Vermunt, 2009). This said, some encouraging developments can be noted here.

One particularly intriguing possibility of training people to show more positive response to potentially threatening out-groups is suggested by research by Kawakami, Phills, Steele, and Dovidio (2007). This program of research focuses on improving people's implicit racial attitudes and their interracial interactions through approach behaviors. For example, in one of the studies by Kawakami et al. (2007), non-Black participants were explicitly instructed to approach Blacks by pulling the joystick toward themselves when presented with photographs of Black individuals and to avoid Whites by pushing the joystick away from themselves when presented with pictures of White persons. These approach and avoidance behaviors are related to what I mentioned in Section 6.3 when discussing the Bal and Van den Bos (2018) research on approach and avoidance of innocent victims.

Importantly, in Kawakami et al.'s (2007) research, participants were engaged in the approach or avoidance task for 480 trials, hence resulting in an extensive training. (In other conditions of the Kawakami et al. study, participants were asked to avoid Blacks by pushing the joystick away from themselves when presented with Blacks and to approach Whites by pulling the joystick toward themselves when presented with Whites, or to push the joystick to the right when presented with Blacks and to the left when presented with Whites, or to push the joystick to the left when presented with Blacks and to the right when presented with Whites.)

Results showed that participants who received the extensive training in pulling a joystick toward themselves when presented with a photograph of a Black person and pushing it away from themselves when presented with a photograph of a White person showed significantly lower levels of implicit racial prejudice than did participants in the other conditions. These findings suggest the possibility that a history of approaching a social category may lower people's levels of prejudice. These results also indicate that implicit attitudes and implicit stereotypes reflect learned habits of mind (Devine, 1989) that can be influenced by practicing to respond in unconventional ways to social groups (see also Kawakami, Dovidio, Moll, Hermsen, & Russin, 2000; Kawakami, Dovidio, & Van Kamp, 2005).

I note here explicitly that the Kawakami et al. (2007) studies have been criticized (see, e.g., Van Dessel, De Houwer, & Gast, 2016; Van Dessel, De Houwer, Gast, Tucker Smith, & De Schryver, 2016; Van Dessel, De Houwer, Roets, & Gast, 2016). Perhaps the questions that were raised about the robustness of the results have something to do with specifics of (some of) the approach and avoidance manipulations that Kawakami et al. used and the rather minimal quality of these manipulations in particular. Interesting in this respect is an intervention program that Devine, Forscher, Austin, & Cox (2012) developed recently that does not rely on a single intervention technique but rather combines five conceptually relevant techniques in order to counter people's startle responses to potentially threatening out-groups.

The prejudice intervention by Devine et al. (2012) taught participants cognitive techniques to overcome nonintentional race bias. Specifically, in the training, non-Black participants were provided with a list of five strategies that people can use in their daily lives. None of the strategies are difficult to implement, and each requires some effort by the individuals using the strategy. The strategies entailed replacing stereotypical responses for nonstereotypical responses, imagining in detail counter-stereotypic

others, preventing stereotypic inferences by obtaining specific information about group members, taking the perspective of a member of a
stereotyped group, and seeking opportunities to encounter and engage
in positive interactions with out-group members. The training of these
five techniques was able to reduce implicit bias up to two months after
the intervention, particularly among those participants who were concerned about discrimination or who reported using the strategies (Devine
et al., 2012).

Part of the success of the training program may come from the notion
that implicit bias is like a habit that can be reduced through a combination of awareness of implicit bias, concern about the effects of that bias,
and the application of strategies to reduce bias. Related to what Figure 6.3
shows, for the intervention to be successful people must be aware of their
biases and be concerned about the consequences of their biases (Devine
et al., 2012). Under these conditions even processes previously thought to
be implicit may be altered by means of repeated and targeted training, at
least among those who are willing to change.

Devine et al. (2012) note explicitly that future studies will need to establish the specific behavioral, cognitive, affective, and neural mechanisms
through which this intervention exerts its effects. Importantly, the authors
argue convincingly that it is likely that there is no single mechanism (no
single "magic bullet," as they put it) that, by itself, prompts the regulation of
people's implicit biases and self-centered responses. Rather, it seems more
likely that several mechanisms work in combination to prompt situational
awareness of one's bias and translate that awareness into chronic awareness,
concern, and self-regulatory effort (Devine et al., 2012). This seems like
good advice to me: When you want to alter complex and probably multifaceted issues such as discrimination or radicalization, do not put your
money on one mechanism only. Instead, rely on multiple mechanisms in
order to create intervention techniques and training programs that are robust across different individuals in different circumstances and at different
points in time.

Figure 6.5 applies these and other insights to the concept of radicalization. The model depicted in the figure summarizes people's reactions

to situations in which they are confronted with the various antecedents of radicalization (such as the perception that things are not fair) and associated impulses (such as the emotion of anger). Figure 6.5 shows that people's impulsive responses can be corrected when people realize explicitly that this is an indication of growing radicalization. If people have sufficient cognitive capacity (such as when their working memory is not overloaded), are sufficiently motivated (such as when they adhere to nonprejudiced or cooperative social values), and are exposed to repeated training of successful self-correction, then self-correction may lead to attenuated radicalization. I hasten to emphasize that although I strive for an "Enlightenment ideal" in which people actively work to fully realize their potentials, I hope to have made clear in this chapter that correction is possible yet can be hard to achieve and hence that correction of first impulses will often be insufficient.

Building on what we have learned in this chapter, I propose that in the case of individual-oriented forms of radicalization (such as important instances of left-wing extremism as discussed in Section 2.4), cognitive control and conscious thought are key (for reviews, see, e.g., Amodio & Frith, 2006; Baumeister & Masicampo, 2010). Furthermore, building on the review in the current chapter, I argue that in the case of group-based radicalization (such as Muslim and right-wing radicalization as discussed in Sections 2.2 and 2.3), the work on group-based stereotypes and prejudice may be especially relevant. This includes the work by Kawakami et al. (2007) and Devine et al. (2012).

The Devine et al. (2012) intervention relied, among other things, on providing meaningful and positive contact with persons from other groups. Indeed, the contact hypothesis has been put forward frequently as one of the best ways to improve relations among groups that are experiencing conflict (Allport, 1954), particularly when people from different groups have to work together to reach important goals (Sherif, Harvey, White, Hood, & Sherif, 1961). However, contact between different groups is also known to not always work effectively, especially not when contact creates anxiety for those who take part. Groups involved must also acknowledge some authority that supports the contact and interactions between the groups and as such support for authorities, law, or customs can help to yield successful interactions between groups.[1]

This is not the time nor the place to dwell on the contact hypothesis in detail (for reviews, see, e.g., Brown & Hewstone, 2005; Crisp & Abrams, 2008; Pettigrew & Tropp, 2006; Tropp & Page-Gould, 2015; Schmid, Ramiah, & Hewstone, 2014; Vezzali, Hewstone, Capozza, Giovannini, & Wölfer, 2014) nor to discuss criticism or nuances of the hypothesis at full length (see, e.g., Barlow et al., 2012; Saguy & Dovidio, 2013; Saguy, Tausch, Dovidio, & Pratto, 2009; Sengupta & Sibley 2013). This said, I do want to note one important issue, namely that Greene (2013) explores how our ethical intuitions play out in within-group versus between-group settings. Greene argues that humans have an instinctive, automatic tendency to co-operate with others within their own social group. For example, Greene notes that in a cooperative investment game, people are more likely to do what is best for the group when they are under time pressure or when they are primed to follow their gut feelings. Inversely, cooperation can be in-hibited by rational calculation in these within-group settings. However, in contexts of intergroup harmony, Greene argues that automatic intuitions run into a problem. That is, the same in-group loyalty that achieves coop-eration within a community leads to hostility between communities.

Thus, within-group morality can easily lead to between-group hostility (see also Insko et al., 1998). I propose here that this also plays a role in "group-oriented" forms of radicalization (such as Muslim and right-wing radicalization) in which one's own group often dictates one's own norms of fairness and one's own loyalty through processes of social identifica-tion as well as in "individualistic" types of radicalization (such as left-wing radicalization) in which moral principles of individuals are shaped by the individuals' subculture with its own moral principles and associated cul-tural worldviews.

Greene (2013) argues that to counter these intergroup tendencies, people need to embrace a sense of morality that encompasses different groups and on which all humans can agree. This can be very difficult

---

1. See https://en.wikipedia.org/wiki/Contact_hypothesis. See also Pettigrew (1998).

but not impossible to achieve, even in the case of heavy and violent past conflicts between different groups (see also Staub, 2011, 2015; Staub & Pearlman, 2009; Staub, Pearlman, Gubin, & Hagengimana, 2005).

Related to this, Hodson (2011) reviews contact interventions among intolerant people. On the basis of this review, he concludes that intergroup contact and friendships work well among intolerant and cognitively rigid persons and that they do so by reducing threat and anxiety and increasing empathy, trust, and out-group closeness. Here I argue that this is also important because cognitive rigidity plays an important role in various forms of radicalization. This is the subject of the next chapter and the next part of this book.

# PART THREE

# Core Components of Radicalization

# Rigidity of Thoughts

## 7.1 INTRODUCTION

Now that the book has introduced a framework to understand radicalization, reviewed several instances of radicalization and theories to understand radicalization, and examined perceived unfairness as a key antecedent of various radicalization processes, especially when these perceptions are combined with uncertainty or other threats and with insufficient correction of self-centered impulses, it is time to focus on core components that characterize what people who have radicalized in some form think and feel and how they behave. This part of the book focuses on these core components of human radicalization.

Obviously, there are many, many different forms of radicalization. Furthermore, people differ immensely as to the extent by which they have radicalized as well as to how and whether they are influenced by their own moral principles, their need for group affiliation, their cultural worldviews, and their identification with or isolation from society. In other words, sketching core components of radicalization is a daunting task. In this book, I therefore limit myself to discussing what I think are key aspects of people's thoughts, feelings, and behaviors that play a crucial role in radicalization processes. To this end, Part Three of this book focuses on people's rigidity of thoughts (Chapter 7), their startled and defensive feelings related to the defense of their worldviews (Chapter 8), and their violent behavioral rejection of law and democratic principles (Chapter 9).

By examining these thoughts, feelings, and behaviors, I do not want to imply by any means that these are the only aspects of radicalization that are important. It is easy to see why it would be a mistake to propose this. Nonetheless, I agree with McCauley and Moskalenko (2008) who noted that "there are many possible meanings of radicalization, but most of the relevant distinctions can be represented with the usual social psychological distinctions among belief, feeling, and behavior" (p. 416). In particular, I argue in this part of the book that "black-and-white" *thinking* (Chapter 7), startled *feelings* and associated hot-cognitive defense of cultural worldviews (Chapter 8), and violent and law-rejecting *behaviors* (Chapter 9) constitute important components of the psychology of radicalization, perhaps even more so than is commonly realized.

Furthermore, the fact that also normal people tend to engage in rigid thoughts, startled and defensive responses, and verbal or even physical aggression (at least in some circumstances and to some extent) allows me to more firmly ground the understanding of radicalization in what is known from solid scientific insights into these issues. It is my goal in this part of the book to use these insights to explore the role of these issues in human radicalization.

Black-and-white thinking or rigidity of human thoughts manifests itself in different ways. In this chapter I examine how people can be tempted to become rigid in their solving of various nonsocial tasks (Section 7.2), how social rigidity can play a key role in people's personal beliefs and their need for social structure (Section 7.3), how rigidity is related to people's need to shield themselves from unwanted thoughts (Section 7.4) and their need to know and understand things, sometimes culminating in illusions of knowing (Section 7.5), and how all this can culminate in rigid radicalization (Section 7.6).

## 7.2 RIGIDITY ABOUT NONSOCIAL STIMULI

One way in which human rigidity is apparent is in people's reactions to nonsocial stimuli. Rokeach (1948), for example, focused on the thinking processes of individuals known to be ethnocentric in their attitudes toward racial and religious out-groups, an issue that plays a role in various forms of radicalization such as right-wing and Muslim radicalization. Rokeach put forward that the thinking processes of these individuals are characterized by rigidity and inflexibility, defined as the inability to change one's response set when the objective conditions demand it, such as is the case when new and simpler solutions to old problems become available.

Rokeach further argued that the rigidity inherent in the ethnocentric person's solution of social problems is not an isolated phenomenon within the personality but is rather an aspect of a general rigidity factor that not only operates in the solution of social problems but also is apparent in the person's approach to nonsocial kinds of problems. To test this prediction, Rokeach (1948) performed several mindset (or *Einstellung*) experiments as tests for rigidity. In these experiments, participants were asked to solve problems. In the first phase of the experiments, participants were confronted with problems that were solvable only by relatively complicated methods. This was followed by another phase in which problems were solvable both by the complicated methods and by more simple methods. The extent to which participants kept on choosing the complicated solution of the problems was taken as an indication of rigidity.

The Rokeach (1948) study found that high-prejudice adults and children, as determined by their responses to a prejudice scale, were significantly more rigid in solving various nonsocial problems than low-prejudice adults and children. In this way, the research showed that prejudiced responses were associated with higher levels of nonsocial rigidity.

In a follow-up project, Rokeach (1950) focused on structural determinants of rigidity. In doing so, he noted that rigidity or fixation of responses increases with the repetition of a given pattern of behavior. He further argued that persons in a hurry will be forced to perceive a problem confronting them narrowly or rigidly, whereas persons in no hurry at all will have time to perceive the problem more broadly and in more flexible ways. The issue of time demands was also highlighted in Chapter 6, where I discussed the relevance of people's taxed working memory and whether people respond to stimuli under conditions of high or low cognitive load (Van den Bos, Peters, Bobocel, & Ybema, 2006).

Providing support for Rokeach's line of reasoning with regard to the effect of time availability on rigidity is work by Luchins (1942), who gave participants a series of arithmetic problems to solve under normal and under speedy conditions. Under normal conditions the participants were given an adequate amount of time per problem. Under speedy conditions the participants were given considerably less time per problem. The results showed that the groups solving the problems under speedy conditions were considerably more rigid than the groups solving the problems under normal conditions.

The research by Rokeach (1950) supported these conclusions, again using mindset experiments. These studies showed that a decrease of time availability leads to an increase in rigid responses. That is, when there was not enough time to approach a problem in an open-minded manner, this increased the chances that people kept using well-learned complicated solutions to problems, whereas easier solutions in fact had become possible in the meantime. Rokeach suggested that these results indicate that differences between persons characterized as rigid and others characterized as less rigid may be attributable, to some extent at least, to differences in time availability. After all, availability of time enables broader cognitions and greater flexibility of behavior, whereas insufficient time availability tends to be associated with narrower cognitions and, consequently, more rigid behavior.

Related to the Rokeach work are more recent experiments by Marien, Aarts, and Custers (2012). These authors studied when people are more flexible or more rigid in switching means to achieve goals. Their research shows, among other things, that when the reaching of the goals was implicitly associated with positive affective states, people more easily switched the means to achieve the goal in situations in which switching the means was necessary for goal achievement. In contrast, when positive affect was associated with well-learned means to achieve the goal, this made it harder for participants to switch the means and hence made their goal-directed behavior more rigid. In other words, feeling good about what you have learned to do can make you more rigid and less likely to consider alternative means to reach your goals.

Importantly, instances of switching versus nonswitching behavior—like we have seen in the studies by Luchins (1942), Marien et al. (2012), and Rokeach (1948, 1950)—have also been found among nonhuman primates, attesting to the robustness of these kinds of responses. For example, in a study conducted by Kret, Jaasma, Bionda, and Wijnen (2016), bonobos completed a dot-probe task during which emotional and neutral pictures of unfamiliar bonobos and control animals were being presented on a touchscreen. In correspondence with earlier dot-probe studies, the bonobos responded faster to a dot presented at their touchscreens when the dot appeared at the location where a picture of an emotional other bonobo had been presented compared with when a neutral-looking bonobo had been presented at the location.

Kret et al. (2016) interpret these findings as evidence for the attention to group members' emotional expressions, which the authors assume is crucial for the maintenance of social bonds and ultimately for group survival. The detecting of dots and other responses to nonsocial stimuli thus may help to uncover the working of various thought processes, including the switching or nonswitching of responses and other indications of rigidity. Rokeach (1960) was able to link these kinds of responses to the issue of human closed-mindedness. This is an issue that will be discussed in the next sections of this chapter.

## 7.3 PERSONAL NEED FOR STRUCTURE

Human rigidity does not only or primarily show in responses to nonsocial stimuli, it also is apparent in people's personal beliefs and their personal needs for social structure. As we have seen in the previous chapter, people live in a complex and information-rich world. Given the fact that people can process only so much information, they often look for ways to reduce the information load. One important way in which they can do this is by attempting to structure the world into a simplified and more manageable form. This can be achieved by creating and using simplified cognitive generalizations of events, individuals, groups, and other social stimuli (Neuberg & Newsom, 1993).

Much research supports the significance of such simple structures, suggesting that people also possess a tendency to maintain such structures. Indeed, some researchers have explicitly suggested the existence of a general need for structure. Neuberg and Newsom (1993) argue that people meaningfully differ in the extent to which they are dispositionally motivated to cognitively structure their worlds in simple and unambiguous ways. Thus, these authors propose that people differ in their needs for simple social structures.

The research by Neuberg and Newsom (1993) operationalizes the construct of people's desire for simple structure. In doing so, these authors define persons high in desire for simple structures as individuals leading a simple, tightly organized life, both cognitively and behaviorally. The contents of the cognitive structures of such persons should be relatively homogeneous, each structure should be well bounded and relatively distinct from others, and such individuals should be relatively uninhibited in their use of their simple structures to interpret new events. These individuals should be especially likely to establish and enjoy routines, prefer familiar social situations, and so on. In sum, such individuals are motivated to seek out simply structured ways of dealing with their world.

In their research Neuberg and Newsom rely on the Personal Need for Structure scale, originally developed by Thompson and colleagues. Thompson, Naccarato, Parker, and Moskowitz (2001) write about this scale that it is designed to assess preferences for structure and clarity in most situations. Ambiguity and "gray areas" are troublesome and annoying for those scoring high on the scale. Such people tend to experience discomfort when they perceive that structure and clarity are missing from social situations. Example items of the scale include, "It upsets me to go into a situation without knowing what I can expect from it" and "I like or enjoy being spontaneous" (the last item is reverse-scored).

In a series of studies Neuberg and Newsom (1993) show that individual differences in the desire for simple structure can have important implications for various fundamental aspects of psychological functioning. For example, findings show that individuals with greater desires for simple structure are especially likely to organize information in simple, less complex ways. Furthermore, individuals with greater desires for simple structure are more likely to apply previously acquired social categories to new, ambiguous situations. Taken together, the findings indicate that individuals differ in the extent to which they are chronically motivated to simply structure their worlds and that this difference has important implications for how people go about approaching and understanding their world and behaving in this world.

People's personal desires for social structure play a relevant role in processes pertaining to radicalization, extreme responses, and terrorism. For example, Routledge, Juhl, and Vess (2010) note that people high in personal need for structure prefer to see the world with simplicity, certainty, and predictability. It should not come as a surprise, therefore, that individuals with greater desires for structure respond to conditions of threat with increased efforts to perceive the world as just and orderly (Landau et al., 2004) and with increased liking of information that confirms their views of how the world should look like (Juhl & Routledge, 2010). Routledge et al. (2010) conclude that people's personal need for structure is key to understanding the rigidity of people's responses to conditions of threat. Under threatening conditions, people high in personal need for structure gain psychological security by becoming more cognitively and attitudinally rigid.

In their research, Routledge et al. (2010) focus on the threat of being reminded about the vulnerability of one's own existence (Becker, 1973). In their analysis this includes the threat of being a victim of a terrorist attack. One reason the threat of terrorism is so anxiety-provoking is that it renders salient the fragility and transience of life (Routledge et al., 2010). Supporting this line of reasoning are studies by Landau et al. (2004), who found that subliminally presenting information about the 9/11 attacks and the World Trade Center led to defensive attitudes. Similarly, Das, Bushman, Bezemer, Kerkhof, and Vermeulen (2009) show that exposure to news stories about terrorist acts increases out-group prejudice.

Related to this, Routledge et al. (2010) show that differences in personal need for structure predict how individuals respond to the threat of terrorism. For individuals with greater desires for structure, the threat of terrorism strongly motivates their defense of their cultural group and their worldview-related traditions. The Routledge et al. findings are important, in part because they suggest that under threatening conditions, such as when your own existence is threatened (Becker, 1973) or when your worldview or culture is threatened by attacks from other groups (Boscarino, Adams, Figley, Galea, & Foa, 2006), "black-and-white" responses and reacting in rigid ways are especially appealing to those with strong desires to see the world in simple terms.

The Routledge et al. (2010) study is grounded in the work on terror management theory, a theory that serves a prominent role in the next chapter. Here I note that another research project that was founded on this theory showed that higher needs for simple structure led people to employ clearly structured conceptions of reality under conditions of threat. Individuals lower in needs for structure did not show this effect (Vess, Routledge, Landau, & Arndt, 2009). In another research project, Goren and Neter (2016) showed that need for cognitive structure (operationalized with a somewhat different measure than Neuberg & Newsom, 1993) was associated with more stereotypical or "black-and-white" thinking among Israeli youth who are vulnerable to post-traumatic stress disorder symptoms following the exposure to terror.

These and other findings support the idea that people who prefer generally simple, perhaps very simple, styles of reasoning are more vulnerable to processes of rigid radicalization. In this way, people's personal belief in simple structures can serve an important role in the psychology of radicalization. Before I discuss the implications of these reasoning styles for instances of rigid radicalization, I wonder what the sources of people's rigid thoughts are. After all, when rigidity of thoughts plays a role in radicalization, as I argue here, then it is good to examine where this cognitive rigidity is coming from. In the next two sections I examine two important sources of people's rigidity of thoughts, namely people's need to shield themselves from unwanted thoughts and their need to know and understand things (which can culminate in illusory thoughts). After this, I explore the implications of the current analysis of rigid thoughts for the radicalization process.

## 7.4 RIGID SHIELDING

One important source of people's rigid thoughts can be their inclination to shield themselves from unwanted thoughts. Indeed, increased radicalization can be assumed to be associated with stronger shielding from unwanted thoughts and intensified avoiding or rejecting information that is inconsistent with the person's worldview.

Neuberg and Newsom (1993) note that through avoidance strategies, people limit the amount of information to which they are exposed. That is, people may be tempted to restructure the information that is coming in (see the previous section), but they may also create barriers that restrict the likelihood that social and environmental information will intrude unexpectedly on their lives. We all do that sometimes, such as when we close the door of our office to not hear our colleagues discussing departmental politics, or when we wear headphones in the gym or at airports to not hear environmental noise and thus try to minimize perceiving what others do in these environments. At other times we do not pick up the newspaper, and we watch a feel-good movie instead of checking out the latest political news in our country or processing information about global warming or human starvation in the world. In this way people may choose not to venture beyond their immediate environments and life spaces, thus reducing exposure to unwanted information (Neuberg & Newsome, 1993).

Thus, normal people engage in shielding from unwanted information, at least at certain times in their lives (see also Arndt, Cook, Goldenberg, & Routledge, 2007; Hayes, Schimel, Arndt, & Faucher, 2010). And when they are compelled to confront and interact with others, people may actively ignore potentially available information, for example, by avoiding eye contact and diminishing the length of social encounters (Neuberg & Newsome, 1993). The point is that radicalized individuals tend to shield themselves in more strict and rigid ways from information that possibly could falsify their ideas about how the world works and what should be done about it. In other words, radicals suffer more strongly from a need of not wanting to know. And they are more likely to engage in rigid processes to ward off threats.

Reflecting on these kinds of issues, Rokeach (1960) put forward the concepts of open and closed systems that people can use to process what is going on in their environments and the world at large. In doing so, he distinguished between belief and disbelief systems. Rokeach (1960) conceived the belief system to represent all the beliefs, sets, expectancies, or hypotheses that a person accepts as true of the world he or she lives in. In contrast, the disbelief system contains all the beliefs, sets, and expectancies that a person rejects as false. Both belief and disbelief systems can be open or closed, and both can operate consciously and unconsciously.

Importantly, according to Rokeach (1960), in a closed belief-disbelief system there is a strong magnitude of rejection of beliefs the person thinks are not true. There is also a greater discrepancy between what the person believes to be true and what the person believes to be false. Furthermore, what the person believes to be false is rather focused and concentrated on one topic or only some topics. As such, there is relatively little differentiation within the disbelief system.

Rokeach (1960) suggests that a basic characteristic that defines the extent to which a person's system is open or closed is the extent to which the person can receive, evaluate, and act on relevant information received from the outside on its own intrinsic merits, unencumbered by irrelevant factors in the situation arising from within the person or from the outside. From this view, growing radicalization can be depicted as increased closing off external information, shielding from outside information, and avoidance of other sources of information and other subcultures.

Most people have systems that are neither completely open nor completely closed. Thus, "open" and closed systems should be treated as ideal types, convenient for purposes of analysis (Rokeach, 1960). Against this background I put forward that it is my assumption that most radicalized people will have adopted closed belief-disbelief systems that are used in part to ward off threats. This is not to say that people cannot change. Indeed, a person's system can expand and contract over time, albeit it within certain limits (Rokeach, 1960).

On a subject that partly anticipates what is discussed in the next section, Rokeach (1960) postulated that belief-disbelief systems serve two powerful and conflicting sets of motives at the same time: the need for a cognitive framework to know and to understand (see Section 7.5) and the need to ward off threatening aspects of reality (the current section). He argued that when the cognitive need to know is predominant and the need to ward off threat is absent, open systems should result. He also proposed that as the need to ward off threat becomes stronger, the cognitive need to know should become weaker, resulting in more closed belief-disbelief systems.

Rokeach further reasoned that for most persons in most situations, both sets of needs operate together to one degree or another. A person will be open to information as far as possible, and will reject it, screen it out, or alter it insofar as necessary. In other words, no matter how much a person's system closes up to ward off threat and anxiety, it can still serve as a cognitive framework for satisfying the need to know. One can distort the world and narrow it down to whatever extent necessary, but at the same time preserve the illusion of understanding it. Thus, if the closed or dogmatic mind is extremely resistant to change, it may be so not only because it allays anxiety but also because it satisfies the need to know (for instance, by the illusion of knowing what is going on). This issue is further discussed in the next section.

The idea is that when warding off threat is a predominant motive, people then are still interested to know what is going on, but only within their own bubble or subculture (Rokeach, 1960). We see this happening all the time. For example, most people will search for information on the Internet, newspapers, or social media such as Twitter or Facebook in such a way that they are likely to find information that confirms their beliefs and their belief systems. In other words, people tend to seek confirmation of what already is believed (see also Garner, 1962, 1970; Kagan, 1972). That said, I propose that compared with normal people, radicalized individuals engage in more rigid processes to ward off threats and, in doing so, tend to engage in stronger confirmation-seeking behaviors and more extreme, black-and-white thoughts.

## 7.5 RIGID ILLUSORY THOUGHTS

Another important source of rigidity of thoughts comes from people's need to know and their will to understand things. Ironically, this epistemic source of cognitive rigidity stems from what normally is a good thing, namely that people want to understand the world, what is going on in the world, and what they should do in the world. Indeed, we humans can be quite good at explaining, ordering, and justifying things (for an overview of the literature, see, e.g., Kruglanski, 1989).

However, there is often too much information about too many things in this world, hence creating conditions of information overload for people. In these conditions of information overload, people want to reduce information. They can do this by means of shielding themselves from information (see the previous section). People can also attempt to structure the world into a simplified, more manageable form (Neuberg & Newsom, 1993). For example, people may establish behavioral routines and rely on formalized social scripts in their encounters with others, thus reducing the amount of information to which they must attend. And they can reduce informational quantity and complexity by cognitive structuring. This process is quite understandable and helps people to manage their complex world. It also can lead to cognitively rigid ways of responding to new or unanticipated information or other information that is inconsistent with what people expected.

Jost, Glaser, Kruglanski, and Sulloway (2003a) integrate theories of authoritarianism, dogmatism-intolerance of ambiguity, epistemic and existential needs, and ideological rationalization to explain political conservatism as a process of motivated social cognition. These authors note that the conservative mind tends to engage in processes of cognitive closure, stresses resistance to change, and is motivated by needs that vary situationally and dispositionally to manage uncertainty and threat. Greenberg and Jonas (2003) argue that the fear- and uncertainty-driven motives reviewed by Jost et al. (2003a) contribute to ideological rigidity independently of whether the ideology is right-wing or left-wing. This suggests that ideological beliefs can help to reduce uncertainty, fears, and anxiety and to mitigate feelings of threat and worthlessness. This effect seems to be a bit stronger among those adhering to right-wing as opposed to left-wing ideology (Jost, Glaser, Kruglanski, & Sulloway, 2003b; see also Adorno, Frenkel-Brunswik, Levinson, & Sanford, 1950).

However, that being said, it is my assumption that in the case of radical individuals (i.e., people who are more extreme than those who merely adhere to right- or left-wing ideology), both radicals on the left and those on the right on average will tend to engage in rigid and dogmatic thinking (see also Greenberg & Jonas, 2003; Van Prooijen & Krouwel, 2017; Van Prooijen, Krouwel, Boiten, & Eendebak, 2015). Related to this, Roets, Kruglanski, Kossowska, Pierro, and Hong (2015) propose that under perceived humiliation (such as when you or your group is treated in fundamentally unfair ways), need for closure increases a response to self-uncertainty and loss of personal significance, which in turn can lead to violent terrorism. This process seems to be relevant for different radical individuals and different radical groups.

The fact that the world is a place in which we often have too much information about many things and at the same time too little information about important things can make our world a sadistic place to live in (Hermans, 1964, 1970). That is, conditions of information overload make it appealing to engage in more rigid, black-and-white thought processes. At the same time, people want to understand things, even when there is little relevant information to understand the complex issues and events that are going on in their world. This is why social psychologists often talk about uncertain situations in which people feel that they do not really understand important features of the situation or that they do not have sufficient information about relationships, agendas, or norms (Garner, 1962; Kagan, 1972; Van den Bos & Lind, 2002).

Fernbach, Rogers, Fox, and Sloman (2013) note that under these kinds of circumstances, political extremism is supported by an illusion of understanding. These authors observe that people often hold extreme political attitudes about complex policies. After all, many important societal issues, ranging from climate change to health care to poverty, require complex policy solutions. The authors note that people typically know less about such policies than they think they do. This is called the illusion of explanatory depth. Furthermore, Fernbach et al. argue that polarized political preferences about these complex policies are enabled by simplistic causal models.

Indeed, research suggests that people have unjustified confidence in their understanding of how complex policies work. Findings also indicate that this illusion of understanding contributes to political polarization (Fernbach et al., 2013). Moreover, Fernbach et al. note that this line of reasoning implies that asking people to explain how a policy works should make them aware of how poorly they understand the policy, which should cause them to subsequently express more moderate attitudes and behaviors. The authors report research results that support this prediction. Fernbach et al. further note that this prediction is related to people's overconfidence in how well they understand how everyday objects work. Asking people to explain in detail how the objects really work shatters this sense of understanding. Fernbach et al. obtained similar findings in the domain of political polarization and extreme political attitudes.

For example, Fernbach and colleagues (2013) asked participants to rate how well they understood different political policies. After participants judged their understanding of each issue, they were asked to explain how some of the policies work and then to rerate their level of understanding. The authors expected that asking participants to explain the mechanisms underlying the policies would expose the illusion of explanatory depth and lead to lower ratings of understanding of the policies. As predicted, asking people to explain how policies work decreased their reported understanding of those policies and led them to express more moderate political views about those policies. Furthermore, participants who exhibited greater decreases in reported understanding of how the policies worked tended to exhibit more moderate political views.

Fernbach et al. (2013) note that previous research has shown that intensively educating citizens can improve the quality of democratic decisions following collective deliberation and negotiation (Fishkin, 1991). One reason for the effectiveness of this strategy may be that educating citizens on how policies work moderates their attitudes, increasing their willingness to explore opposing views and to compromise.

People's rigid cognitive thoughts, including their rigid illusory thoughts, constitute a central part of what humans are. The Fernbach et al. (2013) findings are important because they show these illusory thoughts and suggest possible ways of intervening in the process that is at least partially responsible for these illusions. That is, thinking through in a calm and reasoned way about the possible reasons why a certain policy works may correct several psychological phenomena that make polarization self-reinforcing.

After all, people often are unaware of their own ignorance (Kruger & Dunning, 1999), seek out information that supports their current preferences (Nickerson, 1998), process new information in biased ways that strengthen their current preferences (Lord, Ross, & Lepper, 1979), affiliate with other people who have similar preferences (Lazarsfeld & Merton, 1954), and assume that other people's views are as extreme as their own (Van Boven, Judd, & Sherman, 2012). In sum, several psychological factors increase extremism. Political polarization is therefore hard to avoid. Fernbach et al. (2013) note that explanation generation is no panacea for eliminating extremism. However, it may offer a means that is supported by multiple psychological factors and that may help to counteract a basic human tendency. In that sense, it promises to be an effective debiasing procedure.

## 7.6 RIGID RADICALIZATION

Kay, Laurin, Fitzsimons, and Landau (2014) note that structure is for doing. In line with what I discussed in this chapter, these authors observe that people prefer, seek out, and even selectively "see" structure in their social and natural environments, creating meaning in people's worlds. Structure-seeking has been observed across a wide range of phenomena—from the detection of patterns in random arrays to affinities for order-providing political, religious, social, and scientific worldviews—and is exacerbated under psychological threat. Kay et al. (2014) note that people are motivated to have structure because it allows them to create meaning in their world and to engage in purposeful, goal-directed behavior. Their findings indeed suggest that perceiving structure can facilitate willingness to take goal-directed actions and can increase willingness to engage in goal pursuit (see also Landau, Kay, & Whitson, 2015).

An interesting implication of this line of reasoning is that rigid thinking about nonsocial stimuli (Section 7.2) and personal beliefs (Section 7.3) may function in the shielding from unwanted information (Section 7.4) and how the epistemic need to understand things may lead radical people to engage in illusory thoughts (Section 7.5) because it may help them to derive meaning and plan their behaviors in (sometimes ostensibly) purposeful ways. In other words, just as social thinking is for doing (Fiske, 1992; James, 1890), I argue that instances of rigid thinking (such as rigid shielding and illusory thoughts) serve the goal of creating meaning in one's world and in one's actions in that world. In other words, *rigid thinking is for rigid doing.*

The current section explores the relationship between thinking and behavior—in particular, between rigid thinking and radical behavior. In doing so, I argue that the thinking strategies of radical people are a function of their radical goals and their radical views on the world and how this world can get a sense of meaning. In the case of radical people, the goals they have are achievable by radical means only, and radical, rigid thinking tends to serve the goal of creating meaning in the world (see also Kruglanski et al., 2014).

The notion that thinking is for doing originated from William James' (1890) famous reflections on the principles of psychology. He reasoned that people perceive their environments, and the objects in that environment, for the sake of the current goals that are on their minds. For example, when you want to write, a piece of paper can be used as a surface for inscription. But when you wish to light a fire at your camping site, and no other materials are there, you tend to perceive the paper as combustible material that you can use to reach your goal: to start a fire. Reflecting on these kinds of issues, James (1890) famously noted that "My thinking is first and last and always for the sake of my doing" (p. 960).

People's thinking strategies depend on their goals and how they want to create meaning in their world. Fiske (1992) argues that in the area of social perception, the notion that thinking is for doing is very important. After all, people create meaning and think about each other in the service of interaction. Their interactions depend on their goals, which in turn depend on the social roles they fulfill and the environment and culture or subculture in which they are functioning. Fiske also notes that people create meaning by abstracting relevant essential structures, which then substitute for the original. The familiarity and simplicity of the abstracted structure make it workable for everyday undertakings. This is related to the function of cognitive structuring that I discussed in this chapter and that is prevalent in people's beliefs about politics and social issues (Tetlock, 1989).

Merely talking about what is unfair and not right in society without taking appropriate action can be seen as unjustified and unjust by radicalizing individuals and extremist groups. For example, the *Rote*

*Armee Fraktion* used to say: *Wir haben gelernt das Reden ohne Handeln unrecht is* ("We have learned that talking without taking action constitutes injustice"). This shows another potential linkage between thoughts, injustice, and radical behavior.

Cognitive structuring and rigid thinking also provide meaning to the world. In the case of extreme radicalization, this can take the form of a quest for personal significance that can constitute a major motivational force that may push individuals toward violent extremism (Kruglanski et al., 2014). As discussed in Chapter 3, the quest for significance is defined as the fundamental desire to matter, to be someone, to have respect (Kruglanski et al., 2009, 2012, 2013). Kruglanski et al. (2014) argue that this searching for significance is the general motivating force that underlies the goals to which political radicals, terrorist foot soldiers, terrorist leaders, and suicide bombers are committed. From that perspective, the various specific motivations mentioned in the terrorism literature are special cases of the significance quest.

I argue that the perception of unfairness may trigger this quest for significance in important ways. After all, an important goal that motivates people can be their fight against perceived injustice. Furthermore, the impression that things will or should be fair can fulfill this quest in important aspects. Indeed, perceptions of fair treatment are related to being valued as a full-fledged person (Lind & Tyler, 1988) who is respected by one's group (Tyler & Huo, 2002). People also derive self-esteem from being treated in fair and just ways (Koper, Van Knippenberg, Bouhuijs, Vermunt, & Wilke, 1993; Vermunt, Van Knippenberg, Van Knippenberg, & Blaauw, 2001).

If fairness perceptions are in fact related to terrorists' quest for significance, this could explain and possibly predict the goal pursuit and meaning-seeking behavior of various extremists in meaningful ways. After all, Kruglanski et al. (2014) note that activation of the significance quest can happen (1) through a loss of significance or humiliation, corresponding to the psychology of unfairness (see Chapter 4); (2) through an anticipated or threatened significance loss, corresponding to the psychological construct of threat management (see Chapter 5); and (3) through an opportunity for significance gain, representing the psychological construct of incentive (including the motivational force of the attainment of fair end states; see Chapter 4).

Rigidity of thoughts is also related to extreme political beliefs, which can predict dogmatic intolerance (Van Prooijen & Krouwel, 2017; see also Arendt, 1951). Dogmatic intolerance can be defined as the tendency to reject, and to consider as inferior, any ideological belief that differs from one's own (Van Prooijen & Krouwel, 2017). Van Prooijen and Krouwel (2017) observed high levels of dogmatic intolerance among both left-wing and right-wing extremists in both the European Union and the United States. These authors also found that stronger political beliefs elicited stronger dogmatic intolerance, which in turn was associated with willingness to protest, denial of free speech, and support for antisocial behavior. This suggests that both left-wing and right-wing extremist views can predict dogmatic intolerance.

Again I note that the evidence for both left-wing and right-wing extremists to adhere to rigid thinking styles and dogmatic intolerance is mixed (see, e.g., Adorno et al., 1950; Kemmelmeier, 1997, 2007; Sidanius, 1984, 1985; Taylor, 1960), although evidence seems to suggest that cognitive closure (Kruglanski & Webster, 1996) and support for authoritarianism (Altemeyer, 1998, 2002; Altemeyer & Hunsberger, 1992) are more prevalent among those on the right than among those on the left (Chirumbolo, 2002; Jost et al., 2003b; Tetlock, 1983). For now I assume that both radical extremists on the left and the right engage in rigid and dogmatic thinking (Van Prooijen & Krouwel, 2017), especially when they are prone to defend their group or the values of their subculture in extreme ways and are prone to processes of groupthink to defend the values of their subculture (Tsintsadze-Maass & Maass, 2014).

Dogmatic thinking is also prevalent among Islam terrorists. Gawthrop (2011) proposes that the dogmatic basis for jihad (often defined as "holy war") and martyrdom attacks in the Sunni Tradition of Islam are the core values and themes in Islam's doctrinal texts, the Quran and the Hadiths. Gawthrop argues that the ultimate goal of Islamic dogmatic views is to dominate other religions and ideologies. Furthermore, he notes that means for achieving that goal includes multiple forms of jihad, namely

Jihad of the Tongue (speech), Jihad of the Pen (writings), and Jihad of Wealth (financial support) to feed and fuel Jihad of the Sword (combat, combat support, and combat service support operations). Gawthrop puts forward that absent a moderating interpretation of the worldview, funding practices, and incitement to jihad, dogmatic interpretations of Sunni Islam will continue to attract new generations of responsive, autonomous, and self-actualizing believers (see also Bakker & Grol, 2017).

Gawthrop's (2011) line of reasoning has been criticized, in part because the role of religion in dogmatic thinking and extremist behavior is not entirely clear. For example, Kossowska, Czernatowicz-Kukuczka, and Sekerdej (2017) suggest that both strong beliefs in God (religious orthodoxy) and dogmatic beliefs that there is no God (dogmatic atheism) can function as cognitive responses to uncertainty. These authors also claim that people who dogmatically do not believe in religion and those who dogmatically believe in religion are equally prone to intolerance and prejudice toward groups that violate their important values. After all, prejudice toward these groups may be an efficient strategy to protect the certainty that strong beliefs provide (see also Koomen & Van der Pligt, 2015). The role of religion is further explored in Chapter 11 and in the next chapter, where I discuss the special role that religion can serve in people's defense of their worldviews. Here I note that rigid and dogmatic thinking seems to have a prominent role in right-wing, left-wing, and Muslim extremism.

In closing I note explicitly that tendencies toward rigid thinking and rigid radicalization are most likely to be influenced by a multiplicity of social-cognitive motives. I also explicate that I am not advocating that extremists are always simple-minded people who do not engage in thorough thinking processes. Certainly not. For example, Sidanius (1984, 1985) argued that left-wing and right-wing extremists show greater sophistication in political thinking than those in the political mainstream. Furthermore, some levels of cognitive rigidity can be beneficial to taking a stand and working for the greater good. For example, in my country Reformed Protestants and communists tended to be good resistance fighters in the Second World War. Their perceptions that the Nazi regime was wrong and hence should be fought clearly worked out for the best. Moreover, Baele (2017) proposed that lone-actor terrorists may have thought deeply about political issues and that lone-actor terrorist violence is triggered by extreme anger recurrently triggered by appraisals shaped by cognitively integrated worldviews. The issue of anger and worldviews brings me to the topics of the next chapter.

# Hot-Cognitive Defense
# of Worldviews

## 8.1 INTRODUCTION

After having explored thought processes that are important in human radicalization, with special emphasis on the importance and function of rigid thoughts, the current chapter examines the role of people's feelings in various instances of radicalization. In particular, the chapter studies people's tendencies to defend their views on how the world should look and what role feelings play in these defensive responses. I propose in this chapter that people's inclinations to defend their worldviews involve to a large extent affective processes such as startled feelings, emotions, and what psychologists call "hot cognition" (Van den Bos, 2007).

Cultural worldviews constitute people's fundamental orientations to their immediate environment, the society in which they live, and the world in which this society has a place. As such, these worldviews are humanly created and transmitted beliefs about the nature of reality shared by groups of individuals (Greenberg, Solomon, & Pyszczynski, 1997). Bolstering of these worldviews feels good, whereas violation or threatening of these worldviews triggers negative affective responses. Basically, people hate it when their worldviews are violated or threatened. As we have seen in Figure 5.1, threats in one's environments tend to instigate startle responses. These responses are associated with uncomfortable or aversive feelings and defensive responses such as extreme reactions as a result of identification with an entitative group that has radical opinions.

Furthermore, perceiving that things are fundamentally unfair involves a threat to the worldview of most people (Van den Bos & Miedema, 2000; Van den Bos, Poortvliet, Maas, Miedema, & Van den Ham, 2005). These perceptions can lead to intense emotions. And when perceptions of unfairness are coupled with externally oriented emotions such as anger, this increases the likelihood of violent and offensive behavioral intentions and actual behaviors associated with radicalization.

Moreover, individual differences in affect intensity can aggravate the effects of how people respond to issues that they think are unfair and unjust (Maas & Van den Bos, 2009; Van den Bos, Maas, Waldring, & Semin, 2003). Thus, how people appraise or perceive a situation in terms of unfairness and injustice is one thing. How they respond to these perceptions is another. And it is the combination of cognitive perceptions and affective responses to these perceptions that I assume impact the radicalization process. Perceiving that things are profoundly unfair, combined with strong affective responses to these unfairness perceptions, increases the chances of radicalization dramatically. The combination of people's thoughts and feelings is labeled "hot cognition" in modern psychological science. This topic is discussed in the next section of this chapter (Section 8.2).

After this, I examine three levels of analysis at which feelings play a role in radicalization. One of these levels comprises individual responses. This includes people's attempts to keep their levels of self-esteem at high levels or, when their levels of self-esteem have been lowered (e.g., because of temporary blows to their self-esteem), to increase their levels of self-esteem again. As such, individual defensive responses involve processes of self-esteem perseverance (Section 8.3).

The levels of analysis on which I focus here also entail group responses, including the buffering role of culture. I delineate that worldview-defense reactions tend to be hot-cognitive reactions, consisting of a combination of how situations are interpreted, assessed, and appraised and the feelings associated with these interpretations, assessments, and appraisals (Section 8.4).

As a third level of analysis I discuss the important roles that ideology (Section 8.5) and religion (Section 8.6) can play in various radicalization processes. Ideological and religious concerns often serve important psychological functions that are of special relevance to radicalizing individuals and radical groups and subcultures.

## 8.2 HOT COGNITION

When psychologists talk about "hot cognition," in essence they refer to cognitive processes that are colored by feelings. In other words, hot cognition involves the combination of people's thoughts and feelings (for more extensive introductions, see, e.g., Abelson, 1963; Kunda, 1999). The concept of hot cognition is important for the current purposes because it seems likely that the combination of cognitive perceptions and affective responses to these perceptions influences the radicalization process. After all, there is evidence that hot cognition plays a pivotal role in the fairness judgment process (Van den Bos, 2007), and the current book and other authors (e.g., Moghaddam, 2005) have developed the case that judgments of unfairness are key to understanding radicalization issues. Thus, a central assumption that I put forward here is that when the perception that things are not right and are fundamentally wrong is associated with a strong affective response, this furthers the radicalization process in important ways. The combination of people's thoughts and feelings therefore deserves our attention.

The notion of hot cognition is also important because rationalist theories of fairness, justice, and morality (for an overview, see Beauchamp, 2001) emphasize that reasoning causes judgments of right and wrong to be constructed primarily by means of cognitive processes (Van den Bos, 2007). These "cold-cognitive" processes pertaining to fairness, justice, and morality judgments involve the careful evaluation and weighing of relevant information before a judgment about what is right and wrong is formed (see, e.g., Kohlberg, 1969; Piaget, 1932; Turiel, 1983). Intuitionist notions, in contrast, suggest that notions of right and wrong are strongly influenced by affective factors, that people's intuitive feelings about what is right or wrong cause judgments of right and wrong, and that reasoning pertaining to what is fair, just, and moral is usually a post-hoc construction, generated after judgments about right and wrong have been formed on the basis of people's gut feelings (see, e.g., Haidt, 2001; Kagan, 1984; Wilson, 1993; see also Beauchamp, 2001; Dershowitz, 2004).

Notwithstanding some notable exceptions (e.g., Folger & Cropanzano, 1998; Lerner & Goldberg, 1999; Sinclair & Mark, 1991, 1992; Tanaka & Takimoto, 1997), and in contrast to moral psychology in which a lot of attention has been paid to rationalist versus intuitionist conceptions of right and wrong (e.g., Haidt, 2001; Kohlberg, 1969), the social psychology of fairness and unfairness judgments often has been remarkably silent about the important issue of whether rationalist (such as cognitive) or intuitionist (such as affective) factors constitute the essence of how these judgments are formed. As a result, scientists have ignored this important issue or have implicitly adopted either rationalist or intuitionist assumptions about the fairness judgment process (Van den Bos, 2007).

For example, perhaps the best illustration of an implicit adoption of (in this case, rationalistic) assumptions is the suggestion in the literature that we should understand the fairness judgment process by focusing on calculations (such as logarithm-based functions that include 16 variables or more) that people are supposed to conduct when assessing what is fair and just (see, e.g., Jasso, 1994, 1999; Sabbagh, Dar, & Resh, 1994). I propose to make rationalist and intuitionist assumptions explicit when studying the justice judgment process (Van den Bos, 2003, 2007) and, in doing so, to focus on the combined influence of thoughts and feelings and how this combination influences processes of radicalization.

This is not the time nor the place to discuss in detail whether either rationalist or intuitionist models are true. In contrast, I note here that in some situations people seem to construct fairness judgments in a thorough way, weighing all relevant information carefully in an impartial manner, whereas in other circumstances people's gut reactions seem to lead to snap judgments. Thus, rather than continuing the ancient and ongoing impasse of believing in either rationalist or intuitionist conceptions (see, e.g., Haidt, 2003b; Pizzaro & Bloom, 2003), I propose here that it makes more sense and that it is scientifically more exciting to adopt an integrative approach, in which appropriate attention is paid to both rationalist and intuitionist aspects of judgments of right and wrong (Van den Bos, 2007).

One example of such an integrative approach is to note that it makes sense to focus on the combined influence of cognitive and affective factors on the psychological process of how judgments about right and wrong are formed and to note that this process should be understood as often being a "hot cognitive" process (Abelson, 1963; Kunda, 1999), that is, a psychological process in which cognitive and affective determinants work together to produce people's judgments of what they think is right or wrong. Thus, in the integrative attempt on the radicalization process that I propose here, I focus on the combined impact of both cognitive and affective variables on the psychological process by which judgments of what is right and wrong are formed (Van den Bos, 2007). In adopting this approach I assume that hot cognition is driving processes of radicalization in important ways, including the impact of unfairness judgments on these processes.

The concept of hot cognition is important for the understanding of the psychology of unfairness judgments, in part because modern psychological science distinguishes between two conceptual systems that people use to process information, namely experiential-intuitive and rationalistic-cognitive systems (Epstein, 1985, 1994; Epstein & Pacini, 1999). The experiential way of processing information is intuitive, preconsciously encodes information into concrete images or metaphors, and makes associative connections. In experiential modes, events are experienced passively, and people can be seized by their emotions. The rationalistic way of processing information, on the other hand, is analytic, encodes information in abstract ways, is based on making logical cause-and-effect connections, and requires intentional and effortful information processes. In rationalistic modes, people experience events consciously and actively while thinking things over and making justifications for what happens (Maas & Van den Bos, 2009).

Research on work on individual differences in affect intensity has shown that people differ consistently in the intensity of their affective responses to the same event (Larsen, Diener, & Cropanzano, 1987; Larsen, Diener, & Emmons, 1986). That is, some people consistently experience mild emotional responses, whereas others experience strong emotional responses when exposed to the same affect-related events. These findings are relevant for the psychology of fairness judgments because it has been shown that people's reactions to similar fair and unfair events may differ owing to individual differences in affect intensity (Van den Bos et al., 2003). Individuals scoring high in affect intensity respond with more negative affective reactions to unfair outcome distributions and unfair treatment procedures than those low in affect intensity. These results suggest that individual differences in how individuals respond in affective terms to fairness-related issues play a profound role in explaining people's fairness reactions. In other words, fairness reactions are moderated in important ways by affective processes (Van den Bos et al., 2003).

Maas and Van den Bos (2009) combined the literatures on experiential-intuitive and rationalistic-cognitive systems and individual differences in affect intensity by studying the impact of these individual differences under conditions in which people had been brought into either experiential mindsets in which they react on the basis of their gut feelings or rationalistic mindsets in which they respond in more deliberate and controlled ways. Based on cognitive-experiential self-theory (see, e.g., Epstein & Pacini, 1999), we assumed that the operation of experiential mindsets is intimately associated with affect-related experiences. Supporting this assumption were findings that showed that when participants had been brought into experiential mindsets, individual differences in affect intensity moderated their reactions to fair and unfair events. Furthermore, rationalistic mindsets rely more on cold-cognitive information processing (e.g., Epstein & Pacini, 1999; Van den Bos, 2007), and hence we expected and found that when participants had been brought into rationalistic mindsets, individual differences in affect intensity did not influence their reactions to fair and unfair events. These findings suggest that processes of hot cognition are especially important when people have adopted experiential mindsets, that is, when they process information in intuitive, preconscious, and associative ways (Epstein & Pacini, 1999).

The notion of hot cognition is related to the concept of motivated cognition as studied in the work by Jost et al. (2003a; see also Kruglanski, 1989; Kruglanski et al., 2014). These authors note that in studying the psychological basis of political ideology, it is important to link the contents of specific political attitudes to social and cognitive motives that humans affiliating with these attitudes have. For example, Jost et al. argue that specific motives relating to the management of fear and uncertainty are associated with the ideology of political conservatism. Analyzing political behavior in terms of motivated social cognition helps to integrate seemingly unrelated hypotheses derived from different literatures and to expand on these literatures to further understand the psychology of political attitudes and behavior.

Processes of hot cognition are also associated with the human alarm system, as discussed briefly in Chapters 4 and 5 (see also Figure 4.1). After all, feelings serve as important signals that something might not be good—that something in the environment is possibly wrong and needs attention. This alarm-signaling function of feelings plays an important role in human behavior (Eisenberger et al., 2003; Van den Bos et al., 2008). This also explains why startled feelings are important for people and can make people respond in defensive ways to potentially threatening stimuli (Petrescu et al., 2018).

Eisenberger and Lieberman (2004; Lieberman & Eisenberger, 2004) proposed that the human alarm system is responsible for detecting cues that might be harmful to survival and, after activation, for recruiting attention and coping responses to minimize threat. For example, Eisenberger et al. (2003) have argued that experiencing social exclusion or other self-threatening events may be an experience of social pain. Like physical pain, the experience of social pain may trigger the human alarm system. The working of such an alarm system is assumed to be adaptive in that an activated alarm system would prompt people to act and respond more alertly toward what is going on in their environments (Van den Bos et al., 2008).

Van den Bos et al. (2008) studied the implications of an alarm-system perspective for the psychology of fairness judgments. Building on the literature on the human alarm system, we argued that the process by which fairness judgments are formed may be influenced reliably by the activation of psychological systems that people use to detect and handle alarming situations. Supporting this line of reasoning, we showed that presenting alarm-related stimuli, such as exclamation points and flashing lights, when people are forming fairness judgments leads to more extreme judgments about fair and unfair events than not presenting these alarming stimuli.

Processes of hot and motivated cognition and the working of the human alarm system are probably related to suggestions that information that is easy to process feels good (Winkielman, Schwarz, Fazendeiro, & Reber, 2003; Zajonc, 1998) and right (Camacho, Higgins, & Luger, 2003). In other words, fluency of cognitive processes is related not only to aesthetic pleasure (Reber, Schwarz, & Winkielman, 2004) but also to judgments about right and wrong (Higgins, 2000). When everything is hunky-dory in your environment and information about the environment is easy to process, there is no need to activate the human alarm system.

In contrast, when social information is difficult to processes, cognitive fluency is disrupted. This does not feel right and may signal that something is wrong that needs your attention and may need to be corrected, possibly in radical ways or by extreme means. This brings me to people's tendencies to defend their own levels of self-esteem and their attempts to defend their views on how the world should look. These issues are examined in the next sections of this chapter, in which I assume that many worldview-defense responses are hot-cognitive reactions: combinations of human thoughts and humans' feelings about these thoughts as a result of how they interpret, assess, and appraise social situations.

## 8.3 INDIVIDUAL DEFENSIVE RESPONSES
##     AND SELF-ESTEEM PERSEVERANCE

Hot-cognitive responses are often triggered when individuals' conceptions of self-esteem are threatened. Self-esteem pertains to how positively or negatively you evaluate yourself. More formally, self-esteem is defined as an attitude toward a particular object, namely the self (Rosenberg, 1965). Attitudes are evaluative beliefs that people have about certain objects in their social environments. Thus, attitudes are combinations of beliefs and evaluations of those beliefs. This implies that self-esteem consists of beliefs about yourself and how positively or negatively you evaluate those beliefs. Beliefs are cognitions about the world, for example, subjective probabilities that an object has a particular attribute (Fishbein & Ajzen, 1975). People's beliefs about attitude objects can be patently false. This also applies to their attitudes about themselves—their self-esteem.

Individuals' self-esteem consists of components that are stable across situations and components that vary across situations. For example, Rosenberg (1965) developed a global measure of stable or trait levels of self-esteem. This measure includes items such as "On the whole, I am satisfied with myself" and "At times I think I am no good at all" (reverse-coded). Heatherton and Policy (1991) noted that self-esteem is open to momentary changes. These authors therefore developed a measure of state levels of self-esteem. This measure assesses individuals' levels of performance-state self-esteem with items such as "I feel competent about my abilities." The measure also solicits social state self-esteem with items such as "I am worried about whether I am regarded as a success or a failure" (reverse-coded). And the measure taps levels of appearance-state self-esteem with items such as "I feel satisfied with the way my body looks right now."

Both trait and state aspects of self-esteem matter. Thus, self-esteem is most likely to vary within certain boundaries. As such, James (1890) described self-esteem as similar to a barometer that rises and falls as a function of one's aspirations and success experiences. He also noted that there is a certain average tone to the self-feelings people maintain that is largely independent of objective feedback that might contradict the self-concept. Thus, although momentary self-evaluations may be context dependent, people derive their overall sense of self-esteem by averaging feelings about themselves across a number of different social situations (Heatherton & Polivy, 1991).

Most people try to view themselves favorably, hence striving for high levels of self-esteem or at least keeping their self-esteem from dropping below a certain level. This self-esteem motive may be particularly prevalent in Western cultures (Heine, Lehman, Markus, & Kitayama, 1999; but see Sedikides, Gaertner, & Toguchi, 2003; Sedikides & Gregg, 2008), and high levels of self-esteem are not always a good thing (Baumeister, 1998). Nonetheless, most people seem to be motivated to maintain high levels of self-esteem. How people engage in these processes of self-esteem perseverance has been studied by different social psychological theories, including terror management theory (e.g., Pyszczynski, Greenberg, Solomon, Arndt, & Schimel, 2004a).

My own work on defensive processes has been inspired by terror management theory. My research findings support the theory (e.g., Van den Bos & Miedema, 2000) and qualify the theory in important ways (Van den Bos, Poortvliet, Maas, Miedema, & Van den Ham, 2005). And my conceptual work attempts to further the theory (Van den Bos, 2004), identifies what I think are problems with the theory (L. Martin & Van den Bos, 2014), and suggests solutions for these problems (Van den Bos, McGregor, & Martin, 2015). With this caveats in mind, I do think that the approach of terror management theory to the psychological function of self-esteem

(Pyszczynski et al., 2004a) and how this plays a role in processes of radicalization (Pyszczynski, Solomon, & Greenberg, 2003) is important and deserves our attention.

What I find interesting about terror management's approach to individuals' self-esteem is the notion that people are keenly motivated to maintain high levels of self-esteem and that people are generally motivated to defend their self-esteem when it comes under threat. In answering the question of why people need high levels of self-esteem, terror management theory notes that self-esteem functions to shelter people from anxieties and fears. As such, self-esteem functions as a protective shield designed to control the potential for feelings of anxiety and terror. When self-esteem is strong, this serves as a buffer and allows people to go about their daily affairs and act effectively in the world. When self-esteem is weak or challenged, this instigates various forms of defensive behavior aimed at bolstering self-worth through compensatory efforts (Pyszczynski et al., 2004a).

Building on these propositions, terror management theory argues that self-esteem is ultimately a culturally based construction that consists of viewing oneself as living up to specific contingencies of value that in essence are grounded in a unique individualized worldview by each person. Feelings of anxiety and terror are thus controlled by immersion in a shared conception of reality that imbues life with meaning, certainty, order, and permanence. Self-esteem is important for people because it indicates the belief that one is living up to those standards of value (Pyszczynski, 2008; Pyszczynski et al., 2004a).

Although terror management theory defines self-esteem as resulting from one's own assessment of the extent to which one is living up to internalized cultural standards of value, other people play an important role in the process of maintaining self-esteem. As such, self-esteem is maintained through a process of consensual validation. When others agree with one's conception of reality and evaluation of self, it implies that these conceptions may well be correct and based in external reality. When others disagree with these conceptions, it threatens to undermine this faith and confidence. Thus, from the perspective of terror management theory, self-esteem is a culturally derived construction that is dependent on sources of social validation, is essentially defensive in nature, and functions to provide a buffer against core human fears (Pyszczynski et al., 2004a).

Terror management theory focuses on one important type of anxiety, namely, the fear of death. That is, the theory assumes that humans are aware that death is inevitable yet suppress this potential for paralyzing terror. This fear is assumed to be rooted in an instinct for self-preservation (see, e.g., Greenberg, Solomon, & Pyszczynski, 1997; Solomon, Greenberg, & Pyszczynski, 1991). My own work, although not focusing on self-esteem directly, suggests that feelings about personal uncertainty or insecurity may be underlying at least some terror management findings, especially effects of reminders of mortality on people's defensive reactions (see Van den Bos et al., 2005; Yavuz & Van den Bos, 2009; see also McGregor, Prentice, & Nash, 2009). Furthermore, I note that Leary and Baumeister (2000) criticized terror management theory's analysis of the function of self-esteem (see also Crocker & Nuer, 2004; Leary, 2004; and see Pyszczynski, Greenberg, Solomon, Arndt, & Schimel, 2004b).

Here I note that terror management theory's hypothesis that self-esteem may help to buffer against human anxieties is interesting, and for now I assume that the hypothesis helps to understand processes of radicalization. That is, the pursuit of self-esteem can be quite a normal and often desirable process. However, the process can also lead to clear negative consequences and undesirable behavior, including radical behavior. For example, Kruglanski and colleagues (2013) note how people's quest for significance, which can be related to the psychological function of self-esteem perseverance as discussed here, can result in sympathy for terrorism and associated violent behavior. These significance quests can influence violent extremism (Kruglanski et al., 2014) and can motivate the behavior of suicide bombers (Kruglanski, Chen, Dechesne, Fishman, & Orehek, 2009).

Furthermore, under self-threatening conditions people are more prone to be susceptible to feelings of superiority (e.g., Iyer, Jetten, & Haslam, 2012), including feelings of moral superiority (Peters, Van den Bos, &

Bobocel, 2004; Täuber & Van Zomeren, 2012). As noted in Chapter 4 (see also Figure 4.3), the feeling that one's own group is morally superior has been shown to be associated with radical right-wing attitudes and behaviors (Doosje, Van den Bos, Loseman, Feddes, & Mann, 2012).

Thus, it seems likely that the striving of individuals for high self-esteem can lead to defensive and sometimes extreme responses. This effect can be especially strong among those who on the outside seem to have high levels of self-esteem but in reality have much more fragile self-esteem and may in fact not have very high self-esteem when measured in an unobtrusive or implicit way. Self-esteem that is fragile or implicitly low is known to be associated with black-and-white thinking (Jordan, Spencer, & Zanna, 2005), feelings of insecurity (Kernis & Lakey, 2009), defensive extremism (McGregor & Jordan, 2007), and other defensive responses (Rudman, Dohn, & Fairchild, 2007). The next section examines how these responses hang together with people's identification with groups and the role that culture plays in processes of psychological defense and radicalization.

## 8.4 GROUP RESPONSES AND THE BUFFERING ROLE OF CULTURE

In addition to individuals responding to personally threatening information, people are also part of groups, collectives, and cultures. These social entities color people's hot-cognitive defensive reactions. For example, identification with social groups is more likely when people are uncertain about themselves (Hogg, 2004, 2009), and identification with extreme groups can be especially attractive under conditions of personal uncertainty (Hogg, 2005, 2011, 2014).

People may also go to great lengths to defend their groups and what these groups stand for. This is in part because people interpret their immediate environments and the society they live in by means of cultural worldviews. These cultural worldviews are humanly created and transmitted beliefs about the nature of reality shared by groups of individuals (Greenberg, Solomon, & Pyszczynski, 1997). Cultural worldviews help to buffer against threatening information. Worldviews also play a role in the extreme and hot-cognitive reactions that people can show to defend or bolster their worldviews. As such they deserve our attention.

What I find interesting about the notion of cultural worldviews is that they can help to assuage the anxiety engendered by human vulnerabilities and uncertainties. Cultural worldviews are assumed to ameliorate anxiety by imbuing the universe with order and meaning, by providing standards of value that are derived from that meaningful conception of reality, and by promising psychological protection to those who meet those standards of value. As such, cultural worldviews provide concepts and structures to organize human perceptions and to answer basic existential and sense-making questions in ways that suggest that the universe is stable, orderly, and meaningful (Greenberg et al., 1997).

Cultural worldviews function to protect people from feelings of anxiety, uncertainty, and existential concerns. People are therefore strongly motivated to have faith in their cultural worldview and to defend their worldview against threats. Faith in cultural worldviews is maintained through secular and religious teachings, associated cultural rituals, continual social validation in interpersonal and intergroup contexts, and defensive reactions to those with alternative worldviews (Greenberg et al., 1997). This can be seen in prejudiced and intolerant reactions, as we have noticed in the previous chapter.

According to terror management theory, culture and self-esteem can serve their anxiety-buffering functions only to the extent that faith in the cultural worldview is sustained. Faith in the cultural worldview depends on consensual validation from others. Therefore, individuals or groups who question the worldview or advocate a different worldview threaten our faith in our worldview. Because of the protection from anxiety that cultural worldviews can provide, we respond to threats to the worldview in rigid ways and with strong feelings (Pyszczynski, 2008). As such, cultural worldviews entail a shared conception of reality coupled with hot-cognitive reactions when these conceptions are threatened. Terror management theory thus posits that prejudice and rigid reactions occur because one's cultural worldview, which is so critical as a basis of security, is actually a fragile symbolic social construction (Greenberg et al., 1997).

This analysis suggests that the mere existence of alternative conceptions of reality will be psychologically unsettling because granting their validity either implicitly or explicitly undermines absolute faith in one's own worldview. People respond to the threat engendered by the existence of different others in a number of ways. According to terror management theory, the most common response is to derogate either the alternative worldview or the people who hold that view. By dismissing other worldviews as inaccurate, or the people who hold such views as ignorant savages who would share our perspectives if they were sufficiently intelligent or properly educated, the threat to one's own point of view is minimized. Confidence in one's worldview also can be restored by annihilating those who do not share that view, thus proving the superiority of the victor and his or her worldview (Greenberg et al., 1997).

An important example of people's worldviews is the belief in a just world. This worldview entails that the world is a just place where good things happen to good people and bad things happen only or primarily to bad people (Lerner, 1980). The belief in a just world is developed during socialization as a child in which children learn from their parents and teachers that good deeds in their culture will be associated with good outcomes. After all, the need to believe in a just world develops when children begin to understand the benefits of foregoing their immediate gratifications for more desirable, long-term outcomes (Hafer, 2000b; Lerner, 1980).

Specifically, strong defenses of just world beliefs typically take place when people are dealing with issues of personal uncertainty in delayed-return contexts or cultures (Bal & Van den Bos, 2012), including cultures that score high on the Protestant work ethic (Christopher, Zabel, Jones, & Marek, 2008). After all, a focus on the future enhances intolerance of personal uncertainty. People often have to invest time, money, and energy now in order to obtain a reward later. And delayed rewards are often uncertain, which can lead to feelings of personal uncertainty or self-doubt (Van den Bos, 2009a). Therefore, a strong future orientation can make people more intolerant of these feelings of personal uncertainty, which can lead them to be in higher need of information that bolsters their worldview (such as the view that the world is a just place) and respond in more negative terms to information that threatens the worldview (such as individuals who violate the worldview; Van den Bos & Bal, 2016; Van den Bos et al., 2015).

Similar to important psychological functions of groups and group identification processes (Kruglanski, Pierro, Mannetti, & De Grada, 2006), believing in a just world gives meaning to one's world and a sense of direction (Van den Bos & Bal, 2016). Because worldviews are shared conceptions of reality (Greenberg et al., 1997; Pyszczynski, 2008), sharing the idea with others that something is really wrong can be very upsetting and can be a cause of protest behaviors (Folger, Rosenfield, Grove, & Corkran, 1979). When repeated engaging in social protest does not lead to successful addressing of the unfairness and injustice perceived, this can cause a sense of frustration (Folger, 1977), which can yield extremist behaviors (IVA, 2010).

In these processes of hot-cognitive and radical worldview defense, issues such as group identification, patriotism, and nationalism are very important (McCauley & Moskalenko, 2008). Radicalization may lead to feelings of group superiority. When these feelings that we are part of a special group are coupled with the perception that our group has been unfairly treated and betrayed in an unjust manner, this can lead us to distrust that others will help our group. This can yield the impression that the situation is dire and that our group and our cause are vulnerable and in danger of extinction (McCauley & Moskalenko, 2008).

This explains why activists are likely to feel more sadness and humiliation with group failures, more joy and pride with group success, and more anger and other negative emotions when confronted with enemies of their cause. These feelings are the expression of group identification. We care about what happens to our group, and especially about how other groups are treating or viewing our group. This group can be small, consisting of people that we know on a personal basis, and can be large, containing people whom we do not know personally but whom we identify with nevertheless. Indeed, the human capacity to care about large collectivities as if they were an extended family is an important foundation of mass politics and a key antecedent of national, ethnic, and religious group conflict (McCauley & Moskalenko, 2008).

The issues of ideology and religion are the subjects of the next sections. Here I note that growing radicalization may be viewed as a pyramid. Because terrorists are few in relation to all those who share their beliefs and feelings, the terrorists may be thought of as the apex of the pyramid. The base of the pyramid is composed of all who sympathize with the goals the terrorists say they are fighting for. From base to apex, higher levels of the pyramid are associated with decreased numbers but increased radicalization of beliefs, feelings, and behaviors. Radicalization and terrorism are made possible by bringing individuals into small groups. Sometimes these groups are linked into a larger organization, but not always. The small group is necessary for action, but the organization is not necessary for this. After all, terrorist cells or self-organizing small groups can engage in terrorist attacks (McCauley & Moskalenko, 2008).

## 8.5 IDEOLOGY

A recurring theme throughout this book is the notion that ideology and religion can impact the radicalization process. To this effect, I am paying repeated attention to radicalization of those on the extreme left and the extreme right of the political spectrum as well as to processes of Muslim radicalization. What I would like to do in the current section is examine how ideology (such as left-wing and right-wing ideologies) can color radical views and people's tendencies to defend those views with zeal and passion. In the next section, I examine religion as a potential moderator of radical views and the hot-cognitive defense of those views.

Ideologies can be characterized as integrated and coherent systems of beliefs, attitudes, and values, which are internally consistent and serve to explain one's world, and one's place and experiences within it. Ideologies are widely shared within groups and differ from group to group, and thus they have a powerful identity-defining function. Because ideologies are tied to group identity, they often serve to explain how your own group is treated by another group (Hogg, 2005).

Ideologies are typically relatively simplistic and consensual worldviews that circumscribe thought to answer problematic issues such as why your own group is exploited by another group. Ideologies are therefore associated with beliefs of how strong or weak groups are compared with other groups, and these intergroup power beliefs can legitimize and justify oppression or social change. Because ideologies provide sensible answers to questions of perceived intergroup mistreatment and exploitation, they can help to reduce group-related uncertainties. The more ideological a group membership-based belief system is, the better the job it does at reducing various feelings of uncertainty, particularly uncertainty about oneself in society (Hogg, 2005).

There are numerous examples of appalling human atrocities that are and have been fueled or justified by ideologies. Indeed, many genocides, pogroms, persecutions, and wars are inspired and exacerbated by ideological views (Hogg, 2005). Reflecting on these observations, Frits Bolkestein, a well-known politician from my country with a somewhat conservative-skeptical view on humankind, used to say that "De trein naar Utopia stopt bij de Goelag," which translates into something like "The train to Utopian places stops at the Gulag." This expression conveys the idea that many political ideals, and especially radical and extreme political beliefs, tend to end up with an ideology. Strict adherence to the ideology can easily be viewed by followers of the ideology as being more important than the humane treatment of those who hold other political views.[1]

Ideology serves a vital function for human beings. According to Hogg (2005), this function has to do with the reduction of uncertainty that results from identifying with groups that are associated with ideologies. In Hogg's view, high-entitativity groups have clear boundaries, internal homogeneity, clear internal structure, and common fate. Personal uncertainty motivates identification with groups that are distinct, clearly structured, and internally homogeneous and that have a common fate (Hogg, 2005).

---

1. Interview in *De Volkskrant* on October 29, 2013.

Furthermore, under conditions of pronounced or chronic personal uncertainty, extreme group-identification effects are possible. Hogg (2005)
notes that these extreme effects include: (1) strong and uncompromising
identification and loyalty; (2) a simple, highly focused, and internally
coherent belief system that prescribes normative group behaviors and
provides a cogent ideology to explain and justify group behavior; (3) intolerance of normative disagreement, dissent, and deviance within the
group; (4) a single uncomplicated version of the "truth"; (5) an " 'us-
versus-them" mentality that is highly ethnocentric and views out-groups
as fundamentally wrong, perhaps evil and immoral; and (6) a hierarchical
internal structure that vests authority and power in leaders who are completely trusted to determine the group's destiny and what the group and
its identity stand for.

Extreme or totalist groups (such as extremist political groups, fundamentalist religious groups, and terrorist cells; Baron, Crawley, & Paulina,
2003) have the potential to fulfill many of these extreme effects. Importantly,
these groups all tend to have a powerful ideology that conveys a version of
reality that explains and justifies many, if not all, things without confusing
the mind with subtlety and contradiction (Hogg, 2005; see also Peterson
& Flanders, 2002). Conceptual analyses of terrorist groups indeed suggest
that uncertainty, group identification, and entitativity of groups play an
important role in the formation and maintenance of orthodox totalist
groups with strong ideologies (Hoffer, 1951; Hogg, 2005; Marsella, 2004;
Moghaddam, 2004).

This is in part because such groups have high entitativity and possess
consensual prototypes that clearly define who people are and tightly regulate their thoughts, feelings, and actions. In this way these groups can
help to reduce feelings of subjective personal uncertainty (which may or
may not reflect reality). And the ideology associated with the groups can
help in processes of uncertainty-reduction because ideology is internally
consistent and coherent and serves a key explanatory and justificatory
function that renders the world meaningful (Hogg, 2005).

Relevant in this respect are Hogg's (2005) observations that in the 1920s
and 1930s in Germany, the entire spectrum of radical and conservative

ideologies emerged as a reaction to overwhelming uncertainty and fear of uncertainty. The United States in the 1960s is another example where in the face of societal uncertainty, radical ideologies of social change confronted conservative ideologies of the right. Furthermore, in the late 1970s in Iran, political uncertainty generated revolutionary ideologies and Islamic fundamentalism (Hogg, 2005).

Various social psychological phenomena are related to ideology and discuss its psychological function. For example, right-wing authoritarianism is likely to develop under conditions of uncertainty, and the belief in a just world and the Protestant work ethic are belief systems that tend to function as ideologies (Dittmar & Dickinson, 1993; Furnham & Rajamanickam, 1992; Hogg, 2005). In addition, group-based hierarchies in society are maintained ideologically by legitimizing myths that provide moral or intellectual support for group-based inequality (Sidanius, Levin, Federico, & Pratto, 2001). Furthermore, "people justify and rationalize the way things are, so that existing social arrangements are perceived as fair and legitimate, perhaps even natural and inevitable" (Jost & Hunyady, 2002, p. 119).

The key factor in understanding system-justifying and system-challenging behaviors is that that the belief system is ideological (Feldstein, 2009; Ferracuti, 1990) and is grounded in a distinctive identity that people can use to manage their uncertainties, to define themselves, and to regulate their thoughts, feelings, and behaviors (Hogg, 2005). Indeed, some have argued that there is a postmodern paradox that makes the certainties and absolutes offered by extreme ideologies particularly attractive in a postmodern world of moral and behavioral relativities (e.g., Dunn, 1998; Hogg, 2005). Religion and religious groups play a special role in these kinds of processes, and this is the subject of the next section.

## 8.6 RELIGION

Religion obviously is a strong driver of radicalization processes, especially when strong religious affiliation is combined with high levels of personal uncertainty and insufficient correction of self-centered impulses. Thus, not per se in isolation (see Aly & Striegher, 2012), but when combined with the moderators identified in this book and other relevant variables, religious beliefs are known to have impacted various instances of radicalization. This is because religious beliefs are strongly felt by believers (Durkheim, 1912; James, 1902). Furthermore, religious affiliation includes affiliation with groups and organizations associated with the religion. Moreover, religious people are often strongly motivated to defend their worldview (Hogg, Adelman, & Blagg, 2010).

The psychologist William James (1902) defined religion as the feelings, acts, and experiences of individuals in relation to what these individuals consider to be divine. James circumscribed "divine" to include godlike objects, whether a concrete deity or not, to which the individual responds with solemnity and gravity.

Related to this, the sociologist Émile Durkheim (1912) described religion as a unified system of beliefs and practices with regard to sacred things. By sacred things he referred to things that are set apart. These can be beliefs and practices of a moral community called a Church. However, sacred things are not limited to gods or spirits but can also refer to a mountain, a tree, a spring, a pebble, a piece of wood, and so on. According to Durkheim, religious beliefs are the representations that express the nature of these sacred things.

I treat religion as an ideology (see Hogg, 2005) and note that most religions focus on establishing believers with a worldview that somehow makes sense of what happens after we die and of other things that are not in the materialistic world, whereas most ideologies focus on providing a worldview about the materialistic world. I find it important to note that, personally, I am not a believer and do not adhere to any religion (Van den Bos, 2011). Against this background, I note that as a social scientist and law professor I agree with Juergensmeyer (2003), who stated that religion can give spirit to public life and can contribute to moral and prosocial behaviors but at the same time "needs the temper of rationality and fair play that Enlightenment values give to civil society" (p. 249).

Furthermore, as an academic psychologist I see that religions serve many important psychological functions for believers. Some of these functions are clearly good. And some are definitely bad. For example, believing can lead people to lead better and more healthy lives (see, e.g., Allport, 1959; Batson & Stocks, 2004; Baumeister, 2002), but religion has also been associated with atrocious behaviors, including militant and violent behaviors against those not believing in the same religion (see, e.g., Juergensmeyer, 2003; Stern, 2004).

Interestingly, the social psychologist Michael Hogg relates religion and religious extremity explicitly to group membership and group identification. According to Hogg et al. (2010), religions are social groups that provide ideological and behavioral guidelines for people's spiritual and existential curiosity as well as for their daily endeavors. Hogg and colleagues distinguish between spirituality and religion, whereby spirituality is a personal pursuit of existential understanding and an approach to the divine and sacred that typically revolves around self-transcendence, and religion is a group phenomenon involving group norms that specify beliefs, attitudes, values, and behaviors relating to both sacred and secular aspects of life, which are integrated and imbued with meaning by an ideological framework and worldview.

These aspects of religions make them well equipped to provide consensual validation of one's religious identity and associated worldview. For example, distinctive dress, religious ritual, Church-related activities, and collective prayer routines all provide structure that pervades life and validates social identity. Thus, although individuals can search for their own spiritual path, identification with religious groups reduces uncertainty as described earlier in this book. In other words, religions can be highly entitative (Hogg et al., 2010).

Thus, according to Hogg et al. (2010), a religion often constitutes a group, and religious people are typically those who identify with the group and adhere to its normative beliefs and practices. These aspects are assumed to be similar to many other ideologies, but religious groups differ from other types of groups and other ideologies in an important way, namely that they are related to the sacred (Durkheim, 1912) and the divine (James,

1902) to render existence meaningful and to provide prescriptive moral guidance for behavioral choices, sacred rituals and quests, and daily life (Hogg et al., 2010). In part because curiosity about the nature of existence and the afterlife is a pervasive feature of the human condition, religions endure (Hogg et al., 2010; see also Armstrong, 1993, 2000; Becker, 1973; Hinde, 1999).

Like all groups, religions vary in how they are structured and organized. Some religions are flexible, open, and loosely structured. Other religions are tightly organized with well-established and distinctive authority structures, powerful normative prescriptions about beliefs, attitudes, and behaviors, and rigorous and far-reaching explanatory ideologies (Hogg et al., 2010). Hogg and colleagues also note that people vary in how strongly they identify with a religion and how central the religion is to their sense of self.

Interestingly, organized religions provide a practical moral code and set of principles for daily living that are widely shared across major religions and encourage people to live in harmony and to treat others with tolerance, understanding, kindness, and compassion (Hogg et al., 2010). However, religions can also be intolerant and cruel, with some adherents who claim to be religious committing atrocities in the name of their religion (Juergensmeyer, 2003).

Religious ideologies are assumed to be very effective at reducing uncertainty and giving people a clear identity. Although religious worldviews may feel personal, they typically are shared belief systems grounded in consensus circumscribed by group membership. It is this group consensus that lends a religious ideology its comforting sense of infallibility and absolute correctness. Furthermore, religious ideologies have a greater explanatory reach than most other ideologies because they address questions of existence, ultimate causality, and absolute morality (Hogg et al., 2010).

Religions not only provide well-developed and elaborated ideologies and worldviews but also specify normative practices regarding everyday life choices and behavioral routines. For instance, most religions subscribe to the just world hypothesis, suggesting that good things happen to good people (the just should be rewarded) and bad things to bad people ("sinners" should be punished; Furnham, 2003). Most religions also pre-scribe virtuous human behaviors such as altruism and generosity (Batson, Schoenrade, & Ventis, 1993).

Overall, religions function as powerful, all-encompassing ideolog-ical systems that impart meaning and purpose to existence and daily life and prescribe identity-defining normative practices relating to moral choices, sacred observances, and daily living. They are meaning-making frameworks and moral compasses that serve basic psychological needs ranging from existential meaning to social identification and connection and a sense of certainty and stability. This is precisely what can make a re-ligion an entitative group with enormous power to reduce self-uncertainty (Hogg et al., 2010). Not surprisingly, research shows that religious iden-tification and adherence to a religious ideology help believers deal with stress, anxiety, and trauma (Hogg et al., 2010; see also Inzlicht, McGregor, Hirsh, & Nash, 2009; Laurin, Kay, & Moscovitch, 2008; Van den Bos, Van Ameijde, & Van Gorp, 2006).

Scholars have noted that when religious ideologies and moral princi-ples are grounded in highly structured and distinctive religious groups, they can gain extraordinary power and significance and can assume the status of unassailable and undeniable truths that are rigidly prescriptive and unchanging (e.g., Durkheim, 1912). Religion can facilitate and even encourage a stark dichotomy between right and wrong that religious believers use as a framework for understanding themselves, others, and the world they live in and as a basis for rewarding the righteous and pun-ishing the immoral (Hogg et al., 2010).

Religions, like other groups, vary in how extremist their struc-ture, ideology, and normative beliefs and practices can be considered. Although most religions and most religious people are not extremists, religious extremism has always been with us and has caused great human suffering (Hogg et al., 2010; see also Dawkins, 2006; Juergensmeyer, 2003). Strong religious identification and the belief that the in-group's worldview and associated practices are entirely superior and more absolutely moral than those of out-groups generate profound ethno-centrism associated with in-group protective and promotive intergroup behaviors. These behaviors can become extreme, resulting in intol-erant and violent actions, and can conflict with other, more tolerant ideology tenets (Hogg et al., 2010). In fact, there is a substantial lit-erature that associates societal uncertainty with religious extremism (e.g., Altemeyer, 2003; Batson et al., 1993; McGregor, Haji, Nash, & Teper, 2008). For example, Lewis (2004) argues that in times of strains, faltering ideologies, and other uncertain conditions, Islamic funda-mentalism is especially appealing.

Herriot (2007) defined fundamentalism as an attempt to prevent re-ligious identity from falling victim to modernity and secularism. This author argues that modernity creates uncertainty and that this is a nec-essary condition for religious fundamentalism and for fundamentalist groups to flourish. Interestingly, fundamentalist groups do not fight uncertainty directly, but rather react strongly to those aspects of sec-ular societies that challenge their beliefs, values, and norms of behavior. In other words, under conditions of uncertainty, fundamentalist reli-gious groups engage in strong and hot-cognitive processes of world-view defense.

The notion that modernity triggers uncertainty, which in turn fuels religious fundamentalism, has also been noted by Dunn (1998), who argues that rigid ideological systems are particularly attractive in a post-modern world of moral and behavioral relativities and limitless choice. Furthermore, Kimball (2002) notes that it is in reaction to modernity that members of religions can go to extremes and become prone to orthodoxy, intolerance, and/or violence in attempts to protect their religious identity and associated values and practices.

Taken together, we have seen various instances in this chapter in which hot-cognitive reactions to worldview-threatening events can encourage people to engage in extremist responses and rigid radicalization. These issues are related to people's radical attitudes, consisting of a combination of cognitive beliefs and evaluations of those beliefs. As shown in Figure 4.3, radical attitudes include illusory feelings of superiority, "us-versus-them" responses, and other combinations of what radical people believe and how they evaluate those beliefs. The extent to which these radical attitudes can lead to robust behavioral reactions, including behaviors of radicals who reject the law and democratic principles, and including radical actions that are clearly violent is the subject of the next chapter.

# Violent Rejection of Law and Democratic Principles

## 9.1 INTRODUCTION

After having examined people's radical and rigid thoughts (Chapter 7) and the hot-cognitive defense of their (sometimes radical) views of the world (Chapter 8), in the current chapter I concentrate on the issue of when radical thoughts and associated feelings shift to radical and extremist behaviors. A crucial step in any attempt to understand processes of radicalization is to determine when people will move from thoughts and feelings to behavioral action. And in delineating this topic, a pivotal issue is when people will move from legal and nonviolent behaviors to illegal and violent actions to achieve their desired outcomes that reflect their beliefs and feelings and what they see as the right cause.

This is a crucial issue, in part because it distinguishes radicalization that stays within the law from radicalization that basically views the law as irrelevant or an obstacle to obtaining what is desired. The current chapter discusses these different forms of radicalization. Furthermore, when one understands the psychology of when people are likely to shift toward violent extremism, it also becomes possible to start working on the prevention of violent and illegal radicalization that has many negative aspects for open and democratic societies and for humankind at large. In short, just as the issue of deradicalization needs exploring, the topic of the shift to illegal and violent extremism deserves our attention as does the possible prevention of that shift.

As it turns out, how people move from thoughts and feelings to behavioral action is not an easy issue. The literature on human attitudes teaches us that people's beliefs and their evaluations of those beliefs influence people's intentions to behave in a certain way. Under the right conditions these behavioral intentions can spur people to indeed act in a certain way (see, e.g., Ajzen & Fishbein, 1980; Fishbein & Ajzen, 1975). But the psychological process of how people shift from thoughts and feelings to behavioral intentions and actual behaviors is not easy to get a grip on. And in the case of radical thoughts, radical feelings, radical behavioral intentions, and radical behaviors, this may well be even more difficult (Section 9.2).

This chapter aims to delineate the ontogenesis of radical behavior by arguing that the active rejection of democratic principles is an important phase in various radicalization processes. I argue that rejecting principles of open and democratic societies usually takes place via processes of delegitimization. Thus, when people put their own right before the right of others in open societies, this may well serve as a red flag for those interested in trying to prevent the onset of violent and illegal extremism (Section 9.3).

I further propose that delegitimization is also responsible for the rejection of the rule of law and constitutional states. There obviously can be a gap between what people think is fair and legitimate and what society considers as legal. Furthermore, nonviolent engagement in forms of civil disobedience in which people act in nonviolent ways to convey in an open way their conscientious thoughts and feelings should be distinguished from violent breaking of the law. In this chapter I make this distinction, and in doing so, I reason that how radical people relate to the law plays an important role in processes of radicalization. In particular, whether people stay within the boundaries of the law or deliberately break the law and violate legal rules is a key issue for those interested in the prevention of violent and illegal extremism. This implies that when people are willing to break the law to obtain their goals, possibly by violent means, this is an important signal that something is seriously going wrong (Section 9.4).

When people have formed intentions to engage in violent extremism and reject principles of law in open and democratic societies, they can be tempted to actively engage in violent and illegal extremist behaviors. In this process, evil as a motive and the justification of violence are important antecedents of political violence, religious violence, and terrorism (Section 9.5). The chapter ends with drawing conclusions about the violent rejection of the rule of law and democratic principles and how this enhances our insights into, and possible prevention of, extreme forms of radicalization (Section 9.6).

## 9.2 FROM THOUGHTS AND FEELINGS TO BEHAVIOR

An important social psychological observation is that people's beliefs and feelings do not necessarily predict their behaviors. For example, general attitudes are not strongly associated with specific behaviors, and it is only when specific attitudes about specific behaviors are coupled with the perception that it is doable to perform the behavior in question and that other important people positively evaluate the behavior that people then are likely to form the intention to engage in the particular behavior (Ajzen & Fishbein, 1980). Furthermore, behavioral intentions are only weakly related to people's actual behaviors (Fishbein & Ajzen, 1975). The same applies to radical thoughts, radical feelings, and radical behaviors: There is not always a strong relationship between the thoughts and feelings of radical people and their behaviors (McCauley & Moskalenko, 2008).

Related to this, Mandel (2009) argues that radicalization does not necessarily end in violence. Thus, according to Mandel, radicalization is not a sufficient cause of terrorism because most radicals are not terrorists. Moskalenko and McCauley (2009) note that the perpetrators of political violence, including terrorist violence, are the apex of a pyramid of sympathizers and supporters. There are fewer people at the higher levels of this pyramid, but those at the apex tend to show extreme beliefs, feelings, and behaviors. Furthermore, in their review of the literature, McCauley and Moskalenko (2008) point out that there is a long history of research in social psychology that shows that beliefs alone are a weak predictor of action. Thus, it is not entirely clear when people will move from radical thoughts and feelings to radical behaviors.

In part because radical and extremist beliefs and radical feelings sometimes are and sometimes are not clearly related to radical and extremist behaviors, different approaches to the study of radicalization have emerged in the research literature and in policy decision making. These perspectives are associated with different approaches to counter-radicalization. The distinction between the different approaches boils down to the issue of what endpoint one focuses on in the study of radicalization (Goerzig & Al-Hashimi, 2015). Do you focus primarily on radicalization of beliefs (cognitive radicalization) or beliefs and feelings (affective or "hot-cognitive" radicalization)? Or do you concentrate solely on radicalization of behaviors (behavioral radicalization)?

What endpoint you focus on has important consequences for the prevention of radicalization and what you think is the best way to approach counter-radicalization. Neumann (2013) notes that there is an Anglo-Saxon approach that tends to concentrate mainly on behavioral radicalization and a European approach that seeks to confront cognitive radicalization as well. Neumann argues that focusing on behavioral radicalization alone, as in the Anglo-Saxon approach, entails that freedom of speech is nearly absolute and that people can express their political views, even if extreme, as long as they do so by peaceful means. According to the European approach, extremist beliefs are problematic as well, and democracy has to be protected from extremist forces even before they become violent. European governments therefore do not leave counter-radicalization to counterterrorism, primarily focusing on fighting radical behaviors, but instead connect it to efforts to promote democracy and social cohesion, hence attempting to influence the thoughts of radicalizing persons as well as their behaviors (Goerzig & Al-Hashimi, 2015).

Indeed, there are good arguments to examine radical beliefs and radical feelings, as I tried to explain in the previous two chapters (see also Goerzig & Al-Hashimi, 2015). However, notwithstanding the possible importance of cognitive or hot-cognitive radicalization, it is also crucial to pay attention to behavioral radicalization. In fact, one could well say that understanding the ontogenesis of violent and illegal behavior is a key aspect, and probably the most important aspect, of the study of radicalization.

Relevant in this respect is Moskalenko and McCauley's (2009) observation that a common perspective in seeking the origins of violent extremism and terrorism portrays the trajectory to violence and terrorism as a "conveyor belt" that begins with radical beliefs and grievance and ends in violence. These authors note that this popular conveyor belt metaphor found only mixed support. It is important therefore to emphasize that pathways of increasing radicalization as sketched in this book (see, e.g., Figures 1.2 and 4.3) are not deterministic paths, but in fact constitute probabilistic associations.

Thus, although there is no doubt that some activists become terrorists (Moskalenko & McCauley, 2009), the different pathways identified in this book and in the research literature indicate increased likelihood of radicalization, possibly ending with violent and illegal extremist behaviors. However, when conditions as identified in this book or elsewhere in the literature are met, this does not imply a necessity that violent extremism or terrorism will prevail.

Related to this, Moskalenko and McCauley (2009) show that the readiness to participate in legal and nonviolent political action (political activism) is correlated to but distinguishable from the readiness to participate in illegal or violent political action (what these authors call radicalism intentions, and what others would label as violent extremism). A social psychological analysis of radical thoughts, feelings, and behaviors can help to obtain reliable insight into when people move from political attitudes and beliefs to political action, including violent extremism and terrorism.

A core aspect of such a social psychological analysis involves the issue of how cognitive or hot-cognitive radicalization and behavioral radicalization are related. While some argue that cognitive radicalization does not necessarily lead to violence, others stress that radical beliefs and extremist actions are related (Goerzig & Al-Hashimi, 2015; Neumann, 2013). Furthermore, there are some clear indications that people are inclined to act on their moral beliefs and the feelings associated with those beliefs (Skitka & Morgan, 2014). Related to this, Neumann (2013) quotes the German poet Heinrich Heine, who noted that "Wherever they burn books, they will also, in the end, burn human beings" (p. 891).

Of course, people do not always act on their moral beliefs or on their perceptions that things are not right and fundamentally unfair. Studying the social and societal contexts, as well as individual differences that may serve as moderators of the shift to violent and illegal behavior, is crucial. Thus, I note explicitly that how to study radical behavior and violent extremism is very difficult. Having said that, I also put forward that systematic attention to the social psychology of perceptions of unfairness, the feelings associated with those perceptions, and the delegitimizing effects on law and the adherence to democratic principles can help us to understand behavioral radicalization. In the next sections, I explore how examining the rejection of law and democratic principles via processes of delegitimization may help us to understand and possibly counter the ontogenesis of violent and illegal radical behavior.

## 9.3 DELEGITIMIZATION

What we have seen thus far is that it is difficult to predict radical and extremist behavior. I have also argued that insight into the social psychological processes that underlie radicalization and pathways to violent extremism may help us to get a better grip on these issues. One relevant concern in this respect is the rejection of democratic principles and principles of constitutional state law. To understand why people start to reject these principles, I argue that it is important to understand the psychological process of delegitimization. Delegitimization (also labeled delegitimation in the literature and treated here as synonym) is the psychological withdrawal of legitimacy, for example, from some institution such as a state, from judges in the constitutional democracy in which one lives, or from important principles of democracy in constitutional states. There is evidence that delegitimization of government, law, and other societal institutions plays a crucial role in right-wing radicalization, left-wing radicalization, and Muslim radicalization.

With respect to right-wing radicalization, Sprinzak (1991, 1995, 2009) argues that far-right groups usually start with focusing on other groups, usually minority groups, that they perceive to hold inferior legal and social status. Thus, right-wing extremists believe these groups should be expelled or even eliminated. Sprinzak (1995) argues that this belief in delegitimacy of the other is rooted in deep-seated social psychological processes and cultural traditions. The hated other group may be defined by race, nationality, religion, or sexual orientation. These characteristics cannot be altered easily and make the subgroup intrinsically inferior and deserving of their status (in the eyes of extremists).

According to Sprinzak (1995), right-wing groups at the first stage of radicalization engage in political activities designed to strengthen and perpetuate existing social and cultural mechanisms of discrimination. During this stage, right-wing groups accept the government's legitimacy, even though they are disillusioned with its policies, and seek to accomplish their goals through legitimate political activities. Group violence targeting minorities, such as hate crimes, are sporadic in this stage and only emerge if the group feels threatened (Kerodal, Freilich, Chermak, & Suttmoeller, 2014).

Sprinzak (1995) further argues that when far-right extremist groups become convinced that the government is not using sufficient energy to protect the interests of majority members as legitimate citizens, they progress to the next stage of radicalization. At this stage, the right-wing group loses confidence in the government and its policies. As a result, the far-right extremist group attempts to restore the status quo by engaging in low-level intimidation, such as harassment of the other, minority group. In this stage, right-wing groups may also begin to disobey laws. Political action shifts toward protests, which can lead to unplanned violent altercations with law enforcement. The groups may eventually splinter as the members become convinced the leaders are not radical enough (Kerodal et al., 2014).

Sprinzak (1995) also proposes that if far-right extremist groups become convinced that the government is controlled by the other, minority groups, a third stage of radicalization occurs. In this stage, both the hated minority group and the government are deemed illegitimate, and systematic terrorism could occur. Although Sprinzak (1995) did not believe all far-right extremist groups would follow this pattern, he argued that this framework explained the violent behavior of most far-right extremist groups (Kerodal et al., 2014).

Sprinzak's theorizing about delegitimization has been criticized, for example, for adhering too rigidly to a strict typology, whereas in fact it is not always possible to see clear differences between the different stages of delegitimization as identified in Sprinzak's model (Dzhekova et al., 2016; see also Wilkinson, 1995). This noted, Sprinzak's (1991, 1995) work provides a good theoretical starting point for considering theories of radicalization (Dzhekova et al., 2016). The model has also received at least some empirical support (see, e.g., Kerodal et al., 2014), although it is very hard to reliably assess violent acts against societal institutions in empirical research. I come back to this latter issue in Chapter 12.

Here I note that left-wing radicalization has also been associated with processes of delegitimization. For example, left-wing groups operating within functional democracies often undergo a profound political and psychological change in its members such that they delegitimize politics in their constitutional democracies. This has been observed among members of the Red Army Faction in West Germany (Sprinzak, 1991). The violent extremist actions of the Red Army Faction also spread to the Netherlands. When judging these acts, the relevant court of law in the Netherlands noted that it is completely unacceptable when people engage in violent actions merely because they disagree with the politics and policies of the democratic states in which they live. These acts corrode the basic principles of constitutional law and democratic states (Pekelder, 2007).

Muslim radicalization has also been related to delegitimization of democracy and democratic principles. For instance, Muslim radicalization and support for violence are linked to changing attitudes toward democracy and democratization, which often are associated with negative reactions to modernization. As such, radical Muslim groups ideologically reject electoral democracy as well as the legitimacy of political and ideological pluralism (Ashour, 2009). Ashour states that deradicalization of Muslim groups is primarily concerned with changing the attitudes of armed Muslim movements toward violence, rather than democracy. That is, in his view, many deradicalized Muslim groups still uphold misogynistic, homophobic, xenophobic, and antidemocratic views. Moreover, and very relevant for the current purposes, jihadism is characterized by the rejection of democracy as well as intolerance and the frequent use of violence against political rivals (Ashour, 2009).

## 9.4 REJECTION OF LAW AND DEMOCRACY

What we have seen is that through processes of delegitimization, radicalizing persons distance themselves psychologically from politics, societal institutions such as government and law, and principles of democracy and open societies (Popper, 1945). I argue here that key to understanding the ontogenesis of violent extremism and terrorism is people's rejection of constitutional democracy and the rule of law (Mak & Taekema, 2016).

After all, when it is hard or impossible for you to work within principles of constitutional democracy (such as when you cannot really force yourself to be open-minded about different opinions and at least be willing to tolerate them to such a degree that you try to make your case heard through majority rule or other democratic principles), then you might easily become frustrated that your wishes and opinions are not put into action, and then you are more likely to take action yourself to ensure that things will go your way. Furthermore, violent extremism and terrorism constitute illegal acts, and when you do not care about what the law says, or when you even sympathize with illegal behavior, it is easier to prepare or prompt yourself to engage in illegal actions.

Related to this, Ashour (2009) notes that jihadist groups are those movements that ideologically reject democracy as well as the legitimacy of political and ideological pluralism (see also Hagan, Kaiser, & Hanson, 2016; Nivette, Eisner, Malti, & Ribeaud, 2015; Sampson & Bartusch, 1998). Radicalization of those groups is thus a process in which a group undergoes ideological and/or behavioral transformations that lead to the rejection of democratic principles (including the peaceful alternation of power and the legitimacy of ideological and political pluralism) and possibly to the utilization of violence or to an increase in the levels of violence in order to achieve political goals (see also Meeus, 2015).

Based on these kinds of insights I propose that when radicalizing people start to reject the law in democratic states and open societies, this is a pivotal signal that indicates that something is going seriously wrong. In other words, I do think it is fine when people hold radical opinions that differ from others drastically, but when this is coupled with a certain disdain for law and democracy, this may well serve as an important next phase of radicalization that ultimately may end in violent extremism and terrorism.

A distinction can be made between those people who do not engage in a violent rejection of the law and those who are willing to use violence as part of their not complying with the law, and thus engage in such acts as vandalizing the private property of politicians or other people who are viewed of as symbols that need to be fought. Many people occasionally oppose certain aspects of the law, but this does not lead them to engage in a violent rejection of the law. It is therefore interesting to investigate why some extremists engage in a violent rejection of the law while other radicals oppose this behavior.

It is very difficult to predict the onset of violent and illegal behavior. This also applies to the prediction of violent extremism and terrorism. For instance, of the many people who sympathize with some forms of right-wing, left-wing, or Muslim radical thoughts, most in the end will not actively engage in illegal violence. A key issue to understand the psychology of violent extremism and terrorism may be the psychological rejection of law and democratic principles. This might be even more important, psychologically speaking, than is often realized. I propose therefore that rejection of the law and democracy constitutes a turning point in the radicalization process of many people.

It is important to realize that radicalization refers to the process by which individuals are introduced to an ideological system that encourages movement from moderate, mainstream beliefs toward extreme views. To be a radical is to reject the status quo, but not necessarily in a violent or even problematic manner (Bartlett & Miller, 2012). Some radicals conduct, support, or encourage terrorism, while others actively and often effectively agitate against it (Bartlett & Miller, 2012). Therefore, rejection of and noncompliance with the law (and related democratic principles) are considered key aspects of cognitive and behavioral radicalization. Indeed, the point at which one decides to reject the law (and act accordingly, in violation of rules that protect democratic principles) can be seen as a fundamentally new phase in any process of radicalization.

It is very difficult to predict in advance people's intentions to break the law and their actual breaking of the law. That being said, Parker, Manstead, Stradling, Reason, and Baxter (1992) use the theory of planned behavior

(Ajzen & Fishbein, 1980) to account for people's intentions to commit legal violations. Results showed that when people perceive that it is easy or doable for them to perform the illegal behavior and when they believe that other important people positively evaluate the behavior, then they are likely to form the intention to break the law. This indicates that the relevance of behavioral control and what others think of the behavior in question can be key variables in predicting when people will actually engage in illegal behavior, such as violent extremism.

Another pivotal issue is that people start seeing the law as not really legitimate. We have seen this in the previous section. When people see a gap between what they think is legitimate and what the law states is legal, they are easily persuaded to engage in violating the law (Von Essen, 2016). Viewed from this perspective, people's violation of a perceived illegitimate law may testify to a profound disjuncture between legality and legitimacy.

I hasten to emphasize that violating the law does not need to imply violent breaking of the law. For example, radicals such as the militant feminist Fadela Amara adhere to extreme ideas, uphold conflictual and militant visions, and break the law, but they do not do so in a violent manner (McCauley & Moskalenko, 2011). Related to this, radicals who engage in civil disobedience and as a result of this break the law also provide an interesting case in this respect (Habermas, 1985). I adhere to Schuyt's (1972) analysis of civil disobedience and am inclined to find it acceptable when people engage in civil disobedience when this is done openly, on the basis of conscientious decisions, and without violence and when the chosen action is in accordance with the goals the radical attempts to attain. Modern approaches to human rights also seem to adhere to this line of thinking (see, e.g., Buyse, 2014). Again, I emphasize that when people start to develop a disdain of law, this well might serve as a red flag in most circumstances, albeit not all (Schuyt, 1972). That is, in most situations decreased sympathy for the law and associated democratic principles may indicate for many radicalization processes that something is seriously going wrong, especially when this disdain for the law and democracy is coupled with violent behavioral intentions.

## 9.5 VIOLENT BEHAVIOR

Radicalizing individuals who have developed sympathy for violent extremism or terrorist movements and who have formed associated intentions to fight for the extremist or terrorist goals, perhaps combined with a disdain for law and democratic principles in open societies, can be lured into actual engaging in violent and illegal extremism and terrorism. However, as it turns out, understanding when, why, and how people living in a democracy become radicalized to the point of being willing to use or directly support the use of extremist or terrorist violence against fellow citizens is not an easy issue to get a good grip on. In fact, this question has been at the center of academic and public debate for many years now (Dalgaard-Nielsen, 2010).

Part of the difficulty stems from the observation that when the backgrounds, ideologies, behaviors, and attitudes of violent radicals are compared with nonviolent radicals, many different variables seem to play some role. For example, intellectual, rational, and religious issues are important, as are emotional, social, and status issues (Bartlett & Miller, 2012; see also Bartlett & Birdwell, 2010; Bartlett, Birdwell, & King, 2010). Group processes and mass psychology are also important for understanding violent radicalization, in part because perpetrators of political violence depend on a much larger group who sympathize with and support their cause or grievance (McCauley & Moskalenko, 2011).

Furthermore, many of these different variables apply at least to some extent to both violent and nonviolent radicals. For instance, Bartlett and Miller (2012) note that many of the claims regularly deployed to explain Muslim terrorism apply to nonviolent Muslims as well. For example, many nonviolent Muslim radicals feel a strong, cynical distrust of government and a deep outrage at Western foreign policy. Nonviolent Muslims share a keen perception of social discrimination, especially in employment; experience periods of drift and uncertainty about their own identity; desire in some sense the creation of either the caliph or an Islamic government; and are attached to some level of self-segregation and aspects of a theological just war theory (Bartlett & Miller, 2012).

Bartlett and Miller (2012) also suggest that with respect to homegrown young male Muslims, there is an emotional pull to violent radicalization. To join the battle against the power and authority of Western states is considered risky, exciting, and heroic and taps into a countercultural and antiestablishment tradition exemplified by many youth subcultures, both Muslim and non-Muslim. Furthermore, in-group peer pressure and an internal code of honor can render violence the most obvious route to accrue status, respect, and meaning.

In short, many different variables can play at least some role in explaining and predicting violent radicalization. Here I argue that the key factors discussed in this book—perceptions of unfairness and injustice, uncertainty and threats, and insufficient self-corrections—may help us to better understand, and possibly predict, active behavioral engagement in illegal and violent extremist and terrorist behaviors.

With regard to perceptions of injustice, Della Porta (1995) observed that these perceptions are associated with the degree to which violent behavior is tolerated in various countries across several points in time. Related to this, the more that widespread violence is perceived to be just and is justified, the more that radical behavior appears to be viewed not as deviance but as the norm in various cultures. Furthermore, Staub (1989, 2015) notes that the processes leading to extreme group violence are psychological and social processes, such as identification with groups, high self-esteem, underlying insecurity, and, importantly, a sense of entitlement. These observations are in accordance with the importance of justice and injustice perceptions that I discussed in Chapter 4 and at various other places in this book.

With respect to the issue of feeling uncertain about yourself and responding to self-threatening information, Becker (1975) proposes that people use high levels of self-esteem to buffer themselves against these threats to the self (see also Salami, 2010). He also notes that self-esteem is rooted in cultural worldviews and that because you want your culture to be right, self-esteem is often equivalent to righteousness or feeling right. Although there is evidence that high self-esteem can buffer against violence (see, e.g., Salami, 2010), the hypothesis that low self-esteem is likely to cause aggression and violence is not always supported and seems to be more complicated. For example, Bushman et al. (2009; Bushman & Baumeister, 1998) propose that the highest levels of direct physical aggression are likely to be observed when people think highly of themselves and when these self-views are threatened by other people. In my view, these findings support the line of reasoning presented in Chapter 5 that threats to people's selves can make them uncertain about themselves and can influence or moderate important components of various radicalization processes, including the occurrence of violent radicalization.

With regard to the relevance of self-control, Baumeister (1997) notes that evil can be an important motive of human violence and cruelty. Importantly, he also notes that although many adults have experienced many frustrating events, most have not committed murder or engaged in assault or other acts of violence to revenge their feelings and to ensure that what they think is right is pushed forward. According to Baumeister, this is because most violent impulses are held back by forces inside the person. In other words, self-control prevents a great deal of potential violence. This line of reasoning fits with the analysis I put forward in Chapter 6 of this book.

The social psychological variables discussed in this chapter and this book help to explain various instances of violent radicalization, including violent extremism and terrorism. For example, these factors further our understanding of why social movement organizations sometimes shift from predominantly nonviolent forms of contentious politics to tactics of political violence that include violent means and the justifying of the newly introduced violence (Alimi, Demetriou, & Bosi, 2015). Similarly, this may help to explain why social and political activists sometimes may move from nonviolent to violent civil disobedience (Morreall, 1976).

The factors discussed here are also conducive to understanding the occurrence of religious violence. For example, Niebuhr (1932) wondered when it is permissible for a Christian to use force or violence in defense of justice and a righteous cause. He argued that righteous force is sometimes necessary to extirpate injustice and subdue evil within a sinful world, and that small strategic acts of violence are occasionally necessary to deter large acts of violence and injustice. Similarly, Juergensmeyer (2003) discusses a Muslim extremist who recounted the injustices done against himself, his family, and other Arabs over the years to demonstrate that the experience of victimization had preceded these violent attacks.

The occurrence of extremism or terrorism may also be explained by at least some variables discussed here. For example, Reich (1990) notes that right-wing organizations frequently resort to violence in response to what they see as a threat to the status quo from the left. According to Reich, what is noticeable about terrorists is that they suffer from a psychological trauma that does two things: First, it makes them see the world, including their own actions and the expected effects of those actions, in a grossly unrealistic light. Second, it motivates them to use violence against individuals in its most extreme form—cold-blooded murder. Interestingly, Gurr (1970) notes that many of the attitudes and societal conditions that facilitate political violence may be present and relatively unchanging in a society over a long period. They become relevant to or operative in the genesis of violence only when relative deprivation increases in scope and intensity. If people are intensely discontented, they are susceptible to new ideologies and less complex beliefs that assert the righteousness and usefulness of political violence. Related to this, Stern (2004) proposes that employing unjust means for (subjectively determined) just ends can justify violence for terrorists and can make violence and crime become second nature. As such, a culture of violence breeds more violence and terrorism.

## 9.6 CONCLUSIONS

Understanding human behavior, and especially abnormal, radical, violent, illegal behavior, is an enormous task. Part of the difficulty of this task is caused by the various steps that play an important role in the psychological process, from radical thoughts and radical feelings to radical attitudes, then radical behavioral intentions, and finally radical behaviors. And comprehending and predicting if or when people will shift from radical thoughts to extremist, violent, and illegal behaviors is perhaps even more difficult.

This difficulty is caused in part by the fact that the field of social psychology on which this book builds used to focus on the understanding of behavior but nowadays concentrates on cognitions and associated feelings, and not so much on actual behavior. In all honesty, this implies that the modern social psychological analysis of radicalization put forward in this book fares better in understanding cognitive and hot-cognitive processes of radicalization than in predicting the actual occurrence of extremist and terrorist behavior.

With this important caveat in mind, I do note that this chapter has examined the psychological processes leading to radical and extremist behaviors. In doing so, I developed the case that delegitimization and a certain disdain for law and democratic principles may serve as pivotal turning points in shifting from radical thoughts and radical attitudes to radical and extremist behaviors.

This insight, taken together with what we learned from Chapters 7 and 8, can help us to better understand important shifts in various radicalization processes that can lead people to adopt radical and extreme thoughts (including thoughts that are statistically very extreme and that focus on rejection of the law and open societies; see also Chapter 7), radical and extreme feelings (including extremely negatively outward-oriented feelings; see also Chapter 8), and radical and extreme behaviors (including violent and illegal acts; see the current chapter).

Thus, I argue that notwithstanding the very difficult task of understanding and predicting the actual onset of violent extremism and terrorism, the cognitive, hot-cognitive, and behavioral processes discussed in this book may help to make some progress toward the important goals of the prediction and prevention of various forms of radicalization. The psychology of unfairness judgments (see Chapter 4), how people respond to uncertainty and other threats (see Chapter 5), and how and when they engage in insufficient correction of self-centered impulses (see Chapter 6) can work together to delineate violent rejection of law and democratic principles and how this can ultimately lead to violent extremism and perhaps even terrorism.

I note explicitly here that what also can help us to better understand the issue of violent radicalization is a better insight into evil as a motive of human behavior (Baumeister, 1997) and a better, more fine-grained understanding of aggression and aggressive behavior (Berkowitz, 1993). Aggression often consists of a combination of a positive attitude toward the use of violence and the actual engagement in the aggressive behavior. Furthermore, aggression can be instigated to reach certain goals (instrumental aggression) or can be the result of strongly felt emotions (emotional aggression). Aggression can also be caused by the frustration of desired goals (Berkowitz, 1993).

Aggression is often linked to violent physical behavior but also encompasses verbal aggressive behaviors, such as the verbally strong rejection of law or the insulting of societal authorities or other people. Young men are typically more involved with physical forms of aggressive acts, and women can show strong indirect or verbal forms of aggressive behaviors (Berkowitz, 1993). Group processes also play an important role in aggressive behaviors (see, e.g., Pynchon & Borum, 1999; see also Borum, Fein, Vossekuil, & Berglund, 1999). A better integration of the aggression literature could lead to a better understanding of various radicalization processes, in part because the aggression literature is focused on violent forms of human behaviors, and it is especially this part of the radicalization process that is less strongly developed in the research literature I focus on than the cognitive and hot-cognitive processes underlying many different forms of human radicalization.

This brings me to the conclusions and reflections of this book, including what we learned in this book, what we can do to fight radicalization, what we should or should not do in exploring these issues, how we learn about radicalization in future research and policy projects, and what is next to be studied to solve some of the important limitations that we currently face. The final part and the last three chapters of this book focus on these issues.

# PART FOUR

# Conclusions and Reflections

# Conclusions and Limitations

*What Do We Learn?*

## 10.1 CONCLUSIONS

Now that we have discussed several instances of Muslim, right-wing, and left-wing radicalization, and have reviewed several ways in which perceptions of unfairness can fuel radical beliefs, extremist behaviors, and terrorist acts, it is time to draw some conclusions. It is also time to discuss several limitations of the scientific line of reasoning presented in this book. The current chapter notes some conclusions and discusses important limitations that need our attention.

Perhaps the most important conclusion thus far is that I think it is reasonable to infer that the assumption that perceptions of unfairness play a crucial role in many different forms of radicalization holds up pretty well. These unfairness perceptions include judgments of unfair treatment, horizontal group deprivation, vertical group deprivation, inequity of outcome distributions, perceived immorality, and general impressions that things are not right and that the world is not a just place.

It is important to realize that these perceptions are what they are, namely perceptions. This implies that unfairness perceptions can be biased and distorted in many ways. Nonetheless, when people have come to the judgment that something in their social environments, society, or the world at large is blatantly unfair, this feels not like a mere perception, but instead as real and genuine. Unfairness perceptions thus can have a profound impact on people's thoughts, feelings, and behaviors. It makes sense therefore to examine systematically how people use perceptions of unfairness to fuel radical beliefs, extremist behaviors, and sympathy for terrorism.

To an important extent, perceptions of unfairness are related to objective circumstances, including demographic backgrounds and living conditions of people. Furthermore, of course, unfairness perceptions of radicalizing persons can be correct (fully or at least partially). That noted, a central presumption in the social psychology of radicalization is the notion that what really matters is how these objective conditions are perceived by people. After all, it is these perceptions that impact and drive people's thoughts, feelings, and behaviors. Thus, what interests me highly is how social situations and societal issues are perceived in terms of unfairness, injustice, and immorality. What follows from this fascination is the prediction that it is not the objective or actual circumstances, but rather how these circumstances are perceived, experienced, and interpreted, that makes for important possible antecedents and moderators of radicalization processes.

I hasten to note that although I emphasize the importance of psychological perceptions of unfairness for the understanding, prevention, and combating of radicalization, it is crucial not to exaggerate this sound idea by maintaining that radicalization is nothing but subjective. Thus, I agree with Merton (1995), when he warns against total subjectivism that conceives of social reality as consisting only of social definitions, perceptions, labels, or beliefs and that we would not have any reason to believe in the objective existence of anything.

That being said, it is important to realize that the experienced genuineness of perceived unfairness is an aspect of the psychology of radicalization that is unique and that makes perceptions of unfairness a very important topic to study and to take into consideration when attempting to prevent or combat radicalization. Because these perceptions feel genuine and real, they are likely to influence people's reactions. In particular, when perceptions move from perceptions of unfairness to judgments of injustice and perhaps even convictions that things are immoral, then this tends to be associated with increased certainty that this perception is not really a perception, but instead is something that is real, genuine, and important that deserves to be followed by appropriate action.

Staub (2011) and others emphasize the importance of material resources and how the unequal distribution of these resources may constitute one of the sources of mass societal protest and unrest. This can indeed be important, but the fairness literature shows quite convincingly that often unfairness perceptions do not revolve around distribution of outcomes, but rather involve perceptions that individuals or group members are not treated rightly (Lind & Tyler, 1988) and general impressions that things are fundamentally wrong (Finkel, 2001).

Related to the notion of general notions that things are not fair is the observation by Kruglanski, Gelfand, and Gunaratna (2012) that terrorist ideology consists of a grievance. Inherent in this grievance is some form of injustice, targeted at a culprit or actor assumed to be responsible for the grievance. Part of this grievance is also a method (terrorism) that is considered morally justifiable because it addresses a great injustice (see also Staub, 2011).

Furthermore, most perceptions of unfairness that have to do with rad-icalization may well be relatively simple and not very elaborate. For ex-ample, J. Martin, Scully, and Levitt (1990) content-analyzed the rhetoric of 22 leaders of violent, 20th-century revolutions to examine how they describe the injustice of a status quo system of reward distribution, mo-bilize others to join a revolutionary movement, and envision a perfectly just future.

The authors expected that the leaders would actively compare their own group to their enemies and emphasize perceived injustice. They thought that the leaders would focus on inequality in material outcomes, which would include food, shelter, and jobs. In addition, they expected to find that the leaders would also focus on procedural injustice. For instance, leaders might state that laws have been drafted while not all interested parties were represented. In summary, J. Martin et al. expected to find a complex, emotionally charged delineation of the injustice of the status quo system of reward distribution, including detailed social comparisons and concern both with distributive injustice and with procedural injustice.

Interestingly, however, the data of the J. Martin et al. study suggested that the revolutionary leaders did not focus on complex perceived injustices, but instead kept it very simple. They only focused on one type of distributive injustice, namely "too much inequality between groups," and one type of procedural injustice, namely "a lack of representation in government." Thus, although the content analysis by J. Martin et al. sought complexity and nuance, the revolutionaries' claims of injustice were un-expectedly simple.

The revolutionary leaders offered a vision of a perfectly just future that was unexpectedly simple—even empty. For example, few social comparisons were made in the content analyses presented by J. Martin et al. (1990). The revolutionary leaders also offered an unexpectedly simplified vision of perfect justice. As in the description of the status quo, a wide range of material, ideological, and emotional outcomes were mentioned. However, all these outcomes were to be distributed using pri-marily one simple, general rule: decrease inequality.

This does not imply that these relatively simple notions of injustice are not relevant or would not influence radicals' behaviors. Certainly not. We know from other research that simple justice rules, such as those focusing on equality (Messick, 1993) or general impressions of fairness of treatment (Lind, 1995), may well constitute core components of the psychology of unfairness and societal protest (see also Layendecker, 1981; J. Martin, Brickman, & Murray, 1984; J. Martin & Murray, 1984). This seems to apply especially to radicals who tend to engage in black-and-white thinking, including relatively simple notions of how just or unjust the world is (Van den Bos & Loseman, 2011).

Of course, this observation of black-and-white perceptions of unfairness does not imply that perceptions and violent behavior cannot and will not vary in magnitude and form across different instances of radicalization. For example, Gurr (1970) observes that political violence varies according to how many participate in the political violence, the intensity or destructiveness of the violent acts, and the duration of the violence. Political violence also manifests itself in many different forms. Having said that, Gurr (1970) proposes that relative deprivation tends to underlie many different manifestations and different forms of violence. Part of this predominance of relative deprivation is the notion that people are quick to aspire beyond their social means and quick to anger when those means prove inadequate but are slow to accept their limitations (Gurr, 1970, p. 58).

After all, relative deprivation involves the tension between your actual state and what you feel you should be able to achieve. The intensity and scope of relative deprivation strongly determine the potential for collective violence. Gurr gives a long review of psychological research on aggression and concludes that frustration-aggression is the primary source of the human capacity for violence (Gurr, 1970, p. 36), although aggression is neither necessary nor sufficient. The more intense and prolonged the feeling of frustration, the greater the probability of aggression. Even highly educated radicals, such as those who advocate for human rights in rather radical ways (Jansen, 2015), may switch to extremist behaviors when their goals are frustrated.

In summary, it seems reasonable to conclude for now that perceptions play an important and perhaps special role in various processes of radicalization. As noted, Figure 1.3 summarizes the possible impact of unfairness perceptions on radicalization. This process is moderated by variables such as uncertainty and other self-relevant threats. Figure 1.3 shows this, and Figure 4.1 discusses this in detail. Figure 5.1 also discusses threat reactions and illustrates how these reactions can be turned into possible approach reactions and hence may contribute to the prevention of radicalization and processes of deradicalization.

Here I note that further conclusions will be drawn in Chapter 12, the last chapter of this book. Before I draw these conclusions, a discussion of some of the limitations of this book and the analysis presented here is in order. This will be the focus of the remainder of this chapter. After this, I examine in Chapter 11 some of the practical implications that follow from the line of reasoning presented in this book.

## 10.2 MISSING OUT AND OTHER LIMITATIONS

Because of the complex quality of the many different radicalization processes that are out there, any conceptual model of radicalization is necessarily not perfect. Furthermore, because of the difficulty of predicting rare behavior, explanations of extremist and terrorist behaviors are expected to be imperfect as well. I find it very important, therefore, to be very explicit about the limitations of the current book and the line of reasoning presented in it. After all, this book is definitely not without limitations.

The current book addresses many variables that play a role in various forms of radicalization. I did my utmost best to discuss these issues in a coherent way. I also ensured that these discussions received strong conceptual backup and contained relevant empirical findings, preferably from multiple and different sources. Nonetheless, although I am convinced of the value of the conceptual models presented here, many issues discussed here are conjectures, hypotheses, or even assumptions.

Perhaps the biggest limitation of the social psychological analysis put forward in this book is that although it includes many different variables, it also neglects many other important variables at the same time. The conceptual quality of the line of reasoning presented and the conceptual models discussed here necessarily impose certain boundaries. After all, putting forward a conceptual model necessitates a domain to which the model does and does not hold. So, this is a potentially important limitation. The conceptual focus of the current book is both a strength and a potential weakness.

The conceptual line of reasoning presented here, focusing on unfairness perceptions influencing radicalization processes, gives body to the book. Appropriate attention to moderating variables and other issues provides a nuanced understanding of this central hypothesis. That said, radicalization, extremism, and terrorism are such complicated and multifaceted issues that it is nearly impossible to explain and predict all instances in our world in a satisfying way. Thus, the various models, research findings, and theoretical conjectures presented here are relevant and important, I think, but may also miss out on other important issues not addressed or not discussed at length in this book.

I understand that this open mentioning of the limitations of this book can be somewhat dissatisfying for some readers, but please be aware that radicalization, extremism, and terrorism are complex issues and involve psychological processes that may come about in different ways surrounded with many qualifying variables. In other words, there is a lot of "noise" or "error" to be dealt with when trying to explain processes of radicalization.

For instance, the models put forward here focus to a large extent on Western radicalization processes of people living in Western countries. Thus, although the book also aims to be relevant for radicalization in non-Western countries, such as the Middle East and other parts of the world, there is a possibility that this book includes an overreliance on Western extremist and terrorist movements. This overemphasis may be caused to some extent by a greater scientific literature on these Western radicalization processes, but this nevertheless constitutes a potentially important limitation of the current book.

Specifically, I devoted some space to the notion that extremist groups can turn against a democratic system. But this is not always a central component of radical groups. Rather, a central element of radical groups tends to be that they mistrust the current political powers, whether democratically chosen or not. In the current book, I decided to focus on the parts of the world I am most familiar with. To what extent the current analysis extends to nondemocratic and non-Western societies is an issue that needs further study and may constitute a limitation of the current book.

The current book also relies heavily on psychological science and policy decision-making research. So, the financial and economic conditions under which radicalization takes place need to be taken into consideration as well. This also applies to legal issues pertaining to radicalization, including the prevention of radicalization and attempts to combat radicalization.

There is also the possibility that I may be naïve about certain forms of radicalization such as Muslim radicalization. For example, Dennis Abdelkarim Honing, a deradicalized Muslim in the Netherlands, argues that many scientists and policy decision makers do not realize the many issues that currently are important among Muslims in the Netherlands and in other countries. As a result, scientists such as me may miss out on important antecedents of radicalization and, in fact, may underestimate the occurrence and prevalence of radicalization, including the adherence to extreme Muslim thoughts and extremist and terrorist acts (Abdelkarim Honing & Sterkenburg, 2015).

Furthermore, throughout the book I focused on various instances of extreme Muslim, right-wing, and left-wing forms of radicalization. These represent important instances of radicalization, but they do not cover the whole spectrum. For example, I did not explore single-issue groups, such as extreme anti-abortion groups and extreme animal rights groups, nor other extreme religious groups, such as Sikhs or extreme Christians. Furthermore, future research could examine in detail whether the distinction between lone actors (or lone wolves) and group forms of radicalization deserves more attention. For example, do lone actors perceive the same unfairness? Is the unfairness factor as important for lone actors as it is for group forms of radicalization?

In short, there may be several important limitations of this book, and I do not shy away from explicitly discussing them. Other potentially important limitations that I discuss in this chapter are issues of how to define the various concepts pertaining to radicalization (Section 10.3), the relevance and strength of the general models presented here (Section 10.4), the prediction of concrete instances of radicalization (Section 10.5), and the importance of social media and Internet communication (Section 10.6).

## 10.3 DEFINITIONAL ISSUES

Another potential limitation that needs our attention is how I have defined the core issues that this book focuses on. As noted in Section 1.2, I define radicalization as a process in which people move from staying within the law (as in the case of activism) to deliberately breaking the law (as in the case of extremism), possibly using violent means (as in the case of violent extremism). The ultimate endpoint of radicalization on which I focus in this book is terrorism, which I define as the engagement of individuals or groups in ideologically motivated violence or other destructive acts against persons, property, or the fabric of society. These acts are committed with the aim of bringing about social change and causing public disquiet or influencing political decision making. Furthermore, I propose that terrorism encompasses acts that actually took place as well as acts that are planned or that individuals or groups threaten to engage in.

Notwithstanding the fact that I am adopting a "positive-scientific" position on the issue of radicalization, extremism, and terrorism and that I come from a scientific discipline that does not reflect too much and too long on definitional issues, I do want to note explicitly that I understand that there are many other definitions and approaches possible to try to understand these concepts. Thus, I note that the issue of radicalization may be a contested concept and that there is no universally accepted definition of radicalization or of extremism and terrorism in academia or government.

After all, one of the issues with defining radicalization is the importance of the context to determine what is perceived as radicalization. Therefore, radicalization can mean different things to different people.

I also realize that in my work I aim to contribute to policy decision making and also use insights from policy decision makers. This is both a strength and a possible limitation of my approach to processes of radicalization. After all, in terms of potential limitations or weaknesses, this aspect of my approach makes me vulnerable to criticism that I might be biased toward the status quo. For example, terrorism is defined in this book as violent, ideological acts committed by nonstate individuals or groups. This definition tends to neglect the sometimes-illegal forces that nation-states can exert on their enemies (both other states and individuals or groups of individuals).

In general, radicalization is a process by which an individual or group comes to adopt increasingly extreme political, social, or religious ideals and aspirations that reject or undermine the status quo (Wilner & Dubouloz, 2011). It can also undermine contemporary ideas and expressions of freedom of choice. Radicalization can be both violent and nonviolent, although most academic publications focus on radicalization into violent extremism (Borum, 2011a; Schmid, 2013). There are multiple pathways that constitute the process of radicalization, which can be independent but are usually mutually reinforcing (McCauley & Moskalenko, 2008). The different pathways identified in this book and elsewhere do not imply that radicalization will always follow these pathways or always will develop along gradual lines. Quite the contrary, there is more and more evidence that radicalizing individuals may jump to different phases of radicalization rather quickly, often quite unexpectedly for their previous social contacts, including their families and former friends.

I further note that there can be a difference between creating terror and terrorism. This said, I also state explicitly that how I define terrorism includes that an important goal of terrorist movements is to create terror among the citizens, institutions, or government of legitimate democracies. As noted by Juergensmayer (2003): "Terrorism is meant to terrify. The word comes from the Latin *terrere*, 'to cause to tremble'" (p. 5).

Nonetheless, it is important to emphasize that radicalization is not necessarily bad. For example, there are political parties that have adopted very
radical ideas but combine these ideas with pacifist ideology restraining
them from violent extremism. For example, Mahatma Gandhi is an example of a radical person who fought for change in his country of India
by nonviolent means. Related to this, I also want to note explicitly that
sometimes radical thoughts are needed to create desperately needed societal changes. For example, scholars radically embracing the concept of
Scientific Enlightenment changed Western European countries for the
better (Israel, 2001, 2006, 2011). In the current book, therefore, I draw an
explicit distinction between nonviolent and violent extremism. The study
of radicalization as I put it forward here focuses to a large extent on the
issue of when people are likely to embrace violence, either by having sympathetic thoughts about violence to obtain certain goals or by actually engaging in violent behavior.

## 10.4 GENERAL MODELS

A possible strength of the radicalization analysis put forward in the
current book is that the analysis is aimed to be general in nature. As
such, it was my explicit aim to focus on different instances of radicalization, extremism, and terrorism and to explore some general factors and
specific mechanisms that apply to many different instances of Muslim,
right-wing, and left-wing radicalization processes. I believe this general
approach is interesting, important, and valuable. For example, the general
models presented in this book aim to be relevant for various instances
of radicalization in different circumstances in different countries and
cultures in the past, present, and future. This reflects my ambition to try
to explain many different issues pertaining to radicalization, extremism,
and terrorism.

A possibly important disadvantage of the general models and general
analysis presented here is the relative neglect of differences between various forms of radicalization. This is especially the case because my social

psychological background orients me toward not only extremist and very radical people but also less extremist people. This is fine, but the specific differences between different extremists, terrorists, and other very radical individuals also warrants our attention (see, e.g., De Graaf, 2010, 2012; De Graaf & Weggemans, 2016; Gill & Corner, 2017; Ipsos, 2017; Monahan, 2012).

Another possible limitation of my general models is that they can become too abstract. For example, when zooming in on concrete instances of radicalization processes, it is necessary to specify in detail what exact unfairness perceptions, types of uncertainty, and insufficient self-corrections play a role in these instances. Specifying the precise emotions, behavioral intentions, and types of actions associated with the radicalization processes is also important.

I also note that I focus in my models to a large extent on homegrown radicalization in which perceptions of unfairness grow slowly but steadily, sometimes leading to feelings of frustration and associated violent acts. However, radicalization processes can also develop very quickly. Radicalization is certainly not always a slow or gradually evolving process. For example, spontaneous emotions or the thrill of sensation-seeking may instigate instantaneous forms of radicalization, and this also can occur among people not living in the country where the perceived unfairness is taking place. Thus, it is certainly possible that rapidly radicalizing persons skip certain phases as identified in this book or in other models in the research literature (see, e.g., Horgan, 2017; Horgan & Taylor, 2013). Furthermore, sometimes radicalization strongly resembles the careers of criminal youngsters (especially young men). Insufficient self-correction may be very prevalent among those types of radicalization processes (Dunkel, Mathes, & Beaver, 2013). Notions of pride and violation of honor can be very important in this respect (Feldstein, 2009).

Fundamental criticisms could be voiced against linear and "monodimensional" and "mono-causal" models of radicalization. A chronology of stages suggests a sequence of logical steps that quite often cannot be perceived in current instances of radicalization. Youngsters jump to and fro on the "staircase," miss a series of steps, radicalize far more quickly, or revert the process on a whim. Furthermore, these models are sometimes used and appropriated by authorities to legitimate their "actuarial justice," meting out sentences for individuals allegedly at the first step of the staircase, presuming they will climb the ladder further, but without actually being able to predict that pathway. We should be careful when applying insights from general models (such as the models that I presented here) to actual cases of individual radicalization, for example when dealing with individual criminal court cases (see also 10.5).

The models that I presented here involve many relationships. I think there are good reasons to present these models and these relationships between the different variables put forward here. However, I do not want to argue for the causal relationship among all (or many) of the relationships proposed. Obviously, radicalization processes are influenced in many different ways by many different variables, and many of the relationships proposed in the current book need to be tested in future research projects, especially among new or multifaceted forms of radicalization. As such, the arrows presented in the different figures should not be interpreted as deterministic pathways.

I also state explicitly that many of the issues surrounding radicalization, extremism, and terrorism are complex and potentially complicated. Thus, it is good to realistically expect that the many variables presented in this book may help to systematically explain and predict radicalization processes, but this takes place in contexts in which there is a lot of noise and a lot of issues that are not explained by the variables put forward. As such, it can be argued that the systematic variance (what you can explain as a researcher) is facing a huge amount of error variance (what you do not explain or perhaps do not know at all). I understand that this can be a dissatisfying aspect of the study of radicalization and the line of reasoning presented in this book, but it is a realistic caveat that needs to be taken into consideration.

We also should not exaggerate the specific details of the models or the interrelationships between the different models. After all, this could convey that we can delineate the psychology of radicalization in very specific detail. I am not convinced that this is truly possible. As such, I present my line of reasoning as a conceptual framework that gives some sense of direction in how to understand radicalization and what to do about it.

One of the core issues in this respect is the realization that radicalization is not always a necessary condition for terrorism (Dzhekova et al., 2016). Furthermore, radicalization does not need to end up in terrorism. After all, terrorism is one of the worst possible, but nevertheless avoidable, outcomes of violent radicalization (Veldhuis & Staun, 2009). Relevant to understanding this matter is Sprinzak's (1991, 1995) theory of delegitimization. This theory stresses that, despite major differences, there are some shared characteristics between terrorist groups that allow for generalizations, namely that they have emerged as splinter groups of larger radical movements and also that they have been radicalized into terrorism. As such, Sprinzak (1991) rightfully observes that most modern terrorists have reached their terrorism gradually. As a result, Sprinzak sees terrorism as the product of the most extreme form of radicalization, what he calls "transformational delegitimation." This also constitutes the main feature that distinguishes terrorists from nonviolent radicals.

As Sprinzak (1991) put it: "Terrorism implies a crisis of legitimacy. What terrorists do—and other radicals do not—is to bring their rejection of the regime's legitimacy to the point of challenging it with unconventional violence. However, since terrorism never emerges overnight, this crisis of legitimacy unfolds through a prolonged process of delegitimation of the established society and the regime" (p. 52). The line of reasoning that I presented in this book adheres to Sprinzak's ideas. By focusing in depth on the modern psychology of unfairness perceptions and associated moderators and mediators, the current book also tries to deepen our understanding of radicalization, extremism, and terrorism.

## 10.5 PREDICTION OF CONCRETE CASES

The issues of radicalization, including the possible endpoints of violent extremism and terrorism, warrant an integrative approach that combines many different factors. It is essential that this approach is tailored to fit the understanding of concrete cases of radicalization as best as possible. This understanding should ultimately lead to the prediction of concrete instances of radicalization, preferably including the prediction of concrete cases of extremist violence and terrorist attacks, however difficult this may be.

Related to some of the issues that were discussed in the previous section, I want to highlight here that another possible disadvantage of the general models and the analysis presented here is the relative lack of specific predictions of actual concrete cases of radicalization, including specific instances of extremism and terrorism. The advantage of the overarching models and line of reasoning presented is that they aim to be relevant to multiple cases of radicalization processes. This noted, clearly tailoring these models so that they fit and are applicable to concrete instances is something that needs to be done to understand in detail the possible relevance of unfairness perceptions and relevant moderators such as personal uncertainty and insufficient self-correction. The overarching framework presented here needs to be combined with individually tailored measures to ensure the concrete prevention or combating of concrete instances of radicalization.

I also want to highlight this because this book does not focus only or mainly on extreme or extremist persons. The social psychological inspiration of this book served me quite well in trying to delineate the radicalization process in detail. But this focus does include not only an analysis what extreme persons do but also insights into how normal people tend to respond to issues of unfairness, uncertainty, and self-correction. This is fine, and I consider the resulting in-depth analysis to be a strength of the current book. However, this also implies that the current book is not necessarily very good at predicting extremist or terrorist behavior.

Thus, special attention should be paid to the possible tipping points that shift radical people away from staying within the boundaries of the law toward starting to break the law by engaging in violent extremism or terrorism. This is related to the issue of determining when normal individuals start to engage in abnormal behaviors. As mentioned in the

previous chapter, the understanding and prediction of the actual and concrete onset of illegal, violent, and ideologically driven behavior is relatively
underdeveloped in the scientific research literature compared with what
we know about what normal or not so radical people do.

Relevant in this respect is a report that El-Said and Barrett (2017) wrote
for the United Nations Office of Counter-Terrorism. In the report, the
authors note that there is inevitably a "personal" factor that persuades one
Muslim individual to become a foreign terrorist fighter in Syria while his
neighbor, or even his sibling, although exposed to exactly the same environment and subject to the same conditions conducive to radicalization
and extremism, chooses to remain at home. El-Said and Barrett state that
these personal factors are among the hardest to discover and, although of
great importance to the individual, are likely to be the least susceptible to
any broad-based intervention at the community level.

Related to this, a research review by the British Psychological Society
(BPS) sought to understand why people are drawn to extremist beliefs
and to violent extremist organizations.[1] Not surprisingly for the readers of
this book, the review indicates that perceived injustice and societal marginalization are among the core predictors of extremism. As the review
suggests, many would-be violent extremists bear grievances, sometimes
a sense of humiliation (either personally or on behalf of their in-group),
and a desire for revenge. These persons also feel that their needs and
interests are not recognized by mainstream authorities and the status quo.
Saucier, Geuy Akers, Shen-Miller, Kneževié, and Stankov (2009) analyzed
the mindset of many militant and extremist groups around the world, including the Irish Republican Army (IRA) and the Muslim Brotherhood.
Two key beliefs that stood out among these groups were the illegitimacy
of established authorities and that change can only be achieved through
extreme and unconventional means. This fits with the line of reasoning
presented in this book.

The BPS review also indicates that of 242 jihadi terrorists in Europe, most
were in their late teens or 20s, and just five of the jihadists were women

1. See https://digest.bps.org.uk/2014/10/27/the-psychology-of-violent-extremism-digested.

(Bakker, 2006). Another demographic variable standing out is that most Islamist extremists are from upper-class or middle-class backgrounds and tend to be well educated (Silke, 2008). Interestingly, most extremists do not seem to suffer from clear indications of mental illness (Silke, 2008). Personally, I think this could also have something to do with the difficulty of diagnosing mental abnormalities and the fact that researchers often have to rely on individuals who are willing and able to work with self-reports and other diagnosing instruments (see also Corner & Gill, 2015). That said, it is interesting to observe that Borum (2014) concluded that for now the knowledge of mental illness is of not much use in the prevention and repression of terrorism.

Interestingly, Baez, Herrera, García, Manes, Young, and Ibáñez (2017) had 66 incarcerated paramilitary terrorists (with an average of 33 murdered victims) and 66 control participants from the same region in Colombia complete measures of intelligence, aggression, emotion recognition, and moral judgments. Results from that study showed that on most measures, such as intelligence and executive function, there were no differences between the terrorists and the nonterrorist control participants. However, the two groups differed remarkably in their moral judgments on 24 different moral dilemmas.

Unlike control participants, the terrorists judged acts of intended harm with neutral outcomes (such as intending to poison someone but failing) to be more morally permissible than acts of accidental harm (such as poisoning someone by mistake). In a follow-up, the terrorists also rated attempted harm as more morally permissible than accidental harm, compared with a group of incarcerated nonterrorist murderers.

Baez et al. (2017) conclude that this distorted approach to morality implies a problem weighing intentions combined with an excessive focus on outcomes, and it is similar to the moral perspective taken by very young children and by adult neurological patients with damage to the frontal lobe or temporal lobe of their brain (but not by psychopaths, who do seem to weigh intentions when making their moral judgments). The authors conclude that the profile observed in the terrorists may reflect their fixation on utopian visions whereby only (idealized) ends matter.

That is, their outcome-based moral judgments may be related to the belief that any action can be justified.[2]

This finding fits the line of reasoning presented in this book focusing on the importance of judgments of fairness, justice, and morality. Baez and her colleagues suggest that a promising avenue for future investigation will be to see whether careful tests of moral judgment can be used to predict likelihood of future offending in dangerous offenders and also whether and how radicalization alters the nature of people's moral judgments.

Group-based extremism also seems to be influenced by processes of group polarization, especially by the tendency for groups to arrive at more extreme positions than any individual members would have done on their own. Related to this, a shocking feature of the behavior of many violent extremists is their total disregard for the value of other human lives. This is a process that psychologists call the dehumanization of enemies, a process in which out-group others are seen as unimportant and as somehow less than human. Extremists share this feature with members of violent gangs (Alleyne, Fernandes, & Pritchard, 2014) and also with how normal people react with brain responses to drug addicts and homeless people (Fiske, 2009).

Related to this, when British Muslims felt their primary identity was Muslim, rather than British, they held more sympathetic views toward the concept of jihad and martyrdom (Ansari, Cinnirella, Rogers, Loewenthal, & Lewis, 2006; Silke, 2008). Indeed, a key psychological vulnerability of those drawn to extremism is their need to feel they belong. In radical movements and extremist groups, many prospective terrorists find not only a sense of meaning but also a sense of belonging, connectedness, and affiliation (Borum, 2014). As discussed in this book, a related idea is that extremist groups and their ideologies help people cope with uncertainty about themselves and the world (Hogg, Kruglanski, & Van den Bos, 2013).

A quest for significance also can constitute a major motivational force that can push individuals toward violent extremism (Kruglanski et al.,

2. See https://digest.bps.org.uk/2017/06/06/on-psychological-tests-comparing-66-terrorists-with-controls-one-key-difference-stood-out/.

2014). Furthermore, joining a terrorist group can increase the standing of a teenager or youth in some communities. The lure of danger and excitement, especially to young disenfranchised men, also plays an important role, as interviews with former IRA members suggest (Silke, 2008).

Bal and Van den Bos (2017) propose a model that examines when people stop accepting the status quo and instead start embracing alternative social systems, unconventional worldviews, and countercultural norms and associated organizations. In the model, we propose that emotional and behavioral system rejection are important in understanding growing radicalization. When there is no alternative system available, people can only show emotional system rejection. However, when an alternative system is available (such as when membership of a radical group or terrorist organization is a viable alternative), the scale may tip from emotional system rejection to behavioral system rejection, resulting in significantly higher levels of radicalization. In this way, the model identifies under what conditions tipping points may arise that can tilt people from system acceptance or emotional system rejection to active behavioral rejection of the societal system.

In conclusion, although much more progress needs to be made, it seems safe to conclude that more and more becomes known about the lure of extremism and when and why people become likely to adhere to extremist and terrorist beliefs and behaviors (see also Zahedzadeh, 2017). Another tipping point that needs to be studied further is the point at which people are tempted to start a process of deradicalization. The next chapter focuses on that issue in more detail.

## 10.6 COMMUNICATING UNFAIRNESS

Another issue that I would like to discuss explicitly is the important matter of how people communicate experienced unfairness to others. Being social animals oriented toward interpersonal exchanges, people used to talk in interpersonal communication about what they thought was unfair and unjust, often in face-to-face interactions with other persons. For example,

Hudson, Phillips, Ray, and Barnes (2007) used qualitative research methods in two ethnically diverse neighborhoods in the United Kingdom to explore residents' experiences and relationships. Experienced deprivation and disadvantage played a pivotal role in neighborhood relationships. Respondents talked about the unfairness of resource allocation, such as unfairness regarding employment status and housing conditions. Racial tensions were often driven by struggles for such resources.

There is a good possibility that reality is construed by sharing perceptions of unfairness. Focusing on Muslim radicalization, Githens-Mazer (2008) argues that perceived unfairness is a core reason why people radicalize. Furthermore, unfairness perceptions are confirmed and strengthened by the communication and sharing of those feelings with like-minded people. The author suggests that symbols of how Muslims and Islam are repressed affect radicalization among North Africans living in the United Kingdom. Githens-Mazer further proposes that these symbols are an insufficient but necessary cause in the larger process of radicalization because they provide a basis for perceptions of injustice. As such, myths, memories and symbols of colonial repression, contemporary repression of free political expression in North African states, and current perceptions of Western oppression of Islam may be perceived as rationales for exchanges among different Muslim communities throughout Britain that potentially facilitate terrorist networks.

Another classic instance of communication about unfairness is radical media, by which I refer to generally small-scale media that express an alternative vision to hegemonic policies, priorities, and perspectives. Radical media help to communicate about unfairness perceptions and about how social movements aim to do something about the unfairness (Downing, 2001). Interestingly, contemporary terrorists use digital and social media proactively and reach individuals and the public without communicating throughout journalists (Coombs, Falkheimer, Heide, & Young, 2015). Terrorists used to rely on mainstream media to spread their message. But with the creation of social media, terrorists now no longer depend on journalists. Both traditional and modern social media can serve as platforms for like-minded people to meet and discuss their ideas, and because of this, extremist and terrorist groups are known for their active utilization of both media (see also Section 3.11).

Nacos (2016) notes that terrorists used mass media to get attention, spread fear and anxiety among the targets of this sort of violence, and threaten further attacks. The traditional news media's appetite for shocking, sensational, and tragic stories has always resulted in overcoverage of terrorist events and threats. Furthermore, today, social media outlets, such as Twitter, Facebook, and YouTube, allow terrorists to communicate directly with huge audiences around the globe, spreading their propaganda, radicalizing and recruiting followers, and providing information to lone actors about how to engage in terrorist acts.

Thus, a lot of unfairness is currently shared via social media and people tend to live in their own news bubbles or Internet subcultures. Schmidt et al. (2017) find that the advent of social media and micro-blogging platforms has radically changed the way we consume information and form opinions. For example, despite the huge number of news sources to choose from, Facebook users are typically focused on a handful of pages. This yields a clear-cut community structure among news outlets. As a result, users' polarization seems to dominate news consumption on Facebook.

Given the new environment of incessant media presence and social media production, the question becomes how processes of radicalization have changed under the influence of the new types of media. Is it just their pace, such as a two-weeks' radicalization spell instead of the previous months or years? Or has the quality of the process changed as well? These kinds of issues could and should be studied in more depth in future research.

Furthermore, a lot of perceived unfairness and other emotionally upsetting information is experienced on the Internet indirectly. This information does not involve something that happened directly to the perceiver but instead constitutes events that occurred to others with whom the perceiver identifies somehow (Kramer, Guillory, & Hancock, 2014). Terrorists make use of this and exploit global media networks and Internet platforms to carry news of their violence along with propaganda about why they engaged in their deeds.

In fact, one could say that terrorism, and to some extent violent extremism, involves a war of ideologies of what is just and fair. As such, the notions of justice and fairness clash between the ideology of the status quo and the ideology of the terrorists. Stern and Berger (2015) cite Nasser Balochi, a member of ISIS's social media team, who states that whereas a physical war is fought on the battlefield, an ideological war is fought in the media.

Related to this, Klausen (2015) reports how social media played an essential role in the jihadists' operational strategy in Syria and Iraq. She notes that in particular Twitter is used to drive communications, possibly because Twitter streams from the insurgency give a sense of authentic experiences of people committed to certain causes. However, her research on the Twitter accounts of 59 Western-origin fighters known to be in Syria during January through March 2014 suggests that the online streaming of images and information is managed more tightly than is generally recognized. Evidence exists that the communications of the fighters are restricted and that only trusted militants maintain high-volume social media activities. Klausen's hypothesis, therefore, is that what appears to be a spontaneous stream of self-publication using social media is, in fact, controlled communications by terrorist organizations. Tweeting the jihad thus seems to be a powerful and controlled form of communication about experienced unfairness, ideology, and terrorist acts.

The media serve all kinds of purposes. Also, different forms of radicalization use the media for different kind of reasons. For example, terrorist organizations, especially right-wing and religious ones, are working with the philosophy of "the theatre of terror" (De Graaf, 2010). This concept is related to the Chinese proverb: "Kill one, frighten ten thousand" (Klausen, 2015). Another clear example of how terrorist organizations actively exploit the media is their recruitment of new members, which seems an important goal of al-Qaeda's online magazine *Inspire*.

Stern and Berger (2015) note that compelling evidence suggests that social media outlets tend to discourage extremism in the wider population, but for those already vulnerable to radicalization, they create dark pools of social connections. Thompson (2011) and Chebib and Sohail (2011) conclude that social media, even when not actively used by terrorist organizations to recruit new people, actually turned out to be a perfect facilitator of radicalization. One of the reasons for this is that social media provide a density of information flow and emotional perceptions that create a higher probability for radicalization.

In this book, an underlying assumption is that people experience unfairness that can make them adopt radical ideas. It is written with an idea of a "demand" for radical ideas. However, it is also possible to describe radicalization in terms of a "supply" model, such that when people are vulnerable (e.g., when they are uncertain about themselves), they are more likely to be approached by the suppliers of radical ideas. Thus, from this perspective, it is also important to examine the supply side of radicalization and, for instance, examine how propaganda resonates with an audience.

In short, there are many different reasons why communicating unfairness through interpersonal face-to-face and Internet communication may be experienced as real and genuine and may have strong experiential effects among the perceivers of those communications. These communications may cause feelings of threat among potential victims of the terrorist organization, and they also may appeal to persons who are radicalizing by amplifying their thoughts and feelings and inspiring their future behaviors. The next chapter explores what we can do about growing radicalization.

# Practical Implications

*What Can We Do?*

## 11.1 INTRODUCTION

After focusing in Chapter 10 on scientific conclusions and reflections, including a discussion of some important limitations of the current book, the present chapter aims to explore practical implications that follow from the line of reasoning presented in this book. As such, Chapter 11 focuses on what we can do to prevent radicalization and how we perhaps can combat radicalization after it has occurred.

Obviously, trying to intervene in radicalization processes is important in our modern world with its prevalent instances of various forms of radicalization. It is also a somewhat daunting task. To meet the challenges this task poses, scientists can attempt to delineate an elaborate conceptual analysis of what we think is driving current radicalization processes. After that analysis has been constructed, we can then brainstorm about what can be done and how we can develop important tools of prevention and measures of counter-radicalization, including interventions that aim to influence people's thoughts and behaviors in ways that are beneficial to the greater good. In earlier chapters I focused on conceptual analyses of radicalization. Now it is time to brainstorm about possible solutions and interventions.

In line with the conceptual reasoning presented in this book, these practical implications will focus on taking unfairness perceptions seriously (Section 11.2), processes of uncertainty management (Section 11.3), the possible training of self-control (Section 11.4), ways of preventing radicalization (Section 11.5), and how to fight radicalization after it has occurred (Section 11.6).

Many of the measures that I discuss adopt a proactive stance. That is, instead of using a reactive approach whereby you wait for bad things to happen and only then respond, I advocate a proactive approach in which you actively think at early stages about what you can do to against radicalization, extremism, and terrorism. I also work from the maxim by Popper (2001; after Kant, 1785) that it is a duty of intellectuals and scientists to be optimistic when dealing with difficult issues. In other words, optimism is a moral duty when studying and trying to intervene in issues of radicalization. Let us see what we can do.

## 11.2 TAKING UNFAIRNESS PERCEPTIONS SERIOUSLY

Perceived unfairness, injustice, and immorality are deeply felt by radicalizing individuals and groups. Furthermore, perceptions that things are not right can legitimize the most hideous forms of violent extremism and terrorism. Thus, somewhat ironically, perceiving that certain issues in the world are not right can be associated with future behaviors of the perceivers that clearly are not right. These and other observations in this book warrant the conclusion that there is a good case to make for the importance and relevance of unfairness perceptions in various processes of radicalization.

One of the practical implications that follows from this conclusion is that we need to pay close attention to justice-related symbols. That is, one of the reasons perceived unfairness has such an impact on people is that the unfairness is viewed as an important symbol that signifies how society at large is looking at your cause and the group with which you identify.

For example, in our interviews with Muslims in the Netherlands, we often heard our interviewees remark how important the Sugar Feast is to them. This feast celebrates the end of the fasting period of the Ramadan. Our Muslim respondents noted how much they longed for the Dutch government to stand up for the Sugar Feast and make this an official holiday.

To be very clear: Personally, I find any religion nonsense. I am an atheist, and I do not believe in religion rationally (Dawkins, 2006). And as a person and scientist I have observed many intergroup and intragroup processes associated with organized religion that I do not appreciate at all (see also Altemeyer, 2003; Bushman, Ridge, Das, Key, & Busath, 2007; Harris, 2004; Juergensmeyer, 2003; Stern, 2004). Thus, personally and scientifically I find that there are many good reasons to distance myself from religion and organized forms of human behavior associated with all kinds of religions. I also think it is my right to be a nonbeliever (Cliteur, 2010). And I think that religion can absolutize and moralize political calculations that realistically are made for reasons of self-interest (Juergensmeyer, 2003; Niebuhr, 1932).

Having noted that, I do see the important psychological functions that religion can serve (see, e.g., Allport, 1959; Batson & Stocks, 2004; Baumeister, 2002; James, 1902). Writing about these psychological functions would merit another book. Here I note that as a psychologist I recognize the importance of religiously affiliated symbols such as the Sugar Feast in the Netherlands, the Coptic flag of Christian-Coptic activists in Egypt, and Buddhist temples in Tibet.

Again, I emphasize that as a person I do not necessarily agree with these religious symbols, but as an academic psychologist I see that these and other religious symbols can signify pivotal values for believers of the religions associated with these symbols. This implies that when majority groups and governments would treat these symbols with dignity and respect, while simultaneously communicating basic values of democracy and human rights, this not only could well be the right or polite thing to do (Habermas, 1985) but also could mean that growing radicalization is attenuated, at least among some radicalizing individuals of some important groups. Symbols are important and serve crucial psychological functions for those believing in the symbols. Furthermore, as an intellectual I work from the Enlightenment assumption that I may disagree sharply with what people believe but that I shall strongly defend their right to believe it, as long as democratic values are respected and believers treat nonbelievers with due respect as well (see also Berman, 2003; Cliteur, 2010; Harris & Nawaz, 2015; Huizinga, 1935; Juergensmeyer, 2009; Moghaddam, 2008; Nicholson, 1985; Voltaire, 1763).

I realize that this recommendation can be worrisome for some people. For example, when—in passing—I once noted the issue of the Sugar Feast to a journalist, he made this a big part of his story and sold this to a newspaper that made a big headline of this. This triggered various negative reactions on the Internet. It also yielded stencils hate mail in my university postbox, ventilating that I was selling out Dutch and Western civilized culture.

It is certainly not my intention to sell out what is important about my own culture. Not at all. As I explain in this book, I work from the assumption that the Western Enlightenment process (see, e.g., Hume, 1777; Kant, 1784; Rousseau, 1762; Smith, 1759; Voltaire, 1763) is among the best things that ever happened to humankind and that we should make use of that to fight growing radicalization in our world. After all, the careful reasoning based on solid scientific insight that aims to be conducive for the greater good is among the core assets of our modern world. However, part of the Scientific Enlightenment that I advocate is the notion that we should also include insight from scientific psychology in this Enlightenment process. Careful application from solid psychological scientific insight (including perhaps the positive psychological function of some religious symbols) has a place in tackling the problem of radicalization and how to pursue the prevention of radicalization and to engage in effective counter-radicalization.

As a scientist I try to delineate to the best of my abilities what I think are core issues in processes of radicalization and deradicalization. I also note that perceptions of unfairness drive important reactions of those on the right of the political spectrum. And there is the likelihood that the behavioral sciences tend to miss those insights in many of their studies, in part because many of the participants in those studies do not adhere to right-wing ideologies (Henrich, Heine, & Norenzayan, 2010). Unjust distribution of welfare and decreased access to jobs, housing, and other important outcomes may be among the more important unfairness perceptions that hence may be missed in many important psychological studies on radicalization. Paying appropriate attention to these perceptions is needed to delineate the origins of right-wing radicalization.

Similarly, it would be appropriate and of pragmatic value for governments to pay genuine attention to the basic concerns of left-wing radicals protesting against global injustice in terms of the working of financial organizations and markets, access to good medical care, and other important goods and resources. We should take unfairness perceptions seriously, in part because perceptions tend to have real consequences and because the correct and appropriate treatment of those perceptions in terms of adequate levels of procedural justice may be part of the (beginning of the) solution of the radicalization associated with these perceptions.

Perceived fairness has to do with getting respect from figures that are important to you, including societal authorities. It involves the serious consideration by those figures of your concerns and needs. Thus, fair and just treatment of people means taking them seriously, both in terms of their rights and in terms of their duties. So, fair treatment of Muslim, right-wing, and left-wing radicals does not mean the pampering of those individuals and groups. No. But it does imply giving due consideration to what is on their mind.

Thus, for example, we should pay close attention to people who say they are discriminated or treated in other ways that are unfair. At the same time, we should also take these groups seriously by pointing in gentle yet clear ways to the potential problems these groups face, such as unemployment, instances of criminal behavior, and radicalization. It is of the utmost importance to treat groups and potentially marginalized individuals seriously, with respect, and with due process, while simultaneously engaging in a mature kind of conversation and not allowing people to wallow in self-pity or overinterpretation of instances of discrimination or myths of injustice. Somehow, we should train people to actively engage in processes of self-reliant patterns of behavior. The fair treatment of these people may be part of that solution (Tyler, Schulhofer, & Huq, 2010). Rationally based legal thinking and legal nation-states are also important in this respect.

My attempt to understand how people experience things such as unfairness does not mean that I necessarily approve of those perceptions. Clearly, unfairness perceptions can be over the top and may not closely align with reality. Affective responses to these perceptions can constitute overreactions, making people respond too strongly to things they perceive as unfair. Somehow, we should stop or attenuate this overreacting process. Teaching people to deal with these affective responses by channeling the responses into appropriate behavioral reactions aimed at trying to change what is unfair while simultaneously staying within the boundaries of the law and paying respect to core democratic values may be crucial here.

## 11.3 UNCERTAINTY MANAGEMENT

One of the issues closely related to the experience of unfairness is people feeling uncertain about themselves (Van den Bos & Lind, 2002). Although some think that uncertainty provides windows of opportunities, for the large majority, the experience of personal uncertainty is annoying (Van den Bos, 2009a). People want to get rid of the feeling that they are uncertain about themselves or—at a bare minimum—want to be able to manage the feeling and deal with it in some way. The experience that one is being treated fairly by important authorities can be very beneficial in this respect (Van den Bos, 2005, 2015).

Furthermore, people form their judgments of fairness and unfairness under conditions of informational uncertainty in which they do not know how to interpret the situation at hand, for example, because the information that would be most relevant in forming the judgments is not readily available (Van den Bos, Lind, Vermunt, & Wilke, 1997). Under these conditions of unavailable or insufficient information, the information that is at hand—often procedural fairness information—tends to serve as substitute for the missing information (Van den Bos, Wilke, & Lind, 1998). This provides another reason why fairness information—and especially information about procedurally fair treatment—influences people's responses in uncertain circumstances.

Receiving fair treatment from societal authorities is thus conducive to enhanced participation and successful integration in society. After all, being treated fairly by important members of society signals that you are valued and are considered to be a full-fledged member of society (Lind & Tyler, 1988). Viewed from this perspective, procedurally fair treatment may help to fight unemployment and other conditions of individual and group deprivation (Jahoda, 1982). Thus, our modern world, which is full of different sorts of uncertainties, may provide us with important means to manage these uncertainties when societal and other authorities treat us in fair ways. As such, uncertainty management by means of fairness judgments may be a pivotal tool that we can use to attenuate radicalization, even for those with a strong potential to radicalize within our society (Van den Bos & Loseman, 2011).

When people's certainties are threatened, they have a strong need to affirm their values. In part, this effect is there because an uncertain world is a world in which it is difficult to find meaning. Rovenpor, Leidner, Kardos, and O'Brien (2016) demonstrated that under meaning threat, people who identify strongly with their group strengthened their support for military-based conflict resolutions of intergroup conflicts such as the Israel-Palestinian conflict. These findings are consistent with the notion that when meaning is threatened, people affirm their preexisting values.

One of the values on which people rely is religion. As such, religion can serve important psychological functions. Staub (2011) reviews recent programs to deradicalize captured or suspected Islamic terrorists. He notices that a central component of deradicalization programs is religious authorities engaging in dialogue with detainees about their ideology, such as the nature of their religious beliefs and their relationship to terrorist activities, and promoting a more tolerant and peaceful vision of "true" Islam. Some former militants in some programs indeed seem to be persuaded in this way (Staub, 2011, p. 365).

I hasten to emphasize that religion is often at the core of radicalization and associated problems, so this way of deradicalizing zealous religious believers is far from an easy task. I also observe, however, that Staub (2011) notes that a core reason why deradicalization of religious believers may (or might) work is justice. Staub (2011) argues that "justice is important for healing and reconciliation, with retributive justice (punishment), restorative justice (compensatory actions), procedural justice (an effective justice system), and just relations (fair access for everyone to societal resources) all important aspects of justice" (p. 442).

The social psychology of religious role models also plays a crucial role in the deradicalization of religious radicals. Imams and other religious authorities can lead by example and show peaceful interpretations of the particular religion that may positively affect zealous believers (Staub, 2011). Furthermore, because of its uncertainty-reducing properties, procedural fairness by leaders and societal authorities can yield a constructive and effective approach to conflict resolution, especially for those citizens high in need for closure (Giacomantonio, Pierro, & Kruglanski, 2011; Pierro, Giacomantonio, Kruglanski, & Van Knippenberg, 2014).

When personal uncertainties are a salient concern, there is a strong tendency to think in abstract terms about other people and to dehumanize out-groups (Hogg, 2004, 2011). Furthermore, people tend to morally justify these dehumanization and abstraction tendencies (Bandura, 1990).

Abstract thinking and dehumanization processes can be countered by humanizing out-group members and (potential) victims of violent extremism and terrorism (Hermann & Hermann, 1990). After all, psychological distancing from and thinking in abstract and derogatory terms about potential victims of violent extremism and terrorist attacks are necessary before such acts can be approved. By implication, decreasing psychological distance and attenuation of psychological abstraction can turn out to be powerful tools to counter tendencies toward radicalization.

All these instances of commendable behaviors can be very difficult to achieve for people. However, as Bandura (1999) notes, people are also capable of remarkable moral courage. In those remarkable cases, individuals can triumph as moral agents over compelling situational pressures to behave otherwise. Such moral heroism is most strikingly documented in rescuers who risked their lives, often over prolonged periods fraught with extreme danger. For example, those who worked to save from the Holocaust persecuted Jews with whom they had no prior acquaintance, when they had nothing material or social to gain by doing so. Thus, not only do humans engage in the most revolting sorts of behaviors and the most repulsive group processes, but they also are capable of stepping up and rising above themselves as true moral leaders, even under dire and uncertain circumstances. This brings me to the subject of the next section.

## 11.4 TRAINING OF SELF-CONTROL

Various radicalization processes seem to be exacerbated by radicalizing individuals not being able to sufficiently control their self-centered, affective, and intuitive responses. This suggests that another important aspect of the social psychology of radicalization is insufficient self-control of first responses. When people are not sufficiently controlling their self-centered reactions, radicalization is more likely.

From my personal experience as a lecturer, working at both a psychology department and a law school, I get the impression that controlled responses to self-centered first reactions are possible. For instance, from lecturing not only psychology students, but also judges, public prosecutors, and high-ranked police officers, I know that the latter nonstudent population learned to adopt mindsets in which they respond in more controlled ways to stimuli to which psychology students tend to react in affective-intuitive ways.

For example, compared with the psychology students that I lectured for many years now, the nonstudent, highly educated officials working in areas of law and law enforcement tended to respond in much more controlled ways to instances of the Implicit Association Test (IAT). When taking the IAT, participants are asked to respond as quickly as possible to certain words. The goal of the IAT is to measure people's spontaneous associations between mental concepts in memory (for more information, see Greenwald, McGhee, & Schwartz, 1998).

Although some controversy still exists regarding the IAT and how to interpret the findings resulting from this test, what always strikes me is that in the psychology lecture hall, students show reliable intuitive associative reactions to out-groups. For instance, White psychology students tend to show negative implicit associations to names of Islamic origins, such as Achmed and Mohammed. This effect works every time in the psychology classroom, even when the predominantly liberal students are well aware of the effect, attesting to the implicit quality of what is measured with the test.

In contrast, however, the highly educated officials working in areas of law and law enforcement did not show these IAT effects when using the same setup in their lecture room. Compared with the psychology students, they slowed down their responses, hence making less errors and not showing negative responses to Islamic names. One thing this suggests to me is that training of controlled mindsets and self-control is possible. Indeed, from carefully conducted lab experiments, I know that it is possible to successfully train rationalistic mindsets in which all relevant information is weighed carefully (Maas & Van den Bos, 2009; Van den Bos & Maas, 2009).

Thus, although not undisputed, I work from the assumption that training to control initial, self-centered responses is possible. Furthermore, self-control tends to make you a better person. This is not to say that training of self-control is easy, without problems, and a panacea to most issues surrounding radicalization. Not at all. But I do note there are important developments in the areas of implicit evaluations and controlled responses, such as the work by Kawakami, Phills, Steele, and Dovidio (2007), discussed in Chapter 6.

Furthermore, there is evidence to suggest that spontaneous or intuitive and more controlled processes may work in parallel, such that the former may always be strongly activated, whereas the latter may be more strongly or less strongly activated, depending on situational cues and individual predisposition (Strack & Deutsch, 2004). It is my prediction that future psychological research will show important developments in how people can learn to train their levels of self-control. I hope these insights can be used in meaningful ways to help people with high radicalizing potential to engage in sufficient correction processes.

An insight that can be helpful in this respect is enhanced understanding of the psychophysiological processes underlying the effects discussed here. For example, the startle reflex discussed in Chapters 5 to 7 (see, e.g., Petrescu et al., 2018) is strongly related to activation of the amygdala. The amygdala is traditionally known as the fear center but also consists of many different areas, each with its own different functions. How amygdala activation is turned into more controlled responses is dependent on people's preexisting notions, such as the extent to which they are prejudiced against other groups (Derks, Scheepers, & Ellemers, 2013). More insight into these fascinating processes is needed to yield very concrete practical implications.

One source of practical implications, and how and in what directions to train self-control, can be found in the notion of the social contract. Much can be said about this notion (see, e.g., Hobbes, 1651; Locke, 1689; Rousseau, 1762). Here I argue that in the end we as citizens should strive to close a social contract between ourselves and the democratic society we are living in. In the (hypothetical) contract, the society in turn obliges to take care of our basic needs and to pay due consideration to our concerns. We as citizens respect the democratic society in which we are living and ideally try to ensure that our behaviors correspond with the greater good of the society at large. In other words, we want to be respected and taken seriously by society at large, including societal authorities, majority groups, and government. In turn, we should do our utmost to ensure that we respect those other parties in society. Viewed in this way, respect, fair treatment, and due consideration are a two-way street between citizens and societies and are a mutual concern of all of us.

I place these notions firmly in ideas of what I call Scientific Enlightenment. That is, somehow we need to push ourselves to rely on the immense capacities of the human cognitive system so that we open up to those with whom we disagree and do our utmost to defend their right to speak out. When others' discrepant thoughts stay within the limits of democratic principles and nonviolence, we must control our impulses to quash these discrepant thoughts. We then should strive to act as responsible democratic citizens and control our responses to ideas and persons who are really different from us.

I also think that training programs can be targeted in that direction, teaching people how to open up and respond in more controlled ways to different (democratic, nonviolent) views. This can be difficult, to be sure, but humans' cognitive capacities and motivational forces are quite impressive, when you think of it, and can be used for the greater good by many people (albeit definitely not everyone; Van den Bos et al., 2011; see also Berger & Zijderveld, 2009; Hoogerwerf, 2002).

Of course, these kinds of statements are not without problems and do not come without important caveats. One is that the society in which we are living is sufficiently strong and democratically organized in such a way that it is possible to protect the rights of both majority and minority groups and adheres to solid principles of good government (see also Hume, 1742). Things might be quite different in the case of citizens who are dealing with a clearly nondemocratic and perhaps even illegal government (El-Said, 2015). Related to this, people need to be protected against the power of government (Montesquieu, 1748), and governments should allow citizens to do what their conscience tells them to do, within the limits of solid democratic principles and nonviolence.

Another problem is that it can be very hard for people to start using their enormous cognitive capacities and to respond in rational and critical yet open ways to different and new viewpoints. For example, Shah, Michal, Ibrahim, Rhodes, and Rodriguez (2017) note that there are various reasons why everyday scientific reasoning can be challenging. For example, we as humans are biased by our prior beliefs. Even experts of human behavior suffer from the human foibles that undermine scientific thinking. People's critical faculties are contaminated by their motives and the confirmation bias to seek out evidence that supports their existing beliefs. Shah and colleagues point out that raw cognitive ability in terms of IQ is not a good predictor of a person's ability to think like a scientist. More relevant is mental attitude, including people's need for cognition and their ability or motivation to override gut instinct and reflect deeply. Shah et al. also note that these mental dispositions may be trainable (and more so than basic intelligence). Thus, thinking and responding in a scientifically enlightened way is very hard, but perhaps it is more doable and better trainable than we sometimes tend to think.

Again, I hasten to emphasize that all this is not without difficulties. For instance, clearly people can overreact, and some individuals, cultures, or subcultures are even more likely to do so than others. After all, people can respond with overly intense affective reactions to things they perceive as unfair (Van den Bos, Maas, Waldring, & Semin, 2003). This can result in responses that are overly self-obsessed and self-centered. Self-reflecting and inhibiting your initial responses, as well as not taking yourself and your own perspective too seriously, sometimes can be a good thing (e.g., Van den Bos & Lind, 2002; Van den Bos, Müller, & Van Bussel, 2009; see also Chapter 6).

As Durante, Eastwick, Finkel, Gangestad, and Simpson (2016) write, inhibition refers to the extent to which an individual overrides an urge to enact a particular behavior. One major means through which people inhibit such urges is self-control, the process by which people hold themselves back from engaging in behavior they otherwise would enact. These and other reflections may help in the prevention of radicalization. It is to this important subject that I now turn.

## 11.5 PREVENTING RADICALIZATION

Now that I have discussed why and how we should take unfairness perceptions seriously, as well as how important moderators such as how people deal with their uncertainties and how they can train self-control can impact the radicalization process, it is time to focus on concrete measures pertaining to the prevention and combating of radicalization. In the current section I focus on issues of prevention. I do this in part because all theories reviewed here (see Chapter 3) explicitly note how important long-term solutions are. And they all state that prevention is key to addressing the issues of radicalization, extremism, and terrorism. After all, prevention of radicalization may have better chances of success compared with the challenging task of deradicalization of those who have already adopted high levels of radicalization. Furthermore, the line of reasoning presented in this book is probably most relevant to the possible prevention of radicalization.

Interestingly, Post (2007) argues that an important psychological strategy for countering terrorism is to focus on the life course of terrorists and to try to intervene at key stages of the terrorist's life (see also Sarma, 2017; Sieckelinck & De Winter, 2015; Speckhard, Jacuch, & Vanrompay, 2012). I agree with this suggestion. So, those interested in the prevention of radicalization can use the different steps and processes identified in this book, which are illustrated in the various figures included in the book, and try to come up with meaningful interventions at the various stages, steps, and processes identified.

For example, one recommendation that I have is to focus on preventing people from shifting from having radical thoughts to engaging in radical, violent, and illegal behaviors (see also Alimi, Demetriou, & Bosi, 2015). This also includes prevention of the overly abstract thinking that so often causes left-wing radicals, such as Ulrike Meinhof, to dehumanize the people who are potential victims of their extremist violent behaviors (Aust, 1985, 2009). Thus, prevention measures should also focus on the abstracted, depersonalized thoughts adhered to by radicalizing individuals.

The amount of respect that radicalizing individuals and groups pay to those who hold other beliefs is another issue that needs to be taken into consideration. It is fine when different groups uphold different beliefs, but Stern (2004) argues convincingly that when radical, extremist, or religious groups do not give other groups the same amount of respect as they would like to receive themselves, this is a violation of the Golden Rule, which often can be seen as an indication of intergroup relations going awry (see also 2.6). Differential or insufficient amounts of respect being given to those with different views thus is something that needs to be prevented and fixed.

Effective prevention of radicalization may also be achieved by paying close attention to processes of societal polarization. Azough (2017) notes that the prevention of social conflict and radicalization should occur at early stages. Adolescents and other young individuals can be vulnerable to various extreme and radical opinions that they can encounter in their environments. It is important that professionals (such as teachers) present in those environments can help the potentially radicalizing persons, for example, by listening to their thoughts and opinions and providing them with information. Ideally, this will increase the chances that the youths involved will be motivated to integrate in society and will successfully find their place in society.

Enabling successful integration in society can be viewed as one of the best ways to prevent radicalization of individuals as well as large groups of people. The Dutch government underscores this line of reasoning and argues that prevention of extremism is of the utmost importance. The government further proposes that professionals who work with the youngsters involved should be supported in getting sufficient information and the right tools so that the chances are increased that they will act in the best way possible to help to prevent the radicalization process to grow further. Of course, societal integration is not an easy task and is not a treatment that does wonders for all the kinds of radicalization processes and potential radicals out there. However, prevention focuses on the large basis that potentially is underlying various forms of extremist movements and perhaps even terrorist groups. Within-group persuasion may also help, such as when imams refuse to pray for those who committed terrorist attacks.

Another way in which growing radicalization may be prevented is by paying appropriate attention to meaningful differences between various forms of radicalization and, after this analysis, trying to construct tailored programs of prevention measures. For example, I note that an important distinction can be made between radicalization that is associated with group membership and radicalization that is more strongly linked with individual beliefs and convictions. Processes of group radicalization may be difficult to tackle, but not impossible (e.g., Staub, 2006, 2011, 2015)— for instance, when those who might be likely to identify with extremist groups are pointed to the differences between those groups and comparable other groups. Thus, providing information that al-Qaeda is fighting ISIS (or vice versa) may help to prevent the growth of group-oriented Muslim radicalization processes (see also Nawaz, 2013).

Similarly, the presenting of information that runs counter to the opinions of right-wing groups may be one element that may help to prevent the further growth of people's sympathy for right-wing movements. It is pivotal that factual information is present for societal authorities and other important figures (such as teachers or managers who interact with upgrowing youth) to counter and prevent the growth of unwarranted extremist thoughts of right-wing groups in society.

Individual beliefs that certain things are wrong and that an individual hence has the right to do something about this, even if this means breaking the law in a violent manner, may be much harder to influence. The experience that one is morally right and feelings of moral righteousness may be quite resistant to social influence. Related to this, many Red Army Faction members who spent time in jail for their misdemeanors did not show any sign of regret or remorse when being released from prison after many years.

Nevertheless, it may be possible that social media can help to prevent the growth of many different forms of radicalization. For example, Shelly Palmer writes on LinkedIn that in our complex world where different cultural worldviews clash, evolutionary biology offers a multimillion-year-old lesson that the good guys must simply and decisively overwhelm the bad guys with good information.[1] The good information must be programmed better than the bad information, and it must be propagated in overwhelming amounts. We can select the social media world we want to live in and social-engineer our way back to safety. Palmer notes that he is not suggesting that messaging alone can change the underlying issues that have given rise to this problem, but rather he proposes that messaging can be incredibly impactful, perhaps especially at the margins of society. It is possible that Palmer is naïvely optimistic, but the impact of social media should not be underestimated and may well turn out to be helpful in the prevention of the further spread of radicalization.

In his counterterrorism strategy, the Dutch National Coordinator for Security and Counterterrorism (2016) notes that individuals, groups, and networks must be prevented from perpetrating terrorist acts. This means identifying and tackling radicalization early, before someone actually becomes an extremist or a terrorist. It also means working closely with other sectors in a multidisciplinary approach: intelligence services, local government, security services, police, the private sector, youth care workers, mental health services, teachers, and so on. The challenge is to identify potential terrorists before they can carry out an attack (National Coordinator for Security and Counterterrorism, 2016).

A key goal of preventive measures is to prevent and disrupt extremism and to thwart terrorist attacks. To this end, the various partners should work together closely to minimize fear, prevent the recruitment of new extremists or terrorists, and curb security risks posed by individuals and networks. Specifically, this entails preventing fear of extremism and terrorism in society, preventing recruitment so that extremist and terrorist groups do not gain followers, disrupting threats by weakening radical groups and undermining their activities, and thwarting attacks by warding off attacks and violence in due time.

1. See https://www.linkedin.com/in/shellypalmer/.

Successful preventive measures are comprehensive, threat-focused, tailored to the situation at hand, and sustainable. This translates to comprehensive policy and implementation, with a wide range of interventions (local, national, international, administrative, operational, civil, military, investigative, prosecutorial) by a wide range of partners (including operational services, mental health services, youth care, municipalities, educators, and the armed forces). This also includes targeting interventions toward people and groups that pose the greatest threat according to threat analyses. Because each case of radicalization is unique, dynamic, and multifaceted, this entails tailored approaches and specific implementation practices (National Coordinator for Security and Counterterrorism, 2016).

While acknowledging how hard the successful prevention of radicalization may be, and how difficult it may be to come up with good, concrete prevention programs, I nevertheless argue that we should try to develop these programs. Prevention measures are not "soft" measures, but instead aim to be smart measures. It is the same as with criminal behavior: The legal system needs to complement crime-fighting behavior with smart measures that try to prevent criminal behavior. That said, prevention measures alone are insufficient to counter the abominations of violent extremism and terrorism. As such, combating radicalization is also important, and this is the subject of the next section.

## 11.6 FIGHTING RADICALIZATION

In fighting radicalization, violent extremism, and terrorism, it is essential to use not only preventive but also repressive measures in order to combat radicalization. Early identification of what is going on is key to preventing and combating radicalization. Of course, both the prevention and the combating of radicalization need to take place under the rule of law so that the democratic legal order is safeguarded. Thus, preventive and combative measures need to be able to use all the resources afforded by the law and the rules of democracy. The measures taken must have a legal basis, be proportional, and respect fundamental rights (National Coordinator for Security and Counterterrorism, 2016).

Enforcing criminal law is a vital part of combating violent extremism and terrorism. Criminal investigation, prosecution, and trial can have both a preventive and a repressive effect. Societal authorities can use the powers afforded to them under criminal law to intervene early in order to stop preparatory acts. The priority is preventing a terrorist offense from being carried out. If extremists and terrorists do break the law, criminal justice authorities need to be able to respond appropriately. This includes relying on repressive measures under criminal law, such as detention.

Terrorists want to instill fear among the general public by carrying out attacks (including suicide attacks). Those who are prepared to commit such violence are not usually deterred by the threat of a long custodial sentence (National Coordinator for Security and Counterterrorism, 2016). Therefore, criminal prosecution is also about stopping terrorists before they can carry out acts of violence. If possible, action needs to be taken while acts of violence are still in the planning stage. Furthermore, deradicalizing extremists may be even more important than getting them to simply disengage from terrorist activities, according to Rabasa, Pettyjohn, Ghez, and Boucek (2010), who examined counter-radicalization programs pertaining to Muslim radicalization in the Middle East, Southeast Asia, and Europe. As such, deradicalization is an essential part of fighting violent extremism and terrorism.

Deradicalization of those who have been recruited into extremist groups and movements is a difficult task that entails precise psychological interventions tailored at the specific sort of radicalization at hand. A key question in these kinds of interventions is whether the objective of counter-radicalization programs should be disengagement (a change in behavior) or deradicalization (a change in beliefs) of militants and radicals (Rabasa et al., 2010).

Careful and precise mapping of psychological interventions targeted at important behaviors or beliefs thus is crucial. This implies that a precise understanding of the psychological processes leading to the target behaviors and/or beliefs is necessary (Kok, Schaalma, Ruiter, Van Empelen, & Brug,

2004). After all, interventions targeted only at change in behavior may well entail a focus on different psychological processes and mechanisms than interventions that first target change in beliefs and then change in behavior (Buunk & Van Vugt, 2008).

Furthermore, getting militant radicals to refrain from violence is only part of the process. Preferably, the goal is to get individuals to change their belief system, reject the extremist ideology, and embrace a moderate worldview (Rabasa et al., 2010). Ideally, such an intrinsic change in radicals' beliefs leads to an attenuation of their violent behaviors.

A unique challenge posed by militant Muslim groups is that their ideology is rooted in a major world religion, Islam. This can make it very difficult for Muslim extremists to change their beliefs and their associated behaviors because the requirements of the ideology are regarded as religious obligations (Rabasa et al., 2010). Similarly, ideologically driven left-wing and right-wing radical beliefs may be difficult to change. Thus, we should not be naïve when fighting extreme and ideological forms of radicalization, nor can we be overly optimistic about the success rates of deradicalization and counter-radicalization programs.

Related to this, Ashour (2009) notes on the deradicalization of jihadists that two issues stand out: jihadists' support of violence (radicalization) and their attitudes toward democracy and democratization (reactions to modernization). Deradicalization of jihadists is a process within Islamist movements in which a radical group reverses its ideology and delegitimizes the use of violent methods to achieve political goals while also moving toward an acceptance of gradual social, political, and economic changes within a pluralist context. A group undergoing a deradicalization process ideally abides by democratic principles, but Ashour (2009) notes that deradicalization of jihadists often is primarily concerned with changing the attitudes of armed Muslim movements toward violence, rather than democracy, because many deradicalized Muslim groups still adhere to misogynistic, homophobic, xenophobic, and antidemocratic views. Related to this, Stern (2004) has argued quite convincingly that democratization is not necessarily the best way to fight Islamic extremism.

Having said that, some important progress has been made toward successful deradicalization of at least some radical groups. For example, Bjørgo (1997) interviewed far-right extremists in Scandinavia and found that the majority of neo-Nazis actually become disillusioned with their lives after a number of years. What made it difficult, however, for these people to break away from the right-wing movement was fear of reprisals, social isolation, or disappointing their friends. In his pioneering 1997 book on deradicalization, Bjørgo detailed how neo-Nazis can nevertheless muster the psychological strength to turn their backs on their brutal pasts. This is important because scholars of extremism are often focused on understanding how ordinary adolescents can morph into racist thugs. Bjørgo's insights helps to counter the general idea that you can prevent people from joining extremist groups, but once they have joined these groups, all is lost.

For example, Horgan, Altier, Shortland, and Taylor (2016) describe the disengagement and deradicalization of a violent right-wing extremist. Prison exposed this female extremist to interactions with a racially diverse population who, much to her surprise, began to befriend her despite knowing who she was. The fair treatment that she got from the non-White inmates who treated her like any other person was an important element in the forming of the friendship relations. After she developed a level of rapport with these women, they began questioning her about her beliefs in open and honest discussions. In having to explain these beliefs in this way, she became progressively more uncomfortable defending her commitment to an extreme right-wing ideology. Her decision to pursue an educational degree while in prison also broadened her perspective and challenged her commitment to right-wing extremism. She mentions that in her courses she started learning about various aspects of life that she had not considered before, and she started to realize that the world is so much bigger than her previous beliefs, ideas, and feelings. This realization gave her a terrific sense of freedom and an insight that she could achieve a sense of self-worth and belonging outside of her involvement in right-wing violent extremism. As a result, she started to actively participate with and help out women of all different races.

The issues of fair treatment, opening up, and active participation described in the Horgan et al. (2016) case fit the line of reasoning
portrayed in this book and resemble the case by Nawaz (2013) of successful
deradicalization of a Muslim extremist. They may also be of use when
fighting antidemocratic thoughts present in extremist groups, such as extremist left-wing groups or Muslim extremist groups. For example, based
on the work by Moghaddam (e.g., 2005, 2006, 2008, 2010; Moghaddam &
Marsella, 2004), trainers have been starting to use techniques such as the
democracy circle as a method for the discussion and training of the concept of democracy.[2]

The technique of the democracy circle focuses on the associations
and experiences of participants that they have when answering the
question: "What does democracy mean for me personally, what is my relation, am I critical or convinced by it?" Self-reflecting on their answers and
hearing from the other participants' perspectives can help people to learn
about democracy and other concepts that need self-control. This seems
to work especially well when people are asked to reflect on the following
statements: (1) I can be wrong; (2) I must be critical about everything, even
about what my community thinks is definitely right or what I consider to
be morally right; (3) When confronted with proof otherwise, I will need to
reevaluate my opinions; (4) I need to try to better understand people who
are different from me; (5) I can learn from others; (6) For information and
opinions, I need to search in various different sources; (7) I need to be
open to new experiences; (8) I need to create new experiences for others;
(9) There are principles of right and wrong; and (10) Not all experiences
are equally important.

Again, I emphasize that we should not be overly optimistic about democracy and the learning of democratic values (Stern, 2004; see also Li,
2009). In other words, the democracy circle and other intervention and
training techniques are no panacea to cure every type of radicalization.
Having said that, these kinds of techniques may help people to open up
and respond in more controlled ways to things they perceive to be unfair

2. See http://getting-involved.net/wiki/Democracy_Circle.

and that create emotionally upsetting experiences. I base this insight in part on what happened with followers of extreme left-wing movements in the 1980s. When people such as (some) squatters saw the unjust behaviors of important elements in these movements, they stopped believing in the just cause of the movement, and this helped with the attenuation of the squatters' movement and other instances of left-wing extremism (Demant, Slootman, Buijs, & Tillie, 2008).

The treatment of psychological trauma and the treatment of fears and uncertainties may also be needed to help people to become more open-minded and open up to other ways of thinking and behaving, for example, in the case of people who have been engaged in extreme violence. Fair treatment by societally important authorities may serve as a crucial component in processes of deradicalization and counter-radicalization (Van den Bos & Loseman, 2011).

Other issues that need to be taken into consideration are the reduction of stereotyping and prejudicial attitudes (Berger, Abu-Raiya, & Gelkopf, 2015) and the proper reforming of extreme religious schools (Blanchard, 2008). An enhanced understanding of what exactly leads to aggressive and violent behavior can also be of help here (Baumeister, 1997; Berkowitz, 1993; Borum, Fein, Vossekuil, & Berglund, 1999; Pynchon & Borum, 1999), as well as an understanding of the factors that lead people to renounce violence and instead embrace nonviolent political opposition (e.g., Dudouet, 2013; see also Karagiarmis & McCauley, 2006). We also need to point people not only to their rights but also to the responsibilities that they have as citizens, and people should be encouraged to take up these responsibilities (Altuntas, 2016). Taking these and other kinds of issues into consideration may help us to design successful deradicalization programs (see, e.g., Webber, Chernikova, et al., in press).

Of crucial importance when fighting radicalization and developing respective programs is to identify and tackle the sources of the various radicalization processes that are out there. Thus, I am not against the fighting of violent extremism and terrorism with force of police and military. Quite the contrary. As a Reserve Officer of the Royal Dutch Army, it would be quite weird for me to oppose this. But I also note that it is pivotal that sources of radicalization need to be studied carefully and then taken away. Only this can yield a long-term solution to violent, extremist, and terrorist movements. The final conclusions and reflections pertaining to this line of reasoning are discussed in the final chapter of this book.

# Discussion

*What Is Next?*

## 12.1 INTRODUCTION

It is clear that trying to analyze and deal with radicalization, extremism, and terrorism can pose formidable challenges. This book developed some tentative directions on how to approach these difficult issues. In doing so, I worked from the conjecture that humans are creatures with enormous brain capacities who in principle can behave in disciplined and self-controlled ways. This notion can be contrasted with a strong tendency in the current field of psychological science to try to debunk the role of conscious and controlled processes. I explicitly contrast myself from this view because I think it is misguided and perhaps to some extent simple-minded (see also Baumeister & Masicampo, 2010; Dennett, 2003). I therefore embraced the ideal of Scientific Enlightenment that values cultural and intellectual forces that emphasize reason, analysis, and deliberative and independent thought.

I also contrasted my perspective with postmodern ideas and other philosophies in which "anything goes." Specifically, I proposed the use of an Advanced Golden Rule that argues for treating others with respect and an open mind, emphasizing not only rights but also responsibilities and duties for all parties involved in the interaction. Thus, I put forward the assumption that respectful treatment, coupled with distribution of responsibilities and a mature acceptance of those responsibilities, can be an important aspect of the prevention of radicalization and perhaps also of deradicalization strategies. If this assumption were validated, this would reveal key insight into how open, democratic societies can grow and truly flourish.

The current line of reasoning fits Kepel and Rougier's (2016) account that noted that when a strong feeling of injustice meets an enabling environment, this can contribute significantly to enhanced radicalization. Double standards in how justice principles are seen to be applied in this world may also play a prominent role among radicalizing individuals, such as radicalizing Muslims (Abdelkarim Honing & Sterkenburg, 2015). The crucial psychological quality of unfairness perceptions implies that demographic variables alone are not likely to lead to radical, extremist, or terrorist behaviors. In contrast, how these background variables and other issues in people's worlds are perceived is crucial. After all, we have seen that perceptions of unfairness may lead to a combination of extreme thoughts and strong feelings that may result in decisions to commit illegal behaviors and a gradually evolving or sudden explosion of violence and extremist and terrorist acts.

From what I have discussed, it also follows that cooperative motivation and sufficient cognitive capacities (coupled with adequate education and social coordination skills) are key to understanding and perhaps predicting whether people who run the risk for embracing high levels of radicalization can, in fact, be motivated and persuaded to adopt lower levels of radicalization or (preferably) assume a nonviolent and democratic attitude toward their belief system and the place of it in an open and democratic society. I argued that this applies especially to prevention of radicalization. I examined the potential relevance for deradicalization as well.

In trying to delineate practical insight for politicians, policy decision makers, lawyers and judges, and others, I suggested that to pay careful attention to how situations are perceived and interpreted by people can contribute to the understanding of radical behavior. Politicians and policy decision makers can use this insight, and the specifics described in this book, to better understand and predict the violent behaviors of potentially radical and extremist individuals. In this way the scientific insights presented in this book may help to provide meaningful input that can be used by practitioners to develop measures to counter violent and antidemocratic beliefs and sympathy for extremist and terrorist behaviors.

The conceptual line of reasoning conveyed in this book and the conceptual models that I put forward bring together many topics covered in the chapters of this book. However, conceptual models are always simplified depictions of reality, and this is particularly true for complex and multifaceted phenomena such as radicalization and deradicalization. It is important therefore to discuss limitations of the line of reasoning presented here and mention explicitly the things the presented models do not address. To this end, this final chapter discusses important exceptions and caveats to the standpoints taken in the book.

One important possible limitation of the current book is its relevance to populations of very extreme radicals. In this context I note that the analysis this book puts forward may not be relevant when people are unwilling or unmotivated to correct their self-interested impulses and when they strongly adopt antidemocratic orientations and extreme levels of radicalization. For example, the issue of self-control on which I focus here involves people's capacity and motivation for bringing their first, intuitive, gut-based responses in line with standards, values, and morals that are conducive to values of Scientific Enlightenment, democratic principles, the greater good, and democratic society at large. These kinds of self-correction processes may not be applicable to advanced levels of radicalization, such as is the case with severe extremists and actual terrorists.

Furthermore, people can be too lazy to act in smart and sensible ways. It is true that people's levels of self-control are limited and that they can act as cognitive misers (Fiske & Taylor, 1991). However, although controlled processes are limited by capacity, they are more flexible than automatic processes (Devine, 1989). After all, the capacities of the human brain allow for several controlled processes. Their intentionality and flexibility make them particularly useful for decision making, problem solving, and the initiation of new behaviors.

Notwithstanding the problems with issues of self-control, democratic values, and science and Enlightenment, I propose that our brain capacities can operate successfully as a source of self-control and that democracy and Scientific Enlightenment may be the best things we can offer as a society. Thus, although I agree with Churchill when he stated that "The best argument against democracy is a five-minute conversation with the average voter," I also note that Churchill in addition remarked that "Many forms of government have been tried, and will be tried in this world of sin and woe. No one pretends that democracy is perfect or all-wise. Indeed, it has been said that democracy is the worst form of Government except all those others that have been tried from time to time."[1]

The same applies to issues of Enlightenment. Of course, reasonable issues can be raised about our reasoning capacities and our motivation to use these capacities. But let's not overdo it. People also can be smart creatures who strive for the better good (Van den Bos, Van Lange, et al., 2011; see also Sandel, 1982, 2009, 2012; Staub, 2011). Furthermore, Kant (1784) argued convincingly that Enlightenment is an emergence from self-incurred immaturity. He argued that the immaturity is self-inflicted not from a lack of understanding but from the lack of courage to use one's

1. See https://nl.wikiquote.org/wiki/Winston_Churchill.

reason, intellect, and wisdom without the guidance of another person or party. Thus, he views the motto of Enlightenment as "Dare to be wise"!

On that note, please allow me to discuss some personal reflections, such as that I really detest rigid-minded, bigoted people, and that I really think we should strive for more open-minded reactions, no matter how hard this sometimes can be. I also emphasize that although my line of reasoning clearly points to the importance of psychological perceptions of unfairness for the understanding, prevention, and fighting of radicalization, I am not a big fan of postmodern approaches to radicalization, extremism, and terrorism.

I also want to state explicitly here that insight into radicalization, extremism, and terrorism often relies on empirical findings that are less strong than one ideally wants them to be or that I as a research psychologist trained in experimental social psychology am used to. Thus, I want to note explicitly that the conceptual line of reasoning that I presented in this book needs backup from strong empirical findings. This also applies to the conceptual models that I put forward. For example, more empirical research is needed to test, and hopefully support, Figures 4.1, 4.2, 4.3, 5.1, and 6.5.

The next section focuses in detail on the issue of how to study radicalization and what things to consider in future projects on this issue (Section 12.2). How researchers decide to study radicalization is influenced by whether they assume that radicalization, extremism, and terrorism involve relatively "normal" people or constitute rather "abnormal" individuals. I discuss these normality and abnormality hypotheses in the section thereafter (Section 12.3). How to assess the probabilities of the pathways that are put forward by conceptual models of radicalization should also be considered in future radicalization projects. In realistically assessing these probabilities, models of radicalization should delineate what precise endpoints their pathways lead (and do not lead) to (Section 12.4). Furthermore, when intervening in radicalization processes, legal and ethical concerns deserve our attention. Legal and ethical issues also warrant our attention when studying radicalization and when working together with social stakeholders, policy decision makers, politicians, and in general societal institutions from the status quo (Section 12.5). The book closes by noting that using both the strengths and weaknesses of what this book has to offer can lead to enhanced understanding of radicalization processes and a better grounding of the prevention of (law-violating) radical and (violent) extremist behaviors in society (Section 12.6).

## 12.2 HOW TO STUDY RADICALIZATION

Because I place myself and my account of radicalization firmly in the tradition of Scientific Enlightenment, it is important to reflect on how to study processes of radicalization in a scientific way. In doing so, I consider the strengths and weaknesses of the various scientific methods used in empirical studies on radicalization. I also reflect on the field of experimental social psychology, my home ground.

Studying radicalization obviously can be very difficult. People radicalize about different issues in different ways. The extent to which respondents are radicalized is also important. When studying radicalization, at least a minimum of radicalization is often present among research respondents. However, when radicalized, potential respondents may be difficult to contact and may not trust the interviewer from a university or research institute who hence belongs to the status quo or to groups different from the respondents' groups. Furthermore, ideally one wants to study how radical beliefs transfer into extremist behaviors, but it is often not possible to reliably examine the actual engagement in extremist behaviors, and researchers therefore often refer to assessing sympathy for extremist behaviors among their respondents instead. In short, there are several difficulties when studying the topic of radicalization.

The current book is not a textbook on radicalization research, nor does it aim to provide a full account of the many different research studies that have been conducted on radicalization. Having said that, when you reflect on the scientific study of radicalization, you realize that both micro-oriented approaches to radicalization research (such as quantitative psychological studies on individual processes pertaining to radicalization) and macro-oriented approaches (such as qualitative research from the so-cial sciences and humanities on social and societal issues relevant to radi-calization) suffer from important limitations.

Focusing on quantitative psychological research first, an obvious problem for this field is the fact that data are hard to come by on radicalizing persons. This especially applies to those who are committed to violent extremist behaviors, and the problem is even worse for getting data from terrorists (McCauley & Moskalenko, 2008, p. 418). As a result, systematic data about these groups of respondents are lacking (McCauley & Moskalenko, 2008, p. 426).

Quantitative scientists studying radicalization often have to rely on groups of respondents that can be sampled in a relatively convenient way, relying on voluntary participation and snowball methods in which a radicalizing respondent suggests possible other respondents. These nonrandom sampling methods easily yield problems of differential selection and participation biases and thus quickly violate important assumptions of research designs (Cook & Campbell, 1979; Kirk, 1995; Smith, 1981).

The samples in radicalization studies often tend to be much smaller than what quantitative psychologists are used to or are comfortable with (Webber, Babush, et al., in press). Although it can be argued that the population of radicalizing people (and especially those who engage in violent extremism or terrorism) is relatively small, and hence the sample that is studied does not need to be very large, it is a fact that the power of many samples in radicalization studies is debatable (see Cohen, 1988, 1992; Faul, Erdfelder, Lang, & Buchner, 2007). It can also be difficult to meaningfully compare different persons or groups of respondents and to make sure that these groups are calibrated on important background variables, such as when examining violent and nonviolent far-right groups in the United States and exploring the violent and legal behav-ioral patterns over their life cycles (see Kerodal, Freilich, Chermak, & Suttmoeller, 2014).

Furthermore, it is typically very difficult or impossible to replicate findings of studies that are conducted with radicalized persons such as violent extremists and terrorists. There tend to be too few of these kinds of participants, and how they interpret their individual and contextual background variables tends to vary too much, to be able to conduct meaningful replication studies. The difficulty in replicating results is worsened because issues of radicalization tend to be rather unique. This attests to the difficulty of solid quantitative radicalization research. This is an important limitation for current psychological research in which replication is a very important issue (e.g., Kruglanski, Chernikova, & Jasko, 2017; Schooler, 2014a, 2014b) and in which testing for statistical significance of hypotheses tends to be highly valued (Cohen, 1994). It may also be difficult to share confidential data about radicalized participants with other scientists, hence not contributing to an open science account preferably used in modern research projects.

It also can be difficult to conduct experiments on radicalization, extremism, and terrorism (Hogg, Adelman, & Blagg, 2010). Because there are good reasons why experiments are the most widely preferred and accepted method in modern psychological science, this can be viewed as a potentially serious problem in the study of radicalization, although there are some solutions to this, for example, conducting worldview defense experiments (see, e.g., Hogg et al., 2010). In short, a simple use of quantitative empirical methods may not necessarily work very well when examining processes of radicalization, extremism, and terrorism.

Moreover, the quantitative study of perceptions of fairness and unfairness—the core explaining variables of this book—is not without problems. For example, already in 1990, J. Martin, Scully, and Levitt noted in the flagship journal of scientific social psychological research that "methodological and ethical concerns make it difficult to study injustice under conditions in which economic inequality is extreme, people are severely disadvantaged, livelihoods are at risk, the surrounding context is delegitimated, and feelings of injustice are sufficiently intense to provoke bloodshed" (p. 281). Indeed, in-depth insight into what respondents experience when we interview them in quantitative surveys about what they think is unfair tends to be underdeveloped (Finkel, 2001).

Qualitative approaches to the study of radicalization, such as those conducted in the social sciences or the humanities, are not without problems either. For example, anthropological researchers may sympathize or empathize too much with their radical, extremist, or terrorist respondents. The subjective interpretation is another potential caveat of anthropological studies.

Furthermore, narrative methodologies and the reliance on autobiographies of (former or current) radicals may also suffer from important limitations. For example, Wilner and Dubouloz (2011) note that readers of autobiographies can only interpret the events, characteristics, and relationships the author makes public. Researchers using these autobiographies thus have to rely on the information that the author wants published. As a result, the author of the autobiography controls the scope of the empiricism, not the researcher. Moreover, autobiographies can be self-serving or can portray biased accounts of the author's historical importance.

What most quantitative and qualitative studies of radicalization share is a reliance on self-reports from radicalized persons or individuals who state they have deradicalized. But how can you trust radicalized or deradicalized people to tell the truth? And even if they are inclined to tell the truth, how can you be sure that they have accurate insight into their reactions and behaviors? Having to rely on self-reported data can severely undermine the quality of studies conducted among normal, nonradicalized participants and the validity of the interpretation of the findings that follow from these studies (see, e.g., Baumeister, Vohs, & Funder, 2007; Goldstone & Chin, 1993; Lelkes, Krosnick, Marx, Judd, & Park, 2012). This can be an even bigger problem when interviewing radicalized people (see also Koerner, 2017).

In short, researching radicalizing processes in solid, scientific ways can be challenging. Quite often, empirical studies on radicalization, using either quantitative or qualitative research methods, yield data that are less strong than one wants. This implies that the various accounts on radicalization that are out there tend to be based on a relatively weak empirical basis, that is, a basis that is weaker than most experimental psychologists are used to. This also applies to the account presented in this book.

However, processes of radicalization are too important in this world to leave them alone and to return to the psych lab to focus instead on controllable and hence sometimes somewhat narrow concepts and research topics. In contrast, what is needed, I propose, is to rely on a variety of research methods to address the multifaceted issues of radicalization, extremism, and terrorism. The complexity of radicalization processes brings ambiguity to the interpretation of these processes and how to intervene in the processes. This also implies that it is likely that there is no single "magic bullet" or single research method that will nail down all the various instances of radicalization that are present in our world (see also Devine, Forscher, Austin, & Cox, 2012). Instead, several methods are more likely to work in combination to meaningfully analyze what is going on in terms of radicalization.

This obviously involves more or less qualitative interviews with former lone wolves (Hamm & Spaaij, 2017), incarcerated Middle Eastern terrorists (Post, Sprinzak, & Denny, 2009), and detained Tamil Tigers (Kruglanski et al., 2017; Webber, Chernikova, et al., in press). But this also includes the quantitative study of the spreading of Islamist ideology in different Spanish jails (Trujillo, Jordán, Gutiérrez, & González-Cabrera, 2009) or the application of "Big Data" approaches to processes of radicalization. And in my view, this also warrants the reliance on studies with nonradicals, nonextremists, and nonterrorists, such as many studies reviewed in this book.

I also argue that it is pivotal to complement the insights from these different empirical studies with careful and sometimes perhaps speculative conceptual reasoning. It is fine to speculate about possible notions of radicalization processes, I think, as long as one clearly identifies where inspecting of data stops and where speculation begins. I relied on this multiperspective approach to the empirical and conceptual study of radicalization when writing this book, and I hope that I treated the various empirical findings that have been published correctly and that my conceptual reasoning and theoretical speculations made some sense.

## 12.3 ABNORMAL BEHAVIORS WITH NORMAL AND
##      ABNORMAL ROOTS

How researchers decide to study radicalization is influenced by whether they assume that radicalization, extremism, and terrorism involve relatively "normal" people or constitute rather "abnormal" individuals. In other words, what do they consider to be the roots or the sources of the abnormal behaviors and detestable acts extremist and terrorists engage in? Mental disorders? Psychic problems? Deviant personality traits? Particular combinations of demographic variables and/or personality factors that make up certain profiles? Psychosocial issues?

The issue of whether radical people who engage in violent extremism or terrorism should be regarded as "normal" or "abnormal" individuals is an important subject in the radicalization literature. A lot has been reported about this issue, especially in the area of terrorism research (see, e.g., Ruby, 2002; Silke, 2009). Understandably, many have observed that terrorists engage in hideous acts and do terrible things, quite often on the basis of a readiness to die (e.g., Merari, 1990). It should not come as a surprise, therefore, that authors have argued for the need for proficient mental health professionals in the study of terrorism (e.g., Beutler, Reyes, Franco, & Housley, 2007).

Gill and Corner (2017) recently reviewed this literature and concluded that many early studies on terrorism focused on psychopathy as the core explanatory variable. For example, Pearce (1977) viewed terrorists as sociopaths who are unable to monitor themselves in sufficient ways. Pearce speculated that engaging in extremism provides an outlet for underlying mental health problems. Cooper (1978) argued that terrorists possess psychopathic or sociopathic personalities. He proposed that if terrorists were not engaging in political violence, they would find another outlet for their violent impulses. Similarly, Tanay (1987) put forward that terrorist acts are merely psychopathic tendencies hidden behind political rhetoric to provide the terrorist with an excuse to aggress. In short, early studies on terrorism offered psychopathy as a cause of terrorist involvement and focused on individual drives as a source of people becoming terrorists.

In addition to studies focusing on psychopathy as a cause of terrorist involvement, other early studies on terrorism focused on specific personality types. In fact, many studies explored various aspects of personality, with narcissism the most common (Gill & Corner, 2017). Narcissism constitutes an overinflated sense of self. Many narcissists feel superior to others, possess volatile self-esteem, have interpersonal problems, and are prone to aggression in response to ego threats (Hogg & Vaughan, 2005). Narcissistic injuries, caused by early emotional injuries, lead to a damaged sense of self in adulthood. Incapable of overcoming these early emotional experiences, the individual directs his or her anger toward other targets held to be responsible. Lasch (1979) and Pearlstein (1991) asserted that narcissism is key to understanding the terrorist personality.

Gill and Corner (2017) conclude that despite the popularity of the notion that terrorists are psychologically damaged youths, accounts that focus on the causative nature and prevalence of psychopathy and specific personality types are currently not strongly supported by robust empirical evidence. Thus, as of yet there is no strong empirical support for the notion that terrorists are severely suffering from pathological or personality disorders.

As a result of this empirical weakness, and because of reasons that follow from conceptual analyses of fields such as social psychology, the current focus of many radicalization approaches is on an understanding that involvement with extremist and terrorist groups is a complex process and that involvement with extremist and terrorist acts is usually the outcome of a pathway that includes multiple push and pull factors that differ across various instances of radicalization (Gill & Corner, 2017). The current book aimed to portray such a pathway approach that I hope works across different instances of radicalization, such as Muslim, right-wing, and left-wing forms of radicalization.

Importantly, I argue that it is crucial to distinguish extremist and terrorist *behaviors* from the *processes* that lead up to these behaviors. To be very clear about this, the violent and illegal *behaviors* that extremists and terrorists can engage in are abnormal. You certainly must be crazy to some extent to engage in these kinds of extremist and terrorist acts. These behaviors are also extreme in a statistical sense in that they clearly deviate from what normal people do. In other words, extremism and terrorism are activities with very low base rates (Gill & Corner, 2017). Furthermore, from the perspective of democratic states, violent extremism and terrorism constitute abnormal, detestable behaviors.

In my view it is likely that some aspects of extremist and terrorist behaviors are probably explained by psychopathological factors and deviant personality characteristics, in short by abnormal psychological *processes*. But some other aspects are in all likelihood also explained by psychological processes that are not so abnormal and that extremists and terrorists share with normal people who do not engage in violent and illegal behaviors (see also Horgan, 2003; Silke, 2009; Silke & Schmidt-Petersen, 2015). Thus, I argue that the *abnormal behaviors* extremists and terrorists can engage in are probably the result of both *normal and abnormal psychological processes*. If this assumption were validated in future research, this would imply that a combination of social psychological, psychopathological, and personality factors is most likely to explain particular instances of radicalization in the best way possible.

Viewed from this perspective it makes sense to include conceptual analyses in the study of radicalization that rely on carefully obtained research findings from controlled psychology experiments with nonextremist and nonterrorist participants. Of course, one should not overdo this and rely solely or too much on data from normal participants. However, given the scarcity and difficulty of obtaining reliable data from extremists and terrorists, one should not exclude normal data as well. The controlled process data collected among these participants may contribute to the conceptual analyses needed to yield a robust science of radicalization processes.

I hasten to note that I agree with Moskalenko and McCauley (2009), who explicated that extremists and terrorists constitute a subset of radicals only. The likelihood of moving from endorsing radical beliefs that stay within the law to actively engaging in illegal violence is not accessible in studies of mostly nonviolent respondents. Thus, great care should be used when applying in-depth knowledge of normal processes to the understanding of radicalization and possible interventions against these sorts of behaviors.

Furthermore, Merari (2010) proposes that "by and large, the opinion that terrorists do not have a common psychological profile rests on the absence of research rather than on direct findings. A scientifically sound conclusion that terrorists have no common personality traits must be based on many comparative studies of terrorists from different countries and functions, using standard psychological tests and clinical interviews. As such studies have not been published, the only scientifically sound conclusion for now is that we *do not know* whether terrorists share common traits, but we cannot be sure that such traits do not exist" (pp. 253–254).

Similarly, the studies that are regularly cited as confirming the absence of mental disorders or personality factors are potentially not as rigorously examined as those confirming a relationship (Gill & Corner, 2017). Furthermore, mental disorders or personality factors might be subsumed as a subset of behavior, such as contextual factors like early experiences or social psychological factors like perceived unfairness, experienced uncertainty, motivation for self-correction, and other variables discussed in this book.

Thus, the potential role of mental disorders or personality types, including their possible interaction with social psychological variables, in extremist and terrorist involvement should be examined carefully in future research. For now, it is my conjecture that both the psychology of normal psychological reactions and the psychology of abnormal behavior may best work in combination to explain radicalization, extremism, and terrorism. Furthermore, the psychology of unfairness perceptions and the associated issues of uncertainty management and self-corrections probably play a key role in both "normal" and "abnormal" aspects of radicalization.

## 12.4 REALISTICALLY ASSESSING PROBABILISTIC PATHWAYS

What is also needed in future research is a better assessment of the models presented in the study of radicalization. This includes both increased empirical insight and advanced conceptual analyses. This also entails a realistic assessment of the pathways that are included in many current approaches to radicalization. Thus, I hope that future studies examine in depth the models presented in this book with careful empirical research methods, test in detail the pathways of the figures put forward in the book, and enrich the theoretical and conceptual line of reasoning presented in the book.

The models that are current in the research literature often include pathways leading to increased radicalization (Gill & Corner, 2017). The conceptual and empirical study of radicalization and counter-radicalization should examine in detail the precise pathways that are put forward. In my view these pathways need to be subjected to more fine-grained and more robust empirical examination than currently is the case. Ideally, this empirical study should calculate or estimate with scientific rigor the probabilities of these pathways. The study of radicalization pathways also should include a careful consideration of what endpoints these pathways realistically lead to. These insights should then be used in prevention, deradicalization, and counter-radicalization projects that try to intervene in radicalization processes.

Importantly, the pathway models put forward in this book and elsewhere are not deterministic models, delineating that certain steps will necessary take place in a particular order and that radicalization always will develop in certain prescribed ways. Instead, the models should be treated as conceptual accounts that describe with certain likelihood probabilistic associations relevant to understand increased radicalization. The causal quality of these models needs to be examined by means of careful empirical examination and thoughtful conceptual analysis.

Typically, people are very bad at assessing probabilities (see, e.g., Tversky & Kahneman, 1974, 1979, 1980, 1981, 1983, 1986). This human quality affects all of us, including radicalization researchers and policy decision makers. It also includes me, and it includes you, the reader of this book. As a result, we can systematically overestimate or underestimate the causal probability of certain events. This certainly applies to the study of radicalization and the pathway models used to advance this study. For instance, as the writer of this book, who is enthusiastic about his empirical findings and who is dedicated to his conceptual line of reasoning, it is easy to overestimate the statistical likelihood and causal quality of the probabilistic associations of the models I present. To give another example: For those who are new to social psychology, it is easy to underestimate the impact of people's perceptions on their subsequent behavioral responses. Thus, care should be taken when interpreting and evaluating the pathway models presented in this book and in other publications.

Future research should also aim to reveal when tipping points take place that exacerbate growing radicalization and when tipping points occur that spur the beginning of deradicalization processes. Thus, I agree with Kepel and Rougier (2016) that there is a need for more empirical, comparative, and interdisciplinary research on the social, individual, demographic, and cultural dimensions of radicalization. This includes studies that examine tipping points to violent extremism and terrorism, and projects that reveal when processes of deradicalization become more likely. Furthermore, I note that radicalization is not always a gradually evolving process. Sometimes, radicalization may occur very rapidly. People may also skip certain phases stipulated in radicalization models. All this necessitates not only careful empirical examination but also thoughtful conceptual analysis.

Importantly, I stand in the tradition of "experimental social psychology," founded by people like Kurt Lewin and John Thibaut. Coming from that tradition, I argue for a more thorough empirical study of radicalization processes. Having said this, it is important to note that the word "experimental" does not imply that I am only interested in laboratory studies that involve the random assignment of participants to experimental conditions. Indeed, in contrast to this narrow interpretation, John Thibaut used the term in a far broader sense to refer to a thorough, conceptually well-grounded empirical study of social thoughts, feelings, and behaviors (see Ostrom, 1986). Thus, with Thibaut I am not arguing for any methodological orthodoxy. I am indifferent to whether empirical data are collected in a lab, survey, or field setting, or whether the data are from a correlational or random-assignment research design (see also Van den Bos, 2014). Of primary importance is that empirical data advance the theoretical understanding of the problem under study, in this case radicalization. With this theoretical or conceptual understanding, we can start to implement successful intervention programs. After all, Kurt Lewin argued convincingly that for application and intervention, "there is nothing so practical as a good theory" (Lewin, 1951, p. 169).

Although I ground myself firmly in the approach to experimental social psychology as conceived by Lewin and Thibaut, and while I agree with Gill and Corner (2017) that more robust empirical examination of radicalization processes is needed, I also think it is time to acknowledge that we need to become more modest about what empirical studies can reveal about radicalization, extremism, and terrorism. Quantitative and qualitative empirical studies can tell us only so much about radicalization. This is what it is, and I argue for a careful delineation of what our findings do show and what they do not reveal. Sometimes, we research scientists become too enthusiastic about our scientific methods. As a result, we can overstate the importance of our results (see also Kuhn, 1962; Lakatos, 1976). Thus, without adopting a "postmodern" account or any other overly relativistic version of what science tells us, I do argue for a realistic perspective on what empirical findings can tell us about radicalization, extremism, and terrorism. Science does not produce facts, but instead yields insights that are preliminary and need further testing, made possible by refined thinking (see also Popper, 1957). Empirical findings, therefore, need to be complemented with careful conceptual analysis.

Related to this, a conceptual analysis of radicalization is an interpretation of what is going on in the world and necessarily entails to some extent a simplification of reality. Somewhat grudgingly we need to admit this. And with Einstein and others, I note that in developing scientific models, everything should be made as simple as possible, but not simpler. I hope the present account presents a well-grounded interpretation of radicalization processes and of how unfairness perceptions may fuel these processes.

In arguing for a firm yet realistic assessment of pathway models, the study of radicalization also should include a careful consideration of what endpoints the identified pathways realistically lead to. Understandably,

there is an inclination to focus on what could be considered the ultimate endpoint: behavior. Indeed, radical and especially extremist and
terrorist behaviors are hideous and constitute what you ultimately want
to prevent and fight. Furthermore, many research psychologists in the
end want to be able to predict and explain behavior (see, e.g., Baumeister,
Vohs, & Funder, 2007). Goerzig and Al-Hashimi (2015) note that a major
point of contention regarding the study of radicalization concerns the
end state of the radicalization process. Does the radicalization process
yield merely radical ideas and beliefs, or does it focus on the process by
which individuals ultimately resort to radical action (see also Mandel,
2009; Neumann, 2013)?

I observe that quite often radicalization models are better able to delineate radical thoughts than extremist behaviors or terrorist acts.
Furthermore, empirically it may also be more doable to get a good grip on
thoughts as opposed to behavior. Thus, adopting the firm yet realistically
modest approach to the study of radicalization I developed here, I argue
that the study and prevention may do well not only to focus on behavior as the ultimate endpoint of radicalization but also to pay appropriate
attention to the radicalization of people's thoughts. Similarly, intervention programs may want to consider concentrating not only on behavioral radicalization, but also on cognitive radicalization. I also note this
because radical thoughts about law and democratic values can be dangerous and can constitute pivotal antecedents of violent extremism and
terrorism. This brings me to a discussion in the next section of legal and
ethical concerns when studying radicalization and possibly intervening in
these processes.

## 12.5 LEGAL AND ETHICAL CONCERNS

Radical behaviors can yield hideous acts of violent extremism and
terrorism. Furthermore, radical thoughts can be dangerous as well. For instance, when left-wing or right-wing radicals think that their opinions are
right and what the law says is fundamentally wrong, and that they do not

need to change the law by democratic means but that they can act instead, even when this implies engaging in violence or instilling terror among those who contribute to what is wrong in society, then radical thoughts are psychologically very close to yielding violent extremism or terrorism. Or, for example, when Muslims adopt radical worldviews and as a result want to use democracy to impose oppressive Sharia law that violate rights of civilized culture and values of Enlightenment, then radical thoughts are dangerous as well. We should not be naïve about this.

I therefore think that there are very good reasons to argue that as a society and legitimate democratic constitutional state, we want to do something about radicalization of both thoughts and behaviors. Having said that, when developing and carrying out intervention programs about cognitive and behavioral radicalization, ethical and legal concerns arise (see also Bartlett & Birdwell, 2010; Netherlands Ministry of the Interior and Kingdom Relations, 2007). These concerns deserve our attention and need to be addressed.

One issue of radicalization interventions is whether it is warranted or ethical to try to influence people's thoughts and behaviors. This is a potentially even bigger problem when social influence attempts make use of unconscious processes. After all, then the targets of the intervention programs do not know what is going on and how their thoughts or behaviors are potentially affected by the communicated information they have processed unconsciously.

Paternalism is another important concern of radicalization interventions. After all, I am not arguing that people should always assimilate toward the majority culture. Clearly, majorities can embrace values that are not great (to put it mildly). Human history has seen many important instances of minority influence that turned out for to be better for the greater good in the long run. As noted, I argue that we should take people seriously. This means that we should seriously listen and give due consideration to people's concerns and that simultaneously we should not shy away from pointing people toward their serious duties and obligations to society and toward those who uphold different thoughts than they do. This is related to what Nawaz (2013) states: "Justice, if it means anything, must mean to adhere to your own confessed principles. Of law and democracy, then stick to what you claim and be judged by it" (p. 193).

Working within the rule of law is also important here (Mak & Taekema, 2016). The rule of law protects individual rights and freedoms and shields citizens from the power of government and other powerholders. It constitutes the legal principle that laws should govern a nation, not the decisions of individual government officials. It primarily refers to the influence and authority of laws within society, particularly as a constraint on behavior, including behavior of government officials. The rule of law implies that every citizen is subject to the law. It stands in contrast to the idea that the ruler is above the law, for example, by divine right (Mak & Taekema, 2016). Thus, those governmental agencies and officials trying to intervene in radicalization processes are not above the law and hence should try to prevent and counter radicalization processes while obeying the law and important legal principles, even when this implies that they are fighting radicalization "with one hand tied behind their back."

There can also be tension between privacy concerns and security concerns (see, e.g., Amnesty International, 2017). Related to this, many conflicts are sparked by a failure to protect human rights (including the freedom of speech and religion), and the trauma that results from severe human rights violations often leads to new human rights violations.[2] As conflict intensifies, hatred accumulates, and this makes restoration of peace more difficult. To stop this cycle of violence, states must institute policies aimed at human rights protection. Many believe that the protection of human rights is essential to the sustainable achievement of the three agreed global priorities of peace, development, and democracy (see also Cassese, 1990).

How we deal with citizens' right to freedom of speech is also crucial here. Freedom of speech is a basic and crucial right, but there are also some important limits to this right, such as that people are not allowed to commend violent extremism or glorify terrorism (see also Berman, 2003; Goerzig & Al-Hashimi, 2015; Neumann, 2013). Related to this, under

---

2. See http://www.beyondintractability.org/essay/human-rights-protect.

some conditions a nation-state is allowed to use physical force, but when nongovernmental individuals or groups engage in similar kinds of violent acts, we call this extremism or even terrorism. This can raise some serious issues. Consider the following event:

> Soldiers are looking for a terrorist. During the search process, a young girl, daughter of the terrorist, hides beneath a table. The soldiers are not able to find the terrorist and return to their barracks disappointed.

How do you respond to this? Are you displeased that the terrorist was not found? But now look at this information:

> The "terrorist" the soldiers were looking for was my grandfather. He was a Dutch resistance fighter. The soldiers were Nazi Germans. The young girl was my mother, scared of the big men with guns.

So, yes, things can go wrong with governmental force, and we should not be naïve about this as well. Out of motivated reasons or because of downright stupidity, governments and government officials can engage in the most unwise or foolish kinds of things, and it is essential that appropriate legal measures are taken to protect citizens against too much government intervention, potential invasion of human rights, privacy concerns, and so on. This is important because when studying radicalization or trying to think of possible ways to intervene in radicalization processes, one often works together with government or other powerholders (see also De Graaf, 2017).

Furthermore, one of the core issues in the study of radicalization is what defines a radical. Goerzig and Al-Hashimi (2015) note that researchers face various challenges when conceptualizing radicalization: What is a radical in the first place, who qualifies as radicalized, and how can we operationalize radicalization? Clearly, in the same way that definitions of the term "extremism" and "terrorism" are disputed, so the terms "radical" and "radicalization" mean different things to different people.

The definition employed by the Netherlands General Intelligence and Security Service (2007a, 2007b, 2009, 2014) underlines the relative element of radicalization by defining it as actions or support for actions that threaten the existing order. Following this definition, radicalization can be described as the active pursuit of and/or support for far-reaching changes in society that may constitute a danger to the continuity of the democratic legal order (aim), possibly by using undemocratic methods (means), which may harm the functioning of that order (effect). Clearly, the perception of the existing order is decisive in the evaluation of what is radical (Goerzig & Al-Hashimi, 2015). This brings me to the end of my reflections.

## 12.6 CODA

I hope this book constitutes a scholarly overview of the literature on the psychology of radicalization and comes across as an enthusiastic account of my passion for the unfairness/injustice theme in this psychology of radicalization. Specifically, what I tried to do in this book is contribute to the insights on radicalization, extremism, and terrorism by offering a sharp and distinctive focus to the restive debate on radicalization, deradicalization, and terrorism. That is, with my emphasis on experiences of unfairness and injustice, I took radicalizing persons and their discourse and motivations seriously. I think this is a welcome addition to the sometimes somewhat fragmented debate on radicalization and associated issues. The argument made about the necessity of understanding experiences of injustice and unfairness for our insights into the trajectory of radicalizing individuals is topical, I hope, and offers an urgent and important aspect to the debate on terrorism and radicalization. Reflections on the importance of injustice are not new in the radicalization literature, but the current book attempted to structurally and methodologically unpack its importance and working in various processes of radicalization.

One risk of the current account might be that I overemphasize the role of perceived unfairness. Certainly, perceived unfairness is a core aspect of

radicalization, and I think few scholars will argue against this idea. Still,
I think it is reasonable to say that perceived unfairness is *one* route to radicalization. There are other routes as well, such as the triggering factors that
I discussed in Section 3.3.2. For example, Feddes et al. (2015) argue that
some individuals are mainly attracted by the weapons, violence, and sensation that radical groups can provide (see also Bjørgo & Carlsson, 2005;
Sageman, 2004, 2009). For these sensation-seeking individuals, fairness
perceptions may not matter that much (Van der Valk & Wagenaar, 2010b;
for other factors, see also Horgan, 2003, 2008, 2009, 2017; Kaplan, Mintz,
Mishal, & Samban, 2009).

Furthermore, now that we have seen some evidence for the hypothesis that radicalization hinges on perceptions of injustice and people's
reactions to these experiences, it becomes important to pay more explicit
attention to the historical and societal contexts in which these processes
occur. After all, these processes do not take place in a vacuum, but instead depend on how the state responds and on how groups in society
respond back to instances of repression or alienation. The historical
and societal contexts of these processes of interaction and radicalization matter. It matters where, how, and when terrorism and counterterrorism unfold to explain the next step and stage of the radicalization
ladder. Indeed, other publications have paid ample attention to the the-
atrical aspects and historical context of radicalization processes (see,
e.g., Crenshaw, 1990, 2009; De Graaf, 2010; Della Porta, 1995, 2009;
Hoffman, 1982; Waldmann & Dieterich, 2007). Furthermore, Gergen
(1973, 1980) has rightfully criticized social psychology—my main
area of research training and expertise—as neglecting the historical
processes that are relevant to understanding what people believe, feel,
and do in social contexts. The social psychology of radicalization and
unfairness could profit from a more in-depth examination of the historical and societal contexts in which various radicalization processes
take place.

Moreover, the primary level of analysis on which I focused here is the
individual and his or her relationship with groups, culture, and society.
Indeed, we saw that perceptions of injustice are so important because they

signal how important groups, your culture, and especially society look at you (Lind & Tyler, 1988; Tyler & Lind, 1992). This psychological or in-depth micro-level approach to radicalization processes has many advantages, I argue, but ideally should be complemented with other approaches that focus more explicitly or more strongly on societal or structural factors (macro-level approaches) and group processes (meso-level approaches). The field of terrorism studies generally distinguishes micro-, meso-, and macro-levels of analysis (Della Porta, 1995; Schuurman, 2017). The methodology I adopted in this book starts at the micro-level and includes elements from group-level theories and societal factors when considered appropriate. The added value of this approach may be exactly this methodological bridge: the connection between perceptions and feelings of injustice and the way these "injustice frames" (Della Porta, 1995, 2009; Gamson, Fireman, & Rytina, 1982) are capitalized on by terrorist and radical groups.

In closing, I want to highlight that in this book I delineated my vision on the issue of radicalization, including how I see the occurrence of various instances of violent extremism and terrorism pertaining to Muslim, right-wing, and left-wing radicalization processes. In approaching this issue, I integrated my take on the psychology of judgments of unfairness and how these judgments are influenced in turn by people sometimes feeling uncertain about themselves and being unable to sufficiently correct their self-centered impulses. Taken together, this sketches a picture of why people can radicalize and how unfairness perceptions can impact the various occurrences of these processes.

You could say that in this book I followed Karl Popper's approach to science. After all, I embraced his ideas of rigorous scientific thinking (Popper, 1959), while noting appropriate limitations of what empirical findings can tell us about radicalization. Importantly, this also included Popper's (1957) notion that science does not produce facts, but preliminary insights. Thus, approving of Popper's "critical approach" to science, I realize that I am probably in favor of my own line of reasoning and that I hence need the cooperation of other scientists, scholars, and practitioners to improve the conjectures that I put forward here.

Furthermore, I valued deeply Popper's maxim (following Kant, 1785) that optimism is a moral duty when studying complex issues such as radicalization (Popper, 2001). Moreover, I took inspiration from his notion of the importance of open societies (Popper, 1945). Working from these sources of inspiration, I elaborated my perspective on the science of radicalization by aiming to delineate the sources of radicalization because this in the long run may be the most successful way to study and possibly prevent and fight radicalization.

In developing my perspective on radicalization processes, I combined my training as a researcher trained in experimental social psychology with my knowledge of law and order and my ideas about open, democratic societies. I realize that there are disadvantages of my approach to science and that important nuances may be needed in scientific methods (see also Kuhn, 1962; Lakatos, 1976). That said, I also think there are important advantages of the approach to the science of radicalization presented here.

In this book I aimed to integrate approaches that concentrate on *why* individuals become members of radical, extremist, or terrorist groups with perspectives that mostly focus on *how* individuals become members of these groups. The result is a perspective on both why people radicalize and how this can occur. This is one perspective, my perspective, and I put it forward in a true scientific spirit. As a scientist I try to observe what I see and what perceptions are out there and to explain these as well as I can. I do not necessarily approve of the various radical ideas and extremist behaviors that I am describing in this book. Nor do I always disapprove of radical viewpoints. As a scientist I merely want to understand what is going on and to convey this as clearly as I can.

I explicitly stayed away from reflecting too much or too long on the many, many definitions and definitional debates that are present in the radicalization literature. I know of these issues and respect the importance of them. With that being noted, in the present book I engaged in constructive science, working together with relevant scientific disciplines and societal stakeholders, in an attempt to get a grip on radicalization processes. In doing so, I relied on insights derived from empirical studies while simultaneously noting the limitations of empirical data and highlighting the importance of conceptual analysis. I also paid attention to practical implications and possible interventions against radicalization and noted the caveats surrounding these issues.

This is a book that is firmly grounded in science. It is also an opinionated book. With my emphasis on the role of Scientific Enlightenment and the notion of taking people really seriously (including their serious responsibilities in states organized on the basis of democracy and the rule of law), I do not walk away from putting forward what I think needs to be said. I tried to do this in a very clear yet also respectful manner. Thus, opinions were ventilated and choices were made that some will agree with and some may disagree with. That is fine. I know that I did my utmost best to write a good, solid, and accessible book on the topic of radicalization and how judgments of unfairness may fuel radical beliefs, extremist behaviors, and terrorism. Hope you liked the book.

## ACKNOWLEDGMENTS

A number of people read and commented on earlier drafts of this book or provided meaningful input in other ways. These include Lisa Ansems, Mark Bovens, Antoine Buyse, Janneke Gerards, Hilke Grootelaar, Liesbeth Hulst, Loran Kostense, Elaine Mak, Karoline Mess, Asteria Straathof, Madelijn Strick, Yaron van Keulen, and anonymous reviewers. I thank them all. Special thanks go to Beatrice de Graaf and Bertjan Doosje for their very helpful comments and suggestions. And a big thank you to Jet Klokgieters for her assistance. I also want to thank Carolyn Hafer for her constructive comments on earlier proposals that led to this book. Finally, I would like to thank Abby Gross and Courtney McCarroll of Oxford University Press for their expert help in putting this book together.

# REFERENCES

Abbas, T. (2007). Ethno-religious identities and Islamic political radicalism in the UK: A case study. *Journal of Muslim Minority Affairs, 27*, 429–442.

Abdelkarim Honing, D., & Sterkenburg, N. (2015). *Ongeloofwaardig: Hoe ik mezelf radicaliseerde, en daarvan terugkwam*. Amsterdam: Uitgeverij Q.

Abelson, R. P. (1963). Computer simulation of "hot cognitions." In S. S. Tomkins & S. Messick (Eds.), *Computer simulation and personality: Frontier of psychological theory* (pp. 277–298). New York: Wiley.

Adams, J. S. (1965). Inequity in social exchange. In L. Berkowitz (Ed.), *Advances in experimental social psychology* (Vol. 2, pp. 267–299). New York: Academic Press.

Adorno, T. W., Frenkel-Brunswik, E., Levinson, D. J., & Sanford, R. N. (1950). *The authoritarian personality*. New York: Harper.

Ajzen, I., & Fishbein, M. (1980). *Understanding attitudes and predicting social behavior*. Englewood Cliffs, NJ: Prentice-Hall.

Alimi, E. Y., Demetriou, C., & Bosi, L. (2015). *The dynamics of radicalization: A relational and comparative perspective*. New York: Oxford University Press.

Alleyne, E., Fernandes, I., & Pritchard, E. (2014). Denying humanness to victims: How gang members justify violent behavior. *Group Processes and Intergroup Relations, 17*, 750–762.

Allport, G. W. (1954). *The nature of prejudice*. Cambridge, MA: Addison-Wesley.

Allport, G. W. (1959). Religion and prejudice. *Crane Review, 2*, 1–10.

Altemeyer, B. (1998). The other "Authoritarian Personality." In M. P. Zanna (Ed.), *Advances in experimental social psychology* (Vol. 30, pp. 47–92). San Diego: Academic Press.

Altemeyer, B. (2002). Dogmatic behavior among students: Testing a new measure of dogmatism. *Journal of Social Psychology, 142*, 713–721.

Altemeyer, B. (2003). Why do religious fundamentalists tend to be prejudiced? *International Journal for the Psychology of Religion, 13*, 17–28.

Altemeyer, B., & Hunsberger, B. (1992). Authoritarianism, religious fundamentalism, quest, and prejudice. *International Journal for the Psychology of Religion, 2*, 113–133.

Altuntas, C. (2016). *Regen zonder modder*. Amsterdam: Athenaeum.

Aly, A., & Striegher, J.-L. (2012). Examining the role of religion in radicalization to violent Islamist extremism. *Studies in Conflict & Terrorism, 35*, 849–862.

Amnesty International (2017). *Dangerously disproportionate: The ever-expanding national security state of Europe*. Report Amnesty.org, EUR 01/5342/2017.

Amodio, D. M., & Frith, C. D. (2006). Meeting of minds: The medial frontal cortex and social cognition. *Nature Reviews Neuroscience, 7*, 268–277.

Amodio, D., Harmon-Jones, E., & Devine, P. (2003). Individual differences in the activation and control of affective race bias as assessed by startle eyeblink response and self-report. *Journal of Personality and Social Psychology, 84*, 738–753.

Ansari, H., Cinnirella, M., Rogers, M. B., Loewenthal, K. M., & Lewis, C. A. (2006). Perceptions of martyrdom and terrorism amongst British Muslims. In M. B. Rogers, C. A. Lewis, K. M. Loewenthal, M. Cinnirella, R. Amlôt, & H. Ansari (Eds.), *Proceedings of the British Psychological Society Seminar Series Aspects of Terrorism and Martyrdom*.

Arendt, H. (1951). *The origins of totalitarianism*. New York: Harcourt, Brace.

Ariely, D. (2012). *The (honest) truth about dishonesty*. New York: HarperCollins.

Arkin, R. M., Oleson, K. C., & Carroll, P. J. (Eds.). (2009). *Handbook of the uncertain self*. New York: Psychology Press.

Armstrong, K. (1993). *A history of God: The 4,000-year quest of Judaism, Christianity and Islam*. New York: Ballantine Books.

Armstrong, K. (2000). *The battle for God: A history of fundamentalism*. New York: Ballantine Books.

Arndt, J., Cook, A., Goldenberg, J. L., & Routledge, C. (2007). Cancer and the threat of death: The cognitive dynamics of death-thought suppression and its impact on behavioral health intentions. *Journal of Personality and Social Psychology, 92*, 12–29.

Aronson, E. (1972). *The social animal*. New York: Viking Press.

Ashour, O. (2009). *The de-radicalization of jihadists: Transforming armed Islamist movements*. New York: Routledge.

Associated Press (2001, June 10). McVeigh offers little remorse in letters. *Topeka Capital-Journal*.

Aust, S. (1985). *Der Baader-Meinhof-Komplex*. Hamburg: Hoffmann und Campe Verlag.

Aust, S. (2009). *Baader-Meinhof: The inside story of the R.A.F.* (revised edition). New York: Oxford University Press.

Austin, W., McGinn, N. C., & Susmilch, C. (1980). Internal standards revisited: Effects of social comparisons and expectancies on judgments of fairness and satisfaction. *Journal of Experimental Social Psychology, 16*, 426–441.

Azough, N. (2017). *Weerbare jongeren, weerbare professionals [Resilient youth, resilient professionals]*. The Hague: Ministry of Education, Culture and Science and Ministry of Health, Wellbeing and Sports.

Baele, S. J. (2017). Lone-actor terrorists' emotions and cognition: An evaluation beyond stereotypes. *Political Psychology, 38*, 449–468.

Baez, S., Herrera, E., García, A. M., Manes, F., Young, L., & Ibáñez, A. (2017). Outcome-oriented moral evaluation in terrorists. *Nature Human Behaviour, 1*, article number 0118.

Bakker, E. (2006). *Jihadi terrorists in Europe: Their characteristics and the circumstances in which they joined the jihad—An exploratory study.* The Hague: Netherlands Institute of International Relations Clingendael.

Bakker, E., & Grol, P. (2017). *Nederlandse jihadisten: Van naïeve idealisten tot geharde terroristen.* Amsterdam: Hollands Diep.

Bal, M., & Van den Bos, K. (2010). The role of perpetrator similarity in reactions toward innocent victims. *European Journal of Social Psychology, 40*, 957–969.

Bal, M., & Van den Bos, K. (2012). Blaming for a better future: Future orientation and associated intolerance of personal uncertainty lead to harsher reactions toward innocent victims. *Personality and Social Psychology Bulletin, 38*, 835–844.

Bal, M., & Van den Bos, K. (2017). From system acceptance to embracing alternative systems and system rejection: Tipping points in processes of radicalization. *Translational Issues in Psychological Science, 3*, 241–253.

Bal, M., & Van den Bos, K. (2018). *A process-oriented view on victim blaming and support for innocent victims: Approach and avoidance motivation in dealing with just-world threats.* Manuscript submitted for publication.

Balliet, D., Parks, C., & Joireman, J. (2009). Social value orientation and cooperation in social dilemmas: A meta-analysis. *Group Processes and Intergroup Relations, 12*, 533–547.

Bandura, A. (1986). *Social foundations for thought and action: A social cognitive theory.* Englewood Cliffs, NJ: Prentice-Hall.

Bandura, A. (1990). Mechanisms of moral disengagement. In W. Reich (Ed.), *Origins of terrorism: Psychologies, ideologies, theologies, states of mind* (pp. 161–191). Washington, DC: Woodrow Wilson Center Press.

Bandura, A. (1999). Moral disengagement in the perpetration of inhumanities. *Personality and Social Psychology Review, 3*, 193–209.

Bandura, A., Barbaranelli, C., Caprara, G. V., & Pastorelli, C. (1996). Mechanisms of moral disengagement in the exercise of moral agency. *Journal of Personality and Social Psychology, 71*, 364–374.

Bandura, A., Underwood, B., & Fromson, M. E. (1975). Disinhibition of aggression through diffusion of responsibility and dehumanization of victims. *Journal of Research in Personality, 9*, 253–269.

Bargh, J. (1994). The four horsemen of automaticity: Awareness, efficiency, intention, and control in social cognition. In R. S. Wyer, Jr., & T. K. Srull (Eds.), *Handbook of social cognition* (2nd. ed., pp. 1–40). Hillsdale, NJ: Erlbaum.

Bargh, J. A. (1999). The cognitive monster: The case against the controllability of automatic stereotype effects. In S. Chaiken & Y. Trope (Eds.), *Dual-process theories in social psychology* (pp. 361–382). New York: Guilford.

Barlow, F. K., Paolini, S., Pedersen, A., Hornsey, M. J., Radke, H. R., Harwood, J., Rubin, M., & Sibley, C. G. (2012). The contact caveat: Negative contact predicts increased prejudice more than positive contact predicts reduced prejudice. *Personality and Social Psychology Bulletin, 38*, 1629–1643.

Baron, R. S., Crawley, K., & Paulina, D. (2003). Aberrations of power: Leadership in totalist groups. In D. van Knippenberg & M. A. Hogg (Eds.), *Leadership and power: Identity processes in groups and organizations* (pp. 169–183). London: Sage.

Bartlett, J., & Birdwell, J. (2010). *From suspects to citizens: Preventing violent extremism in a big society*. London: Demos.

Bartlett, J., Birdwell, J., & King, M. (2010). *The edge of violence: A radical approach to extremism*. London: Demos.

Bartlett, J., & Miller, C. (2012). The edge of violence: Towards telling the difference between violent and non-violent radicalization. *Terrorism and Political Violence, 24*, 1–21.

Batson, C. D., Schoenrade, P., & Ventis, W. L. (1993). *Religion and the individual: A social-psychological perspective*. New York: Oxford University Press.

Batson, C. D., & Stocks, E. L. (2004). Religion: Its core psychological functions. In J. Greenberg, S. L. Koole, & T. Pyszczynski (Eds.), *Handbook of experimental existential psychology* (pp. 141–155). New York: Guilford Press.

Baumeister, R. F. (1997). *Evil: Inside human violence and cruelty*. New York: W. H. Freeman.

Baumeister, R. F. (1998). The self. In D. T. Gilbert, S. T. Fiske, & G. Lindzey (Eds.), *The handbook of social psychology* (4th ed., Vol. 1, pp. 680–740). Boston, MA: McGraw-Hill.

Baumeister, R. F. (2002). Religion and psychology: Introduction to the special issue. *Psychological Inquiry, 13*, 165–167.

Baumeister, R. F., & Leary, M. R. (1995). The need to belong: Desire for interpersonal attachments as a fundamental human motivation. *Psychological Bulletin, 117*, 497–529.

Baumeister, R. F., & Masicampo, E. J. (2010). Conscious thought is for facilitating social and cultural interactions: How mental simulations serve the animal-culture interface. *Psychological Review, 117*, 945–971.

Baumeister, R. F., & Tice, D. M. (1988). Metatraits. *Journal of Personality, 56*, 571–598.

Baumeister, R. F., Vohs, K. D., & Funder, D. C. (2007). Psychology as the science of self-reports and finger movements: Whatever happened to actual behavior? *Perspectives on Psychological Science, 16*, 396–403.

Beauchamp, T. L. (2001). *Philosophical ethics: An introduction to moral philosophy* (3rd ed.). Boston: McGraw-Hill.

Becker, E. (1973). *The denial of death*. New York: Free Press.

Becker, E. (1975). *Escape from evil*. New York: Free Press.

Belanger, J. J., Caouette, J., Sharvit, K., & Dugas, M. (2014). The psychology of martyrdom: Making the ultimate sacrifice in the name of a cause. *Journal of Personality and Social Psychology, 107*, 494–515.

Berger, P. F., & Zijderveld, A. C. (2009). *In praise of doubt: How to have convictions without becoming a fanatic*. New York: Harper Collins.

Berger, R., Abu-Raiya, H., & Gelkopf, M. (2015). The art of living together: Reducing stereotyping and prejudicial attitudes through the Arab-Jewish Class Exchange Program (CEP). *Journal of Educational Psychology, 107*, 678–688.

Berkowitz, L. (1993). *Aggression: Its causes, consequences, and control*. New York: McGraw-Hill.

Berkowitz, L., & Walster, E. (Eds.). (1976). *Advances in experimental social psychology, Volume 9: Equity theory—Toward a general theory of social interaction*. New York: Academic Press.

Berman, P. (2003). *Terror and liberalism*. New York: Norton.

Beutler, L. E., Reyes, G., Franco, Z., & Housley, J. (2007). The need for proficient mental health professionals in the study of terrorism. In B. Bongar, L. M. Brown, L. E. Beutler, J. N. Breckenridge, & P. G. Zimbardo (Eds.), *Psychology of terrorism* (pp. 32–55). New York: Oxford University Press.

Bhui, K., Dinos, S., & Jones, E. (2012). Psychological process and pathways to radicalization. *Journal of Bioterrorism & Biodefense*, S5:003.

Bhui, K., Warfa, N., & Jones, E. (2014). Is violent radicalisation associated with poverty, migration, poor self-reported health and common mental disorders? *PloS One, 9*, e90718.

Bjørgo, T. (1997). *Racist and right-wing violence in Scandinavia: Patterns, perpetrators, and responses*. Doctoral dissertation, Leiden University/Oslo: Tano Aschehougs.

Bjørgo, T., & Carlsson, Y. (2005). *Early intervention with violent and racist youth groups*. Oslo: Norwegian Institute of International Affairs.

Blanchard, C. M. (2008). *Islamic religious schools, Madrasas: Background*. Washington, DC: CRS Report for Congress.

Blau, P. M. (1964). *Exchange and power in social life*. New York: Wiley.

Blumer, H. (1969). *Symbolic interactionism: Perspective and method*. Englewood Cliffs, NJ: Prentice-Hall.

Bodanksy, Y. (2001). *Bin Laden: The man who declared war on America*. New York: Prima Lifestyles.

Bongar, B., Brown, L. M., Beutler, L. E., Breckenridge, J. N., & Zimbardo, P. G. (Eds.). (2007). *Psychology of terrorism*. New York: Oxford University Press.

Borum, R. (2011a). Radicalization and involvement in violent extremism I: A review of definitions and applications of social science theories. *Journal of Strategic Security, 4*, 7–36.

Borum, R. (2011b). Radicalization and involvement in violent extremism II: A review of conceptual models and empirical research. *Journal of Strategic Security, 4*, 37–62.

Borum, R. (2014). Psychological vulnerabilities and propensities for involvement in violent extremism. *Behavioral Sciences and the Law, 32*, 286–305.

Borum, R., Fein, R., Vossekuil, B., & Berglund, J. (1999). Threat assessment: Defining an approach for assessing risk of targeted violence. *Behavioral Sciences and the Law, 17*, 323–337.

Boscarino, J. A., Adams, R. E., Figley, C. R., Galea, S., & Foa, E. B. (2006). Fear of terrorism and preparedness in New York City 2 years after the attacks: Implications for disaster planning and research. *Journal of Public Health Management & Practice, 12*, 505–513.

Bourdieu, P. (1977a). *Outline of a theory of practice*. Cambridge, UK: Cambridge University Press.

Bourdieu, P. (1977b). *Reproduction in education, society, and culture*. Beverly Hills, CA: Sage.

Brockner, J., Heuer, L., Siegel, P. A., Wiesenfeld, B., Martin, C., Grover, S., Reed, T., & Bjorgvinsson, S. (1998). The moderating effect of self-esteem in reaction to voice: Converging evidence from five studies. *Journal of Personality and Social Psychology, 75*, 394–407.

Brown, R., & Hewstone, M. (2005). An integrative theory of intergroup contact. In M. P. Zanna (Ed.), *Advances in experimental social psychology* (Vol. 37, pp. 256–345). San Diego, CA: Academic Press.

Buijs, F. J., Demant, F., & Hamdy, A. (2006). *Strijders van eigen bodem. Radicale en democratische moslims in Nederland [Homegrown warriors: Radical and democratic Muslims in the Netherlands]*. Amsterdam: Amsterdam University Press.

Bushman, B. J., & Baumeister, R. F. (1998). Threatened egotism, narcissism, self-esteem, and direct and displaced aggression: Does self-love or self-hate lead to violence? *Journal of Personality and Social Psychology, 75*, 219–229.

Bushman, B. J., Baumeister, R. F., Thomaes, S., Ryu, E., Begeer, S., & West, S. G. (2009). Looking again, and harder, for a link between low self-esteem and aggression. *Journal of Personality, 77*, 427–446.

Bushman, B. J., Ridge, R. D., Das, E., Key, C. W., & Busath, G. L. (2007). When God sanctions killing: Effect of scriptural violence on aggression. *Psychological Science, 18*, 204–207.

Buunk, A. P., & Van Vugt, M. (2008). *Applying social psychology: From problems to solutions*. London: Sage.

Buyse, A. (2014). Dangerous expressions: The ECHR, violence and free speech. *International and Comparative Law Quarterly, 63*, 491–503.

Cacioppo, J. T., Priester, J. R., & Berntson, G. G. (1993). Rudimentary determinants of attitudes: II. Arm flexion and extension have differential effects on attitudes. *Journal of Personality and Social Psychology, 65*, 5–17.

Camacho, C. J., Higgins, E. T., & Luger, L. (2003). Moral value transfer from regulatory fit: What feels right *is* right and what feels wrong *is* wrong. *Journal of Personality and Social Psychology, 84*, 498–510.

Campbell, E. (2015, 30 July). Are IS recruitment tactics more subtle than we think? BBC News. Retrieved from http://www.bbc.com on August 9, 2015.

Carle, R. (2013). Anders Breivik and the death of free speech in Norway. *Society, 50*, 395–401.

Cassese, A. (1990). *Human rights in a changing world*. Philadelphia: Temple University Press.

Chebib, N. K., & Sohail, R. M. (2011). The reason social media contributed to the 2011 Egyptian Revolution. *International Business Research and Management, 2*, 139–156.

Chirumbolo, A. (2002). The relationship between need for cognitive closure and political orientation: The mediating role of authoritarianism. *Personality and Individual Differences, 32*, 603–610.

Christmann, K. (2012). *Preventing religious radicalisation and violent extremism: A systematic review of the research evidence*. Youth Justice Board for England and Wales.

Christopher, A. N., Zabel, K. L., Jones, J. R., & Marek, P. (2008). Protestant ethic ideology: Its multifaceted relationships with just world beliefs, social dominance orientation, and right-wing authoritarianism. *Personality and Individual Differences, 45*, 473–477.

Cliteur, P. (2010). *The secular outlook: In defense of moral and political secularism*. Chichester, UK: Wiley-Blackwell.

Cohen, J. (1988). *Statistical power analysis for the behavioral sciences* (2nd ed.). Hillsdale, NJ: Erlbaum.

Cohen, J. (1992). A power primer. *Psychological Bulletin, 112,* 155–159.

Cohen, J. (1994). The earth is round (*p* < .05). *American Psychologist, 49,* 997–1003.

Cook, T. D., & Campbell, D. T. (1979). *Quasi-experimentation: Design and analysis for field settings.* Rand McNally: Chicago.

Coombs, W. T., Falkheimer, J., Heide, M., & Young, P. (2015). *Strategic communication, social media and democracy: The challenge of the digital naturals.* London: Routledge.

Cooper, H. H. A. (1978). Psychopath as terrorist. *Legal Medical Quarterly, 2,* 253–262.

Copsey, N. (2004). *Contemporary British fascism: The British National Party and the quest for legitimacy.* New York: Palgrave MacMillan.

Corner, E., & Gill, P. (2015). A false dichotomy? Mental illness and lone-actor terrorism. *Law and Human Behavior, 39,* 23–34.

Cramwinckel, F. M., Van Dijk, E., Scheepers, D., & Van den Bos, K. (2013). The threat of moral refusers for one's self-concept and the protective function of physical cleansing. *Journal of Experimental Social Psychology, 49,* 1049–1058.

Crenshaw, M. (1990). Questions to be answered, research to be done, knowledge to be applied. In W. Reich (Ed.), *Origins of terrorism: Psychologies, ideologies, theologies, states of mind* (pp. 247–260). Washington, DC: Woodrow Wilson Center Press.

Crenshaw, M. (2009). The logic of terrorism: Terrorist behavior as a product of strategic choice. In J. Victoroff, & A. W. Kruglanski (Eds.), *Psychology of terrorism: Classic and contemporary insights* (pp. 371–382). New York: Psychology Press.

Crisp, R. J., & Abrams, D. (2008). Improving intergroup attitudes and reducing stereotype threat: An integrated contact model. In W. Stroebe & M. Hewstone (Eds.), *European review of social psychology* (Vol. 19, pp. 242–284). Hove, UK: Psychology Press.

Crocker, J., & Nuer, N. (2004). Do people need self-esteem? Comment on Pyszczynski et al. (2004). *Psychological Bulletin, 130,* 469–472.

Cropanzano, R. S., & Ambrose, M. L. (Eds.). (2015). *Oxford handbook of justice in work organizations.* New York: Oxford University Press.

Crosby, F. (1976). A model of egoistical relative deprivation. *Psychological Review, 83,* 85–112.

Crosby, F. (1982). *Relative deprivation and working women.* New York: Oxford University Press.

Crosby, F. (1984). Relative deprivation in organizational settings. In B. M. Staw & L. L. Cummings (Eds.), *Research in organizational behavior* (Vol. 6, pp. 51–93). Greenwich, CT: JAI Press.

Dalgaard-Nielsen, A. (2010). Violent radicalization in Europe: What we know and what we do not know. *Studies in Conflict and Terrorism, 33,* 797–814.

Das, E., Bushman, B. J., Bezemer, M. D., Kerkhof, P., & Vermeulen, I. E. (2009). How terrorism news reports increase prejudice against outgroups: A terror management account. *Journal of Experimental Social Psychology, 45,* 453–459.

Dawkins, R. (2006). *The God delusion.* New York: Houghton Mifflin.

Dechesne, M. (2001). *Flexible and rigid reactions to reminders of mortality.* Doctoral dissertation, University of Nijmegen.

De Graaf, B. A. (2010). *Theater van de angst: De strijd tegen terrorisme in Nederland, Duitsland, Italië en Amerika*. Amsterdam: Boom.

De Graaf, B. A. (2012). *Gevaarlijke vrouwen: Tien militanten vrouwen in het vizier*. Amsterdam: Boom.

De Graaf, B. A. (2017). Terrorisme- en radicaliseringsstudies. *Justitiële Verkenningen, 2017-3*, 8–30.

De Graaf, B. A., & Weggemans, D. (2016). Na de vrijlating: Observaties en dilemma's in de omgang met (voormalige) terrorismegedetineerden. *Justitiële Verkenningen, 42*, 78–97.

Della Porta, D. (1995). *Social movements, political violence, and the state: A comparative analysis of Italy and Germany*. Cambridge, UK: Cambridge University Press.

Della Porta, D. (2009). Recruitment processes in clandestine political organizations: Italian left-wing terrorism. In J. Victoroff, & A. W. Kruglanski (Eds.), *Psychology of terrorism: Classic and contemporary insights* (pp. 307–316). New York: Psychology Press.

Demant, F., Slootman, M., Buijs, F., & Tillie, J. (2008). *Teruggang en uittreding: Processen van de-radicalisering ontleed*. Amsterdam: IMES.

Dennett, D. C. (2003). *Freedom evolves*. New York: Viking.

Derks, B., Scheepers, D., & Ellemers, N. (2013). *Neuroscience of prejudice and intergroup relations*. New York: Psychology Press.

Dershowitz, A. (2004). *Rights from wrong: A secular theory of the origins of rights*. New York: Basic Books.

Deutsch, M. (1975). Equity, equality, or need? What determines which value will be used as the basis of distributive justice? *Journal of Social Issues, 31*, 137–149.

Deutsch, M. (1985). *Distributive justice: A social psychological perspective*. New Haven, CT: Yale University Press.

Devine, D. J., Clayton, L. D., Dunford, B. B., Seying, R., & Price, J. (2001). Jury decision making: 45 years of empirical research on deliberating groups. *Psychology, Public Policy, and Law, 7*, 622–727.

Devine, P. G. (1989). Stereotypes and prejudice: Their automatic and controlled components. *Journal of Personality and Social Psychology, 56*, 5–18.

Devine, P. G. (2001). Implicit prejudice and stereotyping: How automatic are they? Introduction to the special section. *Journal of Personality and Social Psychology, 81*, 757–759.

Devine, P. G. (2003). Stereotypes and prejudice: Their automatic and controlled components. In A. W. Kruglanski & E. T. Higgins (Eds.), *Social psychology: A general reader* (pp. 97–113). New York: Psychology Press.

Devine, P. G., Forscher, P. S., Austin, A. J., & Cox, W. T. L. (2012). Long-term reduction in implicit race bias: A prejudice habit-breaking intervention. *Journal of Experimental Social Psychology, 48*, 1267–1278.

Devine, P. G., & Monteith, M. J. (1999). Automaticity and control in stereotyping. In S. Chaiken & Y. Trope (Eds.), *Dual-process theories in social psychology* (pp. 339–360). New York: Guilford.

De Waal, F. (1996). *Good natured: The origins of right and wrong in humans and other animals*. Cambridge, MA: Harvard University Press.

De Wolf, A., & Doosje, B. (2015). *Aanpak van radicalisme: Een psychologische analyse* (2nd ed.). Amsterdam: SWP.

Dittmar, H., & Dickinson, J. (1993). The perceived relationship between the belief in a just world and sociopolitical ideology. *Social Justice Research, 6*, 257–272.

Doosje, B., Loseman, A., & Van den Bos, K. (2013). Determinants of radicalization of Islamic youth in the Netherlands: Personal uncertainty, perceived injustice, and perceived group threat. *Journal of Social Issues, 69*, 586–604.

Doosje, B., Van den Bos, K., Loseman, A., Feddes, A. R., & Mann, L. (2012). "My in-group is superior!": Susceptibility for radical right-wing attitudes and behaviors in Dutch youth. *Negotiation and Conflict Management Research, 5*, 253–268.

Doosje, B., Zebel., S., Scheermeier, M., & Mathyi, P. (2007). Attributions of responsibility for terrorist attacks: The role of group membership and identification. *International Journal of Conflict and Violence, 1*, 127–141.

Downing, J. D. H. (2001). *Radical media: Rebellious communication and social movements*. Thousand Oaks, CA: Sage.

Du Bois, W. B. E. (1998). *Black reconstruction in America: 1860–1880*. New York: Free Press. (Original work published in 1935.)

Dudouet, V. (2013). Dynamics and factors of transition from armed struggle to nonviolent resistance. *Journal of Peace Research, 50*, 401–413.

Dugas, M., & Kruglanski, A. (2014). The quest for significance model of radicalization: Implications for the management of terrorist detainees. *Behavioral Sciences and the Law, 32*, 423–439.

Dunkel, C. S., Mathes, E., & Beaver, K. M. (2013). Life history theory and the general theory of crime: Life expectancy effects on low self-control and criminal intent. *Journal of Social, Evolutionary, and Cultural Psychology, 7*, 12–23.

Dunn, R. G. (1998). *Identity crises: A social critique of postmodernity*. Minneapolis: University of Minnesota Press.

Durante, K. M., Eastwick, P. W., Finkel, E. J., Gangestad, S. W., & Simpson, J. A. (2016). Pair-bonded relationships and romantic alternatives: Toward an integration of evolutionary and relationship science perspectives. In J. M. Olson & M. P. Zanna (Eds.), *Advances in experimental social psychology* (Vol. 53, pp. 1–74). San Diego, CA: Academic Press.

Durkheim, E. (1979). *Suicide: A study in sociology*. New York: Free Press. (Original work published in 1897 as *Le suicide: Étude de sociologie*)

Durkheim, E. (1982). *The elementary forms of the religious life*. London: Allen and Unwin. (Original work published in 1912 as *Les formes élémentaires de la vie religieuse*)

Dzhekova, R., Stoynova, N., Kojouharov, A., Mancheva, M., Anagnostou, D., & Tsenkov, E. (2016). *Understanding radicalisation: Review of literature*. Sofia: Center for the Study of Democracy.

Eidelson, R. J., & Eidelson, J. I. (2003). Dangerous ideas: Five beliefs that propel groups toward conflict. *American Psychologist, 58*, 182–192.

Eisenberger, N. I., & Lieberman, M. D. (2004). Why rejection hurts: A common neural alarm system for physical and social pain. *Trends in Cognitive Sciences, 8*, 294–300.

Eisenberger, N. I., Lieberman, M. D., & Williams, K. D. (2003). Does rejection hurt? An fMRI study of social exclusion. *Science, 302*, 290–292.

Ellis, B. H., & Abdi, S. (2017). Building community resilience to violent extremism through genuine partnerships. *American Psychologist, 72*, 289–300.

El-Said, H. (2015). *New approaches to countering terrorism: Designing and evaluating counter radicalization and de-radicalization programs.* New York: Palgrave Macmillan.

El-Said, H., & Barrett, R. (2017). *Enhancing the understanding of the foreign terrorist fighters phenomenon in Syria.* New York: United Nations Office of Counter-Terrorism.

Emerson, S. (2002). *American jihad: The terrorists living among us.* New York: The Free Press.

Epley, N., & Caruso, E. M. (2004). Egocentric ethics. *Social Justice Research, 17*, 171–188.

Epley, N., Keysar, B., Van Boven, L., & Gilovich, T. (2004). Perspective taking as ego-centric anchoring and adjustment. *Journal of Personality and Social Psychology, 87*, 327–339.

Epstein, S. (1985). The implications of cognitive-experiential self-theory for research in social psychology and personality. *Journal for the Theory of Social Behaviour, 15*, 283–310.

Epstein, S. (1994). Integration of the cognitive and the psychodynamic unconscious. *American Psychologist, 49*, 709–724.

Epstein, S., & Pacini, R. (1999). Some basic issues regarding dual-process theories from the perspective of cognitive-experiential self-theory. In S. Chaiken & Y. Trope (Eds.), *Dual-process theories in social psychology* (pp. 462–482). New York: Guilford.

Erikson, E. H. (1968). *Identity: Youth and crisis.* New York: Norton.

Esposito, J. L., & Mogahed, D. (2007). *Who speaks for Islam? What a billion Muslims really think.* New York: Gallup Press.

Expert Group on Violent Radicalisation (2008). *European radicalisation processes leading to acts of terrorism: A concise report prepared by the European Commission's Expert Group on Violent Radicalisation.* Brussels: European Commission.

Farmer, B. R. (2005). *American conservatism: History, theory and practice.* Newcastle, UK: Cambridge Scholars Press.

Farrington, D. P. (1987). What kind of research is needed to advance knowledge about the explanation, prevention and treatment of crime in Canada. *Canadian Journal of Criminology, 29*, 171.

Faul, F., Erdfelder, E., Lang, A.-G., & Buchner, A. (2007). G*Power 3: A flexible sta-tistical power analysis program for the social, behavioral, and biomedical sciences. *Behavior Research Methods, 39*, 175–191.

Feddes, A. R., Mann, L., & Doosje, B. (2013). *Empirical study as part of a scientific approach to finding indicators of and responses to radicalisation (SAFIRE).* Report presented to the European Commission.

Feddes, A. R., Mann, L., & Doosje, B. (2015). Increasing self-esteem and empathy to prevent violent radicalization: A longitudinal quantitative evaluation of a resil-ience training focused on adolescents with a dual identity. *Journal of Applied Social Psychology, 45*, 400–411.

Feddes, A. R., Nickolson, L., & Doosje, B. (2015). *Triggerfactoren in het radicaliserings-proces.* The Hague/Amsterdam: Expertise-unit Sociale Stabiliteit/University of Amsterdam.

Feldstein, S. P. (Ed.). (2009). *Terrorist ideology and the implications of radicalization*. New York: Nova Science.

Fernbach, P. M., Rogers, T., Fox, C. R., & Sloman, S. A. (2013). Political extremism is supported by an illusion of understanding. *Psychological Science, 24*, 939–946.

Ferracuti, F. (1990). Ideology and repentance: Terrorism in Italy. In W. Reich (Ed.), *Origins of terrorism: Psychologies, ideologies, theologies, states of mind* (pp. 59–64). Washington, DC: Woodrow Wilson Center Press.

Finkel, N. J. (2001). *Not fair! The typology of commonsense unfairness*. Washington, DC: American Psychological Association.

Fishbein, M., & Ajzen, I. (1975). *Belief, attitude, intention, and behavior*. Reading, MA: Addison-Wesley.

Fishkin J. S. (1991). *Democracy and deliberation: New directions for democratic reform*. New Haven, CT: Yale University Press.

Fiske, A. P. (1992). The four elementary forms of sociality: Framework for a unified theory of social relations. *Psychological Review, 99*, 689–723.

Fiske, S. T. (2009). From dehumanization and objectification, to rehumanization: Neuroimaging studies on the building blocks of empathy. *Annals of the New York Academy of Sciences, 1167*, 31–34.

Fiske, S. T., & Taylor, S. E. (1991). *Social cognition* (2nd ed.). New York: McGraw-Hill.

Flew, A. (1979). *A dictionary of philosophy*. London: Pan Books.

Foa, U. G., & Foa, E. G. (1974). *Societal structures of the mind*. Springfield, IL: Charles C. Thomas.

Folger, R. (1977). Distributive and procedural justice: Combined impact of "voice" and improvement of experienced inequity. *Journal of Personality and Social Psychology, 35*, 108–119.

Folger, R. (Ed.). (1984). *The sense of injustice: Social psychological perspectives*. New York: Plenum.

Folger, R. (1986). Rethinking equity theory: A referent cognitions model. In H. M. Bierhoff, R. L. Cohen, & J. Greenberg (Eds.), *Justice in social relations* (pp. 145–162). New York: Plenum.

Folger, R., & Cropanzano, R. (1998). *Organizational justice and human resource management*. Thousand Oaks, CA: Sage.

Folger, R., Rosenfield, D., Grove, J., & Corkran, L. (1979). Effects of "voice" and peer opinions on responses to inequity. *Journal of Personality and Social Psychology, 37*, 2253–2261.

Furnham, A. (2003). Belief in a just world: Research progress over the past decade. *Personality and Individual Differences, 34*, 795–817.

Furnham, A., & Rajamanickam, R. (1992). The Protestant work ethic and just world beliefs in Great Britain and India. *International Journal of Psychology, 27*, 401–416.

Gamson, W. A., Fireman, B., & Rytina, S. (1982). *Encounters with unjust authority*. Homewood, IL: Dorsey Press.

Garner, W. R. (1962). *Uncertainty and structure as psychological concepts*. New York: Wiley.

Garner, W. R. (1970). Good patterns have few alternatives. *American Scientist, 58*, 34–42.

Gartenstein-Ross, D., & Grossman, L. (2009). *Homegrown terrorists in the U.S. and U.K.: An empirical examination of the radicalization process*. Washington, DC: FDD Press.

Gawthrop, W. M. (2011, July 6). Dogmatic basis of jihad and martyrdom. *Small Wars Journal, 7*, article 7/06, 1–31.

Gergen, K. J. (1973). Social psychology as history. *Journal of Personality and Social Psychology, 26*, 309–320.

Gergen, K. J. (1980). Towards intellectual audacity in social psychology. In R. Gilmour & S. Duck (Eds.), *The development of social psychology* (pp. 239–270). London: Academic Press.

Giacomantonio, M., Pierro, A., & Kruglanski, A. W. (2011). Leaders' fairness and followers' conflict handling style: The moderating role of need for cognitive closure. *International Journal of Conflict Management, 22*, 358–372.

Gilbert, D. T., & Osborne, R. E. (1989). Thinking backward: Some curable and incurable consequences of cognitive busyness. *Journal of Personality and Social Psychology, 57*, 940–949.

Gilbert, D. T., Pelham, B. W., & Krull, D. S. (1988). On cognitive busyness: When person perceivers meet persons perceived. *Journal of Personality and Social Psychology, 54*, 733–740.

Gill, P., & Corner, E. (2017). There and back again: The study of mental disorder and terrorist involvement. *American Psychologist, 72*, 231–241.

Giner-Sorrola, R. (2012). *Judging passions: Moral emotions in persons and groups*. Hove, UK: Psychology Press.

Githens-Mazer, J. (2008). Islamic radicalisation among North Africans in Britain. *British Journal of Politics and International Relations, 10*, 550–570.

Goerzig, C., & Al-Hashimi, K. (2015). *Radicalization in Western Europe: Integration, public discourse, and loss of identity among Muslim communities*. Oxon: Routledge.

Goldstone, R. L., & Chin, C. (1993). Dishonesty in self-report of copies made: Moral relativity and the copy machine. *Basic and Applied Psychology, 14*, 19–32.

Goren, C., & Neter, E. (2016). Stereotypical thinking as a mediating factor in the association between exposure to terror and post-traumatic stress disorder symptoms among Israeli youth. *Anxiety, Stress, & Coping, 29*, 644–659.

Gray, K., & Wegner, D. M. (2011). Dimensions of moral emotions. *Emotion Review, 3*, 258–260.

Greco, V., & Roger, D. (2001). Coping with uncertainty: The construction and validation of a new measure. *Personality and Individual Differences, 31*, 519–534.

Greco, V., & Roger, D. (2003). Uncertainty, stress, and health. *Personality and Individual Differences, 34*, 1057–1068.

Greenberg, J., & Jonas, E. (2003). Psychological motives and political orientation: The left, the right, and the rigid—Comment on Jost et al. (2003). *Psychological Bulletin, 129*, 376–382.

Greenberg, J., Koole, S. L., & Pyszczynski, T. (Eds.). (2004). *Handbook of experimental existential psychology*. New York: Guilford Press.

Greenberg, J., Solomon, S., & Pyszczynski, T. (1997). Terror management theory of self-esteem and cultural worldviews: Empirical assessments and conceptual refinements.

In M. P. Zanna (Ed.), *Advances in experimental social psychology* (Vol. 29, pp. 61–139). New York: Academic Press.

Greene, J. D. (2005). Emotion and cognition in moral judgment: Evidence from neuroimaging. In J. P. Changeux, A. R. Damasio, W. Singer, & Y. Christen (Eds.), *Neurobiology of human values* (pp. 57–66). Berlin: Springer-Verlag.

Greene, J. D. (2013). *Moral tribes: Emotion, reason, and the gap between us and them.* New York: Penguin Press.

Greene, J. D., Sommerville, B., Nystrom, L. E., Darley, J. M., & Cohen, J. D. (2001). An fMRI investigation of emotional engagement in moral judgment. *Science, 293,* 2105–2108.

Greenwald, A. G., McGhee, D. E., & Schwartz, J. L. K. (1998). Measuring individual differences in implicit cognition: The Implicit Association Test. *Journal of Personality and Social Psychology, 74,* 1464–1480.

Grillon, C., & Baas, J. (2003). A review of the modulation of the startle reflex by affective states and its application in psychiatry. *Clinical Neurophysiology, 114,* 1557–1579.

Grootelaar, H. A. M., & Van den Bos, K. (2016). Naar meer ervaren legitimiteit van de Nederlandse rechtspraak. In R. Ortlep, F. Groothuijse, J. Kiewiet, & R. Nehmelman (Eds.), *De rechter onder vuur* (pp. 275–297). Oisterwijk: Wolf Legal Publishers.

Gurr, T. R. (1970). *Why men rebel.* Princeton, NJ: Princeton University Press.

Habermas, J. (1985). Civil disobedience: Litmus test for the democratic constitutional state. *Berkeley Journal of Sociology, 30,* 95–116.

Hafer, C. L. (2000a). Do innocent victims threaten the belief in a just world? Evidence from a modified Stroop task. *Journal of Personality and Social Psychology, 79,* 165–173.

Hafer, C. L. (2000b). Investment in long-term goals and commitment to just means drive the need to believe in a just world. *Personality and Social Psychology Bulletin, 26,* 1059–1073.

Hafer, C. L., & Bègue, L. (2005). Experimental research on just-world theory: Problems, developments, and future challenges. *Psychological Bulletin, 131,* 128–167.

Hagan, J., Kaiser, J., & Hanson, A. (2016). The theory of legal cynicism and Sunni insurgent violence in post-invasion Iraq. *American Sociological Review, 81,* 316–346.

Haidt, J. (2001). The emotional dog and its rational tail: A social intuitionist approach to moral judgment. *Psychological Review, 108,* 814–834.

Haidt, J. (2003a). The moral emotions. In R. J. Davidson, K. Scherer, & H. H. Goldsmith (Eds.), *Handbook of affective sciences* (pp. 852–870). Oxford, UK: Oxford University Press.

Haidt, J. (2003b). The emotional dog does learn new tricks: A reply to Pizarro and Bloom (2003). *Psychological Review, 110,* 197–198.

Haidt, J. (2012). *The righteous mind: Why good people are divided by politics and religion.* New York: Pantheon Books.

Halevy, N., Bornstein, G., & Sagiv, L. (2008). "In-group love" and "out-group hate" as motives for individual participation in intergroup conflict: A new game paradigm. *Psychological Science, 19,* 405–411.

Hamm, M. S., & Spaaij, R. (2017). *The age of lone wolf terrorism.* New York: Columbia University Press.

Hanley, A. (1997, May 9). The accidental terrorist. *The Independent*.

Harris, C. R. (2004). The evolution of jealousy. *American Scientist, 92*, 62–71.

Harris, S., & Nawaz, M. (2015). *Islam and the future of tolerance: A dialogue*. Cambridge, MA: Harvard University Press.

Hayes, J., Schimel, J., Arndt, J., & Faucher, E. H. (2010). A theoretical and empirical review of the death-thought accessibility concept in terror management research. *Psychological Bulletin, 136*, 699–739.

Heatherton, T. F., & Polivy, J. (1991). Development and validation of a scale for measuring state self-esteem. *Journal of Personality and Social Psychology, 60*, 895–910.

Heine, S. J., Lehman, D. R., Markus, H. R., & Kitayama, S. (1999). Is there a universal need for positive self-regard? *Psychological Review, 106*, 766–794.

Heine, S. J., Proulx, T., & Vohs, K. D. (2006). The meaning maintenance model: On the coherence of social motivations. *Personality and Social Psychology Review, 10*, 88–110.

Heinsohn, G. (2005). *Population, conquest and terror in the 21st Century*. Retrieved from https://www.scribd.com/doc/310265022/Gunnar-Heinsohn-Population-Conquest-and-Terror-in-the-21st-Century.

Henrich, J., Heine, S. J., & Norenzayan, A. (2010). Most people are not WEIRD. *Nature, 466*, 29.

Hermann, M. G., & Hermann, C. F. (1990). Hostage taking, the presidency, and stress. In W. Reich (Ed.), *Origins of terrorism: Psychologies, ideologies, theologies, states of mind* (pp. 211–229). Washington, DC: Woodrow Wilson Center Press.

Hermans, W. F. (1964). *Het sadistisch universum I*. Amsterdam: De Bezige Bij.

Hermans, W. F. (1970). *Het sadistisch universum II: Van Wittgenstein tot Weinreb*. Amsterdam: De Bezige Bij.

Herriot, P. (2007). *Religious fundamentalism and social identity*. London: Routledge.

Higgins, E. T. (1996). Ideals, oughts, and regulatory focus: Affect and motivation from distinct pains and pleasures. In P. M. Gollwitzer & J. A. Bargh (Eds.), *The psychology of action: Linking cognition and motivation to behavior* (pp. 91–114). New York: Guilford.

Higgins, E. T. (2000). Making a good decision: Value from fit. *American Psychologist, 55*, 1217–1230.

Higgins, E. T., Idson, L. C., Freitas, A. L., Spiegel, S., & Molden, D. C. (2003). Transfer of value from fit. *Journal of Personality and Social Psychology, 84*, 1140–1153.

Hinde, R. A. (1999). *Why gods persist: A scientific approach to religion*. London, UK: Routledge.

Hobbes, T. (1985). *Leviathan*. London: Penguin. (Original work published in 1651)

Hodson, G. (2011). Do ideologically intolerant people benefit from intergroup contact? *Current Directions in Psychological Science, 20*, 154–159.

Hoffer, E. (1951). *The true believer*. New York: Time.

Hoffman, B. (1982). *Right-wing terrorism in Europe*. Santa Monica, CA: Rand.

Hoffmann, J. P., & Cerbone, F. G. (1999). Stressful life events and delinquency escalation in early adolescence. *Criminology, 37*, 343–374.

Hogg, M. A. (2001). Self-categorization and subjective uncertainty resolution: Cognitive and motivational facets of social identity and group membership. In J. P. Forgas, K. D.

Williams, & L. Wheeler (Eds.), *The social mind: Cognitive and motivational aspects of interpersonal behavior* (pp. 323–349). New York: Cambridge University Press.

Hogg, M. A. (2004). Uncertainty and extremism: Identification with high entitativity groups under conditions of uncertainty. In V. Yzerbyt, C. M. Judd, & O. Corneille (Eds.), *The psychology of group perception: Perceived variability, entitativity, and essentialism* (pp. 401–418). New York: Psychology Press.

Hogg, M. A. (2005). Uncertainty, social identity, and ideology. In S. R. Thye & E. J. Lawler (Eds.), *Advances in group processes* (Vol. 22, pp. 203–230). New York: Elsevier.

Hogg, M. A. (2007). Uncertainty-identity theory. In M. P. Zanna (Ed.), *Advances in experimental social psychology* (Vol. 39, pp. 70–126). San Diego, CA: Academic Press.

Hogg, M. A. (2009). Managing self-uncertainty through group identification. *Psychological Inquiry, 20,* 221–224.

Hogg, M. A. (2011). Self-uncertainty, social identity, and the solace of extremism. In M. A. Hogg & D. L. Blaylock (Eds.), *Extremism and the psychology of uncertainty* (pp. 19–35). Oxford, UK: Wiley-Blackwell.

Hogg, M. A. (2014). From uncertainty to extremism: Social categorization and identity processes. *Current Directions in Psychological Science, 23,* 338–342.

Hogg, M. A., Adelman, J. R., & Blagg, R. D. (2010). Religion in the face of uncertainty: An uncertainty-identity theory account of religiousness. *Personality and Social Psychology Review, 14,* 72–83.

Hogg, M. A., Kruglanski, A., & Van den Bos, K. (2013). Uncertainty and the roots of extremism. *Journal of Social Issues, 69,* 407–418.

Hogg, M. A., & Mullin, B.-A. (1999). Joining groups to reduce uncertainty: Subjective uncertainty reduction and group identification. In D. Abrams & M. A. Hogg (Eds.), *Social identity and social cognition* (pp. 249–279). Oxford: Blackwell.

Hogg, M. A., & Vaughan, G. M. (2005). *Social psychology.* London, United Kingdom: Prentice Hall.

Homans, G. C. (1961). *Social behavior: Its elementary forms.* New York: Harcourt, Brace, & World.

Hoogerwerf, A. (2002). *Wij en zij: Intolerantie en verdraagzaamheid in 21 eeuwen.* Budel: Damon.

Horgan, J. (2003). The search for the terrorist. In A. Silke (Ed.), *Terrorists, victims and society: Psychological perspectives on terrorism and its consequences* (pp. 3–27). Chichester, UK: Wiley.

Horgan, J. (2005). *The psychology of terrorism.* London, United Kingdom: Routledge.

Horgan, J. (2008). From profiles to pathways and roots to routes: Perspectives from psychology on radicalization into terrorism. *Annals of the American Academy of Political and Social Science, 618,* 80–94.

Horgan, J. (2009). *Walking away from terrorism.* London: Routledge.

Horgan, J. (2017). Psychology of terrorism: Introduction to the special issue. *American Psychologist, 72,* 199–204.

Horgan, J., Altier, M., Shortland, N., & Taylor, M. (2016). Walking away: The disengagement and de-radicalization of a violent right-wing extremist. *Behavioral Sciences of Terrorism and Political Aggression,* 1–15.

Horgan, J., & Taylor, M. (2003). *The psychology of terrorism.* London: Frank Cass.

Hudson, M., Phillips, J., Ray, K., & Barnes, H. (2007). *Social cohesion in diverse communities*. York, UK: Joseph Rowntree Foundation.

Huizinga, J. (2007). *In de schaduwen van morgen: Een diagnose van het geestelijk lijden van onze tijd*. Soesterberg: Aspekt. (Original work published in 1935)

Hulst, L., Van den Bos, K., Akkermans, A. J., & Lind, E. A. (2017). On why procedural justice matters in court hearings: Experimental evidence that behavioral disinhibition weakens the association between procedural justice and evaluations of judges. *Utrecht Law Review, 13(3)*, 114–129.

Hulst, L., Van den Bos, K., Robijn, M., Romijn, S., Schroen, S., & Wever, T. (2018). *Trust in law and society: An experimental approach to interviewer effects among under-investigated participants*. Manuscript submitted for publication.

Hume, D. (1951). *A treatise of human nature*. Oxford: Clarendon. (Original work published in 1739)

Hume, D. (1982). *Enquiries concerning human understanding and concerning the principles of morals*. Oxford: Clarendon. (Original work published in 1777)

Hume, D. (1987). *Essays, moral, political, and literary*. Indianapolis, IN: Liberty Classics. (Original work published in 1742)

Hunton, J. E, Hall, T. W., & Price, K. H. (1998). The value of voice in participative decision making. *Journal of Applied Psychology, 83*, 788–797.

Huo, Y. J., Smith, H. J., Tyler, T. R., & Lind, E. A. (1996). Superordinate identification, subgroup identification, and justice concerns: Is separatism the problem; is assimilation the answer? *Psychological Science, 7*, 40–45.

IJfs, P. (2012, September 22). *Pavlov Radio*. Hilversum: NTR.

Insko, C. A., Schopler, J., Pemberton, M. B., Wieselquist, J., McIlraith, S. A., Currey, D. P., & Gaertner, A. (1998). Long-term outcome maximization and the reduction of interindividual-intergroup discontinuity. *Journal of Personality and Social Psychology, 75*, 695–710.

Inzlicht, M., McGregor, I., Hirsh, J. B., & Nash, K. (2009). Neural markers of religious conviction. *Psychological Science, 20*, 385–392.

Ipsos. (2017). *Segmentatieonderzoek over immigratie en vluchtelingen: Een onderzoek ten behoeve van een effectievere, depolariserende communicatiestrategie over vluchtelingen*. Amsterdam: Ipsos.

Israel, J. I. (2001). *Radical enlightenment: Philosophy and the making of modernity, 1650–1750*. Oxford, UK: Oxford University Press.

Israel, J. I. (2006). *Enlightenment contested: Philosophy, modernity, and the emancipation of man, 1670-1752*. Oxford, UK: Oxford University Press,

Israel, J. I. (2011). *Democratic enlightenment: Philosophy, revolution, and human rights, 1750–1790*. Oxford, UK: Oxford University Press.

IVA (2010). *De strijd voor dierenrechten en tegen asiel- en vreemdelingenbeleid: Een onderzoek naar verschillen en overeenkomsten van radicaliseringprocessen van extremisten*. Tilburg: IVA.

Iyer, A., Jetten, J., & Haslam, S. A. (2012). Sugaring o'er the devil: Moral superiority and group identification help individuals downplay the implications of ingroup rule-breaking. *European Journal of Social Psychology, 42*, 141–149.

Jacques, K., & Taylor, P. J. (2013). Myths and realities of female-perpetrated terrorism. *Law and Human Behavior, 37*, 35–44.

Jahoda, M. (1982). *Employment and unemployment: A social-psychological analysis.* Cambridge, UK: Cambridge University Press.

James, W. (1902). *The varieties of religious experience: A study in human nature.* Auckland: Floating Press.

James, W. (1983). *The principles of psychology.* Cambridge, MA: Harvard University Press. (Original work published in 1890)

Jansen, A. (2015). *Don't let us be bystanders! Anti-genocide activists and the sacralization of humanity.* Doctoral dissertation, Vrije Universiteit Amsterdam.

Jasso, G. (1994). Assessing individual and group differences in the sense of justice: Framework and application to gender differences in the justice of earnings. *Social Science Research, 23*, 368–406.

Jasso, G. (1999). How much injustice is there in the world? Two new justice indexes. *American Sociological Review, 64*, 133–168.

Jiang, Y., & Hong, J. (2014). It feels fluent, but not right: The interactive effect of expected and experienced processing fluency on evaluative judgment. *Journal of Experimental Social Psychology, 54*, 147–152.

Jordan, C. H., Spencer, S. J., & Zanna, M. P. (2005). Types of high self-esteem and prejudice: How implicit self-esteem relates to ethnic discrimination among high explicit self-esteem individuals. *Personality and Social Psychology Bulletin, 31*, 693–702.

Jost, J. T., Glaser, J., Kruglanski, A. W., & Sulloway, F. J. (2003a). Political conservatism as motivated social cognition. *Psychological Bulletin, 129*, 339–375.

Jost, J. T., Glaser, J., Kruglanski, A. W., & Sulloway, F. J. (2003b). Exceptions that prove the rule: Using a theory of motivated social cognition to account for ideological incongruities and political anomalies—Reply to Greenberg and Jonas 2003). *Psychological Bulletin, 129*, 383–393.

Jost, J. T., & Hunyady, O. (2002). The psychology of system justification and the palliative function of ideology. *European Review of Social Psychology, 13*, 111–153.

Juergensmeyer, M. (2003). *Terror in the mind of god: The global rise of religious violence* (3rd ed.). Berkeley, CA: University of California Press.

Juergensmeyer, M. (2009). Islam's "neglected duty." In J. Victoroff, & A. W. Kruglanski (Eds.), *Psychology of terrorism: Classic and contemporary insights* (pp. 419–434). New York: Psychology Press.

Juhl, J., & Routledge, C. (2010). Structured terror: Further exploring the effects of mortality salience and personal need for structure on worldview defense. *Journal of Personality, 78*, 969–990.

Kagan, J. (1972). Motives and development. *Journal of Personality and Social Psychology, 22*, 51–66.

Kagan, J. (1984). *The nature of the child.* New York: Basic Books.

Kahneman, D., & Deaton, A. (2010). High income improves evaluation of life but not emotional well-being. *Proceedings of the National Academy of Sciences of the United States of America, 107*, 16489–16493.

Kahneman, D., Knetsch, J. L., & Thaler, R. H. (1986). Fairness and the assumptions of economics. *Journal of Business, 59*, 285–300.

Kahneman, D., Slovic, P., & Tversky, A. (Eds.). (1982). *Judgment under uncertainty: Heuristics and biases.* New York: Cambridge University Press.

Kant, I. (1784). *Beantwortung der Frage: Was ist Aufklärung?* [Answering the question: What is enlightenment?] Berlin: Berlinische Monatsschrift.

Kant, I. (1959). *Foundation of the metaphysics of morals.* Indianapolis, IN: Bobbs-Merrill. (Original work published in 1785)

Kaplan, E. H., Mintz, A., Mishal, S., & Samban, C. (2009). What happened to suicide bombings in Israel? Insights from a Terror Stock Model. In J. Victoroff, & A. W. Kruglanski (Eds.), *Psychology of terrorism: Classic and contemporary insights* (pp. 467–476). New York: Psychology Press.

Karagiarmis, M., & McCauley, C. (2006). Hizb ut-Tahrir al-Islarni: Evaluating the threat posed by a radical Islamic group that remains nonviolent. *Terrorism and Political Violence, 18*, 315–334

Katz, D., Gutek, B., Kahn, R., & Barton, E. (1975). *Bureaucratic encounters: A pilot study in the evaluation of government services.* Ann Arbor, MI: Institute for Social Relations.

Kawakami, K., Dovidio, J. F., Moll, J., Hermsen, S., & Russin, A. (2000). Just say no (to stereotyping): Effects of training in negation of stereotypic associations on stereotype activation. *Journal of Personality and Social Psychology, 78*, 871–888.

Kawakami, K., Dovidio, J. F., & Van Kamp, S. (2005). Kicking the habit: Effects of nonstereotypic association training and correction processes on hiring decisions. *Journal of Experimental Social Psychology, 41*, 68–75.

Kawakami, K., Phills, C. E., Steele, J. R., & Dovidio, J. F. (2007). (Close) distance makes the heart grow fonder: Improving implicit racial attitudes and interracial interactions through approach behaviors. *Journal of Personality and Social Psychology, 92*, 957–971.

Kay, A. C., Laurin, K., Fitzsimons, G. M., & Landau, M. J. (2014). A functional basis for structure-seeking: Exposure to structure promotes willingness to engage in motivated action. *Journal of Experimental Psychology: General, 143*, 486–491.

Kellen, K. (1990). Ideology and rebellion: Terrorism in West Germany. In W. Reich (Ed.), *Origins of terrorism: Psychologies, ideologies, theologies, states of mind* (pp. 43–58). Washington, DC: Woodrow Wilson Center Press.

Kemmelmeier, M. (1997). Political orientation and need for cognitive closure in German university students. *Journal of Social Psychology, 137*, 787–789.

Kemmelmeier, M. (2007). Political conservatism, rigidity, and dogmatism in American foreign policy officials: The 1966 Mennis Data. *Journal of Psychology, 141*, 77–90.

Kepel, G. (2004). *The war for Muslim minds: Islam and the West.* Cambridge, MA: Belknap Press.

Kepel, G. (2017). *Terror in France: The rise of jihad in the West.* Princeton, NJ: Princeton University Press.

Kepel, G., & Rougier, B. (2016). *Addressing terrorism: European research in social sciences and the humanities in support to policies for inclusion and security—A policy review.* Brussels: European Commission.

Kernis, M. H., & Lakey, C. E. (2009). Fragile versus secure high self-esteem: Implications for defensiveness and insecurity. In R. M. Arkin, K. C. Oleson, & P. J. Carroll (Eds.), *Handbook of the uncertain self* (pp. 360–378). New York: Psychology Press.

Kerodal, A. G., Freilich, J. D., Chermak, S. M., & Suttmoeller, M. J. (2014). A test of Sprinzak's split delegitimization's theory of the life course of far-right organizational behavior. *International Journal of Comparative and Applied Criminal Justice, 39,* 307–329.

Kimball, C. (2002). *When religion becomes evil: Five warning signs.* San Francisco: HarperCollins.

King, M., & Taylor, D. M. (2011). The radicalization of home grown jihadists: A review of theoretical models and social psychological evidence. *Terrorism and Political Violence, 23,* 602–622.

Kirk, R. E. (1995). *Experimental design: Procedures for the behavioral sciences* (3rd ed.). Pacific Grove, CA: Brooks/Cole.

Klandermans, B. (1997). *The social psychology of protest.* Oxford, UK: Blackwell.

Klausen, J. (2015). Tweeting the jihad: Social media networks of western foreign fighters in Syria and Iraq. *Studies in Conflict & Terrorism, 38,* 1–22.

Koerner, B. I. (2017). *Can you turn a terrorist back into a citizen?* Retrieved from https://www.wired.com/2017/01/can-you-turn-terrorist-back-into-citizen/ on January 24, 2017.

Koerselman, F. (2016). *Wie wij zijn: Tussen verstand en verlangen.* Amsterdam: Prometheus.

Kohlberg, L. (1969). Stage and sequence: The cognitive-developmental approach to socialization. In D. A. Goslin (Ed.), *Handbook of socialization theory and research* (pp. 347–480). Chicago: Rand McNally.

Kok, G., Schaalma, H., Ruiter, R. A. C., Van Empelen, P., & Brug, J. (2004). Intervention mapping: A protocol for applying health psychology theory to prevention programmes. *Journal of Health Psychology, 9,* 85–98.

Koomen, W., & Van der Pligt, J. (2015). *The psychology of radicalization and terrorism.* London: Routledge.

Koper, G., Van Knippenberg, D., Bouhuijs, F., Vermunt, R., & Wilke, H. (1993). Procedural fairness and self-esteem. *European Journal of Social Psychology, 23,* 313–325.

Kossowska, M., Czernatowicz-Kukuczka, A., & Sekerdej, A. (2017). Many faces of dogmatism: Prejudice as a way of protecting certainty against value violators among dogmatic believers and atheists. *British Journal of Psychology, 108,* 127–147.

Kramer, A. D. I., Guillory, J. E., & Hancock, J. T. (2014). Experimental evidence of massive-scale emotional contagion through social networks. *Proceedings of the National Academy of Sciences, 111,* 8788–8790.

Kramer, M. (1990). The moral logic of Hizballah. In W. Reich (Ed.), *Origins of terrorism: Psychologies, ideologies, theologies, states of mind* (pp. 131–157). Washington, DC: Woodrow Wilson Center Press.

Kret, M. E., Jaasma, L., Bionda, T., & Wijnen, J. G. (2016). Bonobos (Pan Paniscus) show an attentional bias toward conspecifics' emotions. *Proceedings of the National Academy of Sciences of the United States of America, 113,* 3761–3766.

Krueger, A. B. (2007). *What makes a terrorist: Economics and the roots of terrorism.* Princeton, NJ: Princeton University Press.

Krueger, A. B., & Malečková, J. (2003). Education, poverty and terrorism: Is there a causal connection? *Journal of Economic Perspectives, 17*, 119–144.

Kruger J., & Dunning D. (1999). Unskilled and unaware of it: How difficulties in recognizing one's own incompetence lead to inflated self-assessments. *Journal of Personality and Social Psychology, 77*, 1121–1134.

Kruglanski, A. W. (1989). *Lay epistemics and human knowledge: Cognitive and motivational bases.* New York: Plenum Press.

Kruglanski, A. W., Bélanger, J. J., Gelfand, M. J., Gunaratna, R., Hettiarrachchi, M., Reinares, F., Orehek, E. A., Sasota, J., & Sharvit, K. (2013). Terrorism, a (self) love-story: Redirecting the significance quest can end violence. *American Psychologist, 68*, 559–575.

Kruglanski, A. W., Chen, X., Dechesne, M., Fishman, S., & Orehek, E. (2009). Fully committed: Suicide bombers' motivation and the quest for personal significance. *Political Psychology, 30*, 331–357.

Kruglanski, A. W., Chernikova, M., & Jasko, K. (2017). Social psychology circa 2016: A field on steroids. *European Journal of Social Psychology, 47*, 1–10.

Kruglanski, A. W., Crenshaw, M., Post, J. M., & Victoroff, J. (2008). What should this fight be called? Metaphors of counterterrorism and their implications. *Psychological Science in the Public Interest, 8*, 97–133.

Kruglanski, A. W., & Fishman, S. (2006). Terrorism between "syndrome" and "tool." *Current Directions in Psychological Science, 15*, 45–48.

Kruglanski, A. W., & Fishman, S. (2009). The psychology of terrorism: "Syndrome" versus "tool" perspectives. In J. Victoroff, & A. W. Kruglanski (Eds.), *Psychology of terrorism: Classic and contemporary insights* (pp. 35–53). New York: Psychology Press.

Kruglanski, A. W., Gelfand, M. J., Bélanger, J. J., Sheveland, A., Hetiarachchi, M., & Gunaratna, R. (2014). The psychology of radicalization and deradicalization: How significance quest impacts violent extremism. *Advances in Political Psychology, 35*, 69–93.

Kruglanski, A. W., Gelfand, M., & Gunaratna, R. (2012). Terrorism as means to an end: How political violence bestows significance. In P. R. Shaver & M. Mikulincer (Eds.), *Meaning, morality, and choice: The social psychology of existential concerns* (pp. 203–212). Washington, DC: American Psychological Association.

Kruglanski, A. W., Gelfand, M. J., Sheveland, A., Babush, M., Hettiarachchi, M., Ng-Bonto, M., & Gunaratna, R. (2017). What a difference two years make: Patterns of radicalization in a Philippine jail. *Dynamics of Asymmetric Conflict, 9*, 13–36.

Kruglanski, A. W., Pierro, A., Mannetti, L., & De Grada, E. (2006). Groups as epistemic providers: Need for closure and the unfolding of group-centrism. *Psychological Review, 113*, 84–100.

Kruglanski, A. W., Shah, J. Y., Fischbach, A., Friedman, R., Chun, W. Y., & Sleeth-Keppler, D. (2002). A theory of goal systems. In M. P. Zanna (Ed.), *Advances in experimental social psychology* (Vol. 34, pp. 331–378). San Diego, CA: Academic Press.

Kruglanski, A. W., & Webster, D. M. (1996). Motivated closing of the mind: "Seizing" and "freezing." *Psychological Review, 103*, 263–283.

Kuhn, T. S. (1996). *The structure of scientific revolutions* (3rd ed.). Chicago: University of Chicago Press. (Original work published 1962)

Kunda, Z. (1999). *Social cognition: Making sense of people.* Cambridge, MA: MIT Press.

Laham, S. M., Alter, A. L., & Goodwin, G. P. (2009). Easy on the mind, easy on the wrongdoer: Discrepantly fluent violations are deemed less morally wrong. *Cognition, 112,* 462–466.

Lakatos, I. (1976). *Proofs and refutations.* Cambridge, UK: Cambridge University Press.

Landau, M. J., Johns, M., Greenberg, J., Pyszczynski, T., Martens, A., Goldenberg, J. L., & Solomon, S. (2004). A function of form: Terror management and structuring the social world. *Journal of Personality and Social Psychology, 87,* 190–210.

Landau, M. J., Kay, A. C., & Whitson, J. A. (2015). Compensatory control and the appeal of a structured world. *Psychological Bulletin, 141,* 694–722.

Larsen, R. J., Diener, E., & Cropanzano, R. S. (1987). Cognitive operations associated with individual differences in affect intensity. *Journal of Personality and Social Psychology, 53,* 767–774.

Larsen, R. J., Diener, E., & Emmons, R. (1986). Affect intensity and reactions to daily life events. *Journal of Personality and Social Psychology, 51,* 803–814.

Lasch, C. (1979). The culture of narcissism: American life in an age of diminishing expectations. New York, NY: Warner.

Laurin, K., Kay, A. C., Moscovitch, D. A. (2008). On the belief in God: Towards an understanding of the emotional substrates of compensatory control. *Journal of Experimental Social Psychology, 44,* 1559–1562.

Layendecker, L. (1981). *Orde, verandering, ongelijkheid: Een inleiding tot de geschiedenis van de sociologie.* Meppel: Boom.

Lazarsfeld P. F., & Merton R. K. (1954). Friendship as social process: A substantive and methodological analysis. In M. Berger, T. Abel, & C. H. Page (Eds.), *Freedom and control in modern society* (pp. 18–66). New York, NY: Octagon Books.

Leary, M. R. (2004). The function of self-esteem in terror management theory and sociometer theory: Comment on Pyszczynski et al. (2004). *Psychological Bulletin, 130,* 478–482.

Leary, M. R., & Baumeister, R. F. (2000). The nature and function of self-esteem: Sociometer theory. In M. P. Zanna (Ed.), *Advances in experimental social psychology* (Vol. 32, pp. 1–62). New York: Academic Press.

Lelkes, Y., Krosnick, J. A., Marx, D. M., Judd, C. M., & Park, B. (2012). Complete anonymity compromises the accuracy of self-reports. *Journal of Experimental Social Psychology, 48,* 1291–1299.

Lerner, M. J. (1977). The justice motive: Some hypotheses as to its origins and forms. *Journal of Personality, 45,* 1–52.

Lerner, A. (1980). Orientation to ambiguity. In S. Fiddle (Ed.), *Uncertainty: Behavioral and social dimensions* (pp. 43–58). New York: Praeger.

Lerner, M. J., & Goldberg, J. H. (1999). When do decent people blame victims? The differing effects of the explicit/rational and implicit/experiential cognitive systems. In S. Chaiken & Y. Trope (Eds.), *Dual-process theories in social psychology* (pp. 627–640). New York: Guilford.

Lerner, M. J., & Miller, D. T. (1978). Just world research and the attribution process: Looking back and ahead. *Psychological Bulletin, 85*, 1030–1051.

Lerner, M. J., & Simmons, C. H. (1966). Observer's reaction to the "innocent victim": Compassion or rejection? *Journal of Personality and Social Psychology, 4*, 203–210.

Leventhal, G. S. (1980). What should be done with equity theory? New approaches to the study of fairness in social relationships. In K. J. Gergen, M. S. Greenberg, & R. H. Willis (Eds.), *Social exchange: Advances in theory and research* (pp. 27–54). New York: Plenum.

Leventhal, G. S., Karuza, J., Jr., & Fry, W. R. (1980). Beyond fairness: A theory of allocation preferences. In G. Mikula (Ed.), *Justice and social interaction: Experimental and theoretical contributions from psychological research* (pp. 167–218). Bern: Huber

Lewin, K. (1951). *Field theory in social science.* New York: Harper & Brothers.

Lewis, B. (2004). *The crisis of Islam: Holy war and unholy terror.* London: Phoenix.

Li, Q. (2009). Does democracy promote or reduce transnational terrorist incidents? In J. Victoroff, & A. W. Kruglanski (Eds.), *Psychology of terrorism: Classic and contemporary insights* (pp. 211–226). New York: Psychology Press.

Lieberman, M. D., & Eisenberger, N. I. (2004). The neural alarm system: Behavior and beyond. Reply to Ullsperger et al. *Trends in Cognitive Sciences, 8*, 446–447.

Lind, E. A. (1995). *Social conflict and social justice: Lessons from the social psychology of justice judgments.* Inaugural oration, Leiden University, Leiden, The Netherlands.

Lind, E. A. (2001). Fairness heuristic theory: Justice judgments as pivotal cognitions in organizational relations. In J. Greenberg & R. Cropanzano (Eds.), *Advances in organizational behavior* (pp. 56–88). Stanford, CA: Stanford University Press.

Lind, E. A. (2002). Fairness judgments as cognitions. In M. Ross & D. T. Miller (Eds.), *The justice motive in everyday life* (pp. 416–431). Cambridge, UK: Cambridge University Press.

Lind, E. A., Kanfer, R., & Earley, P. C. (1990). Voice, control, and procedural justice: Instrumental and noninstrumental concerns in fairness judgments. *Journal of Personality and Social Psychology, 59*, 952–959.

Lind, E. A., & Tyler, T. R. (1988). *The social psychology of procedural justice.* New York: Plenum.

Lind, E. A., & Van den Bos, K. (2013). Freeing organizational behavior from inhibitory constraints. *Research in Organizational Behavior, 33*, 79–95.

Linden, A. (2009). *Besmet: Levenslopen en motieven van extreem-rechtse activisten in Nederland.* Vrije Universiteit Amsterdam: Academisch proefschrift.

Livingstone, G. (2004). *Inside Colombia: Drugs, democracy, and war.* New Brunswick, NJ: Rutgers University Press.

Locke, J. (1986). *The second treatise on civil government.* Buffalo, NY: Prometheus Books. (Original version published 1689)

Lord, C. G., Ross L., & Lepper M. R. (1979). Biased assimilation and attitude polarization: The effects of prior theories on subsequently considered evidence. *Journal of Personality and Social Psychology, 37*, 2098–2109.

Loseman, A., Miedema, J., Van den Bos, K., & Vermunt, R. (2009). Exploring how people respond to conflicts between self-interest and fairness: The influence of threats to the self on affective reactions to advantageous inequity. *Australian Journal of Psychology*, *61*, 13–21.

Luchins, A. S. (1942). Mechanization in problem solving: The effect of Einstellung. *Psychological Monographs*, *54(6)*, 1–95.

Maas, M., & Van den Bos, K. (2009). An affective-experiential perspective on reactions to fair and unfair events: Individual differences in affect intensity moderated by experiential mindsets. *Journal of Experimental Social Psychology*, *45*, 667–675.

MacLean, N. K. (1995). *Behind the mask of chivalry: The making of the second Ku Klux Klan*. New York: Oxford University Press.

Mak, E., & Taekema, S. (2016). The European Union's rule of law agenda: Identifying its core and contextualizing its application. *Hague Journal on the Rule of Law*, *8*, 25–50.

Mandel, D. R. (2009). Radicalization: What does it mean? In T. Pick, A. Speckhard, & B. Jacuch (Eds.), *Home-grown terrorism: Understanding and addressing the root causes of radicalisation among groups with an immigrant heritage in Europe*. Amsterdam: IOS Press.

Marien, H., Aarts, H., & Custers, R. (2012). Being flexible or rigid in goal-directed behavior: When positive affect implicitly motivates the pursuit of goals or means. *Journal of Experimental Social Psychology*, *48*, 277–283.

Marigold, D. C., McGregor, I., & Zanna, M. P. (2009). Defensive conviction as emotion regulation: Goal mechanisms and interpersonal implications. In R. M. Arkin, K. C. Oleson, & P. J. Carroll (Eds.), *Handbook of the uncertain self* (pp. 232–248). New York: Psychology Press.

Marsella, A. J. (2004). Reflections on international terrorism: Issues, concepts, and directions. In F. M. Moghaddam & A. J. Marsella (Eds.), *Understanding terrorism: Psychosocial roots, consequences, and interventions* (pp. 11–47). Washington, DC: American Psychological Association.

Martin, J., Brickman, P., & Murray, A. (1984). Moral outrage and pragmatism: Explanations for collective action. *Journal of Experimental and Social Psychology*, *20*, 484–496.

Martin, J., & Murray, A. (1984). Catalysts for collective violence: The importance of a psychological approach. In R. Folger (Ed.), *The sense of injustice: Social psychological perspectives* (pp. 95–139). New York: Plenum.

Martin, J., Scully, M., & Levitt, B. (1990). Injustice and the legitimation of revolution: Damning the past, excusing the present, and neglecting the future. *Journal of Personality and Social Psychology*, *59*, 281–290.

Martin, L. L. (1999). I-D compensation theory: Some implications of trying to satisfy immediate-return needs in a delayed-return culture. *Psychological Inquiry*, *10*, 195–208.

Martin, L. L., & Shirk, S. (2006). Immediate-return societies: What can they tell us about the self and social relationships in our society? In J. V. Wood, A. Tesser, & J. G. Holmes (Eds.), *The self and social relationships* (pp. 161–182). New York: Psychological Press.

Martin, L. L., & Van den Bos, K. (2014). Beyond terror: Toward a paradigm shift in the study of threat and culture. *European Review of Social Psychology*, *25*, 32–70.

McCauley, C. (2007a). Psychological issues in understanding terrorism and the response to terrorism. In B. Bongar, L. M. Brown, L. E. Beutler, J. N. Breckenridge,

& P. G. Zimbardo (Eds.), *Psychology of terrorism* (pp. 13–31). New York: Oxford University Press.

McCauley, C. (2007b). War versus justice in response to terrorist attacks: Competing frames and their implications. In B. Bongar, L. M. Brown, L. E. Beutler, J. N. Breckenridge, & P. G. Zimbardo (Eds.), *Psychology of terrorism* (pp. 56–65). New York: Oxford University Press.

McCauley, C. (2017). Toward a psychology of humiliation in asymmetric conflict. *American Psychologist, 72*, 255–265.

McCauley, C., & Moskalenko, S. (2008). Mechanisms of political radicalization: Pathways toward terrorism. *Terrorism and Political Violence, 20*, 415–433.

McCauley, C., & Moskalenko, S. (2011). *Friction: How radicalization happens to them and us.* New York: Oxford University Press.

McCauley, Clark R., & Segal, M. E. (1989). Terrorist individuals and terrorist groups: The normal psychology of extreme behavior. In J. Groebel & J. H. Markstein (Eds.), *Terrorism: Psychological perspectives* (pp. 41–64). Seville: University of Seville Publications.

McCauley, C., & Segal, M. E. (2009). Social psychology of terrorist groups. In J. Victoroff, & A. W. Kruglanski (Eds.), *Psychology of terrorism: Classic and contemporary insights* (pp. 331–346). New York: Psychology Press.

McClintock, C. G. (1978). Social values: Their definition, measurement, and development. *Journal of Research and Development in Education, 12*, 121–137.

McGloin, J. M., Sullivan, C. J., & Piquero, A. R. (2009). Aggregating to versatility? Transitions among offender types in the short term. *British Journal of Criminology, 49*, 243–264.

McGregor, I., Haji, R., Nash, K. A., & Teper, R. (2008). Religious zeal and the uncertain self. *Basic and Applied Social Psychology, 30*, 183–188.

McGregor, I., Hayes, J., & Prentice, M. (2015). Motivation for aggressive religious radicalization: Goal regulation theory and a personality × threat × affordance hypothesis. *Frontiers in Psychology, 6*, Article 1325.

McGregor, I., & Jordan, C. H. (2007). The mask of zeal: Low implicit self-esteem and defensive extremism after self-threat. *Self and Identity, 6*, 223–237.

McGregor, I., Prentice, M., & Nash, K. (2009). Personal uncertainty management by reactive approach motivation. *Psychological Inquiry, 20*, 225–229.

McVeigh, R. (2009). *The rise of the Ku Klux Klan: Right-wing movements and national politics.* Minneapolis: University of Minnesota Press.

Mead, G. H. (1934). *Mind, self, and society: From the standpoint of a social behaviorist.* Chicago: University of Chicago Press.

Meertens, R. W., Prins, Y. R. A., & Doosje, B. (2006). *In iedereen schuilt een terrorist: Een sociaal-psychologische analyse van terroristische sektes en aanslagen.* Schiedam: Scriptum.

Meeus, W. (2015). Why do young people become jihadists? A theoretical account on radical identity development. *European Journal of Developmental Psychology, 12*, 275–281.

Meinhof, U. (1970, June 15). Natürlich kann geschossen werden. *Der Spiegel, 25*, 74.

Merari, A. (1990). The readiness to kill and die: Suicidal terrorism in the Middle East. In W. Reich (Ed.), *Origins of terrorism: Psychologies, ideologies, theologies, states of mind* (pp. 192–207). Washington, DC: Woodrow Wilson Center Press.

Merari, A. (2010). *Driven to death: Psychological and social aspects of suicide terrorism.* Oxford, UK: Oxford University Press.

Merton, R. K. (1938). Social structure and anomie. *American Sociological Review, 3,* 672–682

Merton, R. K. (1995). The Thomas theorem and the Matthew effect. *Social Forces, 74,* 379–424.

Messick, D. M. (1993). Equality as a decision heuristic. In B. A. Mellers & J. Baron (Eds.), *Psychological perspectives on justice: Theory and applications* (pp. 11–31). Cambridge, MA: Cambridge University Press.

Messick, D. M., Bloom, S., Boldizar, J. P., & Samuelson, C. D. (1985). Why are we fairer than others? *Journal of Experimental Social Psychology, 21,* 480–500.

Messick, D. M., & McClintock, C. G. (1968). Motivational basis of choice in experimental games. *Journal of Experimental Social Psychology, 4,* 1–25.

Messick, D. M., & Sentis, K. (1979). Fairness and preference. *Journal of Experimental Social Psychology, 15,* 418–434.

Messick, D. M., & Sentis, K. (1983). Fairness, preference, and fairness biases. In D. M. Messick & K. S. Cook (Eds.), *Equity theory: Psychological and sociological perspectives* (pp. 61–94). New York: Praeger.

Michener, H. A., & Lawler, E. J. (1975). Endorsement of formal leaders: An integrative model. *Journal of Personality and Social Psychology, 31,* 216–223.

Milgram, S. (1974). *Obedience to authority: An experimental view.* New York: Harper & Row.

Miller, D. T. (1999). The norm of self-interest. *American Psychologist, 54,* 1053–1060.

Miller, D. T. (2001). Disrespect and the experience of injustice. *Annual Review of Psychology, 52,* 527–553.

Mirahmadi, H., & Farooq, M. (2010). *A community based approach to countering radicalization: A partnership for America.* Washington, DC: World Organization for Resource Development and Education.

Moghadam, A. (2006). *The roots of terrorism.* New York: Chelsea House.

Moghaddam, F. M. (2004). Cultural preconditions for potential terrorist groups: Terrorism and societal change. In F. M. Moghaddam & A. J. Marsella (Eds.), *Understanding terrorism: Psychosocial roots, consequences, and interventions* (pp. 103–117). Washington, DC: American Psychological Association.

Moghaddam, F. M. (2005). The staircase to terrorism: A psychological exploration. *American Psychologist, 60,* 161–169.

Moghaddam, F. M. (2008). *Collective uncertainty and extremism: A further discussion on the collective roots of subjective experience.* Paper presented at the 2008 Claremont Symposium on Applied Social Psychology, Claremont, USA.

Moghaddam, F. M. (2010). *The new global insecurity: How terrorism, environmental collapse, economic inequalities, and resource shortages are changing our world.* Santa Barbara, CA: Praeger.

Moghaddam, F. M., & Harré, R. (Eds.). (2010). *Words of conflict, words of war: How the language we use in political processes sparks fighting*. Santa Barbara, CA: Praeger.

Moghaddam, F. M., & Love, K. (2011). Collective uncertainty and extremism: A further discussion. In M. A. Hogg & D. L. Blaylock (Eds.), *Extremism and the psychology of uncertainty* (pp. 246–262). Oxford, UK: Wiley-Blackwell.

Moghaddam, F. M., & Marsella, A. J. (Eds.). (2004). *Understanding terrorism: Psychosocial roots, consequences, and interventions*. Washington, DC: American Psychological Association.

Molano, A. (2000). The evolution of the FARC: A guerrilla group's long history. *NACLA Report on the Americas, 34*, 23–31.

Moll, J., De Oliveira-Souza, R., Zahn, R., & Grafman, J. (2008). The cognitive neuroscience of moral emotions. In W. Sinnot-Armstrong (Ed.), *Moral psychology, Volume 3—The neuroscience of morality: Emotion, brain disorders, and development* (pp. 1–18). Cambridge, MA: MIT Press.

Monahan, J. (2012). The individual risk assessment of terrorism. *Psychology, Public Policy, and Law, 18*, 167.

Monin, B., & Miller, D. T. (2001). Moral credentials and the expression of prejudice. *Journal of Personality and Social Psychology, 81*, 33–43.

Montesquieu, C. L. (1995). *De l'esprit des lois" [The spirit of the laws]*. Paris, Gallimard. (Original work published in 1748)

Moore, D. A., & Loewenstein, G. (2004). Self-interest, automaticity, and the psychology of conflict of interest. *Social Justice Research, 17*, 189–202.

Morreall, J. (1976). The justifiability of violent civil disobedience. *Canadian Journal of Philosophy, 6*, 35–47.

Moskalenko, S., & McCauley, C. (2009). Measuring political mobilization: The distinction between activism and radicalism. *Terrorism and Political Violence, 21*, 239–260.

Nacos, B. L. (2016). *Mass-mediated terrorism: Mainstream and digital media in terrorism and counterterrorism* (3rd ed.). Lanham, MD: Rowman & Littlefield Publishers.

Nagle, J. D. (1970). *The National Democratic Party: Right radicalism in the Federal Republic of Germany*. Berkeley: University of California Press.

National Coordinator for Security and Counterterrorism. (2016). *National Counterterrorism Strategy for 2016–2020*. The Hague: National Coordinator for Security and Counterterrorism.

Nawaz, M. (2013). *Radical: My journey out of Islamist extremism*. Guilford, CT: Lyons Press.

Netherlands General Intelligence and Security Service. (2007a). *Annual Report 2006, General Intelligence and Security Service*. The Hague: Netherlands General Intelligence and Security Service (AIVD).

Netherlands General Intelligence and Security Service. (2007b). *The radical dawa in transition: The rise of Islamic neoradicalism in the Netherlands*. The Hague: Netherlands General Intelligence and Security Service (AIVD).

Netherlands General Intelligence and Security Service. (2009). *Animal rights extremism in the Netherlands: Fragmented but growing*. The Hague: Netherlands General Intelligence and Security Service (AIVD).

Netherlands General Intelligence and Security Service. (2010). *The flames of resistance: Growing opposition to asylum policy*. The Hague: Netherlands General Intelligence and Security Service (AIVD).

Netherlands General Intelligence and Security Service. (2014). *Left-wing activism and extremism in the Netherlands: A multi-faceted, volatile and fickle phenomenon*. The Hague: Netherlands General Intelligence and Security Service (AIVD).

Netherlands Ministry of the Interior and Kingdom Relations (2007). *Van dawa tot jihad: De diverse dreigingen van de radicale islam tegen de democratische rechtsorde*. The Hague, Netherlands Ministry of the Interior and Kingdom Relations. Retrieved from: file:///C:/Users/klokj/Downloads/notavandawatotjihad.pdf

Neuberg, S. L., & Newsom, J. T. (1993). Personal need for structure: Individual differences in the desire for simple structure. *Journal of Personality and Social Psychology, 65,* 113–131.

Neumann, P. (2013). The trouble with radicalization. *International Affairs, 89,* 873–893.

Nicholson, P. P. (1985). Tolerance as a moral ideal. In J. Horton & S. Mendus (Eds.), *Aspects of toleration: Philosophical studies* (pp. 158–173). New York: Methuen.

Nickerson R. S. (1998). Confirmation bias: A ubiquitous phenomenon in many guises. *Review of General Psychology, 2,* 175–220.

Niebuhr, R. (1932). *Moral man and immoral society: A study of ethics and politics.* New York: Scribner.

Nivette, A. E., Eisner, M., Malti, T., & Ribeaud, D. (2015). The social and developmental antecedents of legal cynicism. *Journal of Research in Crime and Delinquency, 52,* 270–298.

Ostrom, T. M. (1986). In memoriam: John Thibaut. *Journal of Experimental Social Psychology, 22,* 505–506.

Parker, D., Manstead, A. S. R., Stradling, S. G., Reason, J. T., & Baxter, J. S. (1992). Intention to commit driving violations: An application of the theory of planned behavior. *Journal of Applied Psychology, 77,* 94–101.

Paulhus, D. L. (1984). Two-component models of social desirability responding. *Journal of Personality and Social Psychology, 46,* 598–609.

Paulhus, D. L., Grae, P., & Van Selst, M. (1989). Attentional load increases the positivity of self-presentation. *Social Cognition, 7,* 389–400.

Paulhus, D. L., Harms, P. D., Bruce, M. N., & Lysy, D. C. (2003). The over-claiming technique: Measuring self-enhancement independent of ability. *Journal of Personality and Social Psychology, 84,* 681–693.

Pearce, K. I. (1977). Police negotiations: A new role for the community psychiatrist. *Canadian Psychiatric Association Journal, 22,* 171–175.

Pearlstein, R. M. (1991). *The mind of the political terrorist*. Wilmington, UK: Scholarly Resources.

Pekelder, J. (2007). *Sympathie voor de RAF: De Rote Armee Fraktion in Nederland, 1970–1980*. Amsterdam: Mets & Schilt.

Peters, S. L., Van den Bos, K., & Bobocel, D. R. (2004). The moral superiority effect: Self versus other differences in satisfaction with being overpaid. *Social Justice Research, 17,* 257–273.

Peterson, J. B., & Flanders, J. L. (2002). Complexity management theory: Motivation for ideological rigidity and social conflict. *Cortex, 38,* 429–458.

Petrescu, D., Van den Bos, K., Klumpers, F., & Kenemans, L. (2018). *Death can be surprising: Mortality salience and attentional control influence startle reactions to outgroup members.* Manuscript in preparation.

Pettigrew, T. F. (1998). Intergroup contact theory. *Annual Review of Psychology, 49,* 65–85.

Pettigrew, T. F. (2015). Samuel Stouffer and relative deprivation. *Social Psychology Quarterly, 78,* 7–24.

Pettigrew, T. F., & Tropp, L. R. (2006). Interpersonal relations and group processes: A meta-analytic test of intergroup contact theory. *Journal of Personality and Social Psychology, 90,* 751–783.

Phelps, E. S. (1970). *Microeconomic foundations of employment and inflation theory.* New York: Norton.

Piaget, J. (1975). *The moral judgment of the child.* London: Routledge and Kegan Paul. (Original work published in 1932)

Pierro, A., Giacomantonio, M., Kruglanski, A. W., & Van Knippenberg, D. (2014). Follower need for cognitive closure as moderator of the effectiveness of leader procedural fairness. *European Journal of Work and Organizational Psychology, 23,* 582–595.

Pizarro, D. A., & Bloom, P. (2003). The intelligence of the moral intuitions: Comment on Haidt (2001). *Psychological Review, 110,* 193–196.

Plant, E. A., & Devine, P. G. (2009). The active control of prejudice: Unpacking the intentions guiding control efforts. *Journal of Personality and Social Psychology, 96,* 640–652.

Popper, K. R. (1945). *The open society and its enemies.* London: Routledge and Kegan Paul.

Popper, K. R. (1957). Philosophy of science: A personal report. In C. A. Mace (Ed.), *British philosophy in the mid-century.* London: Allan & Unwin.

Popper, K. R. (2001). *All life is problem solving.* London: Routledge.

Popper, K. R. (2002). *The logic of scientific discovery.* London: Routledge. (Original work published 1959)

Posner, R. A. (2007). *Countering terrorism: Blurred focus, halting steps.* Lanham, MD: Rowman & Littlefield.

Post, J. M. (1990). Terrorist psycho-logic: Terrorist behavior as a product of psychological forces. In W. Reich (Ed.), *Origins of terrorism: Psychologies, ideologies, theologies, states of mind* (pp. 25–40). Washington, DC: Woodrow Wilson Center Press.

Post, J. M. (2007). *The mind of the terrorist: The psychology of terrorism from the IRA to Al-Qaeda.* New York: Palgrave Macmillan.

Post, J. M., Sprinzak, E., & Denny, L. M. (2009). The terrorists in their own words: Interviews with 35 incarcerated Middle Eastern terrorists. In J. Victoroff, & A. W. Kruglanski (Eds.), *Psychology of terrorism: Classic and contemporary insights* (pp. 109–117). New York: Psychology Press.

Precht, T. (2007). *Home grown terrorism and Islamist radicalisation: From conversion to terrorism.* Copenhagen: Danish Ministry of Justice.

Prinz, J. J., & Nichols, S. (2010). Moral emotions. In J. M. Doris (Eds.), *The moral psychology handbook* (pp. 111–146). Oxford, UK: Oxford University Press.

Pynchon, M. R., & Borum, R. (1999). Assessing threats of targeted group violence: Contributions from social psychology. *Behavioral Sciences and the Law, 17,* 339–355.

Pyszczynski, T. A. (2008, October). *Terror management theory, religion, hatred, and compassion.* Paper presented at the 2008 Conference of the Society of Experimental Social Psychology, Sacramento, CA, USA.

Pyszczynski, T. A., Greenberg, J., Solomon, S., Arndt, J., & Schimel, J. (2004a). Why do people need self-esteem? A theoretical and empirical review. *Psychological Bulletin, 130,* 435–468.

Pyszczynski, T. A., Greenberg, J., Solomon, S., Arndt, J., & Schimel, J. (2004b). Converging toward an integrated theory of self-esteem: Reply to Crocker and Nuer (2000), Ryan and Deci (2004), and Leary (2004). *Psychological Bulletin, 130,* 483–488.

Pyszczynski, T. A., Solomon, S., & Greenberg, J. (2003). *In the wake of 9/11: The psychology of terror.* Washington, DC: American Psychological Association.

Rabasa, A., Pettyjohn, S. L., Ghez, J., & Boucek, C. (2010). *Deradicalizing Islamist extremists.* Santa Monica, CA: Rand.

Rahimullah, R. H., Larmar, S., Abdalla, M. (2013). Understanding violent radicalization amongst Muslims: A review of the literature. *Journal of Psychology and Behavioral Science, 1,* 19–35.

Rasser, M. (2005). The Dutch response to Moluccan terrorism, 1970–1978. *Studies in Conflict and Terrorism, 28,* 481–492.

Reber, R., Schwarz, N., & Winkielman, P. (2004). Processing fluency and aesthetic pleasure: Is beauty in the perceiver's processing experience? *Personality and Social Psychology Review, 8,* 364–382.

Reich, W. (Ed.). (1990). *Origins of terrorism: Psychologies, ideologies, theologies, states of mind.* Washington, DC: Woodrow Wilson Center Press.

Richardson, M. W. (2012). *Al-Shabaab's American recruits: A comparative analysis of two radicalization pathways.* Doctoral dissertation, University of Texas at El Paso.

Rieger, D., Frischlich, L., & Bente, G. (2017). Propaganda in an insecure, unstructured world: How psychological uncertainty and authoritarian attitudes shape the evaluation of right-wing extremist internet propaganda. *Journal for Deradicalization, 10,* 203- 229.

Rock, M. S., & Janoff-Bulman, R. (2010). Where do we draw our lines? Politics, rigidity, and the role of self-regulation. *Social Psychological and Personality Science, 1,* 26–33.

Roets, A., Kruglanski, A. W., Kossowska, M., Pierro, A., & Hong, Y.-y. (2015). The motivated gatekeeper of our minds: New directions in need for closure theory and research. In J. M. Olson & M. P. Zanna (Eds.), *Advances in experimental social psychology* (Vol. 52, pp. 221–283). San Diego, CA: Academic Press.

Rokeach, M. (1948). Generalized mental rigidity as a factor in ethnocentrism. *Journal of Abnormal and Social Psychology, 43,* 259–278.

Rokeach, M. (1950). The effect of perception time upon the rigidity and concreteness of thinking. *Journal of Experimental Psychology, 40,* 206–216.

Rokeach, M. (1960). *The open and closed mind.* New York: Basic Books.

Rosenberg, M. (1965). *Society and the adolescent self-image.* Princeton, NJ: Princeton University Press.

Rousseau, J.-J. (2001). *Du contract social, ou principes du droit politique [The social contract, or principles of political right]*. Paris: Flammarion. (Original work published in 1762)

Routledge, C., Juhl, J., & Vess, M. (2010). Divergent reactions to the terror of terrorism: Personal need for structure moderates the effects of terrorism salience on worldview-related attitudinal rigidity. *Basic and Applied Social Psychology, 32*, 243–249.

Rovenpor, D. R., Leidner, B., Kardos, P., & O'Brien, T. C. (2016). Meaning threat can promote peaceful, not only military-based approaches to intergroup conflict: The moderating role of ingroup glorification. *European Journal of Social Psychology, 46*, 544–562.

Roy, O. (2017). *Jihad and death: The global appeal of Islamic State*. London, UK: C. Hurst & Co.

Rozin, P., Lowery, L., Imada, S., & Haidt, J. (1999). The CAD triad hypothesis: A mapping between three moral emotions (contempt, anger, disgust) and three moral codes (community, autonomy, divinity). *Journal of Personality and Social Psychology, 76*, 574–586.

Ruby, C. L. (2002). Are terrorists mentally deranged? *Analysis of Social Issues and Public Policy, 3*, 15–26.

Rudman, L. A., Dohn, M. C., & Fairchild, K. (2007). Implicit self-esteem compensation: Automatic threat defense. *Journal of Personality and Social Psychology, 93*, 798–813.

Runciman, W. G. (1966). *Relative deprivation and social justice: A study of attitudes to social inequality in twentieth-century England*. London: Routledge & Kegan Paul.

Rutter, M. (1996). Transitions and turning points in developmental psychopathology: As applied to the age span between childhood and midadulthood. *International Journal of Behavioral Development, 19*, 603–626.

Sabbagh, C., Dar, Y., & Resh, N. (1994). The structure of social justice judgments: A facet approach. *Social Psychology Quarterly, 57*, 244–261.

Sageman, M. (2004). *Understanding terror networks*. Philadelphia: University of Pennsylvania Press.

Sageman, M. (2009). Understanding terror networks. In J. Victoroff, & A. W. Kruglanski (Eds.), *Psychology of terrorism: Classic and contemporary insights* (pp. 361–365). New York: Psychology Press.

Saguy, T., & Dovidio, J. F. (2013). Insecure status relations shape preferences for the content of intergroup contact. *Personality and Social Psychology Bulletin, 39*, 1030–1042.

Saguy, T., Tausch, N., Dovidio, J. F., & Pratto, F. (2009). The irony of harmony: Intergroup contact can produce false expectations for equality. *Psychological Science, 20*, 114–121.

Salami, S. O. (2010). Moderating effects of resilience, self-esteem and social support on adolescents' reactions to violence. *Asian Social Science, 6*, 101–111.

Sampson, R. J., & Bartusch, D. J. (1998). Legal cynicism and (subcultural?) tolerance of deviance: The neighborhood context of racial differences. *Law and Society Review, 32*, 777–804.

Sandel, M. J. (1982). *Liberalism and the limits of justice*. Cambridge, UK: Cambridge University Press.

Sandel, M. J. (2009). *Justice: What's the right thing to do?* London: Penguin.

Sandel, M. J. (2012). *What money can't buy: The moral limits of markets.* London: Allen Lane.

Sarma, K. M. (2017). Risk assessment and the prevention of radicalization from nonviolence into terrorism. *American Psychologist, 72,* 278–288.

Saucier, G., Geuy Akers, L., Shen-Miller, S., Knežević, G., & Stankov, L. (2009). Patterns of thinking in militant extremism. *Perspectives on Psychological Science, 4,* 256–271.

Schelling, T. C. (1960). *The strategy of conflict.* Cambridge, MA: Harvard University Press.

Schmader, T., Johns, M., & Forbes, C. (2008). An integrated process model of stereotype threat effects on performance. *Psychological Review, 115,* 336–356.

Schmid, A. P. (2013). *Radicalisation, de-radicalisation, counter-radicalisation: A conceptual discussion and literature review.* ICCT Research Paper, 97.

Schmid, K., Ramiah, A. A., & Hewstone, M. (2014). Neighborhood ethnic diversity and trust: The role of intergroup contact and perceived threat. *Psychological Science, 25,* 665–674.

Schmidt, A. L., Zollo, F., Del Vicario, M., Bessi, A., Scala, A., Caldarelli, G., Stanley, H. E., & Quattrociocchi, W. (2017). Anatomy of news consumption on Facebook. *Proceedings of the National Academy of Sciences, 114,* 3035–3039.

Schooler, J. W. (2014a). Metascience could rescue the "replication crisis." *Nature, 515,* 9.

Schooler, J. W. (2014b). Turning the lens of science on itself: Verbal overshadowing, replication, and metascience. *Perspectives on Psychological Science, 9,* 579–584.

Schopler, J., Insko, C. A., Wieselquist, J., Pemberton, M., Witcher, B., Kozar, R., Roddenberry, C., & Wildschut, T. (2001). When groups are more competitive than individuals: The domain of the discontinuity effect. *Journal of Personality and Social Psychology, 80,* 632–644.

Schuurman, B. W. (2017). *Becoming a European homegrown jihadist: A multilevel analysis of involvement in the Dutch Hofstadgroup, 2002–2005.* Doctoral dissertation, Leiden University.

Schuyt, C. J. M. (1972). *Recht, orde en burgerlijke ongehoorzaamheid.* Rotterdam: Universitaire Pers.

Schwinger, T. (1980). Just allocation of goods: Decisions among three principles. In G. Mikula (Ed.), *Justice and social interaction* (pp. 95–125). New York: Springer-Verlag.

Sedikides, C., De Cremer, D., Hart, C. M., & Brebels, L. (2009). Procedural fairness responses in the context of self-uncertainty. In R. M. Arkin, K. C. Oleson, & P. J. Carroll (Eds.), *Handbook of the uncertain self* (pp. 142–159). New York: Psychology Press.

Sedikides, C., Gaertner, L., & Toguchi, Y. (2003). Pancultural self-enhancement. *Journal of Personality and Social Psychology, 84,* 60–79.

Sedikides, C., & Gregg, A. P. (2008). Self-enhancement: Food for thought. *Perspectives on Psychological Science, 3,* 102–116.

Sedikides, C., & Strube, M. J. (1997). Self-evaluation: To thine own self be good, to thine own self be sure, to thine own self be true, and to thine own self be better. In M. P. Zanna (Ed.), *Advances in experimental social psychology* (Vol. 29, pp. 209–269). San Diego, CA: Academic Press.

Sengupta, N. K., & Sibley, C. G. (2013). Perpetuating one's own disadvantage: Intergroup contact enables the ideological legitimation of inequality. *Personality and Social Psychology Bulletin, 39,* 1391–1403.

Shah, J. Y., Friedman, R., & Kruglanski, A. W. (2002). Forgetting all else: On the antecedents and consequences of goal shielding. *Journal of Personality and Social Psychology, 83,* 1261–1280.

Shah, P., Michal, A., Ibrahim, A., Rhodes, R., & Rodriguez, F. (2017). What makes everyday scientific reasoning so challenging? *Psychology of Learning and Motivation, 66,* 251–299.

Sherif, M. (1954). Integrating field work and laboratory in small group research. *American Sociological Review, 19,* 759–771.

Sherif, M. (1958). Superordinate goals in the reduction of intergroup conflict. *American Journal of Sociology, 63,* 349–356.

Sherif, M., Harvey, O. J., White, B. J., Hood, W. R., & Sherif, C. W. (1961). *Intergroup conflict and cooperation: The Robbers Cave experiment.* Norman, OK: University Book Exchange.

Shiffrin, R. M., & Schneider, W. (1977). Controlled and automatic human information processing: II. Perceptual learning, automatic attending, and a general theory. *Psychological Review, 84,* 127–190.

Sidanius, J. (1984). Political interest, political information search, and ideological homogeneity as a function of sociopolitical ideology: A tale of three theories. *Human Relations, 37,* 811–828.

Sidanius, J. (1985). Cognitive functioning and sociopolitical ideology revisited. *Political Psychology, 6,* 637–662.

Sidanius, J., Levin, S., Federico, C. M., & Pratto, F. (2001). Legitimizing ideologies: The social dominance approach. In J. T. Jost & B. Major (Eds.), *The psychology of legitimacy: Emerging perspectives on ideology, justice, and intergroup relations* (pp. 307–331). New York: Cambridge University Press.

Sieckelinck, S., & De Winter, M. (Eds.). (2015). *Formers and families: Transitional journeys in and out of extremisms in the United Kingdom, Denmark and the Netherlands.* The Hague: National Coordinator for Security and Counterterrorism.

Silber, M. D., & Bhatt, A. (2007). *Radicalization in the West: The homegrown threat.* New York: NYPD Intelligence Division.

Silke, A. (2008). Holy warriors: Exploring the psychological processes of jihadi radicalization. *European Journal of Criminology, 5,* 99–123.

Silke, A. (2009). Cheshire-cat logic: The recurring theme of terrorist abnormality in psychological research. In J. Victoroff, & A. W. Kruglanski (Eds.), *Psychology of terrorism: Classic and contemporary insights* (pp. 95–107). New York: Psychology Press.

Silke, A., & Schmidt-Petersen, J. (2015). The Golden Age? What the 100 most cited articles in terrorism studies tell us. *Terrorism and Political Violence,* 1–21.

Sinclair, R. C., & Mark, M. M. (1991). Mood and the endorsement of egalitarian macrojustice versus equity-based microjustice principles. *Personality and Social Psychology Bulletin, 17,* 369–375.

Sinclair, R. C., & Mark, M. M. (1992). The influence of mood state on judgment and action: Effects on persuasion, categorization, social justice, person perception, and judgmental accuracy. In L. L. Martin & A. Tesser (Eds.), *The construction of social judgments* (pp. 165–193). Hillsdale, NJ: Erlbaum.

Sinnot-Armstrong, W. (Ed.). (2008). *Moral psychology, Volume 2—The cognitive science of morality: Intuition and diversity.* Cambridge, MA: MIT Press.

Skidmore, T. E. (1988). *The politics of military rule in Brazil 1964–85.* New York: Oxford University Press.

Skitka, L. J. (2002). Do the means always justify the ends, or do the ends sometimes justify the means? A value protection model of justice. *Personality and Social Psychology Bulletin, 28,* 588–597.

Skitka, L. J., & Morgan, G. S. (2014). The social and political implications of moral conviction. *Advances in Political Psychology, 35,* 95–110.

Smith, A. (2002). *The theory of moral sentiments.* Cambridge, UK: Cambridge University Press. (Original work published in 1759)

Smith, H. J., Pettigrew, T. F., Pippin, G. M., & Bialosiewicz, S. (2012). Relative deprivation: A theoretical and meta-analytic review. *Personality and Social Psychology Review, 16,* 203–232.

Smith, H. J., Tyler, T. R., Huo, Y. J., Ortiz, D. J., & Lind, E. A. (1998). The self-relevant implications of the group-value model: Group-membership, self-worth and treatment quality. *Journal of Experimental Social Psychology, 34,* 470–493.

Smith, H. W. (1981). *Strategies of social research: The methodological imagination* (2nd ed.). Englewood Cliffs, NJ: Prentice-Hall.

Solomon, S., Greenberg, J., & Pyszczynski, T. (1991). A terror management theory of social behavior: The psychological functions of self-esteem and cultural worldviews. In M. P. Zanna (Ed.), *Advances in experimental social psychology* (Vol. 24, pp. 93–159). New York: Academic Press.

Sorrentino, R. M., Bobocel, D. R., Gitta, M. Z., Olson, J. M., & Hewitt, E. C. (1988). Uncertainty orientation and persuasion: Individual differences in the effects of personal relevance on social judgments. *Journal of Personality and Social Psychology, 55,* 357–371.

Sorrentino, R. M., Hodson, G., & Huber, G. L. (2001). Uncertainty orientation and the social mind: Individual differences in the interpersonal context. In J. P. Forgas, K. D. Williams, & L. Wheeler (Eds.), *The social mind: Cognitive and motivational aspects of interpersonal behavior* (pp. 199–227). New York: Cambridge University Press.

Sorrentino, R. M., & Roney, C. J. R. (1986). Uncertainty orientation, achievement-related motivation and task diagnosticity as determinants of task performance. *Social Cognition, 4,* 420–436.

Sorrentino, R. M., Short, J.-A. C., & Raynor, J. O. (1984). Uncertainty orientation: Implications for affective and cognitive views of achievement behavior. *Journal of Personality and Social Psychology, 46,* 189–201.

Speckhard, A., Jacuch, B., & Vanrompay, V. (2012). Taking on the persona of a suicide bomber: A thought experiment. *Perspectives on Terrorism, 6,* 51–73.

Sprinzak, E. (1990). The psychopolitical formation of extreme left terrorism in a democracy: The case of the Weathermen. In W. Reich (Ed.), *Origins of terrorism: Psychologies, ideologies, theologies, states of mind* (pp. 65–85). Washington, DC: Woodrow Wilson Center Press.

Sprinzak, E. (1991). The process of delegitimation: Towards a linkage theory of political terrorism. *Terrorism and Political Violence, 3*, 50–68.

Sprinzak, E. (1995). Right-wing terrorism in a comparative perspective: The case of split delegimization. *Terrorism and Political Violence, 7*, 17–43.

Sprinzak, E. (2009). The psychopolitical formation of extreme left terrorism in a democracy: The case of the Weathermen. In J. Victoroff, & A. W. Kruglanski (Eds.), *Psychology of terrorism: Classic and contemporary insights* (pp. 317–330). New York: Psychology Press.

Stanski, K. (2005). Terrorism, gender, and ideology: A case study of women who join the revolutionary armed forces. In J. J. F. Forest (Ed.), *The making of a terrorist: Recruitment, training, and root causes* (pp. 136–150). New York: Praeger.

Starn, O. (1995). Maoism in the Andes: The communist party of Peru-Shining Path and the refusal of history. *Journal of Latin American Studies, 27*, 399–421.

Staub, E. (1989). *The roots of evil: The origins of genocide and other group violence.* New York: Cambridge University Press.

Staub, E. (2006). Reconciliation after genocide, mass killing, or intractable conflict: Understanding the roots of violence, psychological recovery, and steps toward a general theory. *Political Psychology, 27*, 867–894.

Staub, E. (2011). *Overcoming evil: Genocide, violent conflict, and terrorism.* New York: Oxford University Press.

Staub, E. (2015). *The roots of goodness and resistance to evil.* New York: Oxford University Press.

Staub, E., & Pearlman, L. A. (2009). Reducing intergroup prejudice and conflict: A commentary. *Journal of Personality and Social Psychology, 96*, 588–593.

Staub, E., Pearlman, L. A., Gubin, A., & Hagengimana, A. (2005). Healing, reconciliation, forgiving and the prevention of violence after genocide or mass killing: An intervention and its experimental evaluation in Rwanda. *Journal of Social and Clinical Psychology, 24*, 297–334.

Stern, J. (2004). *Terror in the name of God: Why religious militants kill.* New York: Harper Collins.

Stern, J., & Berger, J. M. (2015). *ISIS: The state of terror.* New York: Harper Collins.

Stouffer, S. A., Suchman, E. A., DeVinney, L. C., Star, S. A., & Williams, R. M. (1949). *The American soldier: Adjustment during Army life* (Vol. 1). Princeton, NJ: Princeton University Press.

Strack, F., & Deutsch, R. (2004). Reflective and impulsive determinants of social behavior. *Personality and Social Psychology Review, 8*, 220–247.

Sunshine, J., & Tyler, T. R. (2003). Moral solidarity, identification with the community, and the importance of procedural justice: The police as prototypical representatives of a group's moral values. *Social Psychology Quarterly, 66*, 153–165.

Tajfel, H., & Turner, J. C. (1979). An integrative theory of intergroup conflict. In W. G. Austin & S. Worchel (Eds.), *The social psychology of intergroup relations* (pp. 33–47). Monterey, CA: Brooks/Cole.

Tanaka, K., & Takimoto, S. (1997). Effects of interpersonal affect upon fairness judgment. *Japanese Psychological Research, 39*, 312–322.

Tanay, E. (1987). Pseudo-political terrorism. *Journal of Forensic Sciences, 32*, 192–200.

Täuber, S., & Van Zomeren, M. (2012). Refusing intergroup help from the morally superior: How one's group moral superiority leads to another group's reluctance to seek their help. *Journal of Experimental Social Psychology, 48*, 420–423.

Tausch, N., Becker, J., Spears, R., Christ, O., Saab, R., Singh, P., & Siddiqui, R. N. (2011). Explaining radical group behavior: Developing emotion and efficacy routes to normative and nonnormative collective action. *Journal of Personality and Social Psychology, 101*, 129–148.

Taylor, I. A. (1960). Similarities in the structure of extreme social attitudes. *Psychological Monographs, 74*, 1–36.

Tellidis, I., & Toros, H. (2015). *Researching terrorism, peace and conflict studies: Interaction, synthesis and opposition.* Abingdon, UK: Routledge.

Tetlock, P. E. (1983). Cognitive style and political ideology. *Journal of Personality and Social Psychology, 45*, 118–126.

Tetlock, P. E. (1989). Structure and function in political belief systems. In A. R. Pratkanis, S. J. Breckler, & G. G. Anthony (Eds.), *Attitude, structure and function* (pp. 129–151). Hillsdale, NJ: Erlbaum.

Thibaut, J., & Kelley, H. H. (1959). *The social psychology of groups.* New York: Wiley.

Thibaut, J., & Walker, L. (1975). *Procedural justice: A psychological analysis.* Hillsdale, NJ: Erlbaum.

Thomas, W. I., & Thomas, D. S. (1928). *The child in America: Behavior problems and programs.* New York: Knopf.

Thompson, M. M., Naccarato, M. E., Parker, K. C. H., & Moskowitz, G. B. (2001). The personal need for structure and personal fear of invalidity measures: Historical perspectives, current applications, and future directions. In G. B. Moskowitz (Ed.), *Cognitive social psychology: The Princeton symposium on the legacy and future of social cognition* (pp. 19–39). Mahwah, NJ: Erlbaum.

Thompson, R. L. (2011). Radicalization and the use of social media. *Journal of Strategic Security, 4*, 1–26.

Triandis, H. C., & Gelfland, M. J. (1998). Converging measurement of horizontal and vertical individualism and collectivism. *Journal of Personality and Social Psychology, 74*, 118–128.

Tropp, L. R., & Page-Gould, E. (2015). Contact between groups. In M. Mikulincer, P. R. Shaver, J. F. Dovidio, & J. A. Simpson (Eds.), *APA handbook of personality and social psychology* (Vol. 2, pp. 535–560). Washington, DC: American Psychological Association.

Trujillo, H., Jordán, J., Gutierrez, J. A., & Gonzalez-Cabrera, J. (2009). Radicalization in prisons? Field research in 25 Spanish prisons. *Terrorism and Political Violence, 21*, 558–579.

Tsintsadze-Maass, E., & Maass, R. W. (2014). Groupthink and terrorist radicalization. *Terrorism and Political Violence, 26*, 735–758.

Turiel, E. (1983). *The development of social knowledge: Morality and convention.* Cambridge, UK: Cambridge University Press.

Tversky, A., & Kahneman, D. (1974). Judgment under uncertainty: Heuristics and biases. *Science, 185*, 1124–1134.

Tversky, A., & Kahneman, D. (1979). Belief in the law of small numbers. *Psychological Bulletin, 76,* 105–110.

Tversky, A., & Kahneman, D. (1980). Causal schemas in judgments under uncertainty. In M. Fishbein (Ed.), *Progress in social psychology* (pp. 49–72). Hillsdale, NJ: Erlbaum.

Tversky, A., & Kahneman, D. (1981). The framing of decisions and the psychology of choice. *Science, 211,* 453–458.

Tversky, A., & Kahneman, D. (1983). Extensional versus intuitive reasoning: The conjunction fallacy in probability judgment. *Psychological Review, 90,* 293–315.

Tversky, A., & Kahneman, D. (1986). Rational choice and the framing of decisions. *Journal of Business, 59,* 251–278.

Tyler, T. R. (1987). Conditions leading to value-expressive effects in judgments of procedural justice: A test of four models. *Journal of Personality and Social Psychology, 52,* 333–344.

Tyler, T. R. (1988). What is procedural justice? Criteria used by citizens to assess the fairness of legal procedures. *Law and Society Review, 22,* 103–135.

Tyler, T. R. (1989). The psychology of procedural justice: A test of the group-value model. *Journal of Personality and Social Psychology, 57,* 830–838.

Tyler, T. R. (2006). *Why people obey the law.* Princeton, NJ: Princeton University Press.

Tyler, T. R., Boeckmann, R. J., Smith, H. J., & Huo, Y. J. (1997). *Social justice in a diverse society.* Boulder, CO: Westview.

Tyler, T. R., & DeGoey, P. (1996). Trust in organizational authorities: The influence of motive attributions on willingness to accept decisions. In R. Kramer & T. R. Tyler (Eds.), *Trust in organizations: Frontiers of theory and research* (pp. 331–356). Thousand Oaks, CA: Sage.

Tyler, T. R., & Fagan, J. (2008). Legitimacy and cooperation: Why do people help the police fight crime in their communities? *Ohio State Journal of Criminal Law, 6,* 231–275.

Tyler, T. R., & Huo, Y. J. (2002). *Trust in the law: Encouraging public cooperation with the police and courts.* New York: Russell Sage Foundation.

Tyler, T. R., & Lind, E. A. (1992). A relational model of authority in groups. In M. P. Zanna (Ed.), *Advances in experimental social psychology* (Vol. 25, pp. 115–191). San Diego, CA: Academic Press.

Tyler, T. R., Rasinski, K. A., & McGraw, K. M. (1985). The influence of perceived injustice on the endorsement of political leaders. *Journal of Applied Social Psychology, 15,* 700–725.

Tyler, T. R., Rasinski, K. A., & Spodick, N. (1985). Influence of voice on satisfaction with leaders: Exploring the meaning of process control. *Journal of Personality and Social Psychology, 48,* 72–81.

Tyler, T. R., Schulhofer, S., & Huq, A. Z. (2010). Legitimacy and deterrence effects in counterterrorism policing: A study of Muslim Americans. *Law and Society Review, 44,* 365–401.

Van Bergen, D. D., Feddes, A. R., Doosje, B., & Pels, T. (2015). Collective identity factors and the attitude toward violence in defense of ethnicity or religion among Muslim youth of Turkish and Moroccan Descent. *International Journal of Intercultural Relations, 47,* 89–100.

Van Boven L., Judd C. M., & Sherman D. K. (2012). Political polarization projection: Social projection of partisan attitude extremity and attitudinal processes. *Journal of Personality and Social Psychology, 103*, 84–100.

Van den Bos, K. (1999). What are we talking about when we talk about no-voice procedures? On the psychology of the fair outcome effect. *Journal of Experimental Social Psychology, 35*, 560–577.

Van den Bos, K. (2001a). Uncertainty management: The influence of uncertainty salience on reactions to perceived procedural fairness. *Journal of Personality and Social Psychology, 80*, 931–941.

Van den Bos, K. (2001b). Fairness heuristic theory: Assessing the information to which people are reacting has a pivotal role in understanding organizational justice. In S. W. Gilliland, D. D. Steiner, & D. P. Skarlicki (Eds.), *Theoretical and cultural perspectives on organizational justice* (pp. 63–84). Greenwich, CT: Information Age Publishing.

Van den Bos, K. (2003). On the subjective quality of social justice: The role of affect as information in the psychology of justice judgments. *Journal of Personality and Social Psychology, 85*, 482–498.

Van den Bos, K. (2004). An existentialist approach to the social psychology of fairness: The influence of mortality and uncertainty salience on reactions to fair and unfair events. In J. Greenberg, S. L. Koole, & T. Pyszczynski (Eds.), *Handbook of experimental existential psychology* (pp. 167–181). New York: Guilford Press.

Van den Bos, K. (2005). What is responsible for the fair process effect? In J. Greenberg & J. A. Colquitt (Eds.), *Handbook of organizational justice: Fundamental questions about fairness in the workplace* (pp. 273–300). Mahwah, NJ: Erlbaum.

Van den Bos, K. (2007). Hot cognition and social justice judgments: The combined influence of cognitive and affective factors on the justice judgment process. In D. de Cremer (Ed.), *Advances in the psychology of justice and affect* (pp. 59–82). Greenwich, CT: Information Age Publishing.

Van den Bos, K. (2009a). Making sense of life: The existential self trying to deal with personal uncertainty. *Psychological Inquiry, 20*, 197–217.

Van den Bos, K. (2009b). On the psychology of the uncertain self and the integration of the worldview defense zoo. *Psychological Inquiry, 20*, 252–261.

Van den Bos, K. (2010). Self-regulation, homeostasis, and behavioral disinhibition in normative judgments. In D. R. Bobocel, A. C. Kay, M. P. Zanna, & J. M. Olson (Eds.), *The psychology of justice and legitimacy: The Ontario Symposium* (Vol. 11, pp. 205–228). New York: Psychology Press.

Van den Bos, K. (2011). From "is" to "ought": The naturalistic fallacy in the psychology of religion. *Religion, Brain and Behavior, 1*, 242–243.

Van den Bos, K. (2014). *Kijken naar het recht.* Inaugural lecture, Utrecht University.

Van den Bos, K. (2015). Humans making sense of alarming conditions: Psychological insight into the fair process effect. In R. S. Cropanzano & M. L. Ambrose (Eds.), *Oxford handbook of justice in work organizations* (pp. 403–417). New York: Oxford University Press.

Van den Bos, K., & Bal, M. (2016). Social-cognitive and motivational processes underlying the justice motive. In C. Sabbagh & M. Schmitt (Eds.), *Handbook of social justice theory and research* (pp. 181–198). New York: Springer.

Van den Bos, K., Euwema, M. C., Poortvliet, P. M., & Maas, M. (2007). Uncertainty management and social issues: Uncertainty as important determinant of reactions to socially deviating people. *Journal of Applied Social Psychology, 37*, 1726–1756.

Van den Bos, K., Ham, J., Lind, E. A., Simonis, M., Van Essen, W. J., & Rijpkema, M. (2008). Justice and the human alarm system: The impact of exclamation points and flashing lights on the justice judgment process. *Journal of Experimental Social Psychology, 44*, 201–219.

Van den Bos, K., & Lind, E. A. (2002). Uncertainty management by means of fairness judgments. In M. P. Zanna (Ed.), *Advances in experimental social psychology* (Vol. 34, pp. 1–60). San Diego, CA: Academic Press.

Van den Bos, K., & Lind, E. A. (2013). On sense-making reactions and public inhibition of benign social motives: An appraisal model of prosocial behavior. In J. M. Olson & M. P. Zanna (Eds.), *Advances in experimental social psychology* (Vol. 48, pp. 1–58). San Diego, CA: Academic Press.

Van den Bos, K., Lind, E. A., Vermunt, R., & Wilke, H. A. M. (1997). How do I judge my outcome when I do not know the outcome of others? The psychology of the fair process effect. *Journal of Personality and Social Psychology, 72*, 1034–1046.

Van den Bos, K., & Loseman, A. (2011). Radical worldview defense in reaction to personal uncertainty. In M. A. Hogg & D. L. Blaylock (Eds.), *Extremism and the psychology of uncertainty* (pp. 71–89). Oxford, UK: Wiley-Blackwell.

Van den Bos, K., Loseman, A., & Doosje, B. (2009). *Waarom jongeren radicaliseren en sympathie krijgen voor terrorisme: Onrechtvaardigheid, onzekerheid en bedreigde groepen*. The Hague: Research and Documentation Centre of the Netherlands Ministry of Justice.

Van den Bos, K., & Maas, M. (2009). On the psychology of the belief in a just world: Exploring experiential and rationalistic paths to victim blaming. *Personality and Social Psychology Bulletin, 35*, 1567–1578.

Van den Bos, K., Maas, M., Waldring, I. E., & Semin, G. R. (2003). Toward understanding the psychology of reactions to perceived fairness: The role of affect intensity. *Social Justice Research, 16*, 151–168.

Van den Bos, K., McGregor, I., & Martin, L. L. (2015). Security and uncertainty in contemporary delayed-return cultures: Coping with the blockage of personal goals. In P. J. Carroll, R. M. Arkin, & A. L. Wichman (Eds.), *Handbook of personal security* (pp. 21–35). New York: Psychology Press.

Van den Bos, K., & Miedema, J. (2000). Toward understanding why fairness matters: The influence of mortality salience on reactions to procedural fairness. *Journal of Personality and Social Psychology, 79*, 355–366.

Van den Bos, K., Peters, S. L., Bobocel, D. R., & Ybema, J. F. (2006). On preferences and doing the right thing: Satisfaction with advantageous inequity when cognitive processing is limited. *Journal of Experimental Social Psychology, 42*, 273–289.

Van den Bos, K., Poortvliet, P. M., Maas, M., Miedema, J., & Van den Ham, E.-J. (2005). An enquiry concerning the principles of cultural norms and values: The impact of uncertainty and mortality salience on reactions to violations and bolstering of cultural worldviews. *Journal of Experimental Social Psychology, 41*, 91–113.

Van den Bos, K., Van Ameijde, J., & Van Gorp, H. (2006). On the psychology of religion: The role of personal uncertainty in religious worldview defense. *Basic and Applied Social Psychology, 28*, 333–341.

Van den Bos, K., Van der Velden, L., & Lind, E. A. (2014). On the role of perceived procedural justice in citizens' reactions to government decisions and the handling of conflicts. *Utrecht Law Review, 10(4)*, 1–26.

Van den Bos, K., & Van Laarhoven, D. (2018). *On behavioral disinhibition and the interindividual-intergroup discontinuity effect: Reducing cheating behavior by means of reminders of behavioral disinhibition.* Manuscript in preparation.

Van den Bos, K., Van Lange, P. A. M., Lind, E. A., Venhoeven, L. A., Beudeker, D. A., Cramwinckel, F. M., Smulders, L., & Van der Laan, J. (2011). On the benign qualities of behavioral disinhibition: Because of the prosocial nature of people, behavioral disinhibition can weaken pleasure with getting more than you deserve. *Journal of Personality and Social Psychology, 101*, 791–811.

Van den Bos, K., Van Schie, E. C. M., & Colenberg, S. E. (2002). Parents' reactions to child day care organizations: The influence of perceptions of procedures and the role of organizations' trustworthiness. *Social Justice Research, 15*, 53–62.

Van den Bos, K., Vermunt, R., & Wilke, H. A. M. (1996). The consistency rule and the voice effect: The influence of expectations on procedural fairness judgements and performance. *European Journal of Social Psychology, 26*, 411–428.

Van den Bos, K., Wilke, H. A. M., & Lind, E. A. (1998). When do we need procedural fairness? The role of trust in authority. *Journal of Personality and Social Psychology, 75*, 1449–1458.

Van den Bos, K., Wilke, H. A. M., Lind, E. A., & Vermunt, R. (1998). Evaluating outcomes by means of the fair process effect: Evidence for different processes in fairness and satisfaction judgments. *Journal of Personality and Social Psychology, 74*, 1493–1503.

Van den Bos, W., Van Dijk, E., Westenberg, M., Rombouts, S. A. R. B., & Crone, E. A. (2009). What motivates repayment? Neural correlates of reciprocity in the trust game. *Social Cognitive and Affective Neuroscience, 4*, 294–304.

Van der Valk, I., & Wagenaar, W. (2010a). *Monitor racisme & extremisme: In en uit extreemrechts.* Amsterdam: Amsterdam University Press.

Van der Valk, I., & Wagenaar, W. A. (2010b). *The extreme right: Entry and exit.* Amsterdam/Leiden: Anne Frank House/Leiden University.

Van Dessel, P., De Houwer, J., & Gast, A. (2016). Approach-avoidance training effects are moderated by awareness of stimulus-action contingencies. *Personality and Social Psychology Bulletin, 42*, 81–93.

Van Dessel, P., De Houwer, J., Gast, A., Tucker Smith, C., & De Schryver, M. (2016). Instructing implicit processes: When instructions to approach or avoid influence implicit but not explicit evaluation. *Journal of Experimental Social* Psychology, 63, 1–9.

Van Dessel, P., De Houwer, J., Roets, A., & Gast, A. (2016). Failures to change stimulus evaluations by means of subliminal approach and avoidance training. *Journal of Personality and Social Psychology, 110*, e1-e15.

Van Dijk, E., & Wilke, H. A. M. (1993). Differential interests, equity, and public good provision. *Journal of Experimental Social Psychology, 29*, 1–16.

Van Dijk, E., & Wilke, H. A. M. (1995). Coordination rules in asymmetric social dilemmas: A comparison between public good dilemmas and resource dilemmas. *Journal of Experimental Social Psychology, 31*, 1–27.

Van Lange, P. A. M. (1999). The pursuit of joint outcomes and equality in outcomes: An integrative model of social value orientation. *Journal of Personality and Social Psychology, 77*, 337–349.

Van Lange, P. A. M., Agnew, C. R., Harinck, F., & Steemers, G. E. M. (1997). From game theory to real life: How social value orientation affects willingness to sacrifice in on-going close relationships. *Journal of Personality and Social Psychology, 73*, 1330–1344.

Van Lange, P. A. M., De Bruin, E. M. N., Otten, W., & Joireman, J. A. (2003). Development of prosocial, individualistic, and competitive orientations: Theory and preliminary evidence. In A. W. Kruglanski & E. T. Higgins (Eds.), *Social psychology: A general reader* (pp. 371–389). New York: Psychology Press.

Van Lange, P. A. M., & Kuhlman, D. M. (1994). Social value orientations and impressions of partner's honesty and intelligence: A test of the might versus morality effect. *Journal of Personality and Social Psychology, 67*, 126–141.

Van Lange, P. A. M., & Liebrand, W. B. G. (1991a). Social value orientation and intelligence: A test of the Goal Prescribes Rationality Principle. *European Journal of Social Psychology, 21*, 273–292.

Van Lange, P. A. M., & Liebrand, W. B. G. (1991a). The influence of other's morality and own social value orientation on cooperation in the Netherlands and the U.S.A. *International Journal of Psychology, 26*, 429–449.

Van Lange, P. A. M., Otten, W., De Bruin, E. M. N., & Joireman, J. A. (1997). Development of prosocial, individualistic, and competitive orientations: Theory and preliminary evidence. *Journal of Personality and Social Psychology, 73*, 733–746.

Van Prooijen, J.-W., Karremans, J. C., & Van Beest, I. (2006). Procedural justice and the hedonic principle: How approach versus avoidance motivation influences the psychology of voice. *Journal of Personality and Social Psychology, 91*, 686–697.

Van Prooijen, J.-W., & Krouwel, A. P. M. (2017). Extreme political beliefs predict dogmatic intolerance. *Social and Personality Psychological Science, 8*, 292–300.

Van Prooijen, J.-W., Krouwel, A. P. M., Boiten, M., & Eendebak, L. (2015). Fear among the extremes: How political ideology predicts negative emotions and outgroup derogation. *Personality and Social Psychology Bulletin, 41*, 485–497.

Van Yperen, N. W., & Buunk, B. P. (1991). Equity and exchange and communal orientation from a cross-national perspective. *Journal of Social Psychology, 131*, 5–20.

Veldhuis, T., & Bakker, E. (2007). Causale factoren van radicalisering en hun onderlinge samenhang. *Vrede en veiligheid, 36*, 448–470.

Veldhuis, T., & Staun, J. (2009). *Islamist radicalisation: A root cause model.* The Hague: Netherlands Institute of International Relations Clingendael.

Vermunt, R., Van Knippenberg, D., Van Knippenberg, B., & Blaauw, E (2001). Self-esteem and outcome fairness: Differential importance of procedural and outcome considerations. *Journal of Applied Psychology, 86*, 621–628.

Vess, M., Routledge, C., Landau, M. J., & Arndt, J. (2009). The dynamics of death and meaning: The effects of death-relevant cognitions and personal need for structure on perceptions of meaning in life. *Journal of Personality and Social Psychology, 97,* 728–744.

Vezzali, L., Hewstone, M., Capozza, D., Giovannini, D., & Wölfer, R. (2014). Improving intergroup relations with extended and vicarious forms of indirect contact. *European Review of Social Psychology, 25,* 314–389.

Victoroff, J., & Kruglanski, A. W. (Eds.). (2009). *Psychology of terrorism: Classic and contemporary insights.* New York: Psychology Press.

Vohs, K. D., Baumeister, R. F., Ciarocco, N. J. (2005). Self-regulation and self-presentation. Regulatory resource depletion impairs impression management and effortful self-presentation depletes regulatory resources. *Journal of Personality and Social Psychology, 88,* 632–657.

Vohs, K. D., Mead, N. L., & Goode, M. R. (2008). Merely activating the concept of money changes personal and interpersonal behavior. *Current Directions in Psychological Science, 17,* 208–212.

Voltaire (2000). *Treatise on tolerance.* Cambridge, UK: Cambridge University Press. (Original work published in 1763 as *Traité sur la tolérance*)

Von Essen, E. (2016). *In the gap between legality and legitimacy: Illegal hunting in Sweden as a crime of dissent* (Doctoral Thesis, Swedish University of Agricultural Sciences, Uppsala, Sweden). Retrieved from http://library.canterbury.ac.nz/services/ref/apa/thesis.shtml.

Waldmann, M. R., & Dieterich, J. H. (2007). Throwing a bomb on a person versus throwing a person on a bomb: Intervention myopia in moral intuitions. *Psychological Science, 18,* 247–253.

Walster, E., Berscheid, E., & Walster, G. W. (1973). New directions in equity research. *Journal of Personality and Social Psychology, 25,* 151–176.

Walster, E., Walster, G. W., & Berscheid, E. (1978). *Equity: Theory and research.* Boston: Allyn & Bacon.

Walzer, M. (1977). *Just and unjust wars: A moral argument with historical illustrations.* New York: Basic Books.

Wardlaw, G. (2009). Justifications and means: The moral dimension of state-sponsored terrorism. In J. Victoroff, & A. W. Kruglanski (Eds.), *Psychology of terrorism: Classic and contemporary insights* (pp. 409–417). New York: Psychology Press.

Weary, G., & Jacobson, J. A. (1997). Causal uncertainty beliefs and diagnostic information seeking. *Journal of Personality and Social Psychology, 73,* 839–848.

Webber, D., Babush, M., Schori-Eyal, N., Vazeou-Nieuwenhuis, A., Hettiarachchi, M., Bélanger, J. J., Moyano, M., Trujillo, H. M., Gunaratna, R., Kruglanski, A. W., & Gelfand, M. J. (2018). The road to extremism: Field and experimental evidence that significance loss-induced need for closure fosters radicalization. *Journal of Personality and Social Psychology, 114,* 270–285.

Webber, D., Chernikova, M., Kruglanski, A. W., Gelfand, M. J., Hettiarachchi, M., Gunaratna, R., Lafreniere, M.-A., & Belanger, J. J. (in press). Deradicalizing detained terrorists. *Political Psychology.*

Wiktorowicz, Q. (2004, May). *Joining the cause: Al-Muhajiroun and radical Islam.* Paper presented at the Roots of Islamic Radicalism conference, Yale University, New Haven, CT.

Wildschut, T., Pinter, B., Vevea, J. L., Insko, C. A., & Schopler, J. (2003). Beyond the group mind: A quantitative review of the interindividual-intergroup discontinuity effect. *Psychological Bulletin, 129*, 698–722.

Wilkinson, P. (1995). Violence and terror and the extreme right. *Terrorism and Political Violence, 7*, 82–93.

Wilner, A., & Dubouloz, C.-J. (2011). Transformative radicalization: Applying learning theory to Islamist radicalization. *Studies in Conflict & Terrorism, 34*, 418–438.

Wilson, J. Q. (1993). *The moral sense.* New York: Free Press.

Wilson, T. D., Centerbar, D. B., Kermer, D. A., & Gilbert, D. T. (2005). The pleasures of uncertainty: Prolonging positive moods in ways people do not anticipate. *Journal of Personality and Social Psychology, 88*, 5–21.

Winkielman, P., Schwarz, N., Fazendeiro, T., & Reber, R. (2003). The hedonic marking of processing fluency: Implications for evaluative judgment. In J. Musch & K. C. Klauer (Eds.), *The psychology of evaluation: Affective processes in cognition and emotion* (pp. 189–217). Mahwah, NJ: Erlbaum.

Woodburn, J. C. (1982a). Egalitarian societies. *Man, 17*, 431–451.

Woodburn, J. C. (1982b). Social dimensions of death in four African hunting and gathering societies. In M. Bloch & J. Parry (Eds.), *Death and the regeneration of life* (pp. 187–210). New York: Cambridge University Press.

Woodlock, R., & Russell, Z. (2008). *Perceptions of extremism among Muslims in Australia.* Paper presented at the conference on Radicalistion Crossing Borders: New Directions in Islamist and Jihadist Political, Intellectual and Theological Thought and Practice. Melbourne, Australia.

Yavuz, H., & Van den Bos, K. (2009). Effects of uncertainty and mortality salience on worldview defense reactions in Turkey. *Social Justice Research, 22*, 384–398.

Zahedzadeh, G. (2017). Overt attacks and covert thoughts. *Aggression and Violent Behavior, 36*, 1–8.

Zajonc, R. B. (1980). Feeling and thinking: Preferences need no inferences. *American Psychologist, 35*, 151–175.

Zajonc, R. B. (1998). Emotions. In D. T. Gilbert, S. T. Fiske, & G. Lindzey (Eds.), *The handbook of social psychology* (4th ed., Vol. 1, pp. 591–632). Boston, MA: McGraw-Hill.

Zammit, A. (2013). Explaining a turning point in Australian Jihadism. *Studies in Conflict & Terrorism, 36*, 739–755.

# NAME INDEX